Bobby Whitlock

Bobby Whitlock

A Rock 'n' Roll Autobiography

BOBBY WHITLOCK
with MARC ROBERTY

Foreword by Eric Clapton

McFarland & Company, Inc., Publishers
Jefferson, North Carolina, and London

LIBRARY OF CONGRESS CATALOGUING-IN-PUBLICATION DATA

Whitlock, Bobby.
Bobby Whitlock : a rock 'n' roll autobiography /
Bobby Whitlock with Marc Roberty ; foreword by Eric Clapton.
p.   cm.
Includes index.

ISBN 978-0-7864-5894-3
softcover : 50# alkaline paper ∞

1. Whitlock, Bobby.   2. Rock musicians—United States—
Biography.   I. Roberty, Marc.   II. Title.
ML420.W496A3   2011   782.42166092—dc22 [B]   2010049463

British Library cataloguing data are available

© 2011 Bobby Whitlock and Marc Roberty. All rights reserved

*No part of this book may be reproduced or transmitted in any form
or by any means, electronic or mechanical, including photocopying
or recording, or by any information storage and retrieval system,
without permission in writing from the publisher.*

On the cover: Bobby Whitlock today
(Photograph by CoCo Carmel)

Manufactured in the United States of America

*McFarland & Company, Inc., Publishers
Box 611, Jefferson, North Carolina 28640
www.mcfarlandpub.com*

To my beloved wife, CoCo Carmel

CoCo Carmel and Bobby Whitlock.

Table of Contents

Acknowledgments ix
Foreword by Eric Clapton 1
Introduction 3

Childhood Memories 5
The Sixties 26
Joining Delaney and Bonnie 33
Eric Clapton and My Freedom 48
My New Life in England 66
George Harrison and *All Things Must Pass* 73
All Things Must Pass Track by Track 79
Mick's Birthday Party 83
Layla Album Song by Song 94
The Domino Flat 98
Playing Back Home 101
The Johnny Cash Show 104
The End of the Dominos 111
Going Solo 124
C'est la Vie! 131
Going Gold 134
New Home, New Girlfriend, New Adventures 137
Caribou Ranch 143
The Daytona Crash 147
Wakey, Wakey! 153
Leaving England and Eric 155
Fall from Grace in Peach Country 158
Elvis' Caddy 167

My Old Pal	170
Pool of Tears	172
Magical Ireland	173
Back in Memphis	179
Building My Barn	183
Empty Fruit Basket	186
My New Deal	189
The Spiritual Void	193
Meeting CoCo for the First Time	195
Safe at Last	203
Hard Times	209
Lovers	214
Our New Home in Austin	216
The King of Luck	223
The Flow	229
Full Circle	233
Selected Discography	237
Index	245

Acknowledgments

I would like to acknowledge and thank everyone on the Steve Hoffman Music Forum for the insightful questions. You were all a part of the beginning of me writing my story. Everyone who was online with me, and asking those very important questions, was witness to a cathartic experience and the creative principle at work through every one of them, and through me as the vessel that was emptying itself out to the planet. Just that one question started it all. "Who was the girl in the inside of the *Layla* album sleeve?" And I am eternally grateful to whoever it was that asked it. Because of that question, I became a writer.

CoCo was surfing the internet and saw that question. She told me about it and I said that it was Kay Poorboy and to answer it. When CoCo sent it, immediately thousands of questions began to come in. It was a never-ending tsunami that lasted for over two weeks and not once did I get asked the same question twice. It opened me up and an outpouring began that I did not expect at all. I didn't realize that I had been carrying everything around with me all of my life. I thought that they were memories, not burdens. I had an incredible breakthrough and spiritual healing right in front of the world. And it is still there, too! Completely unfiltered on the thread. Honest to the bone and completely frank and candid. I couldn't stop it because I didn't start it. It still flows, as I am sure you can tell.

Marc Roberty had been a member of the forum for as long as we had, two years, and had yet to look at it until a few days after I got started answering questions via CoCo typing them for me. She did that at first then I took over when she went to California to visit her family. Marc came on after reading for three solid hours and told me, "Don't you recognize that this is fate?" A lot of people on the forum were asking if this was going to be a book and I asked Marc for his advice, and he told me that this would be a great book to write. I told him that I didn't know how to start. He said that I already had and that he would do whatever he could to help me, and for me just to let him know what I needed. I didn't know what to ask him for because I didn't know what I needed. I knew nothing about what I was doing, but Marc told me to keep on writing the stories. It hasn't stopped since September 9, 2008, either!

I told him to let me know what he felt would be the appropriate role for him to play in it. He got back after thinking it over and said that he would be my editor because it was my life and I was already writing the book myself. I went online and found out what a developmental editor's role was and it turns out that Marc plays the most important role of all. He is my closest ally. And he makes the thread of continuity in everything flow. His role is a very complex one at best. He makes it read as though I know what I am doing, which I don't. I am just this place where it seems to flow through and I'm writing it down.

I'm the instrument through which it flows. It amazes even me at times. I can't write a grocery list and get it right, much less try to write a book! Just a simple note is always misspelled and pretty much a jumble of incomplete thoughts. The list is never complete. But let me get started on a story and it flows like a river through me. I just love it!

Marc has written more than thirteen books on Eric Clapton alone, so he knows the score when it comes to putting together a story and a book. And I believe that we have a mutual understanding of something greater that is at work here than the sum total of us both. Without each person acting and reacting the way he or she did, I would not be here now and have this incredible story to tell. Doing what I am doing and love to do, which is to write songs and sing and play them, and to write stories about the only thing that I know, my world.

And my world would not be complete without my darling CoCo Carmel. CoCo is my wife and soul mate and musical partner. She held my hand through this whole growing process. She was with me to comfort me when I was going through my darkest hour and was with me when I finally came into my own and saw the light of a new day. She is the love of my life and the light unto it. I certainly cannot go without acknowledging my lifelong friend Eric Clapton and his partner Michael Eaton for their continued support and generosity in this ever-changing world of mine.

Thank you all.
~ BW ~

* * *

I have been a music lover ever since I can remember. Motown, Stax and Atlantic are some of my favorite labels. My tastes are varied, especially so today. But, back in the late '60s I was heavily into Cream. To me, nobody could touch them. So when Eric released his first solo album with Delaney and Bonnie and Friends, it took some time for me to fully appreciate it because I was still after the heavy guitar workouts. In reality, I needed my tastes to mature.

Among the many artists I have enjoyed over the years, Delaney & Bonnie and Friends, and Derek and the Dominos have been constant favorites. Their music had soul and a solid groove and remains, as far as my ears are concerned, as vibrant today as ever. I only knew about the music and never about what was happening behind the scenes. It turns out that a lot was happening, particularly with drugs. If ever you needed a reason to say no, then this is the book for you.

I was lucky enough to stumble upon an ongoing discussion on the Steve Hoffman Forum about the girl that was pictured on the inside sleeve of the *Layla* album. Turns out Bobby and CoCo had answered the question and a torrent of further questions followed for months. Bobby and I got to talking and I told him that his story should be documented in a biography. It was a privilege getting to know Bobby and CoCo over the last 17 months or so. In many ways I was reliving the music from my youth but actually hearing the story through a person who was there. Magic. In my experience not many musicians from this era have such vivid recall, for obvious reasons. It actually made me take out my Delaney and Bonnie and Derek and the Dominos albums and listen to them with a totally new perspective. I was blown away by the detail in the stories that Bobby told me during the time of putting this book together. Whether personal or musical, I found the process of editing these stories about growing up in the American South both fascinating and insight-

Acknowledgments

ful. This is the story of Bobby's life, warts and all, and I hope you will enjoy it as much as I do.

I would like to thank my partner, Karen Daws, for her help in editing along with her patience (forced to listen to Dominos music for a year!) and encouragement. I would also like to thank two photographers in particular who have generously donated some of their photos for the book. Stefan Wallgren took the two shots of Derek and the Dominos at the Marquee Club in London on August 11, 1970. Laurie Asprey provided the two shots of Delaney & Bonnie and Friends from the Fairfield Hall in Croydon on December 7, 1969, where most of their live album was recorded. Thank you to both of you.

~ Marc Roberty ~

Foreword by Eric Clapton

"Come on, man, the sun's up" (or words to that effect). I blearily look out of my bedroom window, and there's Whitlock beaming up at me, bursting with energy, the picture of blooming health, despite the fact that we haven't slept in several days. I have just managed to escape the action for a few hours, and now it's time to come out and play again. To set the scene: The year is 1970, the location, Hurtwood Edge, my new home in the English countryside, and Derek and the Dominos are being born.

I stole the Dominos from Delaney Bramlett, although the official version would be that they left over a pay dispute. Nevertheless, I feel obligated to take the blame for that scenario, since I know I was entirely capable of that kind of maneuver in those days. We met during the Blind Faith tour, in '69 when Delaney and Bonnie were supporting us—Bobby played piano and organ and sang, and was without doubt the most energetic sideman I had ever seen. I would spend every free minute hanging out with Delaney and the guys, sometimes jamming with the band, and after the tour was over, I left Blind Faith and moved in with Delaney and his family. I remember in those early days, Bobby warned me that if I got too close, they would "swarm" on me. Little did they know that in my own quiet way, I was swarming on them.

Fast-forward to the present day. In the corner of the kitchen at Hurtwood Edge is a long thin box which has arrived from America, a present from Bobby W. It remains unopened for six months. I have a nasty feeling it's a fishing rod that I don't want and will never use. My wife finally nudges me to open it or throw it away, as it's cluttering up her kitchen. I bite the bullet and open the parcel. Lo and behold it's a pipe of peace, a beautiful native American artifact. The smile creeps onto my face; I have always underestimated Bobby.

In those early days of the Dominos, we lived a dream that I had only heard of or read about. The notion of the live-in band had always captured my imagination, especially since the emergence of The Band and *Big Pink*. When I got the chance to form the Dominos, I invited them to come and live with me in the English countryside. Jim Gordon, Carl Radle and Bobby Whitlock took to it like fish to the water. We spent at least a year living together, playing together all day and all night, and getting crazy on every substance available with total abandon. We toured all over England, playing clubs and small venues, with no one having any idea of who we were, and it was heaven, just making music for the pure fun of it. We also played on George's *All Things Must Pass* album—in fact, we were the house band. It was a golden period for us all: I finally belonged to a band formed of musicians that I totally respected, and I truly felt that I had to work to keep up with them. We made sweet, tough and soulful music, and the future looked good. It was during this period that I learned what little I do know about writing songs, and most of that I learned from BW. It's all to do with persistence and relentlessness. My inherent attitude is, "If it doesn't come out easily in one go, it's probably not worth bothering about." But Bobby would want to go over and over our ideas until something materialized. It's a tough and sometimes frustrating process, but one that always pays off if you have the tenacity to follow through. Our ride was fast and dangerous, and in the end it chewed us all up pretty badly, so that by the time people had figured out who we were, we were long gone. Jim is still in an institution, Carl left us over twenty years ago, and Bobby and I went a long way into the dark. Thank goodness we came out the other side both still in one piece, and in many respects, better than ever.

The day of our great reunion glimmers now and then, although it hasn't fully happened yet, and of course it might not ever come to pass, but never underestimate Bobby Whitlock.

Eric Clapton, an English singer-songwriter, is widely regarded as one of the most influential blues and jazz guitarists who ever lived. He has been active in the music industry since 1962 and has been inducted into the Rock and Roll Hall of Fame three times.

Introduction

I know that there is a purpose behind everything that happens to us on our journey through this life. We don't always know what it is, or why things are the way that they are, they just are that way for their own reason. I guess it's so that they may be brought into expression in their own due season. I really felt I was before my time when I was twenty-three. I knew it even then. I was just having a problem adjusting to my skin for a few years. It is only just now getting to feel as though it has finally broken in. It's about time, too! I thought that it was going to wear out first. I was a little too early for blooming and was constantly looking for approval from my Dad all of his life and never got it.

Maybe I shouldn't have been looking to him for something that he was incapable of giving me. He could not accept himself, so how could I possibly ever expect him to accept me, and what I was doing? He never even heard me perform outside of singing in his church. Even when I was first starting out and was playing folk music in the coffeehouse in town, just across the tracks from his store, he would never come to hear me sing. It made me sad then and still does. I can't possibly imagine having a child and not being supportive of whatever it was that they did. He would say to me that he was doing his best to get everybody into heaven and that I was busy sending them straight to hell with the music that I was singing.

But all I was singing was soul music. It just wasn't church songs. Then again I guess that would depend on the church that you go to, or carry with you. Personally, the temple I sing in has always been my church.

Childhood Memories

I was born on March 18, 1948. For some reason, my mother used to dress me in dresses until I was about three and I rarely had my hair cut, so it was long with soft curls. My hair is still the same. It just has a little silver in it. I guess that she hadn't quite grown up yet and I was sort of her live baby doll. I tend to believe this to be true. Her name is LaVada "Bitsy" King and she and I grew up together because she was very young when she got pregnant with me. She was fifteen and still a minor and my dad wasn't. He should have been put in jail for statutory rape. My mom had it hard all of her life. I don't know how long she let me wander all over Millington, Tennessee, with nothing but a diaper on but I have memories that go past when I should have already stopped and hadn't. Millington isn't a small place but it's not big either. Crime was something that we never concerned ourselves with. Life was just something that we did while we were living and that was one moment at a time.

I said something to my mother the other day about living by grace. I asked her if she had a clear understanding of the meaning of that. She said that's what we have been living by all of our lives because we couldn't depend on anybody or anything else. I used to wander all over Millington singing and was as happy a child as you could possibly imagine. All of the turmoil that was going down was mostly in my dad's head. He was working on the river so he was gone for real long stretches, sometimes for months. I remember being about five or six and walking from our house on Saratoga across town about two miles to Granny Whitlock's little old shotgun house on Woodstock-Cuba Road. That was on the other side of town, and where we used to live in a boathouse that was out in the middle of a cotton field. Babe Howard had moved it from the Mississippi River for us to live in. He was a family friend and owned the Millington telephone company. He was the only person in the United States to own his own telephone company. He was a short fat man who always wore khaki pants with suspenders. He was a wealthy man but you would never have known it. Babe was a good man who, along with Uncle Woodrow, loved me, and my Mama.

I remember pretty much everything from back when I was a little boy. I have such a vivid memory because pain was inflicted on me at a very early age. I became aware at a very early age. It's kind of like breaking a horse too early. You break his spirit and he's never the same because he didn't get the chance to develop naturally. And he will shy away from the person who broke him every time. My Mama told me that my dad kicked me like a football across the room when I was three months old. I have no reason to ever doubt her because it never stopped, until I stopped it. The only memories that I have of him are terrible. I don't have any fond memories of my dad because they all turned out tragic in the end.

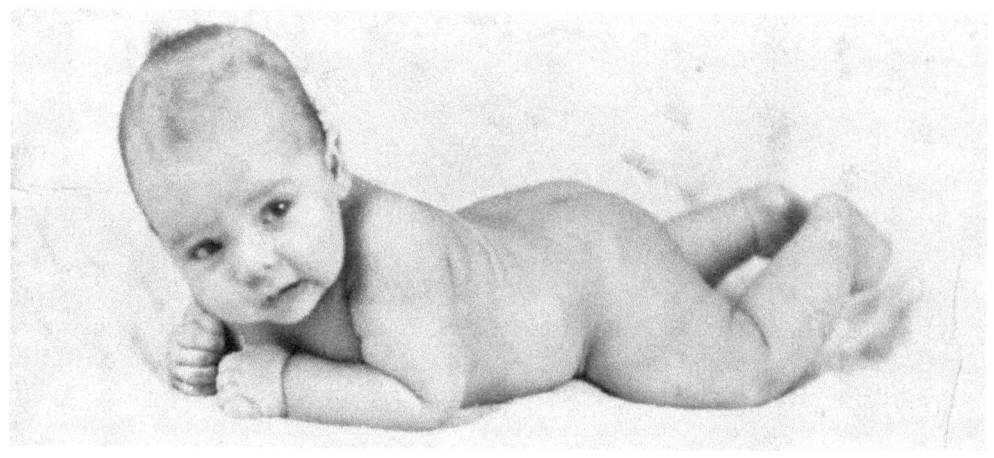

As a baby.

I distinctly remember my mother and my dad having trouble back then. In fact I don't recall him being there very often. He put holes in the bottom of the boat to drain the water because it had been just sitting down there on the river tied up, and nobody looked after it before it was brought up onto dry land. It was a wreck, but it was home. Then rats got up in the holes and they were everywhere! My Mama finally spread a sheet out on the floor and put everything we had in it, which wasn't much, and she tied a square knot in it and threw it over one shoulder and me over the other and we were gone! I must have been only about three when this happened. It's like a picture of an event frozen in time in my mind that I can see so very clearly when the veil is lifted. I believe that we went to my Big Mama's (my mother's mother) for a while but then it wasn't long before we were back at Granny's. She had a black woman named Coreen who worked for her from time to time. I really liked Coreen. I told her one time that the reason that she was so black was because she drank so much coffee. I believed it, too, at my young age. She just laughed and said, "You're a sweet boy, little Bobby." That's what everyone called me, Little Bobby.

I remember when my little brother Alex died and they brought him home. He was in a little crib up on the table. I was three or so and I did not think of him of being any other way except that he was sleeping. I got up in there with him and was lying next to my little brother with my arm around him, talking to him. My mom came and made me get out, but as soon as she left, I was back up in there with him. I'm told that we looked exactly alike. That's probably true because my grandson

Age 1 in 1949, a few minutes before my first haircut.

My first performance, singing "Snowball" to the tune of "Bingo," in kindergarten. I had cut my toe, so I wasn't wearing my right shoe.

looks exactly like me as well. Perhaps he's my brother as well as my grandson, like I believe that my son Beau just might be my firstborn, who was lost. B.J. Alex was there for a few days. Why I don't know, but he was. I never thought he was anything but sleeping the whole time. I didn't know what they were talking about when they were all crying and talking about dying. I have a clear understanding of it now but then again, maybe not. Maybe it was more so then when I was nothing more than an innocent child, pure as the freshly driven snow. It was absolute innocence. We took my little brother to the cemetery to bury him. I didn't know what was going on. All that I knew was that they had my baby brother in that box with the top closed and he was still sleeping. And everyone was crying and holding each other. Everyone was holding everyone but me. I was standing there all

In a yellow outfit my mother made for me.

alone. I stood there at my brother's grave and watched as my uncle and some other men lowered his casket with some long white cloth straps about four inches wide that my mother kept rolled up and in a drawer for years after that. I watched as they lowered him down into the ground into that deep, dark hole. I dreamed of this for years. I thought that he was still in there sleeping. They started to throw dirt in there and they kept on until it was completely full and running over. "My little brother's down in there!" I shouted, "He's down in there and I can't get to him!" I didn't know what to do and I had no idea what had happened to my brother. No one would listen to me. Everyone was busy consoling each other and not watching me at all. I got one of the shovels and started digging him back up out of there as fast as I could until someone walked up to me and said, "What are you doing, Little Bobby?" I said, "I'm digging up my little brother Alex!"

Granny worked as a cook at the Anchor Café, one block from her house. I used to go there and she would make me a hamburger with onions and a slice of melted cheese in a warm bun and a pickle. It was a rarity for me and it tasted delicious. She would give me a Dr. Pepper and a bag of potato chips to go with it as well. I use to go there all the time when I was growing up, but sadly, they tore that place down a few years ago. One day I was as dirty as you could be because I had been being playing in the dirt off the side of Granny's back porch. She told me that it was time for me to start heading back home because Mama would be getting worried about me, so I did. There I was, my little nasty barefooted self, covered with dirt, filthy shorts and no shirt on walking home singing "Bo Weevil." About five blocks past the school there was a little park on the way home that had a slide and some swings and a little round wading pool about a foot deep. It was just for wading. I looked towards the park and saw that there were a lot of ladies all standing around the pool. There were children all dressed up and they were all walking in a circle on the ledge around the wading pool. They were going around and around and it looked like they were having fun so I went over and got up there with them and started walking around and around that wading pool in a circle with all of those other children who were all dressed so fancy. I walked in the circle three or four times and got off and kept on walking home. I didn't even look back. When I got home a little later my mom had made dinner for us. It was nighttime and as usual

With my father at Little Alex's gravesite.

Left: *Granny Whitlock with Rex and me.* **Right:** *LaVada Whitlock, my mother.*

my dad was somewhere on the river and we were at peace, my Mother and me. Two days later there was a knock was at the door and Mama answered it. There were a couple of ladies who had come by to present me with the first place beauty contest trophy! Turns out I had entered a children's beauty contest by walking around that wading pool and didn't even know it! And I won! They gave me a cup that was a small trophy cup that read,

 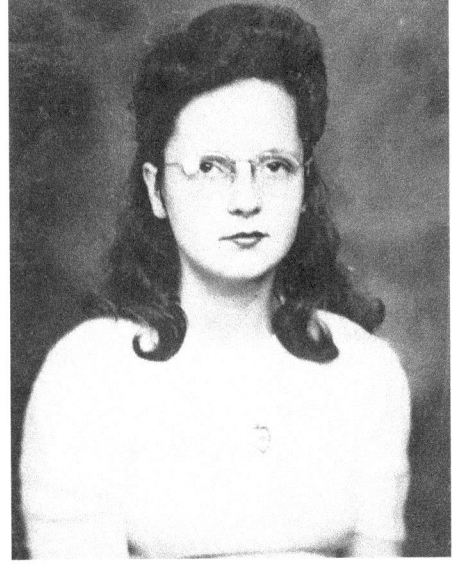

Left: *Jimmy Whitlock, my dad, in Foggia, Italy, 1946.* **Right:** *LaVada "Bitsy" King.*

"King of Oak Park 6–11 yrs ~ 1954 ~ Robert S. Whitlock." I still have it, and it's about four inches tall. The base is long gone but the cup is missing the handles. I was King long before Elvis!

When we were little my Uncle Jimbo, who was only one year older than me, was up a tree and too afraid to come down. He was crying and Big Mama had gone to the store, and we had cornered Aunt Christine on the front porch in her wheelchair so she couldn't see us. My aunt, who was crippled, was as smart as a whip. She would tell on us every time. She couldn't talk like everyone else. Only Big Mama, Jimbo, and my Mama and I could understand her and what she said. It was like we had a language of our own. We did. It was the language of love, that unspoken word that you feel deep within. Jimbo would not even try to come back down because he was too scared of falling. I told him to hang in there because I had a plan. I went into the tool shed and got an axe and chopped the tree down. I laugh recalling it because I can still visualize him when it started to fall. It was like, "Oh, nooooooo!" He was all right and Big Mama wasn't too upset when she got home because she knew that I really meant well, and I did, too.

My Big Mama King used to sit me on her lap and put her metal Dobro in front of me and she would play with her arms wrapped around me. My hands would try to do what hers did as I held the neck with my left hand on the back of the neck and my right arm

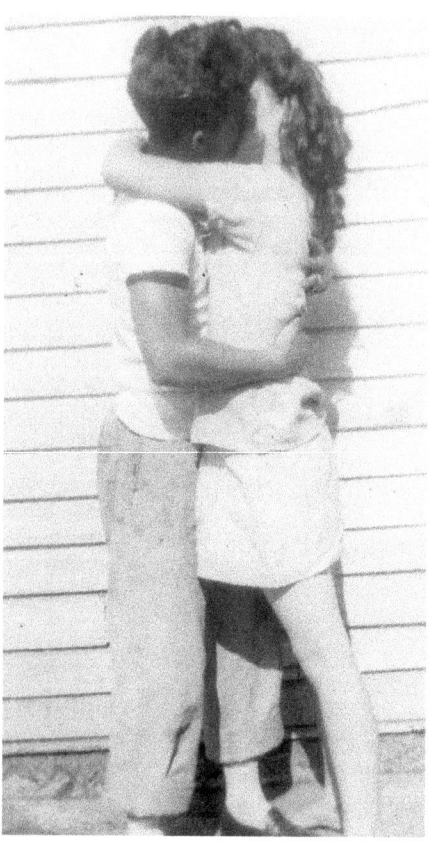 

Left: *As it should have been, Jimmy Whitlock and Mama.* **Right:** *With my dad on Easter Sunday, 1951.*

not long enough to reach over the top of the Dobro. She would sing and swing in that old, well-worn white porch swing. She told me that when I got bigger that she would give me that guitar. She did when I was fifteen years old. I still have it and I had it painted her favorite color, deep red. Her name is on the headstock in mother of pearl. It reads Gladys.

My mother's daddy, Peapaw, was a character for sure. He was a drunk, a hobo and a chicken thief, and he worked on the Mississippi River on a tugboat. He used to jump trains and ride on the flatcars to wherever he was going, and he took the whole family when he did. He'd take Big Mama, who was a bootlegger, my Uncle Troy, Mama and Aunt Christine. He was a hobo and a family man—hobos have families, too. He and a preacher had it all worked out. The preacher would keep the congregation occupied while my Peapaw would go steal everybody's

With Big Mama King, in the back, and Mama.

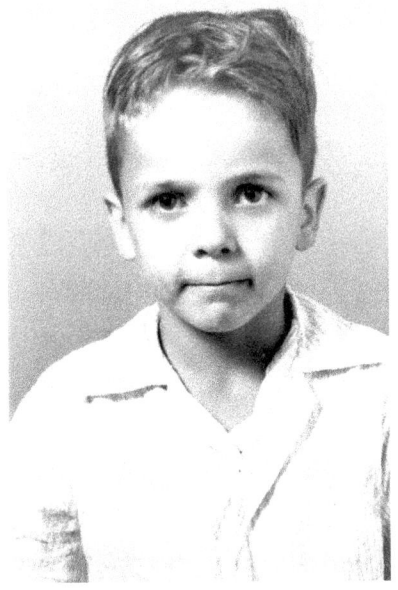

Left: *My trophy for King of Oak Park (photograph by CoCo Carmel).* **Right:** *Me, the King of Oak Park.*

chickens while they were in church. Then he and the preacher would divide their profits after having a fried chicken dinner with mashed potatoes and gravy and biscuits and a glass of iced tea. One time he had the chicken coop in the trunk of his car with the lid tied, and it was so big that it was sticking out halfway. Too many chickens in it this time. It fell out, and chickens went everywhere! Peapaw knocked on the man's front door where he had stolen the chickens. He told him that he needed some help rounding up all of these chickens that fell out of his car right in front of his house. The man obliged and my grandad drove away with all his chickens. He later got a case of conscience and took back some of them and left a note on the man's chicken coop. It read, "I rob from the rich and I rob from the poor. I left you six, to raise us some more!" Cavalier old dude, my granddad.

One time I asked him about working on the river because I wanted to write a song but didn't know anything about it other than he and my dad worked on it. He told me that they would do a run that would last for months at a time. He told me about a time when they were pushing forty barges up river and they broke loose near Cairo, Illinois, and went wild all the way down past the Harahan Bridge in Memphis. Forty huge barges loaded with oil and steel and boxcars, rubber tires and frames for automobiles and all sorts of grain and chemicals, loose and running wild down the Mississippi River. Can you just imagine that? He said that they eventually did get them all back.

The Mississippi is a wild river without anything on it. I was raised on it and I know.

Left: *With Jimbo, right.* **Right:** *Peapaw, my mother's daddy, holds Christine. Troy and Mama stand with them.*

That current runs at least thirty miles an hour. I've seen a whole log twenty-five feet long get caught in a whirlpool, and it would start to spin and then it would stand on end and then it was gone. You wouldn't see it again. That river is dangerous even if you're in a boat. Peapaw said that a run would start out in Cairo and go to St. Louis and then all the way down to New Orleans. That sounded like a good line for a song to me. I asked him what they did while they were out on a run. He said that they drank whiskey and played cards and gambled and fought all night long. I asked which one was the most famous whorehouse in New Orleans and he said, "Hell boy, they're all famous!" My Aunt Dude ran a whorehouse in Memphis, and her place was called The Blue Moon Café. I don't know what was being served in the kitchen but I know what she was serving upstairs!

My dad had this thing about finding churches that had no congregation and most of which were literally falling down. He dragged us from one mud hole to the next and all in the name of God. I think that it had more to do with him finding us a place to live for free than it did about religion. The preacher always got the parsonage thrown in as a part of his deal. And it was always some little old shotgun high-water house sitting in the woods or a bean field or cotton field somewhere in the middle of nowhere. He didn't like to get his hands dirty by working hard at any type of manual labor. Preaching was a natural and came easy for him. He was a great

Peapaw King, Big Mama, my mother, whose nickname was Bitsy, Aunt Christine in the stroller, and Uncle Troy in Richmond, Indiana, in 1938.

My Peapaw King, 1920.

orator and very passionate about what he was doing. Even if he didn't know what it was. One time he had a little old falling-down church that was in the middle of nowhere on a thousand acres of cotton fields outside of Marmaduke, Arkansas.

It sat on a gravel road and across from a great big general store, or company store, as some people called them. It was a two-story building and had a large front porch and the place was white clapboard covered with the dirt from the fields. There was everything in there from feed to saddles to penny candy. I used to go in there just to look. I didn't have the money for gum or anything like that. This was near a place where we lived on the creek in a shotgun house with an outdoor toilet with two holes in it—a large one for Mama and Daddy and a small one cut in it for me and my little sister, Debbie. There were wasp nests up under the seat in the spring and summertime. My sister and I used to swim in the creek with the snakes swimming there with us. They never bothered us and we never bothered them. They would just swim on down the creek. That water was crystal-clear spring-fed water. And that was about it in the way of entertainment in our wretched lives. That falling down church and that general store were the only two buildings within several miles either way down that gravel road. And they were sitting right in the middle of a thousand acres of dry flat dirt with row after row of cotton plants and bean plants, all of which we chopped and picked. Some of those rows were a mile long.

Left: *Aunt Dude*. Right: *Aunt Dude with her appointment book and a john, 1934.*

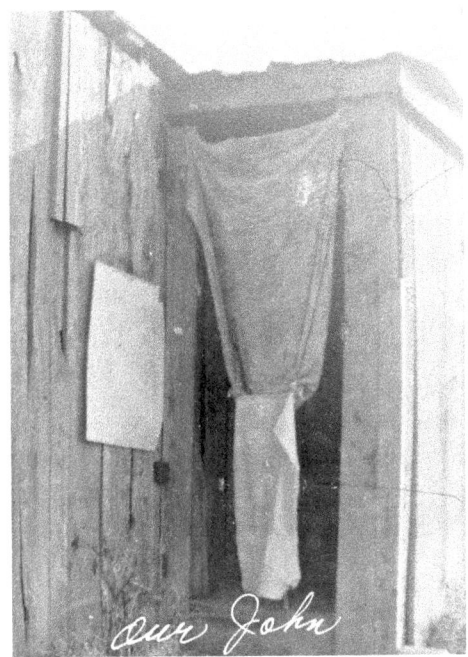

Left: *Home, a shotgun house near the creek near Marmaduke, Arkansas.* **Right:** *The outhouse next to our house.*

My dad's daddy was a moonshiner. He made illegal whiskey. Corn liquor. White lightning. Blue flame. The first time I ever smoked a joint the first person to come into my mind was my Peapaw Whitlock. He lived with us in that little shotgun house. That house had a pot-bellied heat stove in the center of the room, and he would drink boiling hot black coffee in the morning and sit there and spit on that stove and it would foam up as soon as it hit. That was his plan for the morning. Drink boiling hot coffee and spit on the woodstove. He slept in the same bed as me. It was a single bed with springs and was barely big enough for me. He was a tall man, probably six feet tall or so. We slept head to foot. That meant that his feet were in my face while I tried to sleep. I still remember that nasty looking yellow, big toenail staring me in the face every morning. The first thing that he would do after his coffee was to go out on the front

Mama cooking on an old wood stove in her homemade dress, 1956.

porch and whittle and spit. He used to make little tops out of empty thread spools. Mama used to sew a lot. He would bring out a pouch of weed to roll himself one first thing and he would break it out again in the evening. That old dude was smoking pot and making whiskey and running it! And he was living with us! I don't know how it came about that he left but he did.

None of my family ever stayed in one place for very long. I'm still like that. I get to feeling all closed in. I like the idea of the planet being my home. Anyway, Peapaw Whitlock was running some shine across a field down in Mississippi one Thanksgiving. It was to be recorded as the coldest Thanksgiving in over a century. He had taken some whiskey to somebody across a cornfield and got drunk while he was there. Afterwards he was walking back across this fresh-cut cornfield in the dark. When they're finished harvesting the corn they use a huge knife to cut the stalks about two feet off the ground to make it easier to plow when plowing time comes. He had about three-fourths of a pint left in a bottle that he was drinking out of when he tripped on a cornstalk and fell forward and one of them stuck him in the stomach. He rolled over into the middle of the row and froze to death. He was so drunk that he couldn't get up and he died lying on his back with his arms outstretched to the sky above with the rest of that pint of corn liquor by his side with the top off. He didn't spill a drop. Two boys riding the fencerow found him the next day, frozen stiff as a board just the way I described it to you. When he was buried they gave his only possessions to one of my uncles and my Dad. Uncle Tommy got a Prince Albert tobacco can with his picture and a nickel in it and my dad got that bottle of corn whiskey. He used to keep it in his church study up on a shelf and I would go in there and pour a little out in a lid and light it. It would pop when it lit and it burned a blue flame. That meant that it is pure. It wasn't too very much longer that I wouldn't be wasting that whiskey. I started drinking it when I was ten. It was gone six months later. I would take a drink and pour that much water back in it. It got weaker and so did I. So, the first drink that I ever had was out of the bottle that was my granddaddy's last. It was also my introduction to the world of drugs and alcohol.

There was an old man by the name of Ross Turberville whose wife was named Lillian. They were two of the nine or ten people who attended services there. They were raising their grandson Danny, who was a little too wild for his parents, what with James Dean and the Big Bopper and Buddy Holly being the happening things back then. Even in the backwoods of Arkansas every now and then a little light would shine. He was breaking loose and wanted to be free. A change was coming for him. Ross and Lillian were fine folks who lived about five miles down the road from the church, on the same gravel road. I thought that they were rich because they had ten acres and a big old barn and two mules that he used to plow with. Ross had a tractor that he could never get started because it had to be done by turning a hand crank and for some reason he didn't have one so he would have to turn a big round wheel on the side of it. It was tiring for him so he would just hitch up the team. It was nigh on impossible to start that tractor without that crank. Come to think of it, I bet that Danny threw it away to keep from having to drive the tractor and work for his Grandpa. Ross let him take the truck every now and then even though he was all of fifteen, and barely that. He had to sit on a football to see over the steering wheel to drive that old truck. I worked for Ross from time to time shucking corn or riding on the back of the planter that he used. The mules would pull down the rows and I would sit on the back and keep a check on the buckets filled with seed. He also had me looking after his livestock and anything else that he could think of because he knew how bad off we were. My dad, the preacher, just got what was put in the offering plate. And if the sermon wasn't up to snuff they wouldn't put anything in the offering plate except maybe a nickel or a dime.

I can say one thing about that little man, and that is that he sure could preach a sermon. He made it believable. I've seen deacons ducking invisible arrows. He had a sermon called the Devil's Quiver of Arrows. One arrow represented one thing and the other another and when he drew back his invisible bow and let the arrow of lusting after your neighbor's wife fly they all ducked! You have got to imagine that my dad was just five feet tall and he had to stand on two wooden Coca-Cola cases to see over the pulpit properly. It looked funny from behind. That was my favorite sermon of his. I loved to hear him preach because he was so colorful and passionate about what he was saying. He just didn't know what it was himself. He didn't know what he thought he knew and really didn't practice what he preached. He was nowhere near the mark. Instead of money they would usually give us some sort of food like canned goods or some crap that my mom would throw out of the window of the car on the way home. Some of what people gave us was insulting.

I was in the back of the church one Sunday and was looking at a Bible with pictures in it and I got to thinking about a song called "'Neath the Old Olive Tree." I hear the melody as I write this. I got to thinking about one of the disciples getting knocked in the head by something bigger than an olive falling from the tree, like an apple with a worm looking out of it at him, and started giggling in the back of the church. My friend Melvin Pole was sitting next to me and he got to laughing as well. My dad was pissed and I knew it because I had seen that look in his eyes many times before. It was a look that no one else saw that was very private to us. We were just being boys with the giggles busting out

My Dad at his church door shaking hands after he slapped me around.

through our noses and laughing out loud until we couldn't stop. This was not good. He stopped his sermon and came down off of those Coke crates from behind that pulpit and grabbed me and took me outside and around the corner in front of the three or four parked cars there and spun me around and then he hit me in the face like I was a grown man, and then he slapped me and backhanded me. I was six years old. When my son Beau turned six I started crying because I could see myself in him at six and I remembered what it was like to be that young and innocent and dependent on someone that I loved who was undependable, and him beating me outside of that little falling-down church. When he was finished he took me back inside and it was real quiet in there. You could hear my heart beating, for sure. Those old country folks just looked at me with pity as my face began to swell right there in front of them. There was nothing that anyone could do. They were helpless and so was I. He finished his sermon without breaking stride. Like nothing had happened at all. After the sermon he was standing at the door shaking all of their hands as they left that little church. That hypocritical egomaniac preacher who was pilled to the gills would be shaking their hands and smiling like he was some sort of saint. It was just another day in the life of Little Bobby. On the way out the door Ross and Lillian invited us over for dinner. I was happy to hear that because I really liked them a lot and I knew that there would be a lot of really good food there. I knew that there would be a peach cobbler and ham and beans with polk salad and turnip greens and cornbread. Of course there was lots of ice tea. And I just remembered that they would have Popsicles for us kids, and we made our own ice cream. I felt safe there with those lovely old folks.

We hadn't hit the door good and my daddy said, "Get out to that barn, boy!" I knew what was coming. I thought, "Oh, dear God, what's going to happen to me? What is he going to do to me now?" He was right behind me, hot on my heels, and when we got in the barn he shut the door and said, "Get in that corn stall, boy!" There were two fifty-five-gallon grain barrels up against the wall full of corn that I had shucked for the mules and there was a pile of fresh corn in the corner waiting on me for Monday morning. There was a mule team harness that Ross used to plow with hanging on the wall. Dad took down the leader line that runs through and in between the team. It holds them together. It's a piece of leather two inches wide and a fourth of an inch thick and twelve feet long. It's for driving mules, not beating children! He wrapped it around his hand with just about six feet to use and told me to climb that stall wall. It was a board then a space then a board then a space all the way to the ceiling. It was for holding corn. I was terrified and felt hollow inside and as cold as you well may imagine. I had run dry of tears and I had become numb emotionally. I still loved him no matter what because he was the only daddy that I had and I knew that I was supposed to have one, it's just that I never did. When I had climbed to where my feet were about two feet off of the ground I was standing on a board and had reached as far up as I could for the next board. He yanked my feet out and I was just hanging there holding on with my hands. I was holding on with all my strength and was not going to let go. I was terrified and numb and was ready as always for the unexpected. He stood back and whipped me like you see in the movies. He whipped me from the top of my head to the bottom of my legs with that six-foot leather strap. He made me count every time he hit me and I did. Only this time I wasn't crying anymore. He kept hitting me and I kept counting every one of them all the way to thirteen. I didn't even whimper. That took him completely by surprise and he didn't know what to do except finally stop. I just collapsed onto the floor, completely wiped out, physically and emotionally. He went back in and my mother came out soon after to get me. She was so frightened of him that she could do nothing. He kept times like these to himself. It would be just him and me behind closed doors. No one could help us and we could not even help ourselves. It's a wonder that I'm here to tell this story.

By the time I was nine years old we had moved again, this time to a very small town in Arkansas called Diaz. My Dad had a church there that he preached at when he came home from seminary school, which was every weekend. As far as I could tell, the only thing that he learned at that school was how to stay out of a cotton field. We lived in a four-room house that was right next to the railroad tracks. In fact our house faced them and had a great big oak tree in the front yard as well. At that time Diaz was a little place that had only 176 people. It had four cotton gins and a country store, a blacksmith shop, a church and about two dozen little houses sitting in the middle of thousands of acres of cotton fields. That's where we worked, my Mama and me.

My dad would come home on weekends and it was always a nightmare for me because he was an abusive little man that could not help himself, but that is still no excuse for the things that he did to me. He was an expert with everything that had to do with throwing something or using a bullwhip. He knew how to braid leather and how to make a bullwhip. He would either use a hammer handle or a branch as the handle. He would tie four very long strips of leather together at the handle with a long, thick strip going down the middle. Then he would cross one over the other while wrapping each strand around to the other hand and tightening it at the same time. He would continue braiding until he got to the end of the strips and then he would attach a strip of leather or sea grass rope for a cracker. He was amazing with it. He could pick out anything and do with it as he pleased. I hated when he got it out and said, "Let's go outside, Bob. I want you to hold some branches for me." I'm swallowing right now and my heart is beating just like it did then. He would make me hold a branch or usually a Johnsongrass leaf. They're long and sturdy and just right for practicing with a bullwhip. He would stand eight feet away and methodically start cutting it away with me standing there terrified at what he was doing. I would shake and cry and he would tell me to stop crying and shaking and hold that leaf still. He would have me hold it with my arm outstretched while he would start cutting it bit by bit until it would be only inches away from my hand. This is not a pleasant thing to be writing, I can tell you.

On other occasions he would call for me to come outside with him as he grabbed his bullwhip and some newspaper. I guess he had been sitting around thinking of another way to terrify me. We would always be in the front yard doing these things. It was all that I could do to hold myself together when he was doing this to me. He knew how afraid I was of him and he took pleasure in terrifying me. When he would get the bullwhip out my dad would make me hold a piece of newspaper and he would be facing me and I had to hold this paper and not move. He would cut it into two and then I would drop one half and hold the other with my other hand. He would cut that one into and I would have to hold it as it got smaller and smaller. One day he said for me to come outside and he got his whip and a sheet of paper. I told him that I didn't want to do it anymore because it scared me and I couldn't take it anymore. He made me go outside anyway and hold that newspaper while he cut it in two. It kept getting shorter and shorter and I started begging him to stop. He kept screaming at me and telling me to suck it up and stop shaking and then I was holding it by my fingers and my thumbs and they were about two inches apart and he was eight feet out in front of me, his ten-year-old terrified son, and screaming at me for crying and he let it go one last time and POW! My wrist exploded! Blood went everywhere! He couldn't believe that he had hit me. But he blamed me! He said that if I had held still he wouldn't have hit me. It was my fault for shaking and crying. We never did it again. I still carry a scar to this very day that is shaped like a cross on my left wrist.

Another one of his favorite ways of tormenting me was with a baseball. He would stand about twenty feet away from me and throw the baseball at me as hard as he could. He could really fire a ball as well. He could place it right where he wanted it to go. He would throw it very hard and I would have to catch it. Then we would take one step forward and he would throw it the same way again. I had to keep my eyes on the ball or I would be hit in the head with it. Then we would step forward and this would continue until I could not take any more and would be crying and completely engulfed in fear. He would literally be standing eight feet in front of me and throw that ball at me as hard as he could. I caught it most of the time. When I didn't it was bad news physically and mentally for me. I would get hit by the ball and then get berated for missing it or dropping it. I grew up in fear and was a grown man with children of my own before I realized that fear was just an image in thought and had no power over me.

I worked in the fields outside of Lepanto, Newport and Diaz, Arkansas, and I actually still have family on my Mama's side who live there. I used to walk many a mile pulling a cotton sack or carrying water for the field hands. Before that I would sharpen the hoes. That was before I got big enough to pull my weight down a row. The first time I got to chop cotton the boss man told me to just thin it out. I had been watching everyone do it and thought that I had it down. I was going to make my first row look like the shining example I thought that it should be when I got finished. I thinned it all right, but the problem was that it was just a little too thin. I had chopped down nearly every stalk of cotton on that row, so I was back to carrying those water buckets and sharpening hoes for a while longer. The boss said that I was a little too short in the britches just yet.

At the time I didn't know that we were poor. My two best friends were a couple of black boys named Rabbit and L.C. We were as thick as fleas. We went everywhere together. They would stay over at my house sometimes and I would stay over at theirs. They lived across the tracks back up in the woods. Their Mama was a fine woman and

That's me holding a string of fish in Diaz circa 1958–1959.

loved her children. As a matter of fact she loved everyone's children. That would include me, too. We used to take a two-man handcart down the track to the old railroad trestle a few miles away and catch crawdads. It was a platform with four wheels and a teeter-totter hand-operated unit. I'm sure you've seen them in the movies. It was supposed to take two to operate it but one could do it if he worked at it. We would get a #2 washtub full of crawdads and take them home. My Mama wouldn't let me bring them in the house so I played with them on the porch. Rabbit and L.C. took theirs home and their mama would boil them for her family to eat. We didn't know that they were edible. My mother wouldn't have cooked them for us to eat in the first place.

Rabbit and I used to get up in the top of those cotton gins and smoke old cigarette butts that we found on the ground. We used to smoke grapevines too, but that stopped when I got a mouth full of red ants. It's a wonder we didn't burn the place down. Luckily, it never happened. The cotton was separated from the hull in those gins and the hulls would go out a chute that was seventy-five feet up in the air. The result was a mountain of cotton hulls about fifty feet tall. We used to climb to the top and hold our knees close to our chests and tumble down. It was a lot of fun and all we did was get covered in loose cotton. All day long we would climb up those hull hills and tumble down. Other times we would go out and find sapling trees that were tall but sturdy enough to support the weight of a nine-year-old. I would get to the top, or as high as I could, and then it would start to sway. I would ride it back and it would straighten back up and go over to the other side and back and forth it would go until eventually it would let me back down on the ground. The tree would end up growing crooked, though.

One time Rabbit and I had been up in the cotton gin smoking those old butts. Later that same day my dad took me fishing down the road a ways. We were standing on a graveled road, fishing off of a bridge into a creek. Out of the blue he asked me, "Have you been smoking?" I said, "No, sir." He asked me again, "Have you and Rabbit been smoking cigarettes?" Again I lied to him. He said to me, "If you tell me the truth you won't get a whipping. But if you lie to me boy, I'm gonna beat you to death!" I quickly said, "Yes, sir, I've been smoking!" He never said another word, not until we got home, that is. I knew something was up because I could see it in his face. His little brain was working overtime. I knew that it wasn't going to be good for me whatever it was he was cooking up in there. Sure enough, when we got back to that little shack by the railroad tracks in Diaz he told me, "Get in the bedroom!" My Mama said, "Jim, why don't you at least wait till after supper?" Here I am getting ready to have I don't know what done to me and she says wait till after supper. I think she was just trying to buy me some time. As a matter of fact I'm sure that she was because she piled my plate high with turnip greens and she knew that I hated turnip greens. He had told me that we would take care of this after we finished eating. That sanctimonious hypocrite started praying and this was one time I was glad that he was pilled up. When he was wired he would pray forever. The food would always get cold. We would all sit there with our eyes open looking at each other and picking out our piece of chicken while he was praying to some hole up in the sky to some invisible God that wasn't helping anybody, especially my Mother and me and my little sister. When everyone else had finished eating but me he told me he wanted to see me in the bedroom when I had finished all of those greens that my mom had so thoughtfully piled so high on my plate. He was trying to prolong the agony and was torturing me because he knew that I hated greens. I finally finished, and Mama said, "You had better go on in there, son." When I walked into the room he was pretty worked up because I had taken my time eating. He had a wide work belt that he had doubled and was bringing his two fists close together and then yanking them out real hard, and the belt made the sound of a whip cracking: Pop! Pop! Pop! It was intimidation in the first degree, especially as I was ten years old. I told him, "You said that if I told you the truth that you wouldn't whip me." He replied, "This is for lying to me in the first place." He enjoyed playing mind games with a child. It was a lose-lose situation for me. He made me lie across the bed and he began to beat me with that three-foot piece of two-inch-wide doubled leather strap from the top of my shoulders to the bottoms of my feet. He made me count every lick and if I had the misfortune to stop or lose count we would start all over with, one, two, three. I dared not stop counting. This kind of nightmarish living would continue until I left that godless man and that godless life. Even a happy occasion became a nightmare very quickly. His temperament would change with each thought that might float through his twisted little mind. If the mind is an avenue of awareness his was a long dark winding road.

Angels All Around Us

When I was a little boy all of my teeth were rotten. I have lived with pain in my face ever since I can remember. I was 10 or 11 when we moved to Kansas City, Missouri, my dad had us living in the worst part, down on Tracy Street in the projects by the railroad yards. He had borrowed someone's truck in Diaz, Arkansas, to move us up to Kansas City. When we pulled up there and he got out of the truck, the first thing that happened was a young boy hit him with a rock and called him a son of a bitch. Then a couple of days later after we had unloaded it, he took the truck back to Arkansas and never returned. He had a revival meeting in Wynne, Arkansas, that lasted for two weeks. That would be two weeks of preaching to a bunch of people who didn't have a clue what he was saying! When he left us we had no money and absolutely nothing at all to eat. It was winter, and it was freezing in that apartment, and we had no food. He had just taken us there on another of his whims and left us there to fend for ourselves while he was preaching away down in Arkansas. My mother had been left with less than a dollar, and there was no food in the house. When I spoke with her recently about this, she said, "I couldn't fix a can of beans for us. There wasn't a drop of anything in the house to eat." There were a few neighbors who saw and recognized my mother's dilemma and brought us something to eat. The snowdrifts up against our end apartment were twelve feet tall, but we played outside during the day to keep warm. My mother had no other option but to start taking us every day when the sun went down to the mission to wait our turn in line to eat with the winos and the street people. We had trays with a plate and a cup and were served a bowl of chicken broth with a piece of bologna floating in it, some mashed potatoes and beans with slice of white bread, and a cup of hot tea without anything in it. And there was an apple on the tray for last. We walked all the way there as well, and it was a hell of a long way, too.

When we were taken to Kansas City by my dad we had no idea that it was going to be so cold, and we didn't have winter clothes at all. A neighbor gave my mother two tickets for my sister and me to go to the circus downtown. There was four feet of snow and we weren't dressed to be going out in that cold weather, but my mom scraped together enough money for us to take the bus downtown and back. She had to stay with my nine-month-old baby brother, Nathan, so she walked us to the bus stop and it was already starting to get dark. Deb and I were alone in Kansas City, 10-year-old big brother Bobby and little

6-year-old sister Debbie. We got to the circus and watched the whole thing. We were probably among the very last out the door and when we got outside an ice storm had turned the entire place into something like the set of *Doctor Zhivago*. There were hardly any cars on the iced-over roads, and there were lines down everywhere. It was absolutely freezing and the wind was cutting into us at that bus stop. My sister and I stood at the bus stop, smack dab in the middle of downtown Kansas City, waiting on a bus that seemed as though it was never going to come. We were freezing, and she was crying and would not stop. She couldn't because she was so cold. All that she had on was a little short ruffled dress and a sweater. The legs of my pants were solid ice, like stove pipes of ice around my legs. Debbie couldn't stop crying so I stood by the wall next to the building because I was embarrassed. People just walked right past us. They were all so indifferent to my sister and me. The bus finally did come, but it took a very long time for it to arrive because of the slick streets. I remember

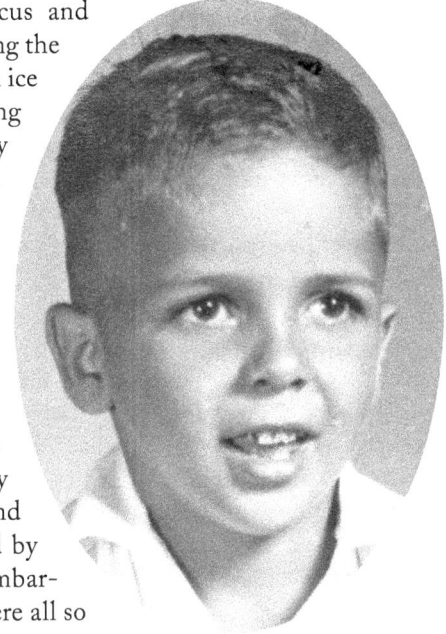

My rotten teeth.

how warm it was when we got on. It took a while to get back, and when we were pulling up I could see my mother standing there anxiously awaiting our return. She had been so worried about us, and I could see it in her eyes. Two weeks went by and my dad finally sent us $100 via Western Union. Here we were with no money for food and he sends us money to Western Union, which was all the way across town! Mom managed to get some cash to get just enough gas to get us to the Western Union station. Mama said, "We had to park a long ways away because we didn't have money for the parking meter. It was a very long walk to the station, and my feet were killing me by the time we got there!" When we got back to our apartment my mother threw everything that she could fit into the station wagon and we were headed back home to Memphis and Big Mama's house. We stopped and got some groceries, and we stopped at a park on the way out of town and she fixed us some bologna and cheese sandwiches with tomato, lettuce and mayonnaise and we had some potato chips and a Coke. When we got back in the car and she started to pull away I told her that angels were watching over us. They were, too, because I could see them all around us!

    I don't have a lot of old friends. I have a lot of friends who are old, though. One of the oldest is Joe Delaney Schenk. He and I were best of friends when were growing up, and still are. He played piano with Carl Perkins up until the day Carl passed. Joe Delaney can play that piano, to be sure. We were living in Tiptonville, Tennessee, and his daddy was a big cotton farmer. He owned 6,000 acres. So Joe ran the farm and played with Carl. Tiptonville was a little nothing of a town a mile off the Mississippi River, the same place my daddy had his breakdown. Main Street was one mile from one end to the other, with a railroad track at the end where sits a sign proudly proclaiming, "The Home of Carl Perkins." His childhood home had been moved to town some years ago in hopes that it would be a big tourist attraction. I used to sit on that front porch when the house was in the middle of a bean field and Ma Perkins would give me fried peach pies and a glass of sweet tea and tell me stories about her famous son. Old man Perkins never said a whole lot. He just walked around in his overalls with a brown hat, head held down, kind of sad like. I don't even remember his face. And that's saying something because I'm good with names and faces. I have difficulty putting them together sometimes, but I remember everybody and every name I ever knew and every place I've ever been in my whole lifetime. It takes a little prodding sometimes but it never leaves. The doors to my mind have never been closed, and there is an infinite storehouse there. Full and spilling over, so it would seem.

I had another friend there by the name of Chuck Stevens. We used to go snake hunting at the big Reelfoot Lake. It was formed in the early 1800s by the New Madrid earthquakes, and the Mississippi River flowed backwards for over 24 hours to fill it. It's a huge lake. We took a couple of toe-sacks and a snake grabber—it was really his grandmother's jar-getter. We took what we had out in the lake in a jonboat, which is made to ride up over the cypress knees. That lake's full of them. It's a beautiful lake and eagles nest there. Great fishing as well. We would spend the better part of the morning catching water snakes. They're harmless and not poisonous. One time, we had just about filled both sacks full of snakes. I don't know what we had intended on doing with them. We were just going to let them all go and watch them go back into the water, I guess. That was what we always did. But we didn't have a plan that day. We must have had about 150 snakes of various lengths and sizes and colors. Then I remembered that there was a baseball game going on that afternoon right after church, when everybody was still all dressed up for God. The bleachers were full of about 35 or so of the local Baptist and Methodist congregations, all sitting smug, pious and hypocritical—poor rich folks, as I saw them. We had the two sacks full of snakes in the trunk of the car. We opened it up behind the stands and let them all out. All 150 of them went straight under the bleachers and came out from under the front and a woman screamed, "Snakes! Snakes! Snakes!" The players all took off running and left their gloves on the field. The stands were emptied and everyone was screaming and running in every direction, and the women all left their purses. All of the men went first—left their wives like they didn't even know them. Tearing out of there running from what has now turned out to be known after all of this time as "thousands of snakes." A couple of fun-loving boys had become the root of a mythological urban legend. The game was over. Chuck and I just laughed at the chaos we caused. Nobody ever found out who the culprits were. But you all know now!

Uncle Woodrow Wages

Woodrow Wages really wasn't my uncle, but I felt closer to him than I did any man in my world. He was about 6-foot-4, a big man in every way, and especially his heart. He had a place for me in there. He always had a cigar holder with a stogie stuck in his mouth. He had a ring and a watch that Elvis had given him. He owned the Millington Furniture store, and his wife's name was Gertrude, or, as she was affectionately called, Gerdie, and they had two sons, Wilson and Dennis. He had known my family all of my life and he loved me and knew what my mother and I were going through. He knew that my dad was a nut case and told me that Dad was just a very sick man. He gave me a job so that I could help my mother out with the groceries and just living. I would put together furniture when it arrived at his store there in Millington, Tennessee, and I worked with two other men, Willie and Raymond, delivering furniture to the military families in Mud Flats. They would generally rent furniture because they were always on the move. One day Uncle Woodrow called me into his office. He said, "Little Whit, come on in here, I want to talk to you." That's what everyone called me, Little Whit. Even when I was head and shoulders taller than my dad they still called me that. And some still do to this very day, or Little Bobby. I went into his office, and he had his feet crossed and was reared back in his

Playing the guitar that Uncle Woodrow bought me.

chair. On his desk, he had a book with guitars pictured in it. He asked me to pick one out because he didn't know anything about guitars and was going to get Wilson one for his birthday. I remember asking myself, "Why is he getting this for Wilson? He's not interested in music other than just listening to it, and he wants to be a lawyer." Wilson is a judge now. I picked out a beautiful rosewood acoustic and went back to work. Two or three weeks later Uncle Woodrow called me back into his office again. This time he had a guitar case on the top of his desk. He said, "Open that up and tell me what you think of it." I thought that this is torture for me. All that I had was that old metal National Dobro that Big Mama had given me. I opened it up and it was beautiful. He asked me to take it out and play it for him. I remember thinking how lucky Wilson and Dennis were to have him as their dad. And how fortunate Wilson was to be getting this beautiful guitar. I took it out and started playing it for him. He just reared back and smiled at me. When I finished he said to me, "Well, what do you think?" I told him that it was the most beautiful guitar I had ever seen and that Wilson was one lucky boy. Then he told me that it was for me. It makes me cry right now remembering how kind and generous he was to me and my mother. I'm not surprised at these tears. There have been a lot of them shed while writing this book. I loved Uncle Woodrow and still think of him often. Uncle Woodrow died in a plane crash in New Orleans. The landing gear didn't come down and when it touched down it caught on fire. It was a small private plane and he could not get out of the escape window because he was too big. He was able to help a young boy out of the window, though. A finer man on this earth I have never met. I only hope that I can be as generous and giving in my life as he was in his. I'm sitting here right now with tears running down my face, knowing that he knows I am writing him into this book of my life. I'm really proud to have had him in my world and that he is still such a part of me.

The Sixties

In 1965 I was just 16 and still in school. I had one more year to go until I graduated. I was not sure even if I would. As it turned out I barely did. I pretty much charmed my way through school. My singing and playing was my way through life even then. That is all that I have ever done except for when I worked in the fields as a boy and then for Uncle Woodrow helping Willie deliver furniture to the military base in Millington, Tennessee. That's where I was living with my folks in 1966 until the exact day after my graduation from school. My mom had the suitcase that I had gotten as a gift from her at Christmas packed and sitting by the back door the morning after I graduated. She had made me a great big breakfast of three eggs and her famous biscuits and ham and bacon and a sliced tomato. I had a glass of juice and some coffee. It was the biggest breakfast that she had ever made for me. She was standing there waiting as I ate my breakfast. She said, "Hurry up and finish and I'll take you to town." She had packed my suitcase just like she said that she would do after I got out of school. She set me free. My mother believed in me and wanted me to have a better life. She knew that all I needed was to be out on my own singing and playing and away from my dad. He would stifle anything that I would do. He was not supportive of my life or what I did with it. As far as he was concerned I was selling my soul to the devil. With him being a Southern Baptist preacher that remark didn't surprise me at all. He never did see or hear me perform. Not even on *The Johnny Cash Show*. He wouldn't come to Nashville and didn't watch it when it aired on the television. I'm sure that he regretted that through the years after me becoming famous and a rock star. After breakfast Mama took me to Memphis, dropped me off at Poplar and Stonewall, gave me $50 and drove away. She gave me my freedom and I got my start in life at the corner of Stonewall and Poplar in Memphis with a suitcase and a harmonica and $50 in my pocket and a ham sandwich from home.

I went to a friend's apartment that wasn't too far away and knocked on his door. He answered it and invited me in and told me to take the other bedroom. I had a roof over my head right away. His name was Stan Cecil. He was in the band called the Short Cuts, who would eventually become the Counts. They featured a black soul singer, Eddie Harrison who could dance and sing like Jackie Wilson. Eddie is still a great singer and lives in Memphis. I had my first band, Out of It. We called ourselves that because everywhere that we went to get matching clothes they were "out of it." I stood out front and sang and played a chromatic harp. I was very good at it as well and played "Fingertips Part 1 and 2." I'm still a pretty good harp player. It came very natural to me as does playing most anything. Our drummer was Roy Yeager, and keyboard player Bobby Sowell played the bass as well with his left hand. He still lives in Memphis and is still playing that rock 'n' roll boogie-woogie piano that he plays. The Counts already had a hit record in 1965 or

1966 with "Stormy Weather." Then they lost their lead singer to the dentistry profession. Later they asked me to join. It wouldn't be too much longer before the old bass player and guitar player from the Short Cuts would be in the band as well. We promptly made Wayne Thompson, our guitar player, our road manager. He was much better at that than he was at playing guitar. And he was the only one of us who had any sense about business. We started doing all soul music and rock 'n' roll. But it was mostly all of the Stax music that I was really into. We also did "Expressway to Your Heart" by the Soul Survivors and some Young Rascals material and "Gimme Some Lovin'" by the Spencer Davis Group. It was really about Steve Winwood's singing and organ playing as far as I was concerned. We opened up on several occasions for Hank Ballard and the Midnighters at some colleges. He always showed up with a doo rag on his head and his hair was just so. It was right in place, as was his wardrobe. He always carried a separate change of clothes for the show.

Age 16.

He had a hair dryer and a suit bag and had it all going on when it came to being prepared for the stage. When it was show time Hank was ready. I took my cue from him and started carrying a change of clothes and a hair dryer after that. It made a whole lot of sense to me to get dressed at the gig. I had never thought about that. Until I watched Hank I never knew what to do about getting ready for the stage. When I joined up with Eric Clapton I was schooled in how to look, how to act, and how to be a rock star. So the way I look at it, Hank got me dressed and Eric put me out on the world stage.

I really enjoyed playing in and around Memphis between 1965 and 1968. It was a great time and town for music then, especially soul music. It was real rhythm and blues. Albert King R&B, that's what I'm talking about. It was loose and all about music everywhere that you turned. I would talk my way into the various studios in Memphis and got to know many musicians and producers. I first met Phil Walden when I was hanging out at Stax studios one day in March 1967. At that time he managed Otis Red-

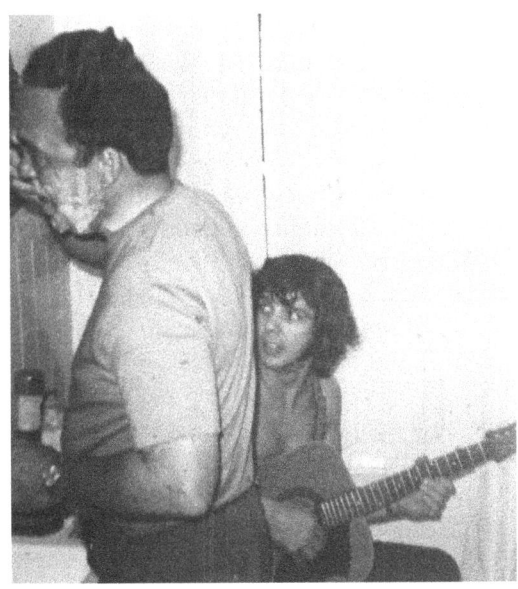

The only time I could get my dad to listen to me play.

The Counts at the Cabaret Lounge in Memphis. That's me on the left, Stan Cecil on the bar, Richie Simpson (standing) and an unknown guitar player (photograph by Jerry Hankins).

ding. Otis was the only somebody that I never saw but once, and that was when they were getting on the bus to go to the airport and on to Europe to do that great *Live in Europe* record. I was living in the heart of rhythm and the blues. What a great way to start your career. Before all of the racial tension and the Beale Street riots, you could sit on the curb of East McLemore and eat hot chicken at 3 in the morning and nobody would bother you—you felt quite safe. I met and became friends with Albert King, Sam and Dave, the Staple Singers, William Bell and every other somebody who came and recorded at Stax. I was the fly on the wall, and I was there when the Staples Singers did "Long Walk to D.C." and Albert King did "Crosscut Saw." I probably saw Booker T. Jones more than any-

I'm out front singing with the Counts: Wayne Thompson on tambourine, Stan Cecil on bass and Richie Simpson on drums.

body else, and he would always let me stand behind him up against the studio brick wall and watch and listen as he and the MGs recorded. I watched them do "Hip Hugger" and "Slim Jenkins' Joint" and many others. I was also often there when Booker T. was in the studio playing by himself. I watched as he used the drawbars to create different nuances of sound and combined the Leslie and the rotation of it to create moods and to color a piece. That's where I learned my technique. Only I took what I had learned and made it mine and developed my own style and way of doing things. I learned an awful lot from just being afforded the opportunity to hang around and watch a great engineer like Ron Capone at work. He was the guy who got that Stax sound. He had the ears, and they all had the playing ability. They all had the sound out in the studio, and Ron knew just how to translate that in the control room and finally down on to the master pressing disc. That's how far back I go in this music business. Stax had an eight-track machine that sat in the corner for a very long time because they were so used to the four-channel machine. It went straight down to two-track and then straight onto the acetate right in the control room. The whole process took place right there in the studio and the control room—there was no going somewhere else to master it. It was a master when we were finished and it became the master disc immediately after that. I felt really lucky that I was welcome everywhere that I went when I was learning my craft in Memphis.

Albert King and I became very good friends and stayed in touch over the years. There was a time later in the mid-'70s when Albert opened a few shows for me at Poet's Music Hall in Memphis that my wild second cousin Bobby Kaiser used to own. Bobby had jailhouse tattoos all over him and always had a huge roll of cash. It was a loud event to be sure. Albert came pulling up in his old bus with his name written in the side, and he was driving with that pork pie hat and that pipe stoking. He had a big grin and was waving as he pulled up, and then he went inside and sat down on the couch backstage and went to sleep. When it was time for his first set, Bobby came up to Albert and shook him and said that it was time to play. Albert woke and said, "Where's my money?" Bobby had to pay him first, then Albert counted it out, and then he did his first set. He couldn't read or write but he knew how to count his money. Then after he finished playing he came backstage and went to sleep again. We did our set and when I walked off the stage Bobby walked up to Albert and shook him again and said that it was time to do his second set. Albert looked up at him and said, "Where's my money?" Bobby forked it over and Albert tore the house down. I loved Albert King. He was the King of the Kings in

Albert King, in 1992 on the barge (photograph by CoCo Carmel).

my book. Every time Albert would be introduced to someone by me he would always say, "I remember Little Bobby when he could barely see over the console down at Stax when he stood in front of it." Every time he would meet someone, that would be the line that he used, and I'm real glad that it was me in those special moments.

I came back from England one time and had to go through New York and then down to Atlanta to fly back up to Memphis, which really pissed me off because I could see my farm below as we flew 36,000 feet over it to Atlanta. I was very tired and would have jumped out of the plane if I had had a parachute. When I arrived at the Atlanta airport I had to change planes to go to Memphis and then drive on home to Mississippi. When I walked on the plane there sat Albert with his pork pie hat on and his pipe sticking out of his mouth. It wasn't lit, he just had it clinched between his teeth and was grinning and standing up and saying "Hey there, Little Bobby!" as he was hugging me. He made my whole experience of going and coming back the long way from England all worthwhile. He told me about recording his last record and how the producer took it back and by the time he finished that it didn't even sound like him. He was very upset about it. I told him that I had just read an article in *Rolling Stone* in which Eric had said that he used Albert's lick sped up for the signature guitar lick of all time. I told Albert that he probably had a ton of money due him for his input on the song "Layla." He told me, "I don't need that boy's money. He can have that lick, I've got a lot more where that came from." When we arrived in Memphis someone was there to meet me, and when I walked off of the plane with Albert I introduced him and he said, "It's nice to meet you. I've known Little Bobby since he could just about see over the console at Stax." What a lovely man.

By 1967 there was absolutely no sign of racial tension in Memphis. That all changed when the infamous garbage strikes by the African American sanitation workers took place in February 1968. Dr. Martin Luther King came to Memphis and offered his support for the strike as part of his Poor People's Campaign, which was an effort to take the grievances of the poor directly to Washington. A change was coming and you could feel it in the streets. The band carried on playing in Arkansas and in Mississippi. There was no freeway system yet, so it was all two-lane roads that wound their way through every hog wallow between Memphis and wherever it was that we would be playing. One of the places I remember was at the VFW Club in Greenwood, Mississippi. It would take two days to get there and then we would set up with our stage clothes on and start playing. We had two Christmas tree lights that were circular and had four colors that changed as they rotated. That was our light show. I stood out front and sang and played harp. We had a great guitar player named David Priola who played a red Gibson. We were a good little rock band.

One day I was at the Amro Music store on Poplar Avenue in Memphis just looking at the instruments and killing time. My friend Stanley walked in and I was playing "Moon River" with three fingers on an old upright piano. He played bass with the Short Cuts and knew that I sang and blew a harp but he had never seen me playing a piano before. He asked me if I played an organ and I said, "Sure I do." In fact, I only knew how to play "Moon River" with three fingers. That was it! That was the extent of my keyboard expertise. I knew that I could play, though, because I was confident that there was nothing that I couldn't turn my hand to. I could feel it within my soul. I knew that I was supposed to be doing what I was doing because that was all that I could embody and nothing else made any sense to me. He said that they were in a tight spot: their organ player had quit and they needed an organ player for some gigs. He asked me if I would be interested in playing and I said yes with no hesitation. The first gig was at Skateland just outside of Memphis on that coming Saturday. This was Tuesday! He said rehearsals were at his mama's house the next day. I arrived there early and had no choice but to break the news to Stanley that I couldn't play because I didn't know how. I told him that I would be fine if only I knew how to make a chord. He showed me how to make a C chord and the different inversions of it and then showed me that the next chord was F and then G. Then by moving one finger it becomes a minor and adding one finger it becomes a minor seventh. After my quick lesson I had it and sat down and started playing right away. It came as natural to me as writing songs did. I had already been steeped in R&B from knowing Duck Dunn and Booker T. and hanging out at every studio in Memphis that would let me in, and they all did. In fact Sam Phillips recorded me in his studio on the same equipment that he used to record Elvis. Those tapes are floating around somewhere and I'm sure will surface one day. His cousin, Dewey Philips, lived behind Big Mama King's house one door down. I had known Dewey ever since I was a little boy. He was one of rock 'n' roll's pioneering disk jockeys and had the "Red Hot and Blue" radio show in Memphis. He was the top DJ there for years. He had red hair and was directly responsible for Elvis' early success. Dewey played "That's Alright (Mama)" for forty-eight straight hours on his show. I saw Dewey scratching records in the early '60s. He would go back and forth to find the exact start and the turntable would be spinning and he would be holding the record in place with his fingers and talking away. When he was through he released the record and the song. He was his own cue master. I was eventually asked by the Short Cuts to play with them and I accepted. I played organ and sang background and duets with Eddie Harrison dancing and singing out front. We all had pirate shirts with big sleeves and very thick belts with huge brass buckles. We were four white dudes and one black dude on the road playing honky-tonks and frat parties down in Mississippi when the lid was just about to blow off the racial jug, and here we were dressed like pirates. When we were in Mississippi we couldn't stay in hotels because Eddie was black. So we would park outside the hotel in the dark and someone would go in and get the room. Once we got in the room we flipped a coin to see who would get the floor. Most of the restaurants in the South, especially in Mississippi and in Arkansas, did not serve blacks, so we would just park outside and send someone in for a sack full of cheeseburgers and some Cokes. When we were going through the South playing and Eddie was in the band it got pretty heavy and hairy at times. I couldn't believe it: Churches everywhere and we couldn't have safe passage through Mississippi because of the racial prejudice. If you were hanging out with black folks in parts of the South you were discriminated against. All of my family were

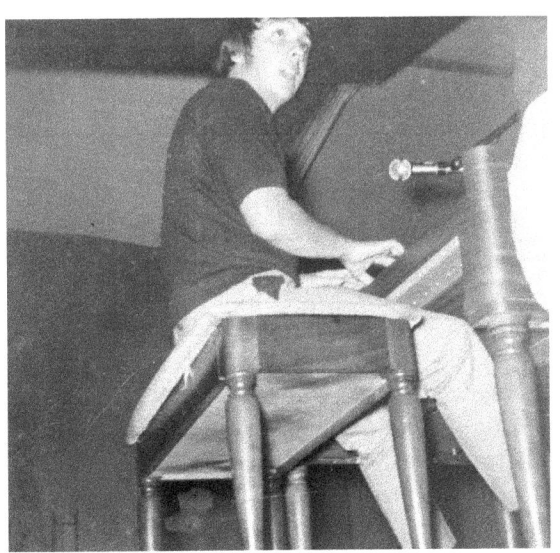

Me on my B3.

from Mississippi, in that very low state of consciousness. A few of them still are that way, too.

A show that will stay with me forever was in Jackson, Mississippi, where we played at a college. After our gig we loaded the Chevy van and trailer and headed back for the very long and very dark ride through the night to Memphis. We were listening to the radio when the news of Dr. Martin Luther King's death came on. We could not believe what we were hearing. There were riots in Memphis and the whole of Beale Street was in blazes. Unbeknownst to us, martial law had been imposed, and no one could be out on the street after dark. We were on our way to a war zone called home and I can tell you it was real eerie. Eddie had to keep his head down when we pulled into Memphis. It was about 3 in the morning and there were only guys with helmets and guns everywhere. We were stopped and told to get off the streets immediately. I can hardly believe that I was around when such behavior existed with our fellow man and I'm not sure much has changed. That would be the end of me eating hot chicken at 3 in the morning down on East McLemore Street.

We used to play a club exactly on the state line between Texas and Arkansas. The Pines Ballroom was in Texarkana and had a white line drawn down the middle. One side was Arkansas and the other was Texas, and there wasn't but one door to the place. You had to fight to get your way in and out of there. They dressed in their finest there on a Friday night. I still vividly remember a guy with white lightning stripes on the sides of his shoes dancing with his girlfriend, who had on a shoestring strap light blue dress. I'll never forget the scene, her in that blue dress just swaying around to the music and not even thinking about where she was or who she was with. She looked completely out of place. She was. She belonged wherever the place was that she was fantasizing about. That's where she was, there, all alone in her head, with him shouting up to us, like Dale on *King of the Hill*, while we were playing our soul music, "Play something new, like 'Kansas City!'" We played "Kansas City" all night long for them. Another great night was opening a show for Mitch Ryder and the Detroit Wheels in Little Rock, Arkansas, in 1966. That guy closed his eyes and sang his heart out and blew me away. I thought that he was the very best white singer that I had ever heard. "Devil with a Blue Dress On" and "Jenny Take a Ride" are just two of his many hits. Mitch had it all going on at that time as far as I was concerned. I thought that he was great. I didn't try to sing like him or take up any of his ways, I just had this tremendous respect for this white dude from Detroit up there in a three-piece suit without a tie, standing on his own exposing his soul through his voice. He was completely soaked with sweat when he was finished with his set. Awesome!

As I mentioned earlier, every day that the door was open and when I wasn't somewhere else playing, I was down at Stax. I knew Homer Banks, Betty Crutcher, Isaac Hayes and David Porter very well. Every time the Staple Singers were in town I would be there, watching and listening and learning everything that I could. The first performance of mine that was ever recorded was clapping hands with Isaac Hayes and David Porter on Sam and Dave's "I Thank You." That was me clapping my way into history. I was always surrounded with greatness, it seems. Duck Dunn and Steve Cropper were my close friends back then. They were with the MGs, Duck was my first producer, and I taught Steve's son, Stevie, how to swim at their house. There was a jukebox there and "Paperback Writer" and "Wild Thing" played at full volume all day long. I worked as a Lifeguard for a couple of summers to get some extra cash and taught little kids to swim. I worked during the day and then played soul music in the honky-tonks at night. I also had a great tan. It doesn't take me but about five minutes in the sun and I'm good to go for the whole year.

Joining Delaney and Bonnie

Delaney Bramlett came from Pontotoc County in Mississippi. His father was a sharecropper who ran off, leaving his mother to raise him and his brother. The house he lived in had no running water. They would have to use the pump in the front yard and boil it up on the stove for bathing. He learned how to play the guitar at a young age from R.C. Weatherall, an old black guy who taught him everything there is to know about the blues. Delaney would later write a song about him, "Poor Elijah," and it became a staple in Delaney and Bonnie and Friends set. Delaney joined the Navy at the age of sixteen. He knew that he would only have to do two years service and, more importantly, it would keep him out of the Vietnam draft, as well as getting him out of Mississippi. He thought he would get to see the world but ended up doing half of his time on land at Great Lakes, Illinois, in boot camp. He finished the rest of his service in Norfolk, Virginia. After his discharge from the navy, he moved to Los Angeles because of the thriving music scene and he knew that that was where the money was. His first job only paid him $8 a night serving beer in a country and western joint in the San Fernando Valley. Eventually he gave up the bar job and started playing the small clubs in the LA area. One night at the Palomino Club in North Hollywood he was asked by Jack Good if he'd like to appear on *Shindig*, a pilot television show for ABC. That was how he got his first break, and Delaney became a member the Shindogs duo with Joey Cooper. They were the house band for the popular ABC-TV series that became the ground-breaking prime-time TV show twice a week for the hip and young, and the first to feature live rock 'n' roll as its main focus. Later the Shindogs' lineup expanded to a full band.

I must admit that I didn't know much about Delaney's career when he was on *Shindig*, except that I was watching him on TV and didn't even know it. As a matter of fact, I was watching the players as a whole. Don Preston played guitar and sang with a unique voice. He never really played with Delaney & Bonnie for some reason. He was a tall handsome blond-haired dude from Tulsa, Oklahoma, and played his butt off. He was also an incredible singer. He was able to split his voice, making it sound like two people. Taj Mahal can make it sound like four! I can do it when it's called for. My voice is in between Don's and Taj's. Leon Russell was in the Shindogs as well, and he ended up with a very successful solo career. Joey Cooper, the other guitar player and singer, never went much further than he did on that show for some reason. Delaney was the bass player and Chuck Blackwell was the drummer. Delaney still had his Dan-Electro bass that he used on that show and he was so damn proud of the fact that he had never changed the strings on it. He would boil them in hot water. Seems to me that he could have just bought some new ones. That bass sounded terrible!

Delaney's future wife, Bonnie Lynn O'Farell, came from Alton, Illinois. Her parents divorced when she was very young. Her father would take her to Stallings Park Tavern. She was only twelve but she would get up on stage and sing with a band called Pickers and Grinners. She loved singing and spent a long time in St. Louis playing wherever she could. She even sang with Ike and Tina Turner as an Ikette. That was pretty much a one-shot deal. She had a real talent for singing, and she, too, was drawn to Los Angeles and moved there in 1967. She met Delaney at a Shindogs gig at the Carolina Lanes Bowling Alley when she was playing on the same bill. After a whirlwind romance she married him a week later.

I was still living in Memphis in the summer of 1967 and would often go to my good friend Duck Dunn's house. Duck, his wife, June, Don Nix and I would listen to music or just hang, but Duck nearly always had something new for me to hear, like the flip side of the Small Faces' "Itchycoo Park" single, "I'm Only Dreaming." Duck and Don were interested in producing a record for me as a solo act, and when Stax started their HIP label to sort of get in on the English invasion, they signed me up. Thing was, they had no idea of what white music was at all. Their concept of a white act certainly wasn't Mitch Ryder, or me, for that matter. It was completely bubble-gum music. Their idea of presenting me to the world for the first time was with a song written by Leon Russell and Donna Washburn, "Raspberry Rug." It had a bunch of trombones playing all over it. I was mortified when it was released. Luckily, although I did not know it at the time, I would soon be leaving my solo deal behind me. Duck had gone to L.A. and found Bonnie and Delaney Bramlett, this white couple, singing in a bowling alley in Hawthorne, California. They actually started out as Bonnie and Delaney. Everyone always called them that until Delaney raised so much hell that nobody could stand it. At this stage they had no representation. Duck had brought Bonnie and Delaney over from Los Angeles to Stax to meet Jim Stewart, the president and part-owner of Stax. He's the ST in the name and Estelle Axton was the AX. Everyone there had heard about Bonnie, who was already known as an amazing chick singer who had the reputation of being the white Aretha Franklin.

I had assembled the little band we called The Counts and was touring local clubs. Duck, Steve (Cropper) and everyone from Stax would come to see me play and would sit in from time to time because I did every song that came out of there. I was completely into soul music. I was not into the Beatles, or the Rolling Stones, or Cream, or any other music but soul music and what I called rock 'n' roll. To this day I haven't listened to any Cream songs except for the songs that we did when we first started Derek and the Dominos. And even then, we just started playing them without listening to any recordings. So it's safe to say that I really didn't know who Eric Clapton was until after I got to know him, and it didn't matter then, because the only way I have ever known him is the way I always have, as a real cool dude with a lot of class and style. And he's a great guitar player!

The first time I met Delaney and Bonnie was when I was playing at the Cabaret night club in Memphis. It was down on Southern and Highland, right next to the railroad tracks. You could hear the trains as they rolled by in the middle of your song. They'd blow their low, mournful horn as they passed because there was a crossing. The trains moved very slowly and were quite long, sometimes over a mile. I loved the rhythm that the wheels made as they rolled across the ties. I could get through three or four songs with that train as a background before it had completely passed. I loved it. I loved the sound and the feel of it as it rumbled past. You could feel it in your feet on the floor and the room kind of shook a little with it. We played right on through it, rumble and horn and engine and all. Duck had brought Delaney and Bonnie along to see me play one Wednesday night after their meetings with Jim Stewart. They were sitting at a table for four a little ways back in this long, narrow brick room. The stage was on one end, and the front door was on the other, and you could see the cars pass by on the street while you played. I did my usual set of "Midnight Hour," "Sunny," "Soul Man," "Gimme Some Lovin'," "Groovin'," "634-5789," "Knock on Wood" and "Try a Little Tenderness." After my set, I went out and sat down, and Duck introduced us. I had heard about them, and had heard some of their music. So I was well aware of who they were and what they sang like. Delaney said that they were going to put together a band in L.A. and asked if I wanted to come out there and be a part of it. After my disappointment with the direction HIP wanted me to go in I jumped at the chance and said yes, immediately, right in front of Duck. I felt bad about letting Duck and Stax down, but it seemed like too good an opportunity to miss.

I had never been past the Arkansas line, and I knew that there had to be a better life waiting for me. Little did I know what was in store for me when I left three days later for California. When I arrived, I slept on the Bramletts' living room couch. It was a real small place in Hawthorne, with only two bedrooms and one bathroom, a living room and a kitchen. There was Delaney and Bonnie, who had just given birth to Bekka, Bonnie's daughter Susanne and Delaney's mother, Mamaw, and Delaney's daddy, Preston, who was living out in the garage. We were packed in there like sardines. It was a hell of a deal I'll tell you. You sure do get to know somebody when you live with them in close proximity for a while. I swear it was the *Beverly Hillbillies* all over, and those two couldn't last a day without having it out. On top of that, there was a constant stream of people running through their house. It never stopped, ever!

Bonnie is a fine woman. She and I never had a cross word and laughed all of the time. We had a lot of fun together and it used to piss Delaney off for some reason. We were always up to something innocent, like hiding the pot or getting Delaney to shave his beard and take out his teeth. We did that one time and it wasn't that long after I had moved out there to be with them. Bonnie had taken out some pictures to look at. Family photos and the like. She ran across this picture of Delaney when he was eighteen. It was a color picture that was a small poster size. He was clean-shaven and was rather handsome with his hair all slicked back. We told him, "Hey, Delaney, why don't you shave your beard off! I bet you're still as good looking as ever!" Those last five words did it for us, as good looking as ever—I always knew the right words to say. Stroke that ego of his and it will work every time. We were playing him like a fiddle and he was going right along with it. He went immediately into the bathroom and cut his beard off! Lathered up and shaved. When he came back out, it was a bad scene. He hadn't taken into account all of the whiskey, pills and cocaine that he had done since he was eighteen. He was twenty-eight, and ten years is a lot when you're slamming. He was looking pretty rough, and that intimidation factor he had was gone. We didn't let on right away because we weren't finished just yet. Bonnie had told me that he wore false teeth, so we talked him into taking them out and doing a Gabby Hayes imitation for us. It was too much and we all busted out, laughing our heads off, and then it wasn't so funny real fast. He realized that we all were laughing at him and how helpless he looked, and in his mind, he immediately grew his beard back that second. He got straight back into the intimidation mode without the beard. He was just plain pissed off at us and himself at how ridiculous he looked. In hindsight, it was pretty cruel of us to do that, but we were just trying to have fun. Bonnie did her dead level best to please him, but that was impossible. He was a perfectionist and a self-centered, abusive person, and nothing was ever good enough for him.

When we first got together in Hawthorne, we didn't do a lot of anything but sing and play. Sometimes we'd roll some pot and go to the drive-in movie in their VW, just Bonnie and Delaney and me. She was the one who showed me how to roll a joint. I had never seen it done until I moved in with them. She showed me how to use a newspaper to get the seeds to roll out. We would take some peppermint liquor and a little weed and go see horror movies.

At first there was no band. It was only Delaney and Bonnie and me. He played acoustic guitar and sang all of the lead vocals and Bonnie sang the second harmony. He also "allowed" her to sing a solo number every now and then. As for me, he had me singing a third part falsetto like a chick background singer. I had only ever sung lead, and here I had come all this way to sleep on their couch and sing chick parts. I was broke and I felt like dying. I had left Duck and my solo deal with Stax to come out to California, to sing third part harmony with two people who were at each other's throats from the moment I walked through the front door. I didn't know about all of this at first. And I sure as hell didn't know about the third part vocals or I would have stayed in Memphis for sure.

Bonnie didn't have anything to do with writing while I was with them, except for one song. She and I share writers' credit on "Alone Together," the first and only song that we were to ever write with Delaney, written when I first arrived. I do believe that Delaney did it just to lure me in, and it worked. We never talked money. That wasn't a part of our relationship. We were family then, or so I thought. I was living with them and money never really came into the picture with us. I guess it's because we started it all and I wasn't in it for the money. I was in it to grow and learn. Boy, did I ever!

Stax were all prepared to put their machine behind Bonnie and Delaney. In their eyes, they were going to be the biggest soul duo singing couple ever. They were putting all of their focus on Bonnie at that time. Stax wanted Delaney to play the role that Ike Turner was playing behind Tina. Delaney wasn't going to let that happen for one second. His ego was way too big for that. He wanted to be the star. Bonnie's chance at becoming the next Aretha was shot down in flames by her own husband and his massive ego. That would be the undoing of it all in the end. Delaney would say one thing and act one way when he was around a person, and then he would turn it all around when he was not anywhere within earshot. From that day on, they became Delaney & Bonnie. Bonnie was philosophical about it, though, and told the influential *Rolling Stone* at the time, "You don't say Missus and Mister, do you? You always say the man's name first. That's the natural way."

Once the deal with Stax was done, Delaney and Steve Cropper started writing songs out at Jim Stewart's house. That's where Bonnie and Delaney were staying. They went into the studio and I sang background vocals along with Bonnie. I sang back then the same way that I do now. It's just that I have now what I seriously lacked then — experience. I could sing and play, but I had no life experiences. All that I knew was what I had been subjected to in my then relatively short existence here on earth. And, sadly, being around those Bramletts didn't lift things in the state of consciousness area one bit. They still carried their upbringing around with them. When we were at Stax studios recording *Home*, our first album, I felt about three feet tall and I was totally embarrassed because of the way I had to sing. Stax's house musicians, including Donald "Duck" Dunn, Steve Cropper, Booker T. Jones, and Isaac Hayes all played on the album. Steve and Duck had been listening to me sing with my bands as well as out in the front of the M.G.'s, and here I was singing like a woman. I was mortified. These guys were my friends as well as my heroes, and I felt like a dwarf that day in the session. I felt like crawling under the table. I was ashamed because I had walked out on them to go sing girl parts and be a sideman with Delaney & Bonnie. *Home* was a great record, though, and they should have had a brilliant future as Stax artists. However, it all went south very quickly. When Delaney got back to Los Angeles, he found a manager and started negotiations with another label. He felt that the album was just another Stax-sounding record, and that was not the direction he wanted to be going in. As a result Stax released Delaney and Bonnie from their contract and lost all interest in them and shelved *Home*. You can't blame them. Why would they spend their time, energy and money promoting an artist who is no longer signed to their label?

I finally moved out of Delaney & Bonnie's Hawthorne house and the couch that I had been sleeping on, and I ended up in the San Fernando Valley area at a place called the Plantation. It was anything but one. It was more like a commune with around thirteen people living there. But that was where I moved to when I left. In the new place lived drummers Jimmy Karstein and Chuck Blackwell, and I ended up with a room that had a round bed that was left there by God knows who. I woke up lying in a different direction every time I got out of bed in the morning. I was always getting turned around when I had to get up in the middle of the night to go to the bathroom. I had to leave a little crack in the curtains so I could see. Jimmy ran the house and paid Mr. Swan, the landlord. Jimmy had a great collection of 45s and we all used to gather upstairs in his room and smoke pot and listen to stuff like Johnny "Guitar" Watson's "Gangster of Love." Great fun. I vividly recall that on one occasion someone whipped out a couple of amyl nitrate capsules, and after we broke them open my heart felt like it was just about come out of my chest. This was going on while the music was blaring. I had never seen or done anything like that before, or since. But back then everything was all new to me and I was happy to experience it all because I felt I was invincible. You do when you are young. I was still in my teens and I had flown only twice before, and that was only to Macon, Georgia, and back home. My ride out to L.A. was my third time to be in an airplane.

JJ Cale also lived at the Plantation, in the apartment in the garage out back. He wrote songs all the time. He played an acoustic guitar with a pickup. He sure had Willie Nelson beat when it came to a guitar with a hole. The whole back of Cale's was gone. I guess he just got tired of the feedback and took the back off. It sounded great, by the way. He never once, that I can remember, came in the house to hang. He was, and probably still is, a real quiet man. I don't think that I could tell you anything that he ever said, and I've known him a very long time. He was real soft-spoken and a lovely man. His companion ended up being one of my dearest friends. She was the one he wrote "Magnolia" and all those great songs about. Once she and I were in a hotel room in L.A. visiting someone, and somebody was in the bathroom shooting up smack. She said to me, "I'd rather be a good girl and live back in Georgia than to be a junkie in L.A." Right then I sang back a slightly different line and a song was born, "Straight Life." It was on my first solo record. She passed some years ago with cancer, but I got to talk with her before she parted. I'm a better man for having been friends with her. She told me about and showed me the real side of living a tough life. It was to be a dead-end street for her. I think of her from time to time. Lovingly.

Another person who lived at the Plantation was a one-legged dude named Billy D. He was from Tulsa. In fact, everybody was from Tulsa there. I liked him, even though he was a bit strange. When I moved in I didn't really have but a few shirts and a couple of pairs of jeans and one pair of zip-up Italian boots. I have always had a thing for nice things. Even if it is only one nice thing, I would rather have one beautiful shirt than a dozen cheap ones. I prefer quality over quantity and always have. I guess it's because I never really had anything and what little I did have, I had to work very hard to get. Things of quality seem to last longer, like relationships. I had only two things other than what I could carry, and they could walk. It was my cat Peaches and my little dog Bekka. Yes, I named her after Delaney and Bonnie's new baby girl, who is now a great singer in her own right. One day I was looking up in the top of my closet and a wooden leg fell on top of me. It took me back a bit until I realized what it was. I went into the front room and said, "Who does this wooden leg belong to?" Then here comes Billy down the stairs in his boxer shorts with only one leg: "It's mine." I didn't know that he had a wooden leg, I just thought that he had a gimp leg and walked funny. That explained why he never flinched or said anything when my little dog was down there messing with it.

One of the Plantation residents told me one day that I was going to have to get rid of my dog and cat because there were too many people in that house and there was not enough room for them. I understood and called and asked Delaney's mother, Mamaw, if she would take Peaches and she said that she would. Delaney came and picked me up in their VW and we headed for Hawthorne. I had Peaches in my lap when we got on the freeway, and the temperature was way up there. Sure enough, about five minutes later the traffic stopped because there was some sort of a wreck up ahead. Delaney started cussing and carrying on and got Peaches upset so that she couldn't hold herself and she let go right on my chest and pants. I had fed her earlier and she couldn't help it. It was terrible. About a hundred and ten degrees, no air-conditioning and covered in feline feces with him yelling and the windows down, stuck in traffic on the Ventura Freeway. It was a hell of a scene. I took off all of my clothes and threw them out the window while we were still sitting there. We hadn't moved an inch. Peaches freaked and got up in the back window and stayed there. We finally got there and Mamaw was standing in the yard when we pulled up. Delaney tore out of the car gagging. He was about to throw up because of the smell. I got Peaches and held her in my arms and handed her over to Mamaw. I must have looked a sight standing there in my white underwear, my Ray Bans and my white socks and Italian zip-up boots.

When I got back to the Plantation, Bekka was gone. I looked everywhere but I couldn't find her. I asked the man, "Have you seen Bekka?" He said that he had gotten rid of her. I was stunned. I could not believe what I was hearing. This man just takes the only thing I loved that I have left in the world and does away with her! I went into my room and closed the door and cried like I'm doing right now as I write this. I felt betrayed and all alone. I didn't know what to do. There was nothing that I could do. It was already done and she was gone, but not in my heart. Even today I still carry my love for her. I got my Dobro guitar, the only consolation that I had and one of the few things that I did have, and started playing the only three chords that I knew. Just sitting there, thinking of how much I miss her. The words just came out. I finished it and then went into the kitchen where he was standing and I said to him, "Hey, man, sit down and let me sing you a song that I just wrote." I sang it and then he said, "That is beautiful, Bobby." Then I said to him, "One day I'm going to get to record this and every time that you hear it, you will know that you are the 'Thorn Tree in My Garden.'" Little did I realize that it was going to go on the end of one of the most well-known and influential records of all time.

Shortly after I first moved into the Plantation in late 1968, I met Leon Russell. He and Marc Benno were recording the album *Look Inside* as the Asylum Choir. That stuff was great. Leon lived on Skyhill Drive up off the Valley floor. When you went through the front door there was a big snake running down the hall, an electrical snake full of wires. To the left, it had been turned into a studio. As a matter of fact, the whole house was. There were wires running everywhere. Pianos, organs and drums were set up, and mikes were on stands all over the place. I especially recall them recording the number "Black Sheep Boogaloo," that appeared on their album. Great song. Marc and I hit it off right away and became fast friends. Both Marc and Leon liked the way that I sang and took me into the studio to record once without anybody knowing about it. We did a very cool song, "So Long for My Baby." It was great, real swampy sounding. I can still remember it and I hear it in my head as if it were yesterday. When Delaney found out about it, he nearly lost it. If he hadn't been in such a bind with me being such an important part of the sound, I'm sure that he would have fired me. I probably would have been real happy if he had. I always had a gut feeling that Marc and Leon had been talking about me joining them. I don't know for sure, but I just had this feeling. Now that I look back, I was probably right.

Thinking back, I met a lot of musicians when I lived at the Plantation. One of them was Jesse Ed Davis, who was the guitar player with Taj Mahal "Indian Ed," I used to call him, because he was a full-blooded Kiowa. This was around the time we were putting the Delaney and Bonnie band together. I really liked Taj's band and I especially loved Jesse Ed Davis' playing. He played slide, lead and rhythm, but he wasn't what you would call an "on fire" guitar player, rather he was more of a smooth player and just right for Taj. What a gentle, beautiful human being he was. With long straight black hair down his back, he really looked like an Indian warrior. Real proud, with a mouth full of teeth that lit up his warm smile and lovely brown eyes. Just downright handsome. Everyone loved and respected him. He would later play with George Harrison at the famous Concert for Bangla Desh at Madison Square Garden in 1971, and he also got to record with John Lennon on his *Walls and Bridges* album. I remember Eric Clapton telling me how much he admired him as well. Eric not only played with him at the Bangla Desh show, he also played on his first solo album.

One of the musicians at the Plantation was running women in and out of there on a daily basis. I had never seen anything like it. I couldn't get one girlfriend and this guy had women everywhere. One, Kay Poorboy, was a petite thing with long brown hair, a really pretty little ol' gal. She was completely in love with Carl Radle but that was never to be. But that didn't stop her from getting it on every day with that musician. She and her friend Francine were both from Tulsa. It seemed that there were a lot of people from Tulsa showing up at the Plantation. They were topless-dancers at the Classic Cat strip club on Sunset Boulevard. They never let me go there; I guess that they would have been embarrassed to let me see them dancing. I don't know why because they both had no problem trading off with each other and sometimes they would double up and have an afternoon threesome with that musician. It was a hell of an eye-opener for me. I didn't have to see anything because I could hear everything that was going on in that room quite easily. I imagine everybody in the neighborhood could. A whole lot of very loud sex was happening behind that closed door. This would be going on right in the middle of the day. One day, another dude from Tulsa comes pulling up in the drive and the girls started scattering and everybody was very busy trying to straighten up fast. This guy pulling into the drive was Kay's boyfriend, fresh in from Tulsa, and he was angry. I had heard stories about this guy and how crazy he got when he was drinking and that was all the time. He didn't even make it into the house because the musician came out on the back porch with a .22 pistol in his hand. It was some sort of act of macho bravado, but it accidentally fired and shot a tiny hole in the trashcan that was across the yard outside of JJ Cale's door. There wasn't a fight, no one was shot, and there certainly wasn't a shoot-out. Nonetheless, Leon Russell wrote the song "Shoot Out on the Plantation," which was about the altercation. Leon heard what had happened and he asked me to tell him the story and I did. It was probably close to what I just told, except that I almost left out Mr. Swan, the landlord. I never saw or met the man. So it was just a song that was made up out of an exaggerated story about a drunk man who was tired after a long drive from Tulsa, Oklahoma. Just looking for his girlfriend who was fresh out of the bedroom of one of his very best friends.

We started to get a band together and prepared to hit the road after rehearsing at the Plantation. Carl Radle, another guy from Tulsa, was one of the first to join. He was a very gentle and unassuming guy. He was the first and only bass player to play with Delaney and Bonnie as an original member of the band. In fact, he was the second person to be recruited into that fiasco. It was me, Carl, then, Jimmy Karstein, JJ Cale and Bobby Keys. Carl lived right down the street from the Plantation, about six blocks away. He had a Triumph motorcycle that he would let me use to find my way around Los Angeles. He was a lovely man and had a red Irish Setter named Dixie. It's funny that I remember that dog. Carl's girlfriend's name was Judy, and she had long dark hair. I remember her as being sort of possessive of Carl. She was left behind very shortly after we started playing together on the road.

We landed a semi-permanent residency at Snoopy's on Laurel Canyon Boulevard in the Valley. It was a real small bar with a small stage, and my organ sat on the floor next to it. The room had one pool table and only had about eight small four-top tables for patrons. We never had more than eight or ten people there and they were all drunk! That's probably why we got to play there a lot. But we didn't get paid a lot either, or so I was told. We did five nights a week, five sets a night and I got paid $5 a night. All that I remember is Delaney telling me when he came up with this high dollar gig was that I better have a B3 there by the time we start or I could go back home to Memphis. He used that a

Kay Poorboy in front of Sunny Heights, Ringo Starr's house, where I lived in 1970 and 1971.

lot. That was his usual threat to me, to send me back to where I came from. I should have taken him up on it right then and there and gone back and stood out in the front of Booker T. and the M.G.'s and the Memphis Horns and sung soul music. I didn't have any money to get anything, much less a Hammond organ. Luckily, Jimmy Karstein said that he knew a keyboard player, John Galley, and he might be able to help me out. I called him and sure enough, he had a B3 for sale. I explained to him that I didn't have any money. He told me to take the organ and pay him as I could. That's exactly what I did, too. At the time of writing this it is still over at Delaney's old studio, where I left it all those years ago.

We played everywhere and anywhere we could get a gig. Delaney and Bonnie were sort of a revolving door to a lot of players back then, and Jimmy Karstein was the first to voluntarily leave. He showed up at the gig one night with a high-hat, a snare and a bass drum. That was it! Delaney was pissed, but it was show time. After the gig he said something to Jimmy about it and Karstein said, "Hell man, this is all I need! If I can't cut it with this, I can't cut it at all." He stayed a while but left to go play with Ricky Nelson. And later he joined JJ Cale, who had also left us to pursue a successful solo career. Gram Parsons, who had been a member of the International Submarine Band, the Byrds and the Flying Burrito Brothers, had spotted the band at Snoopy's. He liked what he heard and became an early champion of Delaney and Bonnie. He introduced Delaney to Alan Pariser, one of the architects of the 1967 Monterey Pop Festival. He was also the heir to the Dixie Lily Sweetheart Paper Cup Company fortune and was loaded. Alan had the best pot and cocaine in Los Angeles. He knew everybody in the business and was really hooked up. He's the one who gave Jimi Hendrix the LSD and the lighter fluid to set his guitar on fire during the Monterey Pop Festival. Alan really loved Delaney and Bonnie and became their manager. He took responsibility for all of the money and all of the connections and what limited success Delaney & Bonnie & Friends ever had. He financed everything for them, including their house and daily living expenses. He paid for the band, the road crew, the equipment, rehearsal place, photo shoots, studio time and just about everything else concerning them. That was supposed to make them free to create. They were free to create, all right. Over the years, they created more heartbreak for Alan than he could ultimately bear. He finally quit the music business and started building race boats. I spoke with him a few years ago, shortly before he passed, and he wouldn't even mention their names.

As soon as Alan became Delaney & Bonnie's manager they started to work out a whole new deal with another label. That new deal was with Jac Holzman, owner of Elektra Records. Although previously known for their small folk label image, they had found recent success on the West Coast with the Doors and Love. They had demonstrated that they were now a label that could handle rock acts and were known as one of the hippest around. Although Jack had misgivings, especially about Delaney, he overlooked them because he loved their southern soul music. Their contract gave them full artistic control of their records, along with the artwork, which was quite unusual at the time. Once the ink had dried, Delaney & Bonnie would cut their second record using their own musicians, namely all of us so-called "Friends," and it was going to be called *The Original Delaney & Bonnie & Friends Accept No Substitute*.

Ahead of that, Delaney & Bonnie and I went on a radio promotional tour in February 1969. We had gone on the road with Alan Pariser, to the top radio stations all across the United States. Just the three of us. We'd stop in and say that we wanted to play on the air. We didn't have a record out yet but it was soon to come. We were laying the foundation for our new album and letting them know that we would be back with a band. On this promotional tour, I remember that Delaney had talked somebody into getting him a prescription of Seconal reds, a barbiturate derivative drug. He sent Bonnie and me to find our way through downtown Atlanta, with me driving a rented car, to find this obscure pharmacy in a seedy part of town to pick up the dope. Legal, but still dope. He was always hogging the drugs, and this time we thought that we'd beat him to the draw. She opened the bottle and took out one for each of us. We took them right there and then and started driving back to the hotel, then all of a sudden everything started looking pretty grim. Those were more powerful than we were ready for. It buckled me at the knees and I was sitting down! We barely made it back to the hotel alive because I was going all over the road. This was all going on in the middle of the day as well. When we finally arrived back at the hotel, out comes Delaney looking more excited than I'd seen him for some time. We pulled up knowing there was going to be trouble. He said, "Where have you two been and why did it take you so long?" We weren't even out of the car yet and he was going off at Bonnie. He could see that we were pretty loopy. What we didn't know is that while we'd been getting his drugs, Alan had run into Ann-Margret and her husband, Roger Smith, in the hotel bar and we were due to go to their room to play and sing for them—ten minutes ago. We all went straight up to Ann and Roger's room, and they were still waiting for us. We went in and I'm sure that they could tell how wasted we were. Delaney was extremely pissed off but he had to keep it to himself in front of the movie stars. Bonnie sang like I had never heard before or since. I guess that she was doing an especially good job to keep from getting punched yet one more time. We finished and Delaney went straight to Leon Russell's room—he happened to be in the same hotel. Delaney locked the door on us. Closed it right in our faces.

Bonnie and I went to Alan's room, and he rolled us a couple of fat joints. We always had the Ozium out, with towels under the door and everything! You could easily tell who was smoking pot, because you just had to follow your nose to the Ozium spray. After a while, we went down the hall and listened through the door while Delaney and Leon were working on a new number, and then banged on the door for them to let us in, but they wouldn't. So we went back and smoked the other joint. You could hear them singing all the way down the hall. We heard that song come together, echoing down the hall. So did everyone else. We were all so very fortunate and didn't even know it. We were all listening to musical history in the making and were completely unaware of it. We sang all of the time, any and everywhere and nobody ever complained. It would have done them no good anyhow: Delaney would have just played louder and sung louder. When they were finished we all got to go in and Delaney said, "Y'all sit down and listen to this." We said, "We have been." It was incredible listening for the first time to that beautiful piece of music. It was called "Superstar (Groupie)." It was a top 10 hit for the Carpenters and was also covered by many other people including Rita Coolidge.

The Friends had changed some again, and were now Carl Radle playing bass, Jim Keltner on drums, Jerry McGee on guitar, Bobby Keys and Jim Price on horns, with Bonnie and me singing background to Delaney. I also had my saving grace, my Hammond B3 organ. Leon Russell, another former Shindog, whom I already knew from the *Asylum Choir* session, also joined along with Rita Coolidge. We would later have drummer Jim Gordon join Jim Keltner, both playing at the same time. You couldn't have asked for nicer people. The only person that ever caused any discord was Delaney. His ego was massive, and it ruled every decision that he made. I never had any trouble with him though, because I never took what he said too personally. We recorded the *Accept No Substitute* album at

Elektra Studios in Los Angeles. It was the first for our new label, and it also signaled the beginning of the end for Delaney & Bonnie & Friends. I remember those sessions very well. We got to record "Superstar" in the studio. That was right after Leon and Delaney had written it and after we came off of the radio tour. David Anderle was connected to Elektra at the time and was the supervising producer of the record because Delaney couldn't be in two places at once. He couldn't be behind the glass and out in the studio. David also produced and dated Rita Coolidge. That's how her version came to be. Another thing that I recall was that Bonnie sang it live. When we did the background vocal overdubs, which were the only overdubs, I got to sing in my natural voice. I remember Leon starting it off and it rings as clearly in my inner ear now as it did when it was first being played. It was a stone-cold smash record then and still is to this day. That was the best studio performance that Bonnie ever did in her life. Singing "Superstar" like it was hers, because it was. Or at least it should have been because it was written for her by Delaney and Leon. What a magical moment that was captured in the studio. The rest of the session was like all of the rest, pay attention and don't mess up, get it down in the second or third take and go home and leave Delaney to do his thing. Anyway, Bonnie's version was held back from being on the album because they wanted to get the hit by letting other performers record it. Of course the biggest hit was the version sung by The Carpenters. It was all about the money. Bonnie's version was eventually relegated to the B-side of our "Comin' Home" single. It nearly killed her. I felt for her and I'm sure that her career would have been different had she been the one with the hit. But that, too, was never to be, because Delaney was jealous of even his own wife.

Dr. John walked into Elektra Studios one day out of the blue and said to Delaney, "I have a song for you and Bonnie." He sat down at the piano and played, "When This Battle Is Over." Mac—that's his real name, Mac Rebennack—knew Bonnie and Delaney very well. He had sat in with us a few times also. I am sure that he wrote that song especially for them, because the subject matter was them! Just looking at the list of the songs on that record, you can tell where their heads were and what was happening in their personal lives by the titles. "Get Ourselves Together," "When This Battle Is Over," "Someday," "Dirty Old Man," "Love Me a Little Bit Longer," "I Can't Take It Much Longer," and "Do Right Woman." That list kind of says it all. As good as the album was, it was not an easy record to make. Delaney was often drunk and making unreasonable demands and Bonnie was mad most of the time. I can tell you that when it hit the fan, everybody got hit. It went everywhere. Everyone was subjected to his personal relationship nightmares. There was no such thing as a private little talk with them. Hell, no! It was all-out war sometimes between those two. And they would usually have me between them, Delaney yelling at Bonnie and Bonnie crying on my shoulder. One time, she threw the keys out of the car window while we were stuck on the freeway. That was just another day in the life of those two. I just got out the car and walked all the way back to the Plantation and let them get on with it. What a life!

Alan Pariser was a friend of George Harrison's. He had given George a tape of *Accept No Substitute* and he was very impressed. So impressed in fact, that he offered Delaney & Bonnie a contract with the Beatles' newly formed Apple Records in England. Incredibly, Delaney signed the deal, despite already being signed up to Elektra. Apple actually went as far as manufacturing some test pressings of the album, which are now worth a fortune. Of course, the Apple contract became null and void when they found out that a deal which included worldwide rights for the album was in place with another label. A furious Jac

Holzman berated Delaney and told him in no uncertain terms that he was not in Mississippi now and that he could not simply walk out on a contract because he loved the idea of being signed to the Beatles' record label. The *Accept No Substitute* album was released to glowing press reviews and gave Elektra even more credibility among musicians, both in the United States and in England. Meanwhile, Stax, realizing that Delaney and Bonnie were getting a lot of publicity paid for by their new label, decided that it was a good time to finally release *Home*. They had to recoup their recording costs for the album, so why not capitalize on the blaze of publicity and get their revenge at the same time? It caused confusion with the record-buying public, who assumed that it was our second album, when in reality it was our first.

Elektra had been getting fed up with Delaney's attitude for several months. It didn't help that the studio was left in a mess every night with empty beer cans and greasy food wrappers left on various consoles, much to the displeasure of Elektra staff. On top of that you had the constant fights and demands. The final straw for Jac Holzman came when a drunk, abusive and frustrated Delaney called him in the middle of the night threatening to kill him because he could not find any copies of *Accept No Substitute* in his father's hometown record store. Delaney ordered him to immediately rectify the situation. Not surprisingly, this soured the relationship between Elektra and Delaney and resulted in the band's immediate release from their Elektra contract, much to the relief of everyone at the label.

George Harrison had played the album to as many friends as he could, including Eric Clapton and Mick Jagger. Everybody in England loved the sound. That was the record, combined with all that went with it, that would be the key that would open the door to the world for them. Trouble was, they didn't know how to use it. Everything was coming to Delaney and Bonnie without them having to go and get it—the money, the success, and all of the people necessary for the fulfillment of their dream. But they were to squander what had so freely come their way. They would use and abuse the very people who had come into their lives and were to be their allies. While George was spreading the word about us in England, we were on the road in the United States. By now, we had Dave Mason as our lead guitarist. He sat in with us several times before being offered the gig. He had been in Traffic in England, but had split and moved to Los Angeles. Alan knew him and became his manager. We played the Whisky A Go Go in L.A. and a couple of other clubs, but they are of no particular significance in anyone's memory. Certainly not mine, anyway. We played some really cool festivals as well, like the Atlanta Pop Festival in July 1969, which stands out for me. All the big names of the day were there, including Led Zeppelin, Johnny Winter, Canned Heat, Blood Sweat and Tears and Janis Joplin. I recall Janis had already played her set at the festival and was drunk and funky smelling and sitting in the back of a black limo making out with Delaney. It was in the middle of the day in the middle of the summer in Georgia and they had it all steamed up and you could see the car moving from the outside. Well, I got in, innocent, and was having a ball with some mescaline I had taken a little earlier only to find those two looking extremely guilty. Bonnie was coming up right behind me! Delaney hadn't known where Bonnie was, but you can believe that she knew exactly what had been going on in there. Bonnie was not happy. Again.

We did a festival in California when all of a sudden there was this incredible thunderous noise. It was the Hell's Angels, about a hundred of them. There was an area in front of the stage with a barrier 50 feet deep to keep people from getting too close. There were thousands of people there. It was a sea of heads. The Angels roared around from the back of that stage to the front and filled the barrier area. Nobody said anything to them, not the cops or security or anybody. I thought that they had come to grab Delaney off the stage in front of everybody to humiliate him for sucker-punching one of their top guys a few weeks earlier in a bar. Delaney, Bonnie and I were at a bar in the Valley in the middle of the afternoon about two weeks prior to the concert. There was this guy and a couple of his friends across the room having a beer and shooting pool. They were flying their colors and they were with the Hell's Angels. One of the dudes really wasn't a big bad looking guy. He was far from that, in fact. He looked like a nice guy. He was more like my size, not too big and not really small. Anyway, he walks up to us at the table and said something in the course of his conversation that Bonnie had been hearing every day. He wasn't directing what he was saying to any one of us in particular, he was just talking and was using some pretty graphic expletives. Delaney said to him, "Watch your mouth you motherfucker!" and hit this guy in the face from across the table. It wasn't a hard right, which surprised me, because I thought by the way Delaney always talked and acted that he was a real badass. Not the case! This guy started coming over the table and Delaney was crawdaddin' big time, backing right up against the wall because he couldn't get back any farther any faster. The dude's friends started yelling at him and grabbed him and said, "Hey man, that's Bonnie and Delaney!" The guy backed off immediately and Delaney apologized. "I'm sorry, man, I'm sorry!" Turns out that the dude was the head of the Hell's Angels in that area's chapter! It certainly got my attention. It was real quiet in that Volkswagen on the way home, I'll tell you. Not a word was said. Bonnie and I just kept looking at each other with this look of wanting to say something, but not wanting the backlash from Delaney. We were almost busting out laughing, but we couldn't. He was real solemn. He did not say one word. He just kept looking straight ahead, just driving. This man had no problem hitting women or children or shooting the dogs with a BB gun. But when it came to hitting a man, he was a coward. It would still be a very long time before I was to lose my respect for Delaney. Not that of the artist, but rather of the man that I thought he was.

The Vietnam War was on, and I had been going to different doctors getting tested and examined, and changing my home address from Memphis to Los Angeles in order to try to buy some time to keep from having to go kill someone. When we were on the road with Delaney and Bonnie my mother got in touch with me and told me about a yellow envelope with my name on it from the United States government. I was being called up for the draft, and they wanted me real bad and real fast. I flew back to Memphis and went down to the draft board. I was pretty much on the run from them and didn't really know it. I knew that I was up for it, but didn't know that I had already been called. I had not kept in close touch with my family for several years after I left home. I was too busy living, and I certainly didn't want to die in some jungle or in some rice field. When I was standing in line at the induction center waiting for my name to be called, there was a tall black dude standing right next to me. He was solid as a rock and about six and a half feet tall. He had come up from the woods in Mississippi. We were all standing there in our underwear. There were about fifteen or twenty of us standing there, all in a row, two lines deep. Some were happy to be there and some of us weren't so happy about it, me being one, for sure. The sergeant called out someone's name and he wasn't there, and then he called out someone else's name and he stepped forward, and then he called out Elizabeth Smith's name and everyone busted out laughing. Everyone except me, and Elizabeth, that is. He was standing right next to me and when he stepped forward, even the sergeant stopped laughing. My name was called and I went to see the man at the desk and he said to me that they had been one city behind me for two months. He said that I had been evading the draft and was sure to go to the front because of it. He asked me if I wanted to go to war and serve my country. I told him no and that I could better serve my fellow countrymen by playing and singing for them. I did not want to be going out there and shooting some other mother's son. I told him that I was far better off holding a guitar in my hands serving my country that way than I would be holding a rifle in my hands and killing my brothers. He had no emotion in his expression as I explained all of this to him, and he sent me straight to the army doctor. I had to go out to the Veterans Hospital for examination because they were sending me away. It seemed like my career as a musician would have to go on the back burner for a while. They took me into a room and poked me with a couple of needles and got some blood from me. Then they had me drink barium and stand behind an X-ray machine. I was strapped to a table that turned me upside down behind the X-ray screen, and they were taking pictures the whole time. After it was finished, the doctor told me to get my clothes on and get out of there. Apparently I had an active stomach ulcer and they rated me 4F, which means not suitable for the army. They didn't want me because of my health and said that the road had taken its toll on my stomach. I think that the road didn't have so much to do with it. It was more than likely the stress of living on it with the Bramletts. The doctor had given me a whole lot of stuff that I was supposed to take every day, and I did, too, for about two days after that. I felt fine. I had suddenly become free and didn't have to worry about getting shot any time soon. It was the best feeling in the world. I had so much freedom that I didn't know what to do with it.

    I was staying at my parents' house in Millington while all of this was going down. A girl I attended school with lived on a farm about two miles out of town. Her name was Cathy Wright, and her dad was a cotton farmer who had a house full of girls all different ages. She and I had known each other for years, but she was a year older than me and graduated the year before me. I was always kind of struck on her but we never really dated. We were just good friends. I was due to go back out to California in about four days, so I had a bit of spare time and went out to visit her the day after I got my release from the army. I guess that I was overcome with old memories when I asked her if she wanted to get married. She said yes, then she packed her bag, and I went to my mom's and got mine, and we went down the road to Reelfoot Lake. That's the lake that I called "Snake Lake." That is what the song "Snake Lake Blues" was going to be about lyrically, but it was never finished. I didn't know then how to convey this story into a song. She and I stopped along the way there and got married at some justice of the peace, and then went to the lake and spent the night. We consummated our marriage there, and the next day we drove the hundred miles back and she went home to her parents' farm and I went home to my mom's house. The next day I got up and went to the airport and caught a plane back to California and went home to the Plantation. I told Bonnie and Delaney what I had done and they couldn't believe it, but we never really took it as being very serious. Not until about two months later, when we had come back off of the road and Bonnie said to me, "When are you going to bring your wife out here so that we can all meet her?" I was so totally involved with myself, and what we were doing, that I didn't even think about anybody else. But being from my background, which was one of ignorance and a displaced sense of loyalty, I brought Cathy out to live with me. But I had to get another place because my room at the Plantation would have been too small for the two of us. She had never been away from home. At least I had been around a bit since I had a preacher for a dad and had traveled all over the South playing and singing. Now I had to bring her out to my new life and world in California. Bobby Keys had a friend who had another friend who knew a couple who were living in John Garfield's old house on Bronson Canyon Drive in the Hollywood Hills. He said that they were looking for a boarder and would probably be very happy to rent us part of the house. Their names were Mike and Shelia Visletear. We became good friends and we had our half of the house, and they had their half, and we shared the kitchen. Mike had a grand piano in one of the rooms that looked out and up to the guesthouse. The place was a Spanish villa and quite beautiful, with twisted pillars and a huge fireplace in the front room of this multi-leveled house. When I was playing piano I could look out the windows to my left and could see the guesthouse where Rita Coolidge and Jim Gordon wrote the piano coda for "Layla." They tried to get me in on it, but I didn't hear it and thought it anything but a rock 'n' roll song, which it wasn't. And still isn't.

Eric Clapton and My Freedom

Alan got us on the tour as the opening act for Blind Faith. This was a real big deal for us and would get us some great exposure. Blind Faith were the first of the supergroups, so-called because their members were comprised of stars from different bands. In this case it was Cream, Traffic and Family. That's when we first became friends with Eric Clapton. He was hanging out with us more and more during the tour. He and Delaney really hit it off. And Eric got along well with everyone in our band. The first show we played was in New York's famed Madison Square Garden on July 12, 1969. That was the biggest arena I had ever played in. I didn't realize just how significant this place was. I was completely blown away when our tour bus pulled up outside the venue and the sign on Madison Square Garden had our name on it. We drove into the cavernous garage under the venue and everybody got out of the bus. We all went our separate ways before reconvening a couple of hours later to start getting ready for the gig. We hadn't checked into a hotel or anything just then, since our road manager was seeing to all of that. I stayed around the Garden and went exploring. I managed to get myself pretty turned around and was way up in the top of the place. It was nearing sound check time, so I started heading back down to the dressing room area. The escalator was turned off and the stairs were very long and high, so I decided to sit on the handrail and slide down. Unfortunately I didn't take into account my new jeans and the slick plastic handrail. I sat on it at the very top and started to slide down. It was like ice—I was going so fast down that escalator handrail that my hair was blowing back like I was on a bicycle. I couldn't stop, and when I reached the end I zoomed across the marble floor and tumbled right up to the doorway of the front of the place. I was a little panicked, but other than that, I made it down and escaped with a few scrapes and a very bruised ego. We had our sound check before heading off to the dressing room to wait for our slot. It was finally show time and we were ready to get out there and rock the house. The Garden had a round stage that slowly revolved so that everyone would get to see the acts head-on. Delaney was especially fired up because it was New York City and Madison Square Garden. The lights went down and right after they announced us, the entire PA system went out. The house lights came back on while they were trying to get the PA working. The monitor system was still working for some reason, so Delaney seized the opportunity to get out there, PA or not. He and Bonnie and I walked out there in front of that packed arena with the house lights on and sat on wooden folding chairs and sang through the monitor system as the stage revolved. I kept seeing the same faces pass from one side of my peripheral vision to the other, smiling and waving time after time after time. Around and around we went singing "Poor Elijah." The PA came back on and the whole band came on and we did our set.

We were blowing Blind Faith away most nights. We had Jim Keltner and Jim Gordon

Performing with Bonnie and Delaney. We opened up for Blind Faith at Madison Square Garden in July 1969, but the PA system went out, so we sang using the monitors.

on drums, Carl Radle on bass, Leon Russell on piano and Rita Coolidge singing backing vocals, Dave Mason on guitar, Bobby Keys and Jim Price on horns, me on organ, and Bonnie and Delaney. That was one hell of a band, especially when Eric started sitting in with us. I still remember how exciting it was to be a part of it when it was rocking—and that was whenever we played. It was actually exciting even when we weren't playing. We would be in the hotel room or on the bus singing and laughing and just enjoying each other's company, especially when Eric was around, which was becoming more and more frequent. After we played our concert in Toronto at Varsity Stadium on July 18, 1969, Delaney and I stood out in the front listening to Blind Faith do their thing, with Ginger Baker pounding away on his massive double kit and looking completely pissed off. He seemed to be just playing for himself rather than the band. But not Eric. He always stood out. He was the star without even trying to be. Delaney turned to me and said, "What do you think about him playing in our band?" I said, "That would be great, but he's going to have to do something about those pink silk pants!" Eric had on high-heeled snakeskin boots, pink silk pants, a flowered silk shirt and a velvet vest. He looked great. We all wore jeans and cowboy boots and didn't look anything like rock stars. Eric, on the other hand, had it all going on right about then. He was a bona fide rock star. It would be a year later that I would have several pairs of silk pants. None of them pink, mind you. Actually, I like velvet trousers and silk shirts and Italian boots. Some things never change.

Ginger Baker was not the nicest person. He seemed angry all the time. His face was always twisted up. He was doing a lot of dope then as well, so that probably had him a bit edgy. Not to mention the fact that it must have difficult to walk out on stage after you had just had your socks blown away. Everywhere we played we blew Blind Faith away. It was in every paper every time we played: "Blind Faith was upstaged by their opening act, Delaney & Bonnie and Friends." Jim Gordon was a tough act to follow if you're a drummer, and I would imagine that Ginger was a little intimidated with Jim's expertise. Ginger was not very friendly to anybody, including his own band mates. I never saw him smile but a couple of times, and even then I wasn't sure if he was smiling. He only rode on the bus with us once and couldn't wait to get to the gig and get off. Their band wasn't a band at all in that respect. They were four individuals up there playing for themselves. The rest of Blind Faith were great, though, and they all warmed up to us and we all got along famously.

Alan Pariser had arranged a new deal with Atlantic Records after we had unceremoniously been dumped by Elektra because of the Apple fiasco and Delaney's drunken outburst with label president Jac Holzman. Alan was friends with Atlantic's Jerry Wexler and introduced Delaney to him. They were very alike, Delaney and Jerry. I guess that's why they got along so well. He became Delaney's champion and vice versa. As soon as the Blind Faith tour ended, Delaney invited Eric to our recording session for our first single for Atlantic. The A side was a number called "Comin' Home." Delaney had written that on our bus while we were on the Blind Faith tour. He used to have a set of headphones that were really for playing your electric guitar through. You just plugged them into the guitar and nobody could hear you and you couldn't hear anything but the guitar. He was singing at the top of his voice and that's all that you could hear. No guitar at all, just Delaney singing it word by word, line by line. I was just listening to it all go down. Then he said for me to put the headphones on and listen. He was playing "Comin' Home" to me through the headset and was singing across the aisle from me while he was playing his guitar. I had one earphone pulled slightly back so as to hear his voice. What an incredible experience for me. Delaney always made it his business to make it mine. He was always busy writing and singing up there in the front seat on the left hand side of the bus, right behind the driver. It wasn't a special tour bus like everyone has now. This was just a bus. No big deal except that it used to be an old Greyhound bus and that the name had been painted over. I had written ballads, but I had never written a rock 'n' roll song and wanted to more than anything. I was in the presence of a great songwriter, so I asked Delaney, "How do you write a rock and roll song?" He said to me, "Put it in a different tempo and change the beat." I said, "Wow! That's it? That's all I have to do? No problem! I've got it!"

I was still living in the Hollywood Hills in John Garfield's house with my wife, Cathy. One day Mike and Sheila were down in the front room in front of the fire and Cathy was in the kitchen trying to cook something for dinner. Cooking was not one of her strong points. As a matter of fact, I never really knew what any of them were. We were both in our teens and really had no idea about relationships. We hardly ever talked and when we did it was without substance. The only thing that we knew about each other was what we knew when we were going to high school together. And she was a year older than me so she was gone before I graduated. I was gone as soon as my feet hit the ground and I was free to start living. But I never saw being married to her coming at all. That afternoon I sat down at the piano and started playing a little rolling thing in the key of C. C, F and G. That was all. It was to be a song about our relationship and I was thinking about how Delaney had told me to just speed it up into a different tempo. I started to rock it a bit and started to sing what I had written down. "Honey when we're together, it seems like we both got a whole lot of nothing to say. But I know if we try, we can work it out someday." I had started my first rock 'n' roll song! The rest of the lyrics just fell out after that. "And I believe, if there's a will, there's got to be a way." Then, "We got to get ourselves together. A little less talking we'll have a lot more to say. Because when we're alone it's going to happen anyway." I had written my first rock 'n' roll song and was over the moon! I played it for everyone but they had heard it as it was coming together. What an exciting time for me then. I just had to call Delaney and play it for him over the phone and tell him how it all came as the result of me following his advice. I did and he said that it was great and that we were going to do it on the show. I couldn't believe it, that I was finally going to get to sing my song with them. Little did I know that when we rehearsed it that he was going to be the one to sing it. I actually learned more about singing and writing songs and playing rock 'n' roll from Delaney than I will ever be able to recount. There was so much to learn from him if you just paid attention. I always did. No one understood the import of the matter like I did. Everyone else was there trying to make a living, and I was there living. I was all ears and eyes when I was around Delaney, and everyone that he was around. He told me to "Surround yourself with people who are as good at what they do as you are at what you do." I took that one step further, though, and I try to surround myself with people who are better at what they do than I am at what I do. And I'm real good at playing a Hammond B3 and singing.

Cathy and I moved into a house across the street and one door down from Delaney and Bonnie. It was a busy time and it made sense to be near them. In the meantime, Eric left Blind Faith and wanted to record a solo album, and he asked Delaney & Bonnie & Friends to be his backing band. He thought it would be great for all of us to come to Europe for a tour and fit in sessions for his album at the same time. Alan organized everything along with Eric's manager, Robert Stigwood, and we flew to England in early November 1969. Eric had generously invited all of us to stay at his country home, Hurtwood Edge, deep in the Surrey countryside. The whole of the Delaney & Bonnie & Friends entourage were there and pretty much everyone that you see on the back of the *On Tour* album were at his house. There were a few exceptions, but that was because the photo shoot took place in January 1970 and some of the members had left.

When we left L.A. for England and Eric's house, some band members were already well into the blow. Since they had no connections for it overseas, they had to think of a creative way to get it across the Atlantic. CoCo, who I have known since 1994 and is now my wife, was with Delaney for thirteen years and married to him for nine of those. She told me that when she read this story she remembered Delaney laughing about it and telling it many times and that he was very proud of the fact that he and Alan had pulled it off. What happened was this: A friend got several ounces of pure cocaine and rented a studio for a night. I was there and saw this go down. They had a couple of two-inch tape reels ready. They then reeled off approximately three-fourths of each reel very carefully onto the floor, cut a slice out of the middle of it big enough to fit the blow into. Then, they reeled it back on, and it was sealed inside very close to the end of the reel in the middle. You couldn't tell just by looking, because the reel looked like it was full of songs. The final touch was to put Eric's name on the outside of the box, so nobody would be likely to inspect it at Heathrow Airport when we arrived because they were Eric Clapton's tapes. Holy mackerel! The tapes were carried onto the airplane by hand and sat right in the seat next to Alan and Delaney. When we arrived, the first stop for someone was a studio, to get that blow out of there. The rest of us had headed for Eric's house and were set up in the front room for playing. But there wasn't a lot of that going on. More like playing around than actually playing music. In fact, just as soon as the wheels of the plane had hit the ground at Heathrow, Delaney and Bonnie's attitudes changed. They were suddenly big stars, but only in their own minds. I had never seen them act that way before and it didn't get any better.

Robert Stigwood had booked some studio time for us and for Eric at Olympic Studios in Barnes, a suburb of London. We managed to record around five or six numbers over a few days for Eric's album, but our minds were on the tour, and there really was not enough time to devote to the project. We were pretty busy having fun. Eric had bought a Safari Land Rover just to haul all of us around, and some nights we all went into London to the clubs.

Robert Stigwood sent someone from the office out to check on things at Hurtwood, and things weren't good. A lot of drugs were being used, everyone was up most of the time, and there was lots of booze—it was just a constant party. As far as Delaney and Bonnie were concerned, they were the top dogs. They treated Eric's home with total disrespect and total disregard. They were steeped in total ignorance and were an embarrassment to be around. I came from people who had chickens roosting in their bedroom and pigs walking in and out of their house, but they didn't know any better. These people knew better and still acted like poor white trash in the presence of the most influential people in the music world. I kept my head hanging down most of the time because of the way those two acted.

Towards the end of November, we did a BBC television show called the *Price of Fame or Fame at Any Price*. It was a weekly entertainment show starring Georgie Fame and Alan Price. They would perform some of their songs as well as have special musical guests. The show credits list Delaney & Bonnie with Eric Clapton and Bobby Whitlock. In fact, Dave Mason was also there, but they forgot to mention him for some reason. The great thing about the show was that it was all live—there was no miming, as was often the case with those sorts of shows in the '60s. It was also filmed in color. We actually recorded it as a five-piece acoustically. Can't remember why, maybe they could not fit the whole band in the studio or we would have been too loud. Eric and Delaney were playing Martin guitars and Dave Mason played a Dobro. We were seated on stools in a semicircle and I was next to Bonnie singing backing vocals. We got to play two songs, "Poor Elijah" and "Will the Circle Be Unbroken." I guess that was the first ever "unplugged" show. We were on fire that night.

Robert Stigwood had organized a German tour with the Lippmann and Rau concert agency. This was really a warm-up for our important forthcoming UK tour. Our band—and that's how I looked at it, too—on the German tour was Rita Coolidge, Bonnie, Tex Johnson the conga player, Delaney, Bobby Keys, Jim Price, Carl Radle, Jim Gordon, Dave Mason, Eric Clapton and me. What an incredible band we were. Our first appearance in Germany was for the famous *Beat Club* television show at Radio Bremen Studios in Bremen on November 26, 1969. We were allocated a three-song set and we played "Comin' Home," our latest single, "Poor Elijah/Tribute to Robert Johnson" and "Where There's a Will, There's a Way." Once again, we played live. A lot of bands at the time did not feel comfortable trying to recreate their sound live and ended up miming on these sorts of television shows. Unfortunately, the rest of the tour did not go as smoothly as our television show. There were problems in Germany because the promoters had wrongly advertised the concerts as Eric Clapton shows on the posters. Although Delaney and Bonnie were pictured on the posters, the wording stated clearly "Eric Clapton introducing Delaney and Bonnie." It was a little misleading, and at a gig in Cologne it got quite nasty. When Eric didn't get out front and sing and play Cream songs, the crowd started booing and kept at it until we had to walk off the stage. Soon after, a riot ensued because they weren't expecting us at all. It was bad news. I know Eric was embarrassed and angry because he felt he was the host and his guests had been humiliated.

We came back to England and knew that we would be better welcomed there. Our first show was at the prestigious Royal Albert Hall in London. Eric, Carl, Jim and I came out to play a couple of numbers to warm up the audience. Looking back, that was the first appearance of Derek and the Dominos, only we did not know it. We did a great version of "Gimme Some Lovin'" which was a huge hit worldwide for the Spencer Davis Group. When I was singing "Gimme Some Lovin'," I just happened to look up when I started the third verse and there stood Steve Winwood! He was standing there watching and listening and I'm sure that he was waiting for me to do what I'm sure everybody else did, fake it through the third verse. And I did just that! No one could ever figure out what he was saying, and to this day I still don't know! It was our first concert in England, and we were really well received by the audience. Robert Stigwood threw a party at his London mansion for us after the show. His house was incredibly beautiful. I had not seen anything like it before. The main entrance hall was massive, and there was a bathroom in the middle of this huge room, but it was so big that you did not know what was there. The toilet was a throne. A real throne! I had never seen anything like it. He had a spread laid out that was amazing. The table looked just like the table off of the Rolling Stones' *Beggar's Banquet* record sleeve. At one point I was in the dining room by myself with all five or six of Robert's dogs sitting in a row at my feet. I was feeding them bits of ham and steak and just about everything that was on the table. I was doing this when Robert and Eric walked in and caught me feeding the dogs. It reminded me of that scene in *Tom Jones* when the guy was throwing food to his dogs in the house. Luckily, "Stiggy" thought that it was sweet that I was feeding his dogs my food—well, actually, it was his very expensive food. He was always an absolute gentleman, debonair, suave, an all-round classy guy. Delaney and Bonnie were totally out of their league. They did not know what to do or say, so for once they were reserved. There was an aura around Robert that silently commanded respect. He was a lovely man and the very person responsible for us all being there. On the other hand, Delaney and Bonnie acted as if they were the ones responsible for us being there. I don't recall them ever showing any gratitude towards Robert Stigwood. But I did thank him for what he had done for us. What an incredible opportunity it was.

George Harrison knew about us through his friendship with Alan. He had championed our cause in England and was at our Royal Albert Hall show. He was going through a hard time with the Beatles and needed some R&R—rock 'n' roll, that is—and we were just the ticket. Eric asked him if he wanted to join us for the rest of the tour and he jumped at the chance. George didn't come and rehearse. We just picked him up at his house in Esher. Delaney had a bad habit of asking people to give him guitars, or anything he saw that someone else had that he wanted. He thought nothing about saying, "Why don't you give me that?" or, "Let me have that guitar." He had already asked Eric for one and I heard him do it. It was downright embarrassing, but Eric, wisely, never handed one over. Alan was aware of this, and to save any further embarrassment he warned George that Delaney would probably ask for a guitar. When we pulled up in our tour bus outside George's house, he came walking out with the guitar that he had played on the roof at Savile Row with the Beatles for their *Let It Be* album and film. And when he got on the bus the first thing that he did before even saying hello was give that guitar to Delaney straight away. George was all class. It was a brown rosewood Fender Telecaster, a very beautiful guitar that was made especially for George. When George was diagnosed with cancer, Delaney tried to auction that guitar. Nobody bid for it out of respect to George. But in 2004, Delaney put it up for auction again and, this time it sold for nearly a half million dollars. It would turn out that Olivia Harrison was the one who quietly bought it back. Now the guitar is back home, where it should have stayed. When George got on the bus, it was the best thing to have happen to us. He had a leveling influence on the whole scene, and he always carried a sense of well-being and serenity with him everywhere that he went. He was very quiet and was always smiling and laughing while being very serious about what he was doing at the same time. I loved the way George played. He was a real straight player with a fine touch. He told me that one time that he very nearly quit playing guitar because he wasn't as good as Eric. He told Eric and Eric told him that it was nonsense and that he was a great guitar player. That was when he asked Eric to play on "While My Guitar Gently Weeps."

When we were on the stage with Delaney & Bonnie & Friends the horns were always to my left and next to Bonnie who was next to Delaney. He was always center stage. Jim and his drums were in the middle in the very back, and Carl was to his left. George and Eric were standing to Delaney's left. What a band! I can hardly believe that it was me who was in it playing organ and singing. Bobby Keys had this cool little thing that he did when he lit his cigarette on stage, or anywhere else that he had an audience. He would take out a cigarette from the pack in his shirt pocket with his left hand. Then he would stick it in his mouth and he would go back into his pocket and take out a book of matches. Doing this all with one hand. His left. I have seen him do this many times in a bar or at a party when he was trying to impress someone. He would open up the matchbook and bend one match forward and close the book back with the wrapper behind the one and between the other matches. He would strike the bent match on the striker and would light his cigarette and then blow out the match and open the book back up and fold the one match back in its original place and close the book back. A very complicated procedure just to light his cigarette, but he made it look cool. When he started doing it you couldn't keep your eyes off of him from wondering what he was going to do

George Harrison's 1969 rosewood Telecaster (photograph by Gary Conaughton).

Me in the shadow of Delaney and Bonnie and Friends, at Fairfield Hall in Croydon, England, December 7, 1969, where most of their live album was recorded (photograph by Laurie Asprey).

next. One night we were really rocking on stage, I can't remember just where, but George and Eric were both with us. Bobby chose this particular night to perform his elaborate cigarette-lighting ceremony while we were in the middle of the drum solo on "Where There's a Will There's a Way." He did his usual thing while holding his sax with his right hand, and it was all going quite smoothly. He got it out and lit his cigarette and he blew the match out and folded it back into its original place and closed the book and put it back in his pocket. No problem. Then he filled the air around us with smoke after he took a long drag off of it. Then it was the horn section's time to come back in. Just as they started to blow their first note his shirt

Delaney Bramlett, left, and Eric Clapton at the Croydon concert (photograph by Laurie Asprey).

pocket lit up with a woomph! He didn't fully extinguish the match and it ignited the whole book of matches and his shirt pocket exploded like it had a pack of fireworks in it. The next thing you know, Bobby's shirt caught on fire right in the middle of the song. He was banging away on his chest, and the band kept on playing right through his dilemma. Bobby was on fire and so were we! We were cooking and so was he! He came out of his shirt and was stomping it out and we kept on playing. And so did he, without his shirt on and with a great big burn hole where the entire book of matches had seared through his pocket and had adhered to his chest. It was a hell of a deal. After the song finished he put it back on and it looked like it had been set on fire and stomped on. Bobby Keys, what a guy.

The U.K. shows were generally well received and several of them were recorded for a proposed live album, but by the end of the tour we were all pretty tired and had had enough. I know I did. We had been playing two shows every night, and it started to take its toll. Still, undeterred, we moved onto Scandinavia for a couple of concerts. Our show in Copenhagen on December 12, 1969, at the Falkonerteatret was filmed for Danish television. It was not a great performance. Eric had on dark glasses and so did Bonnie. Hers were round and pink. We were all so messed up on coke and booze. It was unbelievable! Now it's all out there on YouTube for all to see. They should have thought everything through, but they didn't. I never did see George do any blow at all on that tour. He was a straight dude then. After we played our Scandinavian shows with Eric and George, we all came back to Hurtwood. We were all there when the phone rang and it was John Lennon. He had seen us at the Royal Albert Hall, and he asked Eric if he would bring everyone down to the Lyceum to play with him and Yoko and the Plastic Ono Band. The "Peace for Christmas" concert was to take place on December 15, and was a charity show in aid of the United Nations Children's Fund. Of course, everybody was all excited—everyone but me, that is. It was ego time at Hurtwood, and the Bramletts' egos were getting bigger by the day. Eric, on the other hand, was low-key and humble and totally respectful towards the new-found friends that he had welcomed into his home. After John called, I took Eric aside and asked him if it would be all right with him if I stayed behind at Hurtwood alone. He said that it would be fine with him. I explained that I really needed a break from them and he said that he understood and for me to make myself at home. "Feel free to go everywhere," he told me. Little did I know that I was to be coming back there a few months later and that it really would be my home for a long time to come. They all left and I watched them as they drove away down the drive. Everybody waving their arms, hootin' and hollerin'. The hell-raising had begun, and I was very happy to see them all disappear off into the dark. When I went back into that big old cold house, I built a roaring fire in the front room and had a nice cup of tea and just sat there in a state of wonderment. It was just me and Jeep, Eric's beautiful Weimaraner, and Morris, Eric's grandmother's parrot. It was lovely being there, all alone in that secluded big old place in the English countryside. Everything was all so alien to me, coming from the American South. Don't forget it was my first time out of the United States. Eric's place had beautiful rhododendron lining the drive, and the gardens were so beautiful that you would have to see them to believe it. I was enjoying the solitude, but the calm stopped as soon as they all came back. They were louder and more wasted. I could not wait for it all to be over.

George never saw Delaney and Bonnie again and only called Delaney once, in 1971, to ask if he would help him with his court case. George had been accused of plagiarizing the melody for his worldwide hit "My Sweet Lord" from the 1963 hit single "He's So Fine" by the Chiffons. Delaney refused to help him. Now, I was on the bus when George started playing that "My Sweet Lord" riff, yet Delaney would later say that George stole that idea from him, and he told me that himself! Incredible! But, of course, George didn't. That's the real reason why Delaney didn't want to show up in court.

When we went on the road and toured Europe with Eric Clapton, Dave Mason and George Harrison, I only made $96.50 a week with $12.50 a day for expenses. That was the most money that I ever made during my time with Delaney and Bonnie, $96.50 a week. Unbelievable! I'm sure that all the rest of the band got a hell of a lot more than me. I did say earlier that I wasn't in that band for the money, and that's probably the reason they didn't pay me any more than that paltry amount. Not surprisingly, I had spent most of it in Europe, so when we all flew back to America via New York's JFK airport, I hardly had any money left in my pocket, probably $125. I had bought a rabbit skin coat for Cathy, who I had left at her parents' farm outside of Memphis. I had to declare what I had bought at the customs desk there in New York, and I put down the correct amount that I had paid for it. They took all but five cents of my money! That was all the money that I had left, five cents! Five cents in my pocket and returning from our big European tour with some of the biggest names in the world! I had to borrow a dime from a stranger who stood there waiting for it back. I had to use the telephone to make a collect call to make sure someone was there in Memphis to pick me up. The stranger got his dime back.

One of the first things we did on our return was to go into the studio to review the U.K. tour tapes. It was a real eye-opener because they sounded terrible, nothing like the way we remembered the shows at all. Delaney had to replace all of the lead and background vocals. His singing was off, and he redid most of his guitar work as well. He had to because they had done too many drugs and drunk too much whisky and it showed. It was pretty amazing what we had come home with: a ragged, hollow shell of what started out as a tight, well-oiled machine. I guess it sounded like everyone felt, because they were just looking for an end to it all and couldn't wait until it was over so that they could go home. Drugs and booze will do that to you. After Christmas, Eric flew to Los Angeles to continue the recording of his first solo album. Only one track from the Olympic Studio sessions in London would make the finished album. The remainder would be done in Los Angeles. Since his return to the United States, Delaney had been working overtime writing songs for Eric's new record.

Ahmet Ertegun had introduced us to King Curtis when we were in New York one time. Ahmet played a big role with Delaney and Bonnie as well and was very good at hooking different artists up. He knew who and what would work well together. King Curtis was a gracious, kind and gentle man. He was who you see when you see a picture of him laughing or smiling. I was truly saddened at his passing. Thanks to Ahmet, Delaney was asked to produce a track for the forthcoming King Curtis *Get Ready* album at Sunset Sound in Los Angeles. As Eric was in town, he was asked if he would like to play on the track. "Teasin'" was pretty much made up on the spot with Curtis and Eric playing twin parts. The band was really cooking. It is one of my favorite tracks. Eric's wah wah guitar and King Curtis's soprano sax playing in unison together sounded like one completely unique instrument. When we had finished recording, Eric and everybody else left and went back to the hotel. As usual I had to hang around and wait until Delaney was finished. For some reason he would always keep me there with him no matter where we were and not let me leave until he said so. He really was a father figure, and I looked at him that way many times. He was knowingly giving me an education and he told me so many, many times. As a matter of fact he wouldn't let your attention drift for one second when the creative process was happening, and that was pretty much all of the time. For some strange reason Delaney and Bonnie liked to have me around them at all times when we were out in public. I probably balanced things out and gave them a more wholesome image. But behind the image, they were running wild as hell and completely out of control. Those two were fighting it out every day that the sun came up and they managed to get me in the middle of it. It was exhausting for me, but I believe that I probably kept them grounded for some of the time.

Delaney and Curtis were overdubbing their parts again after Eric had left and out came this huge bag of blow. Delaney liked to stay in a studio and go over something many times until he thought it was right. It was just a waste of money and was no more than an ego trip, because in the end the music came out great no matter what. He could play around with our tracks forever and, sometimes, it felt like that was just what he was doing. Delaney didn't care because it wasn't his money that he was spending, or so he thought. He forgot that the record company always gets theirs first. I have a very clear picture of King Curtis sitting in a chair with his sax across his lap and Delaney standing right next to him and they're laughing. Curtis has an ounce of cocaine in his left hand and a $100 bill in his right hand. It's folded in the shape of a large scoop and he just rammed it in the bag and without looking, stuck it under that great hole of a nostril, and every bit of it went up his nose. Then what wouldn't fit up there just spilled down his face and onto his chest. Then he did the same thing again to the left side. He never broke his stride. It was like he was doing it without even noticing that he was doing it or even giving it any thought whatsoever. He just kept talking and laughing and shoveling that stuff up his nose. I had never seen anything like it. He had a huge grin on his face and looked like he had a white Fu Manchu mustache. He just sat there holding that bag of cocaine and that $100 bill, smiling. I waited for something to happen but it didn't. I thought for sure that he was going to explode or go into a cardiac arrest. But it never happened. I wasn't into doing all of that cocaine at that time. They kept it from me. Not for any other reason than that they were serious about keeping it to themselves, I think. It was a very rare occasion that I would ever be offered any. And even then it would be only a match head. That was one time that Delaney was outdone. Even he marveled at what Curtis had just done. That is the last picture that I have in my mind of Curtis, sitting there in that chair with cocaine running down his face.

The sessions for Eric's solo album were a whole lot of fun and an incredible learning experience for me. For once, there was no alcohol and not too many drugs in the studio during those sessions. It was all business with everyone being there on time and totally together. Delaney was at his creative best and really, all anyone had to do was just stay out of his way and follow his lead. He really was right on about then. All one had to do was just fit in the groove because it was all happening without anybody's help. Delaney thought that it was him, but it wasn't. It was everyone as a whole becoming one solid unit. Kind of like putting seven different colors of paint side by side on the end of a board, and then mixing them all together and watching it all flow into one new color that is a combination. It's a beautiful experience to be one of those colors in a piece of music. Delaney knew very well what the financial rewards were for the publishing of such songs, no matter if he wrote them with Eric or with someone else, just so long as he had his songs on it. He was the producer, and had the band, and was writing the songs and had the publishing on them. It seemed like a pretty cool deal, and it was for a while. Then it went cold. Eric knew what Delaney was doing all along. He knew that Delaney was just using him because of his fame, but he wanted to sing like Delaney was singing. Not to sound like Delaney but to sing like him, from that special place.

We recorded Eric's album at Village Recorders in Los Angeles. We would first record the tracks with Delaney singing and after, Eric would put his voice on, a very simple process. Delaney didn't make Eric do anything that he wasn't already doing before he had ever heard of him. What Delaney did was to get Eric high on LSD and then scare him by telling him that if he didn't use his voice that God would take it away from him. Eric was doing a fine job singing with Jack in Cream and later in Blind Faith with Steve Winwood. More has been made about Delaney's influence on Eric's singing than is due. Eric still sings like Eric Clapton. What Delaney did do, however, was to give Eric the confidence to sing by himself. JJ Cale had written "After Midnight," and he played it for Eric at the start of the sessions after being introduced to him by Delaney. Eric recorded a version of it and it later ended up being a hit single. Eric has continued to cover JJ Cale's songs throughout his career, and they even recorded an album together in 2006 and attempted another in 2009. Leon Russell was also at the sessions and brought along a song written especially for Eric called "Blues Power." Eric loved this number and played it in concert throughout the '70s and '80s. Another Delaney song, "Bottle of Red Wine," was written on the way to the studio one day. It was such a creative time. Jerry Allison and Sonny Curtis from Buddy Holly's Crickets were there as well. I recall I used to ride Carl's Triumph motorbike over to see Jerry when I first moved into the Plantation. He was the drummer with the Crickets and I always liked him. They appear in the picture on the back of the record cover as well as Edward James Olmos. He was an aspiring singer at the time but later turned out to be a very successful actor. That was his calling, to be sure. All of us involved with the album were photographed as a large group for the back sleeve. That was one mighty fine record to have for your first solo album, that's all that I can say.

Our live album, *Delaney & Bonnie & Friends on Tour with Eric Clapton*, was due for release and they needed some artwork urgently. The front sepia style cover has a Rolls-Royce on it with someone's feet hanging out of the window. That Rolls belonged to Albert Grossman, who managed Bob Dylan and the Band. The feet sticking out of the window are Barry Feinstein's, the photographer who was one of the partners in Group Three, our management company. Besides Alan and Barry was Sid Keiser, a rotund man who always had a smile on his face. Barry was responsible for doing many memorable album covers such as George Harrison's *All Things Must Pass*, Eric's first solo album and my first solo album, among many others. The artwork and photography arm of the company was called Camouflage Productions. The front cover was already in their archive from a previously unused session. It had been shot in the desert at Joshua Tree and Barry decided to take all of us there for the back sleeve shoot in order to match the back cover up with the front one. I never knew what the fascination was with this place except that everyone used to take LSD or some other kind of drug and go there. Gram Parsons used to go there all of the time. The place was hot and there was nothing there but rocks, snakes and one tree on a hill. I just didn't get it. I didn't see what folks got all excited about. I couldn't figure if it was the place or the mystique or the drugs. As for us, it seemed that drugs were taken no matter where we were. The idea to go to the desert was a good one though because we didn't have far to go and all it would cost was gas money and film. A very cheap photo shoot and album cover to produce. Barry just had us all grab a guitar or something and walk toward him. That was it, nothing spectacular or magical about it. Just walk towards the camera and don't trip and fall down. It took longer to get there than the actual shoot took. This was in January 1970, and we were getting ready to go on our U.S. tour, and that is why the band on the back cover is missing a few members who were with us in England for the recording. They had left as soon as we got home. I recall the day that Barry brought the picture out for us to see. We were up at Alan's house that overlooked Hollywood and where we later recorded part of the *Motel Shot* record. They also had the house next door and used that as an art studio for Camouflage Productions. Everybody loved the artwork.

Delaney had talked Eric into going on the road for a short tour of the United States after we finished his record. That tour started on the February 2, 1970, and carried on to March 3, 1970. Everyone was enjoying themselves and playing together, but then again, that's what we did. Eric had just finished Cream and moved straight into Blind Faith and then straight into Delaney & Bonnie & Friends. He really did live his life out on the road. He went from one experience into another and has done it up to this day. On that tour we started out in Toronto, Canada, at Massey Hall and then played the popular *Dick Cavett Show* at ABC Television Studios in New York City on February 5, 1970. Delaney and Bonnie were interviewed by Dick and we all played "Comin' Home," an acoustic version of "Poor Elijah/Tribute to Robert Johnson" and a powerful rendition of my song, "Where There's a Will There's a Way." We later heard that a lot of people complained that Eric's guitar was lost in the mix. Televisions were not really able to deliver great sound in those days, and a lot of engineers were not used to dealing with large bands with loud sound. The next day we pulled up in front of the Fillmore East and it was freezing! We were in a regular bus that severely lacked heating, and I clearly remember my feet being so cold in that bus. But that didn't seem to matter because this was the great Fillmore East, one of the hippest venues of the time. The bus driver stopped so that we could all get a look at our names up in lights on the marquee that read "Tonight! Delaney and Bonnie and Friends featuring Eric Clapton." I still feel the feeling that I had in my chest then. I remember this as if it were yesterday. I was about halfway back on the bus on the left side next to a window. I was looking up at the sign and when I redirected my eyes back to the ground I locked eyes with a dude standing with his girlfriend right next to a two-foot block of ice. I said that it was cold there at that time and it was! He had a sign that read, "TICKETS?" He didn't have a ticket for himself and his girlfriend. But he did have on a great leather shirt with very long fringe. It was absolutely beautiful, and I had to have it. I had the driver wait and I got two tickets and two backstage passes from Bruce McCaskill, our road manager. I went across the street and told him that I would give him the shirt off of my back and my jacket and two tickets and two backstage passes for his shirt. He peeled it off right there on the street and handed it over. I took my leather jacket and shirt off and handed them over to him along with the passes and the tickets. He was very happy and so was I. Everyone applauded me as I walked back on the bus wearing the shirt. It's the same shirt that I am wearing on the back of Eric's solo record and the same shirt that Jim Gordon is wearing on our *Derek and the Dominos Live at the Fillmore East* record. I gave it away in the early '70s to a roadie who worked for me.

We were playing two sets a night again on this tour. We followed New York with a couple of dates in Boston at the legendary Tea Party Club and then we went straight to the Electric Factory in Philly, followed by the Symphony Hall in Minnesota. We made our way across the States playing pretty much every night. We did an amazing four-night run at the great Fillmore in San Francisco from February 19 until February 22, and our last show was at the Civic Auditorium in Santa Monica California on March 3. Everywhere that we played we blew everyone away. We really jelled as a band. "Where There's a Will There's a Way" and "Comin' Home" come immediately to mind as good examples. In particular, the drum section in those songs is killer. Unfortunately, it got very tiring because no matter how good a band is, it starts to fall apart when the leader is making it all about himself. Band members became so many faceless musicians passing through Delaney and Bonnie's lives. Playing with Delaney and Bonnie was a personal thing with everyone they had with them. They made it that way. You were told that you were loved, and then treated liked hired help, and talked about to others as if you were an equal when that wasn't the case at all. And it never changed either. Even Eric, who was a seasoned road warrior, was ready to go home. Toward the end of the U.S. tour everyone was talking privately among themselves. To me, it was pretty obvious what was happening, but Delaney and Bonnie were oblivious to what was going on because they were so absorbed with themselves. In reality everyone was making plans to go be with Leon Russell and Joe Cocker's Mad Dogs and Englishmen after we all got back to Los Angeles. I wasn't included, I would imagine, because they were going to use Joe's guy, Chris Stainton. I wouldn't have gone even if they had asked. I wasn't interested in what they were doing. It sounded too much like a circus with all manner of folk all living together on the road. That just didn't sound like fun to me. I had just got off of that not so merry-go-round. And truth be told, I still had a sense of loyalty towards Delaney and Bonnie, however misplaced.

Atlantic wanted a new studio album, but Delaney did not have enough new songs ready. It was decided to record the *To Bonnie from Delaney* album in Miami with Tom Dowd as producer. It was to be a big production number with a lot of great names participating. Jerry Wexler wanted the album to be a mixture of choice covers as well as originals. I was in Jerry's houseboat when he played a whole lot of songs for Delaney and Bonnie. We must have listened to over a hundred songs. He had picked out a few gems that had never been heard or recorded by anyone. "Soul Shake" and "Free the People" were the two that were to become hits for them. They were the ones that Jerry selected. Delaney's well had run dry in the songwriting department. He had hit a wall, and his ego would not let him include anyone else in his songwriting. He was just making songs up that weren't songs of substance, unlike the earlier "The Ghetto" and "Superstar," which were classics. That's when and why Jerry and Ahmet and Tom stepped in. They wanted Delaney and Bonnie to be a commercial success. At least they weren't looking to mold them into something that they weren't. Ahmet and Jerry loved Delaney and Bonnie and only wanted the best for them, as did everybody else. I do believe that Jerry brought us to Miami so that he could really get involved in the creative process and help Delaney to see past himself. Duane Allman played on the album, as he and Jerry were very close. Jerry was perceptive enough to realize that his guitar skills would add some sparkle to the sessions. They also could take over a session and produce it themselves if necessary. Ahmet was so in tune with that kind of thing. He wrote "Mess Around" for Ray Charles, so he knew great material when he heard it. Jerry and Ahmet had the ability to hear who would be right for each other and which songs would bring them all together. They had the ability to see the big picture. They were visionaries, which is something that is seriously lacking in the industry today.

Jerry also knew Little Richard very well. He was playing a residency in Miami and Jerry arranged for us to go to the show. Little Richard was happy that we were there and had already been briefed as to who we were, but he had already heard of us. Delaney was as personable and likeable as you could possibly imagine when we first were introduced to

The band who recorded **To Bonnie from Delaney:** *from left, me, Bonnie Bramlett, Delaney Bramlett, Ron Tutt and Jerry Sheff.*

Little Richard in his hotel suite. I was pretty much blown away just to get to meet him. The meeting was set up by Jerry because he wanted Little Richard to get to know us all. Jerry could already hear what was about to take place. Little Richard kept the guy who worked for him very busy while we were there in his room: "Percy, hand me my hair spray!" and all manner of orders. We all were standing in the room while Little Richard was dressing for his show. It wasn't ten minutes before the idea of him coming over and recording with us came up. He agreed to do it and was going to meet us after the show. We stayed for the set and then went straight to the studio and waited for him to show up. He pulled up in a limo in the front of the studio, came in and immediately sat down at the piano in the main studio and started playing "Miss Ann." He didn't wait for anybody to say anything or count it off. He just started playing and he played that song for twenty-five minutes without stopping. Everyone just joined in and tried to keep up. Delaney edited it down to five minutes for the record. It was a hell of a job and a real jigsaw puzzle for him to piece together because it was a very long medley originally. What an incredible experience that was for me. Getting to go up into his room and meet him, and then having Little Richard play with us on our record was to be one of the favorite memories of my career. The basic band for the sessions was Ronnie Tutt on drums and Jerry Scheff on bass. They were a drum and bass team who played with everyone and eventually wound up playing with Elvis until the end of his days. Duane Allman was playing slide and I was playing organ. I think Ben Benay played guitar on some tracks. He had a bent thumb on his left hand that wouldn't straighten out. It was perfect for him, being a guitar player. He didn't have to work at keeping it there and was a natural lefty, so to speak.

Duane Allman really hit it off with Delaney and Bonnie and became an occasional "friend." When he would come around to their house, he was treated the same way that Eric Clapton was treated. He was swarmed by the two of them, but mostly by Delaney. So, just like Eric, I knew Duane from a distance. They had him so preoccupied that he could barely go to the bathroom alone. As a matter of fact there were a lot of times when he didn't. Cocaine was around, but no one would let me in on any of it at first. They said I was too young. I've got to hand it to them, I had never seen any drugs at all until I went to the Bramletts' house in Hawthorne. I hadn't known until then that's what Peapaw Whitlock had been smoking and I certainly hadn't seen cocaine. In those days I didn't drink a lot and never when I performed. Maybe afterwards. Anyway, the others kept what they were doing to themselves, and kept Duane to themselves as well. So he and I never really got close like brothers until the *Layla* sessions in 1970.

Early on during the *To Bonnie from Delaney* sessions, Delaney had arranged to get cocaine from some guy at a jewelry store not far from the studio. He had given our road manager the money to go get it. Delaney asked me to go with him to get it. I figured carrying a gram wouldn't be much to worry about. We pulled up to this building that stood all by itself in the middle of an otherwise vacant lot. There was a very tall chain link fence around it with a small opening in the front. It looked ominous and had a strange vibe about it. The band's helper I went with asked if I would run in and pick it up. He said that they were waiting and all that I would have to say is Delaney's name and the guy would hand it over. I was thinking that this all seemed to be getting pretty involved for a simple transaction. I reluctantly agreed and was handed the money. When I checked the amount I realized it was over $1000 in cash! This did not look good, but I took it anyway and went inside the front door. It was a very small room with one jewelry case holding only a chain or two, with some cheap earrings and some other crap. This really wasn't looking good at all. A guy came out through the door behind the case and asked if he could help me. I told him my name and then told him that I was sent there by Delaney Bramlett to pick something up for him. He told me to follow him. We went through the door and into a huge room that was stark white. It had a very long table that ran up the middle and tables that ran around the walls on two sides. On the table in the middle were huge piles of cocaine and bags to put it in. There were scales on that table as well as the other two tables that were also piled high with Peruvian flake cocaine. There must have been five or six kilos in that room alone. They were cutting it in that room and weighing it on the other tables. There were two other guys in that room and by now my heart was pounding like it had never done before. All of my senses were heightened, and I was alive like never before. Not a word was said as I took in all of this surreal scene. It looked like something out of *Scarface*, totally surrealistic. Then this dude tells me to come with him. We went into another room, and there was a guy sitting with his feet propped up on a wooden schoolteacher's desk. I'm sure that your teacher had one just like it, but I bet she didn't have a sawed-off 12-gauge pump shotgun sitting in the corner next to her. By this point I was petrified, and I just started to feel that there was a strong possibility that I would not be walking out of there. He asked me if I had the money and I said yes. He asked for it and I handed it over. I was playing it very cool and was concealing my anxiety well. At least I thought I was. The cold sweat coming out of my head and rolling down my face probably gave me away, though. He took the money, counted it out and opened a drawer and pulled out an ounce bag and set it on the table in front of me and said, "That's for your boss." Then he reached back into drawer and said to me, "And this is for you!" I thought for sure that I was going to get shot right then and there. I had never been in such a situation and stopped breathing momentarily, not knowing what he was going to do. He pulled out another bag of cocaine and laid out two lines for me to do. I had to do them or I most certainly would have been shot-gunned right then and there. Each line was exactly as long and as round as my pointing finger. He handed me a plastic straw and said, "Do it all!" He was a cold dude, I'll tell you. He never smiled the whole time and just looked at me as though he were looking right through me. He never blinked and kept his eyes on mine at all times. I had never seen that much cocaine, much less been told to suck it all up my nose. I did, though. I had no other choice. It took me several attempts to get it all, and I had to snort it all or I wasn't leaving of my own accord. That was made very clear to me. It was kind of like blowing out the candles on a birthday cake but only backwards. I kept having to start over and over until it was all gone. I thought that I was surely going to die from the amount that I had just ingested. It had to have been several grams. Crazy. He handed over Delaney's bag of coke and said, "You can go now." I turned and walked out, not knowing if I was going to be shot in the back as I left. My insides were shaking so badly that I was throwing up in my mouth and swallowing it back down because I couldn't do it on the floor. He would have killed me for sure. The man who I thought cared for me sent me out to do that job for him knowing what could happen to me if things went wrong, and they almost did. I took his dope back to the studio, tossed it across the room to him in front of Jerry. I told him, "Run your own errands next time." I can't believe that I even stayed that night there, much less stayed to finish the record. That was the beginning of the end for me. I had stayed with Delaney and Bonnie out of a displaced sense of loyalty and love, despite all the tantrums I had put up with through the last few years.

I would have left them in Miami but I had no place else to go and not enough money to get there. So I was stuck until we got back to Los Angeles. When we did get back, they were doing everything that they could to please me because they knew that I was going to leave and why. After much persuasion from Delaney and a river of tears from Bonnie, I decided to stay for their last album, *Motel Shot*. Sadly, they pretty much continued right where they had left off within about two days of me agreeing to stay. They were at each other's throats with me right in the middle of them.

We started *Motel Shot* pretty much straight away, although we didn't record any of it in any motels. The idea was to try and create some of the loose jams we would have while on the road and playing acoustic guitars and anything that came to hand in our motel rooms. The sound was a melting pot, including rock, gospel, hillbilly, country, blues, and soul. It was recorded in two days. One day at Bruce Botnick's house and the other at Alan's house. Alan's was one of those very cool Hollywood Hills houses that looked like a chalet with a big main room with cedar beams and a stone fireplace at the end and tall windows on either side. That main room was large with a vaulted ceiling, and the kitchen was right there in the room with the bar. The bedrooms were away from the main part of the house. Very cool house with driftwood here and there. It looked out over Hollywood, and on a clear day you could see the ocean. His house was supported by steel poles because it hung off the side of the mountain. The only thing attached to the ground was the front edge of the house. It was chosen because of its great acoustic qualities. Bruce was one of the premier recording engineers of that era and had a good ear for sound and the different nuances. There was a long couch that Bonnie and I sat on, and Delaney sat in a chair to Bonnie's left, playing his Martin. Bruce was miking our feet tapping on the floor, and us playing our knees with our hands and clapping. I played the inside of my thighs with cupped hands. We did the same thing on "Never Ending Song of Love" as well. It all sounded great when it all got going. There were no electric instruments or drum kits. In fact, the loudest sounds were handclaps and tambourines. Duane Allman was across from Bonnie and me, just to my right, playing his Dobro with his Coricidin bottle. We were always very loose in a structured way. None of the regular recording processes were ever really involved with this album. It was always something real simple, like Delaney banging on a briefcase or something else out of the ordinary. He was looking for a pure percussion sound. He was into all sorts of weird stuff, like recording his heartbeat followed by one strange thing after the next. But nothing could top him recording Sandy Konikoff playing on his stomach using his own invention, the sphincter-phone. This was basically a mike the size of a finger and worked by sticking it up one's butt. This was just way too much for me. I had to leave the room. Delaney had outdone himself this time. My happiest memory from those sessions was when we did "Goin' Down the Road Feeling Bad." It was just Delaney and Bonnie with me and Duane Allman. It stands out because it was one of the few songs that we did where I sang in my natural voice. Gram Parsons was on that number also, smacking his lap. I should mention some of the other guests, like an uncredited Buddy Miles, who was using a briefcase for percussion, and Joe Cocker banging loudly on the side of the piano.

Once the session was over, I felt a sense of relief. I knew that this would be the end of the road for me, but I did not know where to go or who to turn to. I felt totally lost and directionless. So I called my old friend Steve Cropper and told him that I had had enough of those two driving me crazy, and that I wanted to leave because of everything that had gone down but I didn't have a clue what to do. He suggested I call Eric Clapton and ask him if I could go and spend a bit of time with him in England to clear my head and gather my thoughts away from everything that was familiar to me. I told Steve that I didn't have any money, even if Eric was to invite me over. He told me to call him anyway, tell him what was happening and see what Eric said and to call him right back. So I called Eric at Hurtwood and explained what was going down and asked if I could come and stay with him. He said that it would not be a problem and that I would be welcome. I hung up from Eric and immediately called Steve back and told him what Eric had said. Steve told me that there would be an airplane ticket for me first thing in the morning. I told him about my wife needing a ticket to get back home to her folks and he said that it would be there as well. I crossed the road and went to see Delaney and Bonnie to tell them I was leaving. I was standing in their front doorway with it still wide open as they were telling me that they would call the new album "Delaney and Bonnie and Bobby" if I stayed. They promised me that I would get a share of everything. I was supposed to, anyway, in our original deal. In the end it didn't make any difference to me what anybody said or did because I was leaving those two. I was leaving behind all of their drinking, doping, fighting, lying, cheating and stealing. I was no longer going to allow them to use me up. Bonnie started crying and Delaney started cussing me out. I simply turned and walked away. The next morning an overnight delivery of two airline tickets arrived at my door. One for Cathy to go back to Memphis when she was ready, and the other, a one-way ticket to England. I gave her the ticket and left with the clothes on my back for the airport. I left Cathy there in the house across the street from Delaney and Bonnie and caught a plane for England. She got a divorce without me being there. It was more than likely not even a real marriage in the first place. That whole experience seemed incredibly surrealistic at the time and still does. When it happened I was very high on mescaline so for a while I wasn't sure about my feelings. After I came back down, I tried to do what I thought was the right thing for her and for myself. It would seem that I made the right choice.

My New Life in England

I never called Eric to tell him when I was coming over. I just left because he had told me to come on over whenever I wanted, and I couldn't wait to get away from Los Angeles and the Bramletts. I was taking a leap of faith. I was following my destiny and didn't even know it. When I first arrived at Heathrow airport in London, all that I had with me were the clothes on my back and $300 in my pocket. I truly was only going to stay for a week or less and then head back home. To what, I didn't know. But, for the moment, I was looking to kick back with Eric and stay right there at Hurtwood Edge and not even go to London. I got a black cab at the airport and told him where I was headed. He was quite excited to be going to Mr. Clapton's residence. I gave him the address and we were off to Eric's house, a gorgeous Italian villa that sits high atop a ridge.

You can see for thirty miles or more out across the rolling Surrey countryside on a clear day. About an hour later we came up the drive. I was glad to be pulling in there, too, as his meter was eating up every bit of what little money I had in my pocket. I had already gone through a major shock when I exchanged my $300 and they gave me back whatever it was at the time, about 125 pounds. After I paid the cab, I had about 50 pounds left. I knocked on the big door and Eric came to the front window of his house and then to the door and said, "What are you doing here?" I told him, "You said to come on over, so here I am!" I would later read somewhere that he said that my coming over was an instinctive move on my part. He was right. He shook my hand, put his arm around me and welcomed me into his home. He told me that I could have my choice of bedroom. The house was very large, although not huge like George's house, Friar Park. That place is massive. Eric's house had a more homey feeling. I always felt at home when I was there. He made it like that. A house should be so much more than mortar and stone. It was what Eric had brought to that place that made it so very comfortable. He had only just bought it a few years before, in 1968, with his earnings from his Cream days. It had no central heating and was freezing in the winter. But it didn't matter because the warmth that was there was the welcome home for me every time I crossed the threshold.

A man named Don was living there. "One-eyed Don," I called him. He was a little hunched-over guy with only one eye and looked exactly like Marty Feldman. Eric had George's psychedelic-painted Mini at the time, and Don drove that back and forth to London and the village down the road. It was a Radford Mini Cooper and was very fast. He would do errands for Eric. He was his right-hand man. Actually, I think he was one of those people who Eric had a fondness for taking in. Don was just one of the many that Eric took into his home and gave a job, and a life. That would include me, too. Eric was always bringing some derelict home for a while, and he would feed him and get him good and drunk and then have Don take him to the village or somewhere and drop him off. I'm told that he continued doing that for a very long time. Yes, old One-Eyed Don was a character, all right. He would drive that Mini to London with Eric and me at 110 mph and I would tell him, "Don't take your eye off of the road!"

Don lived up in the smallest room at the very back of the house. He would get up real early and build a fire in the front room. That's if Mrs. Eggby hadn't already done it. There were a few people who were there looking after Eric and the house. Mr. and Mrs. Eggby lived in the gate house over the garage by the entry gate. Mrs. Eggby looked after the house and cooked a bit for Eric. He was a real easy keeper and did his own ironing. They would come in and build a fire early in the morning, or get one ready for you so all you had to do was light it. Most mornings the one in the front room would be lit and roaring by the time we got up. Mrs. Eggby would make some tea and some breakfast for us and make meals later on if needed. She was never in the main house except to work. Mr. Eggby and Arthur, the gardener, were always in the gardens working away, keeping them looking as beautiful as they were. I was enthusiastic, to say the very least, and had more energy than I knew what to do with. I asked if I could help out in the garden with Mr. Eggby, and Eric told me to ask him. Mr. Eggby told me that there was a tree that needed to come down. I told him that I was very good at handling that sort of chore. And I am, normally. There is a certain way to make your first cut that directs the fall of the tree. Unfortunately, I must have been a little off to the left, because as I shouted "Timber!" it fell straight across an iron trellis. It was full of roses and ran the entire path down into the gardens. The top of the tree was on the ground and the rest was lying across the trellis, about seven feet in the air. They got it cleaned up, but the trellis remains to this day with a big tree-shaped indention. That was the start of me going through little bumps here and there. The next was with a mini bike. I was running down the hill into the garden and then back up and jumping it up in the air. Eric came out to watch and as soon as he did, I ended up going a bit too fast and the bike went up into the air without me on it. It did a few back flips and landed in a crumpled heap at Eric's feet. He had a Honda 350 motorcycle as well. That was the first thing that I went off the property with, but I got confused big time on the road. I didn't know which side I was on and didn't know if I was coming or going. Eric very wisely suggested that I stay off the roads with the bike, so I went out into the woods near his house. I had been out there riding for about ten minutes when a very official and angry looking man came up on his bike. He asked me what I thought I was doing and I told him I was just having some fun riding in those woods. He said that they belonged to the Queen and that I was trespassing. I went back to Eric's and as I was pulling into the gates, One-Eyed Don was tearing out of them. We didn't see each other until it was too late: We went straight into each other. I flew over the top of the Mini and the bike stayed lodged into the front of it. The bike was bent up pretty bad and the Mini had the grill smashed. I was OK and got only some road burn and grass stains on my jeans. Eric didn't say anything about the wrecked bike or the damaged grill on the Mini, which belonged to George Harrison, a Beatle! All of this was going on and I hadn't even been there a week. Amazingly, Eric's only concern, ever, was that I was all right and didn't get hurt. If there was something to be knocked over, or dropped, or wrecked, you can be sure it was probably going to be me behind it. Not intentionally of course, it's just that I was at that gawky age and I was just finding my way. If I reached for something at the dinner table, such as wine glasses and HP sauce bottles, they would get knocked down.

I had chosen my favorite room from when I stayed there before when the band went to play with John Lennon. I walked all over that beautiful place and went into every room, and I probably looked in places that Eric hasn't seen yet. Inside and outside, I covered every square foot of that place. I knew where everything was around there. It had become my home for a while. The bedroom that I chose was at the top far end, with its own balcony. On a very clear day you could see for miles across the stunning rolling countryside to the sea. It was absolutely beautiful and very peaceful.

Even though I was there with him I was still lonely and missed something about where I had come from as well as Cathy. My relationship with her was the beginning of me starting to write songs about my life's experiences. Had it not been for her I would have never been inspired to write "A Game Called Life" or "The Scenery Has Slowly Changed." Both songs were to be on my first record. And she was the inspiration behind both. I wrote those songs just after I arrived. I remember going into the television room and playing them for Eric and Pattie Harrison one day. She had come by for a visit. When I played him "The Scenery Has Slowly Changed" he asked me where the chords came from. I told him that I just made them up. They are still very difficult for me to form with my left hand. I believe that he really understood where those songs came from. Pattie was a regular visitor at that time, and it became very obvious that Eric was madly in love with her. But it was an impossible situation for him as she was married to one of his best friends, George Harrison. Not only that, he was a Beatle. They were like royalty in England, and you did not want to mess with that. It was a situation that would dominate the entire time I was with Eric and was the catalyst for our first album.

Eric and I got to know each other by picking up where we had left off, having a very ordinary casual conversation and a cup of tea like we had known each other all of our lives. We did everyday things that we both loved to do, like play with cars and guitars and talk about girls and played rock 'n' roll music. But these cars were Ferraris, and the rock 'n' roll wasn't Buddy Holly singing "Peggy Sue." We were playing serious rock 'n' roll. These were our songs now, and this was our music that we were playing. He and I were a natural songwriting team and partners in a band that we hadn't put together yet. Eric was interested in my background, and I was interested in his as well. He told me about his mother, Pat, who he thought for years was his sister. And his grandmother Rose was his mother, he thought, until he found out that Pat was his mother and Rose was really his grandmother. And his father was his grandfather, but not really, because his dad was a Canadian airman. Pretty confusing for an adult, let alone a boy. His grandfather was a stonemason and was his central father figure. He passed away during the *Layla* sessions, and Eric went home for a few days for the funeral. It was just one thing after the next with Eric. He was a lot like me in that he was raised in a confusing environment. I was raised by my mother and both of my grandmothers and every other family member that would have me. Then I was put off on strangers. My mother didn't know what else to do sometimes. We didn't have food and the basics to survive at times. She did the best with what she had to work with. My daddy was never around, thank goodness.

Eric and I sat around and played his guitars and watched television at night. And we went all over the countryside in his Lilac 365 GTC Ferrari. He showed me how to drive on the left side of the road in that car. This was March, and the weather was lovely and cold. We would bundle up and go out at night just to go walking in the gardens in the dark. We went to the movies in Cranleigh on occasion. That was really funny because all of the locals knew who we were and this theater held about fifty. Here we were, Ferrari sitting outside in the snow, and we're watching a funny Norman Wisdom movie in this very quaint little village. For a boy from Memphis, I was living in a fairytale dream. When we got back we might have a nice cup of tea or have a few brandy and dry gingers and sit by the fire in the living room where it was warm. We finished "I Looked Away" on an evening just like the one I just described. The following day we were out driving somewhere and stopped at a truck stop café. I'm not sure where it was but I remember there was an overpass and a trucker store, and the head table had Daddy's fruity sauce and HP. A "greasy spoon café," they call them in England. Eric liked to eat at those places because no one recognized him there and nobody really cared that we had long hair. I think that it kept him in touch with his sense of his origins. Also, the sausages were great and the tea tasted as it only can in a place like that. They used steamed milk. Don was there with us having a Cornish pasty and some tea. I had a sausage roll as well. When the check came I reached into my pocket and pulled out what I had left to count because I wanted to get the bill. I didn't have enough to pay the cost of lunch for us. I was so embarrassed. I had always been poor all of my life, but somehow I always knew that poverty was just a state of mind. So money wasn't an issue in my life. I had never had it, so I had no respect for it. I had spent what little I thought I had on I don't know what. I told Eric that I was going to have to get ready to go back to America in the next couple of days, that I had run out of money and it was time for me to go. He said, "I thought that you and I were putting together a band!" Then he said, "I don't have any money either. When we get back home I'll call the office and we'll go see Robert [Stigwood] and we'll tell him that we are putting together a band and that we need a little pocket money while we're doing it." He did and we went to London the next day. Robert Stigwood asked, "What can I do for you boys?" We told him what we had in mind, and he was very pleased and set us both up with a 150 pounds a week wage each. I couldn't believe it. I had just come off of a tour with Delaney and Bonnie and Friends and I was only being paid around $100 a week, so 150 pounds a week was a fortune to me then. Eric was already on a wage. He was getting 200 pounds a week, and he just used to send his bills to the office, even grocery bills. We really didn't need a whole lot of cash. We would tend to get into trouble when we had a little too much in our pocket. It would start to burn a hole in it, and we would start to figure out ways to spend it. We would head out to Deborah & Clare in Beauchamp Place, Knightsbridge, and do some shirt shopping before heading off to the Chelsea Antique market to get some pants and scarves and some very cool English boots with wooden heels. I had several pairs. One was blue suede and the other was burgundy patent leather. Both were zip-up boots. If we weren't doing that, we were off visiting some of Eric's more eclectic friends who were in the art world. He knew some very interesting people in London. He told me about when he was living down on the docks and was making a week stew. Not a weak stew, but one that lasted a week. Eric had a hard go of it in the beginning. Not a lot of people know that he was very nearly living on the street at one point in his career, when he was making his transition from the art world of stained glass making, to playing rock 'n' roll. It hasn't always been as glamorous for Eric as it appears from out here, looking there through the glass darkly. He told me that he used to add some different vegetables every day to keep it going for a week. It would be cabbage one day, and potatoes the next, then carrots and onions the next. I'm sure that it was mighty fine eating about the third day.

 By this point I felt like I was sitting on top of the world. I finally had a best friend. We were soul mates, we were young and talented, good looking and ready for life. At least we thought we were. We continued to write together and it flowed through us like water. It does when you stand aside and let it work for you. I come from people who are steeped in the lowest state of human consciousness that you can possibly imagine. They will be watching television and the commentator on the news says, "You are watching station WNEW Little Rock at Six." Uncle Elvin would turn to Aunt Berthie and say, "Now just how do they know that?" Seriously. All of the people that I was raised with are still back there. They have never left and never will. What a place. That's all it ever was to me, just a place, never a home. I never had one of those until I moved into Hurtwood. It wasn't that I wanted it to be my house. It was just that it was the first place that I had ever been where I wasn't judged and felt comfortable and welcome.

I recall Eric had to run into town one day and he asked if I wouldn't mind staying behind. I thought that was strange as he always took me everywhere he went, especially to London. But I told him "no problem," and he left with One-Eyed Don down the drive. Morris the parrot kept me company, just as he had that night they all went off to play with John Lennon. I'm a bird guy—I like and get along with all of God's creatures, really, but I've got this thing for birds. Eric said that Morris was very old and belonged to his grandmother. She really liked me. She could see how fresh into this world I was, and we got on really well. He said that Morris had never been out of his cage. Ever! I had that big roaring fire going and I went over to see Morris and talk to him. He'd say, "Where's Eric?" I was standing there having a little talk with Morris and I decided to get him out of his cage and put him on my hand. He was a big green tatty-looking bird that looked like he possibly could have been Long John Silver's bird and had been at sea too long. His feathers were a mess. I opened the cage door and he crawled up on top of it and sat there all ruffled up and pissed. He didn't want anything to do with getting on anybody's hand, that's for sure. Morris was a little upset that I had come along and was trying to get him to do tricks and talk when all he wanted to do was get out of that prison and bite me. He was hissing at me and spread his wings. I backed off immediately. You don't want a parrot mad at you, especially if he's loose. He looked at me and said, "Where's Eric?" I told him, "I don't know." He said it again, but this time with more feeling, "Where's Eric?" I told him, "I don't know!" And with that, he spread his wings and took off for his first flight, straight across that huge room directly into the fire! The fireplace is very large, and Morris was standing in the back behind this roaring fire, smoking. He was roasting right in front of me. I didn't know what to do. There was nothing I could do. I just stood there, watching him smoking, when all of a sudden he just walked around the side of the fireplace out to me as pretty as you please. You know how birds walk kind of pigeon-toed? Well, he was real funny looking, and his wings were just little sticks as he came waddling out from behind that fire, smoking. I was just glad he was out and so was he. He got right on the back of my hand and I set him on the top of his cage so he would be able to make his own mind up about going back in. He went back in, but I left the door open. I heard Eric coming back from afar. I could hear him going through the gears. I went outside to greet him as he pulled up, and he was in a brand new orange Porsche 911S 2.2. I told him, "Just what you need, another great car." As I said it he tossed the keys over the front of the hood and said, "No, this is yours!" The keys sort of stopped in mid-air. In all of my days on earth I had never had anyone be so generous and kind and loving to me as Eric was. He never asked anything of me. He really didn't have to because he knew there was nothing that I wouldn't have done for him. But he never asked anything of me other than just being his friend.

The Rolling Stones, Eric, George Harrison and other rock stars really did hang out together in those days. It was like a special club. Eric introduced me to every one of his friends. There were people everywhere, and everybody seemed to have some sort of a job to do. Even if it was to look after Eric's cars and Ronnie Wood's, and now Bobby's, too. Yep, I had my own personal mechanic, Mick Byatt. He was a Ferrari guy, and he looked after all of Eric's, Ronnie's, and Keith Moon's cars. Not bad work if you can get it. And he stayed busy.

Eric and I went to see Stevie Wonder at the Talk of the Town in London. The theater was beautiful. It had built-in high-backed leather booths and chandeliers everywhere. There were big round tables with reserved signs, and right in the middle in the front was where we sat. At first it was just Eric, Catherine James and me at the table. Then in walked Mick Jagger, Keith Richards, Ronnie Wood, Charlie Watts and Bill Wyman, and they all had dates. Champagne all around, and flowing all night, while we all listened to Stevie Wonder. Sometime later a young man walked up to the table and asked if everyone wouldn't mind signing autographs on the night's handbill. Everyone happily agreed. It started with Mick and made its way round the table back to Mick. When he started reading all of the names, including their date's names, he said, "Who's Rocky the Flying Squirrel?" It was me. I'd signed that instead of my name. I didn't feel like my name belonged on that list of rock stars' names. I didn't feel worthy.

Our manager, Robert Stigwood, was "the" premier manager, producer, agent of all time, in my opinion. Everything he touched turned to gold, *Evita*, the Bee Gees, *Saturday Night Fever*, *Grease*, *Jesus Christ Superstar*, Cream, Eric Clapton and Derek and the Dominos. If you have never read up on him it would be worth the read. He is an incredible survivor. It's one thing to lose your money, but it's an entirely different thing to lose your dream. Money comes and goes, but poverty is a state of mind. He was right in the middle of the valley when I arrived on the scene in London, but you couldn't tell by looking around at his world and his office at 6-7 Brook Street in London's Mayfair. It was a very old and beautiful tall white building with columns and black iron fencing. He looked and acted like he was on top of the world, and he was. It's just that his finances were depleted at the time. But never judge by appearances! He wore tailor-made clothes, beautiful suits and handmade shoes with gold buckles and was chauffer-driven everywhere. And at that time he lived in an incredibly beautiful old mansion on a huge estate on the outskirts of London. You could park a dozen cars in front of it—and we used to line our cars up in front. It looked very, very cool!

I really miss the camaraderie that Eric and I once shared. We had a lot of fun together and did a lot of growing together as well. Stiggy's (Robert Stigwood) house had a go-kart track in the front garden, and not a small one either. It was there for all of us boys to play with. That's what we were, just boys with grown men's toys and getting around in young men's bodies. Life was a ball and one big party. Rock 'n' roll, Ferraris, silk shirts, velvet pants, high-heeled boots and girls were all that we had on our minds, and the only thing we cared about. It was all about being young and free. We were living out our fantasies. Robert was always an elegant man with grace and style and impeccable taste, and a hunger for success like no other I have ever seen. He had a way of turning the negative into the positive by not losing his head. When he started RSO (Robert Stigwood Organisation), he didn't have any money to do it with. He used Dominos earnings to start his new record company. In fact, Eric asked me one time if I wanted to invest in it, and I said no. Sadly, I didn't have an understanding of the concept of being able to diversify myself. I thought that I could only do one thing and that being part of a company would make me a businessman. I figured that would mean me having to wear a suit and cut my hair. That was not going to happen. All I wanted to do was to play. He got David Shaw, a financial banker and a wizard with money, to be his partner. David was to be the financial controller of RSO. He was a lovely man who, like Robert, was a sharp dresser. Only David drove himself around London in his white Rolls-Royce Corniche convertible. I would become friends with Moonie (Keith Moon) later and he had one, but I couldn't ride in it because it made me sick. It was so smooth that you couldn't feel the road. After a few brandies, it was, "Pull this thing over, Doogle [his chauffeur], I've got to throw up!"

George Harrison and All Things Must Pass

When Eric and I were talking about putting together a band, word seemed to have gotten out, and Delaney and Bonnie were each calling separately, asking us to let them in our band without the other one. Eric wouldn't speak to either one of them. I fielded the calls for a while and then we stopped answering the phone altogether. Those people would cut each other's throats to further themselves. It would have been so much easier to just love one another.

George Harrison had telephoned Eric in early April to say he would be recording a solo album in May. He wanted to know what Eric and I thought about putting a band together to back him on his record. Eric and I had already been talking at length about forming a band, and after a lot of debating, decided we wanted to get Jim Keltner on drums and Carl Radle on bass. So Eric told George we would love to do it. But our first real session in the studio was for P.P. Arnold. She was one of the support acts on the Delaney and Bonnie tour. She had previously been with Immediate Records and had a huge hit with "The First Cut Is the Deepest." The label went under and she ended up being signed to Polydor. Robert Stigwood asked Eric to produce and play on a session for her, and I think the idea was for us to do a whole album, but I just remember a session for a single. Besides, we had to get our own band together. The day of the P.P. Arnold session was when Jim Gordon had stormed over. Eric and I talked about him later, saying, "Should we just go ahead and ask him or wait on Keltner? Well, he's here now and we want to play now, so let's go ahead and ask him to play with us." That's exactly how it went down and I'm glad to be able to tell it. Jim had heard about what was going on from Carl Radle and he was going to get in on it, so he came over to play with somebody, but it wasn't supposed to be us. We were waiting for Jim Keltner, who was in L.A. finishing a session for a Gabor Szabo album. He was only weeks away from being finished, but we could not wait. Carl was not at the session because he got lost on his way to the studio. So Eric borrowed Steve York from Manfred Mann's Chapter Three, who were recording next door, to play bass. The single and album were never released for some reason.

As soon as news leaked out about George recording a solo album, there was a real buzz going around the music world. This was major news. Everybody started showing up from out of the blue. Until I went over there, and Eric and I started writing and playing together, no one had even thought of going to England, much less move there. But word of what we were doing spread like wildfire. Bobby Keys came over and got a house and then Jim Price got a flat. I love England, and I still have a place in my heart for that country. I feel like I belong there and in Ireland. That's probably why I have moved back and forth so many times since 1969. I have had five different houses in England and two in Ireland. My ancestry has been traced to Berkshire to a criminal named Samuel Whitlock in the late twelfth century. Not surprising. It is my understanding that he was deported because he was a rebel and went against the monarchy and wound up in America married to an Indian woman. It sounds reasonable to me. It seems like deporting Whitlocks goes back a long way with the British.

At Friar Park, George had been running through all of the material that he had. I heard every song that he had intended on doing before we went into the studio to record them. I was dating Pattie's sister, Paula Boyd, so I was at Friar Park a lot of the time. When I would stay over, which was quite a lot, I would stay in the very top of the place. Pattie said that it was room number 101. He played all the songs to me and asked what I thought of them. He showed me some different changes on the song "Run of the Mill," and I still remember those changes. They weren't used on the song, either. He showed me a lot of things on the guitar. George was a really great guitar player. He just didn't think he was. He told me that he almost quit one time because he couldn't play as well as Eric. He said that Eric just had this feel and touch. George really wanted to play like that and told me so, many times. But who wouldn't?

One day, George pulled open a drawer in the cabinet in the dining room and it was full of Beatles 45s—gold records. That's where they all were, stuck in a drawer. I thought it was all pretty amazing, but it gave me a perspective on the true value of those things. He had just gotten Friar Park and he and Pattie were still living in the gatehouse and were working on the big house before and during the recording of *All Things Must Pass*. So, not only was he doing a record and redoing a 101-room house at the same time, he was also balancing the Beatles' break-up and all of the friendships with all of them. Then there were the dealings that he was having with Allen Klein and ABKCO. That's who George is referring to in the song "Beware of Darkness." There were also 50 Hare Krishnas hanging out at Friar Park, and he had that nut case Phil Spector to deal with. All of this in a day in the life of George Harrison. He was still kind of in the Beatles because there was so much to resolve with band issues and ABKCO and the money aspect of it all, which had turned out to be not so much. George told me that the Beatles split one penny four ways. That's all that they saw at the end of the day after taxes, management and the record companies. They divided one penny on the pound. John and Paul would only allow George one song per Beatles album, this despite the fact he had several great songs that at the very least matched theirs, and possibly even bettered on occasion. "Something" and "Here Comes the Sun" are just two that come to mind. It worked out perfectly for George in the end, though. He had managed to stockpile some of the finest material that they overlooked because they thought George an inferior writer.

One beautiful spring day at Friar Park, I was in the kitchen with Pattie while she was making a curry dish with rice for lunch. She always was looking after everybody, including me, when I was there. And that was quite a bit when I was in England and hanging with George. You may just have been staying for a while, or just visiting—no matter, she was the consummate hostess. I would just sit at the table and we would talk while she prepared whatever it was. On one occasion, Terry Doran came running in dripping wet and said that a baby had fallen into the fountain. Terry said that the Hare Krishnas wouldn't try to save it! They said that God would save it. He jumped in and rescued the baby before it drowned. I guess that he was God at that moment. He was wet and very upset, as was everyone. That was the end of the Krishna invasion at Friar Park. Up to that point, every time I turned around there would be three or four of them with their little bags and their robes and shaved heads and a pocket full of peanut butter cookies, dancing through whatever door that led to wherever George was, throwing rose petals and singing and banging on drums. During the *All Things Must Pass* sessions they were coming in, throwing rose petals everywhere and burning lots of incense. I enjoyed those people. I thought that they were harmless—useless, but harmless, just a bunch of moochers. George had bought a main Krishna leader a great big house for his birthday. I went to the party and sat on a cushion and ate peanut-butter cookies and listened to him talk about love. He was a macho phony dressed in a skirt using religion as a way of getting by. He had women waiting on him hand and foot. Literally! He said, "What is love? Love is George Harrison giving me this beautiful estate and home, and I give him a flower. That is love." My daddy should have gotten into that Krishna thing!

Eric and I were doing some serious playing, and our first real killer session was for George's solo album. We arrived at Abbey Road studios in St. John's Wood in Eric's Lilac Ferrari 365GTC. The Apple Scruffs were hanging at the gate and sitting all along the wall. They weren't really scruffy. They just wanted to see you or touch you, or just get an autograph, and they were always there, every single day. I thought that they were sweet and I was always real nice to them, as was everyone else. I remember Mal Evans taking some tea and sandwiches out to a couple of them once. He was the assistant to the Beatles and was helping with tea and everything else that came up that needed to be done. Mal was a big guy and wore black Buddy Holly–style glasses and was always smiling. He was a lovely man and I really liked him. The sessions usually started late afternoon. When Eric got me the Porsche I decided to drive myself to the sessions, and George came out and said, "I love that car, Bobby! Well, you and Eric have put together a wonderful band and you're going to be a rock 'n' roll star and that's just the car for you!" George had his blue 365GTC Ferrari parked there as well. As soon as you went through the doors at Abbey Road, you went up the stairs and into the front of the studio. The tearoom was to the right, as was another small room with a harmonium. That was the room where we listened to and did the acoustic versions of "Let It Down" and some other songs. And to the left was studio A. When you walked through the double doors the main room was set up for two drummers on two different risers, and they were facing you as you entered the room. There was a very large sound stage with 30-foot ceilings, and the control room was to your left as you walk in. The piano was in the front of the glass facing the drummers and sitting next to it was the Hammond. The pump organ that I also played was against the wall on the left just this side of the glass. Eric was to my right as I was playing the Hammond with George in the center facing us. Everyone was in the room at the same time and it was all happening live. The only overdubs, really, were the horns and the hanging bells that I played and, of course, the background vocals which were done by Eric and me a lot of the time. We were the O'Hara-Smith singers. He was O'Hara and I was Smith. Everything else was live. It was awesome when we were doing "The Art of Dying," Eric on that wah-wah and it was all cooking, Derek and the Dominos with George Harrison. That's what it was for the most part. It was Eric, Jim, Carl, George and me. And everything that we did was always first or second take. Then there were assorted other guests at different times, like Billy Preston, Gary Wright and Gary Brooker. They would alternate on different keyboards other than what I might happen to be playing. We were the core of it, so everyone else had to work around what we were doing. My main thing is and was the Hammond organ, although I did play piano on "Beware of Darkness." That was the first time I ever played piano in my life. All of the jams on the Apple Jam record have me on organ and then me learning how to play piano. I was and am an organ player. They are two different animals all together, so I learned a heck of a lot in those sessions. It's amazing what you can do when you are put to the task—we always seem to rise to the occasion. George asked if I could play piano with a gospel feel on "Beware of Darkness" and I said that I could. I had heard my Mama every week at the house and in church, so I knew how it was supposed to go. I sat down and it just happened naturally. I wanted to do a great job, playing piano for the first time and being recorded, not to mention doing it with George Harrison on his record, no less. I was playing the keys very hard even though it was a slow song, because it was a very powerful sounding song in my head. So I wanted it to sound the way that I heard it. It was a matter of dynamics. It was very hard and very precise. The lowest C note on the piano has a string the size of your little finger, and that's the finger that was on the key when I played it. I hit it at one point in the song while we were recording take 1 and it broke. And when it did, it went all through the piano. Of course we had to stop and get someone in to put a string on it. The guy could not figure out how a bass C string could have ever broken—it was a first in his very long career stringing pianos. It must have been that right touch of mine, or that heavy left hand. I tend to think that's probably more the case than not. That is probably the reason that the bottom end on that particular song sounds so good, it had a brand new string, and that is a very big deal sonically. So what initially was a bit of an "oh-oh" moment turned out to be just what the doctor ordered. My first recording on the piano with George Harrison and the first thing that happens is that the whole session is brought to a screeching halt. "Little Bobby" strikes again!

There were other guests, Badfinger, an Apple band, who were against the wall on the far right end, all playing acoustic guitars. George was always in the middle facing everyone, and there was an electric piano in between the two drummers facing George and the studio entrance doors. That's what I played on "Wah-Wah" because I arrived late for the session at Abbey Road due to traffic. As I walked into the room I could hear Phil shouting, "Phase the Drums," "Phase the piano" followed by "Phase everything!" The piano and Hammond organ had already been taken by Billy Preston and the two Garys (Brooker and Wright), so the only thing open was the electric piano. Everyone was playing on the downbeat with Ringo and Jim Gordon on drums, with me sitting right between them, and Klaus Voorman and Carl Radle playing bass. That was perfect for me—no other keyboard left to play but the electric piano, and no other place left to play except where no one else was already playing, and that was everywhere. I took the only open spot there was, the upbeat. It was awesome, I was out there all by myself on the upbeat! The ses-

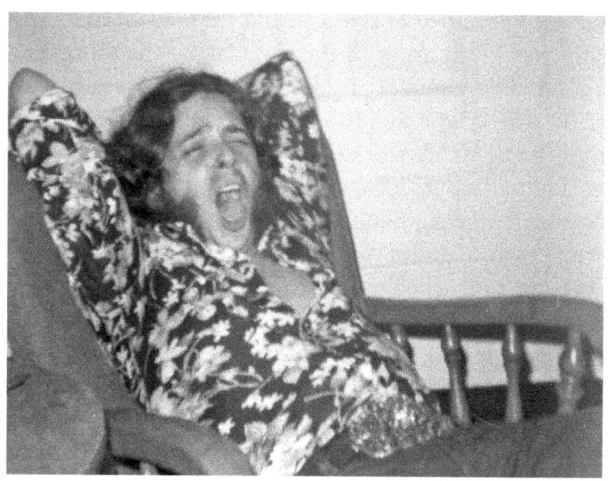

The velvet rock star.

sions felt very comfortable, and George made sure that everybody was happy. I recall the wonderful tandoori chicken that was delivered to the studio. In fact, every night was a huge Indian feast, complete with Hare Krishnas dancing around in the room clanging little cymbals and banging drums. There was a constant sweet aroma of burning incense, rose petals were scattered around the floor, and there were large trays of peanut butter cookies. It all created a serene atmosphere. George's sessions were always spectacular in every way. From the Hare Krishnas bursting in, to John and Yoko showing up dressed in army fatigues complete with helmets. I've got to admit it made me laugh to myself—we were all sort of extremists then. They were very serious about running around in faded fatigues complete with boots and helmets. I don't know what the significance was, but John Lennon looked cool in anything, except the nude. They brought along their *Two Virgins* album cover for us all to check out. They could have left it home, but I guess I'm glad that I can say that John Lennon and Yoko Ono showed us all their naked selves in the front and rear. Front cover and back cover. The record label would only approve the cover if it was sold in a brown paper bag so as not to offend anyone. I remember how proud George was after John left the studio that night. He had a great big smile. John got his socks blown off by all of us, and George's new album was better than anything that John had ever done, and he knew that as well.

Phil Spector's productions are known for echo and reverb, but he didn't add all that until after we were done. There was a bit but it wasn't washed out like the record. Phil was a very strange guy. He was pissed off because he didn't have his gun. They wouldn't let him carry his gun into the country. He never left the control room, but he got along with George and everybody. He wisely recorded everything, even the jams. And that's what initially gave me the idea of keeping everything and the tape rolling at all times during the *Layla* sessions.

The whole thing was an experience each and every night. Every song had meaning that was relevant to the climate of the room. Eric and George both knew, as did I, the deep nature of some of those songs. These were subliminal messages, going back and forth, between two good friends as a way of healing and setting each other free. Saying what they could not say any other way except through a song. I have always known that the better part of those songs were directed to Eric, just like Eric's were to George on the *Layla* record. It really hurt Eric that he had been put in that position. He was the one being used in that whole deal. But that's just from my perspective and what I know and from whom it was told. George was not unaware of what was going on around him. I was in the inner circle and everyone trusted me because they all knew that I was the youngest and was innocent and could be trusted with their deepest secrets. Eric and Pattie were open with me about their relationship and George would tell me of his feelings about it all, his indifference to it. I do believe that he had a bigger kettle of fish to fry, rather than get down with what he had no control over anyway. Pattie told me one time that being married to George the Beatle was like being so much excess baggage, just an extra piece of luggage. He wanted children and she couldn't bear any. He really did have a lot going on, but she knew that coming in. He was a Beatle and suddenly she's not getting enough attention? Well, there's Eric. He's real handy and they are already close. Especially after all of these years, it's perfectly clear. I was in the middle of it with all of them. I have always been in the middle of everyone's strife for some reason.

Eric had given Pattie an ultimatum, to leave George or he would start taking heroin. Pattie was not ready to leave George and was using Eric to make George jealous. But Eric had decided that he was bound and determined to do heroin at those sessions. I didn't do it the first night but I did it with him the second night. I don't know why he chose to start doing smack at George's session. You would think that he would have done it at home with just us, or by himself. I was with him when he first did it, in the tearoom at Abbey Road. A black guy brought it in to the studio. It was pink Chinese heroin and was absolutely pure. Eric did it first. He snorted it. He asked if I wanted to try it, but I told him that I wanted to see what it did to him before I tried it. I waited a minute then I asked him how he felt. He told me that he felt warm all over, as if there was a cotton wool cushion under his head and soft pink cotton wool around him, and he felt very secure. We went home after that as we had already finished playing for the night. The next evening, we brought it with us, and Eric laid out four long pink lines. He did two and I did two and my life changed that instant. As soon as I snorted it, I was sick and had to throw up. But then I did some more and it felt very smooth and this warmness enveloped my body. I understand completely why it is said that heroin is the best drug that there is. It is also very dangerous and addictive. It is so subtle and sneaky that the next thing you know you turn around and you're either in rehab or dead. There was no turning back for me. I wouldn't have even if I could because I was committed to Eric and the heroin now. I remember it well, even at this writing I can still taste it and smell it and remember how it made my insides rush. It was heavy-duty strong stuff. I got right into it with him. We were going to see it through together. But we didn't see through it until it was too late, and then the drugs came between Eric and me. We were both islands in the same sea. We could just about see each other from a distance through the fog and the haze, but we weren't close like we were before, when there was no fog or haze. I stopped doing heroin in 1973, and it's been thirty-seven years since I have done any of it. I can't believe that I ever did that to my body and my soul.

All Things Must Pass
Track by Track

After thirty years George was finally able to say in the end what he couldn't in the beginning. On the first page of the book inside of the 2001 box set he wrote, "I was fortunate to have drum, bass and keyboard players, namely Jim Gordon, Carl Radle and Bobby Whitlock, that had come to England to hang out with Eric Clapton and who were soon to become Derek and the Dominos." He goes on to mention that we recorded the first two Domino songs, "Roll It Over" and "Tell the Truth," during the sessions. And he said, "It was really nice to have their support in the studio and it helped me a lot."

The Album

Over the years people have often asked me what tracks I played on and with whom. So here we go.

"I'd Have You Anytime": I was playing pump organ and Eric was playing guitar, Carl was on bass and Jim was on the drums. George was playing rhythm guitar. This track was live, vocals, solos and all. That was some of Eric's finest guitar playing. His playing was very fluid. The vocals, except for the second part that George added, were live. You can tell because the guitar and the vocal melody are right together. This wasn't worked out, it just happened.

"My Sweet Lord": George is on the main rhythm acoustic and slide guitar and I'm on pump organ or harmonium. The background singers are George and myself and George on the original version. On the "My Sweet Lord (2000)" version it is Sam Brown singing background. It's not Eric and George and me. Ringo is playing drums and Klaus is on the bass. All of the different names on the fade are the different synonyms of the word Krishna or God, Buddah, or Mohammed, whatever you may wish to call it.

"Wah Wah": George and Eric are playing electric guitars. Eric is playing the wah-wah that he gave George. I have always understood this song to be written especially for Eric. Listen to the lyrics now that you know the story of Layla, and it suddenly all makes sense. I'm playing the up-beat electric piano. Jim and Ringo are playing drums and Carl is playing the bass. George is singing all of these particular vocals. I remember him coming in after the sessions and telling us how exhausting it was with Phil going over and over all of those different parts.

"Isn't It a Pity": Billy Preston is playing piano and I'm playing a phase-shifted pump organ, or harmonium. George is playing acoustic guitar, Ringo is playing drums and Klaus is on bass. The string line in the solo is my organ part. That organ is the one that the Beatles used on their recordings. It was a great pump organ. It came naturally to me because my mother had one at home that I used to play all of the time. I guess that old pump organ paid off after all! You can really tell Ringo has tea towels on his drums, especially now that you know he does! That was one of his little things that he did to get that sound. It sounded like "Revolution."

"What Is Life": This was Derek and the Dominos with George playing the fuzzy lead part. Eric is playing his Stratocaster as the electric rhythm guitar and I'm on Hammond and one of the Garys (Brooker or Wright) is on the piano and Bobby and Jim on horns. I think that this song has two bass players on it. It sounds like it.

"If Not for You": I'm playing the Hammond and Billy Preston is playing the piano. It is Jim is on drums and Carl is playing bass and George is on guitar. George is playing all of the harmonica on the whole record.

"Behind That Locked Door": Getting Pete Drake to play on this was my idea. It came from a whistle that I was doing on the playback of the song "All Things Must Pass." I was whistling the part while we were listening back and Phil said, "Who's that?" I thought that I was in trouble but I said, "It's me." He asked me to whistle it on tape and I did. It just didn't sound right the first go-around, so I told both George and Phil when we were listening back that they should call Pete Drake in Nashville. He was there two days later, and there were two special Pete Drake sessions. The part that Pete plays is from the old gospel song "Hallelujah Thine the Glory." Sing along with the pedal steel and the organ with those words and see if they don't work. Pete recognized the organ part because of his church background and he capitalized on it. He told me so when we talked about it many years later at Maude's Courtyard in Nashville. I know what I'm talking about because I have played and sung that song a thousand times in my daddy's church. I'm playing the Hammond and it's Klaus on bass and Ringo on drums with Billy on piano. Let's not forget George on acoustic.

"Let It Down": We rehearsed this in the little room next to the tearoom where they kept the pump organ, and it was strictly a ballad. Right away when I heard it I told him that we ought to rock it right there when it says "Let It Down!" George was completely open to everything that we had to say because he knew that we were all about the music. George plays the hot guitar on this, and I've got the Hammond organ and Leslie cranked! Ringo and Jim are on the drums and Billy is on the grand piano and it is Eric and myself singing the background vocals. We were the original O'Hara-Smith Singers, Eric, me and George. We did all of the backgrounds on the original record. This is one of my favorites on this record. It's live and I'm singing the third part background harmony and Eric is singing the second part and George is singing the melody. Now you know who is singing what.

"Run of the Mill": George is playing all of that beautiful acoustic guitar, and it is Jim and Ringo on drums, and Carl's on bass. I'm on the pump organ, and Billy Preston is on piano, Bobby Keys and Jim Price are playing the horns.

"Beware of Darkness": The first time that I ever played a piano was on this song. Eric and George are playing the electric guitars, Jim's on the drums and Carl is playing the bass. Gary Wright is playing keyboard effects unit.

"Apple Scruffs": George is playing the acoustic guitar and the harmonica. He asked me but I could not play it to sound simple enough, so he played it, and played it like he was a child and it was his first time. It was! He had never played harmonica before. The Apple Scruffs were always waiting at the gate at the studio. They'd be sitting all along the wall there with their hair all done up and all made up to be a rock star's girlfriend someday. All they really wanted was to touch us or just have an autograph. Mostly it was just to see us and give us a flower. That would make them happy. They were all very sweet and cute. That track was all George except for the very old and tall metronome with a little effects added to it.

"Ballad of Sir Frankie Crisp (Let It Roll)": This song is about the very eccentric man who built Friar Park. George told me that his ghost is still there and can be seen coming down the stairs. I never saw it, though. This track is swimming with the two Garys, and Billy is playing grand piano. Klaus is on bass and Alan White is on the drums. And of course George is on the guitar and Pete Drake is playing the steel guitar.

"Awaiting on You All": Eric and I are singing the background vocals. I'm singing the high part and he is the second part harmony. I really like the falsetto part. It all worked very well together. We really had a good time singing all of the parts on this record. We made them all up ourselves. George gave us complete creative freedom. This song is live and has Ringo and Jim on the drums and Carl on bass with Eric and George on guitars. I'm on the Hammond.

"All Things Must Pass": Ringo is playing the drums and Klaus is playing bass. I'm on the pump organ and Billy is on the piano. George is playing acoustic guitar. This is the song that I whistled on in the studio that day when we recorded it. That whistle became this part and it got Pete Drake over to England. Eric and I are doing all of the background vocals on the original version. Jim Price is playing the trombone, and that part is also my arrangement. George asked me to help do all of the horn arrangements because he had no experience at doing horn parts. He told me that I knew more about it because of who I had been working with and my R&B background at Stax. Bobby and Jim weren't real happy about it, but George asked me to do it and I was more than happy to. That's what I told Bobby and Jim as well. They never did their own horn parts with Delaney and Bonnie. Horn parts are an extension of the organ and piano parts. That was probably the only stumbling block during this whole session. But it wasn't a problem for very long.

"I Dig Love": This song has Ringo on drums and Carl on bass, Billy on piano and I'm on the Hammond. Eric is playing a slide part, not the lead slide, but a subtle little movement. You can tell by the sound of the Stratocaster.

"Art of Dying": Eric kicks this rocker off with some killer wah-wah guitar! This song is Derek and the Dominos with George playing rhythm guitar. I'm playing the tubular bells. They were hanging, and I used a leather hammer on them. The feel of this song reminds me of a horse at full gallop.

"Isn't It a Pity (version 2)": It has Derek and the Dominos with Ringo and George. I set a real long ring on the percussion on the Hammond that worked out beautifully. We phased the Leslie and the piano a little as well. Billy is playing the piano. This song is all live. George is playing acoustic guitar. Eric is playing through a Leslie.

"Hear Me Lord": This has Ringo and Jim on drums and Carl on bass. I'm on the Hammond and Billy's playing piano. George is playing some great guitar and singing all of the background vocals.

The Jams

"It's Johnny's Birthday": A little ditty based upon "Congratulations" by Martin and Coulter. George on his own.

"Plug Me In": That jam is where I am starting to learn how to play piano. I had never played rock 'n' roll piano until these sessions. Eric was very encouraging, and I'm glad that he was. At the time I wasn't real happy about it but it opened my vision and broadened my scope. That's why you hear it on our live record (*Derek and the Dominos in Concert*). It sounds like I just heard a little Jerry Lee Lewis and a little Little Richard! That's also where Dave Mason enters the picture on the record. He didn't play on the body of *All Things Must Pass*. He came in at the end on our Domino thing when we recorded "Tell the Truth" and "Roll It Over" and these jams.

"I Remember Jeep": This is Jim and Ginger Baker on drums, Klaus Voorman on bass, Eric and George. I'm playing Hammond, Billy is playing piano. I remember it well! That was a fun jam!

"Thanks for the Pepperoni": This jam was done after about six or seven pizzas had been delivered and were devoured by us all. I'm playing my beginner rock 'n' roll piano. It is George and Dave, Eric and me and Carl and Jim.

"Out of the Blue": I love this spaced out number. I'm on the Hammond organ and Billy's on the piano. Jim is on the drums and Carl's on bass and then there's Bobby Keys on sax, George, Dave and Eric on guitars. I love how it gets completely spaced out at the end. Everyone is really listening to each other.

It was an honor and I was privileged to be a part of it. When we did George's *All Things Must Pass* record we all split equally writer's credits and royalty shares on each of the five jams that we were on. He just gave it to us without saying a word. George was a very generous man. I still receive money from him every three months.

A lot of people wanted us to play on their records, so we did quite a few sessions around that time. One was for Dr. John at Trident Studios in London's Soho for his *Sun, Moon and Herbs* record. There was a room full of musicians playing live. Mac's band was the core of it, so he had the drummer and bass player already and another guitar player as well. Eric was also playing guitar, and Mick Jagger and I were singing background vocals on "Where You At Mule," and some others that I can't recall. Doris Troy and PP Arnold were singing background with us as well. There were a lot of other players on this record because it was supposed to be a three-record set. Jim Gordon and Carl Radle were on it also. Of course Mac was playing the piano. There were a lot of players on the floor at once, and it was very crowded. The drums and guitars, the horn players and the tuba—it looked like a circus in there. And with his grand piano right in the middle of the room, it left very little space for any dancing around. It was very hot and sweaty. Mick and I were on one mike and Doris and P.P. Arnold were on the other one. It was all done live and came off remarkably well. The atmosphere made for some magical music. Mac was in his era of the good doctor. Dr. John was the hoodoo voodoo man and was in full dress and make-up. He brought along his mojo hand and it gave the customs officials quite a start. He had a mummified head that was part of his voodoo gear. I saw it myself. It was a real mummified human head. It gave me the willies. He is from New Orleans and grew up around all of that kind of nonsense. He had his face painted and had fluorescent gris-gris powder on himself and everyone around him. It was everywhere. Kind of like those Krishnas, with their rose pedals and peanut butter cookies. When I first saw him at the session he painted a cross on my forehead with his thumb and it had some sticky gris-gris on it. I had a sparkly cross lighting up on my forehead every time I passed under the amber lamps that lit up the motorway on my way home. Thank God the police never stopped me. Not sure how they would have reacted to my story.

Mick's Birthday Party

Life seemed like it was one long party back in the '70s, and we played somewhere in between. I don't know how we managed it but we did. It seemed that there was always something going on, and that would usually include some sort of party. When I first arrived at Hurtwood Edge, Eric was seeing Catherine James off and on. I didn't really know if they were anything other than just good friends. Eric had a lot of female friends at that time and everybody loved Eric. She told me she had first met him at Cream's first show in New York back in 1967 and they had stayed in touch. We had a big bash for Jim Gordon's birthday at Eric's home and George and Pattie were there as was Mick Jagger. He fell for Catherine pretty much straight away. Catherine was back and forth a great deal at Hurtwood after that. One day Eric said for me to get ready because we were going into town as soon as Catherine got there. We were headed to Mick Jagger's house on Cheyne Walk, Chelsea, for a not-so-surprise birthday party for him. We piled into Eric's lilac Ferrari 365GTC. It was a two-seater, so I got in the back and rode sideways all the way to London. Eric was driving with Catherine in the passenger seat. When we arrived it turned out to be a casual event. A very lovely place with large cushions with little mirrors for everyone to sit on. Mick's place was full of antiques and tapestries. It looked just like you might imagine Mick Jagger's London townhouse to be, very high dollar and top drawer all the way. Keith was there as was Bobby Keys. He had worked his way into the Stones camp by way of his friendship with Keith. They had the same likes and dislikes. Mick and I had talked earlier that very day about Bobby being in their band and I told him that he was the perfect addition to their band. The rock 'n' roll that he played was right up their alley. I had nothing to do with him getting the gig. That was just what my conversation with Mick that day was. Later on, Bobby came walking out of Mick's drawing room after a private meeting with him and said to me, "If you want to be in the Rolling Stones, Mick said for you to come on in and talk about it." I told him that I wasn't interested in being in the Rolling Stones and becoming their piano player because Eric and I were already putting together a band. I didn't want to be a sideman again. I was glad that Bobby got the gig because he had asked me about playing with us and I told him that we didn't want any chick singers or horn players and that Eric and I were putting together a four piece band. I knew that the Stones were the center of it all and Mick and Keith were the main focal point. They had Nicky Hopkins for their recording purposes and then they had their original piano player and roadie Ian Stewart. Ian was an original member and one of the nicest people you could ever hope to meet and was still with them, but no one ever saw him. He was always in the dark or playing behind the speakers. You could hear him but you couldn't see him. Mick and Keith said that Ian didn't look the part. He didn't look like a rock star. How one would go about defining that when you look at Keith at the time baffles me. Everyone at the party was very laid back and was very civil. Mick is a class act and so is everyone in that band. The Stones are all lovely guys who are very warm and accommodating when they know you.

When they were in Memphis some years ago when I was still out on my farm down in Mississippi I went to their concert. Chuck Leavell is their piano player and musical director and he and I go back a long ways. I went backstage to their trailer and everyone was there when I walked in. I flung the door open wide for a big hello, not knowing Mick was standing right behind it against the wall. When I closed it he was standing there and said, "Hello, Bobby, I'm Mick." Like I would have not recognized him in the dark. I got away from the story a bit, but it was a short party. We left right after the invitation from Mick, by way of Bobby, for me to be in the Stones. I chose to be a Domino, not a Rolling Stone. And poor Catherine was to be dumped shortly after the party because Mick had met Bianca. But that's another story.

Our first studio session as a group was for our first single. It was recorded during the *All Things Must Pass* sessions. "Tell the Truth" was to be the A side. It is one of those special songs that just seemed to happen, as if it were a dream being lived out. I was at Hurtwood Edge one day and Eric and I had been playing around as usual. An idea here, a lick there and a song title here. We were just having a day like all of the rest of our days. No pressure and everything was just flowing. We weren't pressed for time and had no deadlines to meet so we were taking our time with whatever it was that we were doing. It always seemed to work when we were out of the way of the activity of it, allowing ourselves to be the avenue through which it flowed. And it did that a lot with Eric and me. It's a special connection that certain people have with each other and their source. Duane Allman had showed me how to tune to an open chord when I was with Delaney and Bonnie. I broke every string on every guitar in Eric's house messing around with all of the different tunings. I tried to tune an open chord to every key there is. I finally settled on open E. Eric got tired of listening to me tuning for hours on end and went to bed while I stayed at it all night long. There was a little blow left and I kept dipping into it. I was just fooling around trying to make up a chord and get my fingering and positioning right. Finally I landed on a configuration that was completely backwards. The first chord was in the second position, the second was in the third and so on and so forth. It wasn't but three chords and a solo, and it was just three done the same way. A completely unique and very cool chord progression, kind of like something Keith Richards might play. The sun started to come up and it was a moving feeling, seeing the early morning mist rising up off the ground of those beautiful gardens and that rolling English countryside. I wrote the whole thing with all of this unfolding along with the realization of how my world was changing. It was all finished except the last verse. Eric came down that morning for breakfast, and I said, "Hey, Eric, I wrote this great rock 'n' roll song last night!" He said wearily, "I know, I know, I've got my part already written." His bedroom was right above the living room and I had been up all night long high as a Georgia pine singing "Tell the Truth" at the top of my voice and had kept him up all night as well! He had been up there listening to me and he wrote the last verse from listening through the floor.

Our first live show as a band was to be a charity event for Dr. Spock's Civil Liberties Legal Defense Fund at the Lyceum in London on June 14, 1970. When we were putting together the Dominos and were rehearsing at Hurtwood Edge with Dave Mason it was a heck of a lot of fun. We all knew each other really well by then from the sessions for George's album, and it wasn't a pressure situation at all. We had all been playing together for quite a while so it was very casual in a get-it-done sort of way. We just let it flow as usual and we were very tight. We were just playing and enjoying life, being who and what we were at that time, young and full of it and ready to go play at the drop of a hat. As for our song selection, Eric had an infinite blues well from which to draw, as did we all. So when it came to material there was always an abundance of it. It would just depend on which direction we wanted to go and how we had approached rehearsing whichever particular song that we were going to be doing. When we did the Lyceum gig we had planned on doing a couple of acoustic numbers. It was just Eric and Dave and me playing acoustic guitars and singing. We were standing rather than seated, as Eric is for the most part when it comes to playing his acoustic set nowadays. We did several numbers and then Carl and Jim came on and we all plugged in and rocked the house. I recall we played "Easy Now" in the acoustic set and it was absolutely beautiful. Our vocals blended so well together that it is a memory that will stay with me forever. We were a great band no matter the configuration because everyone was a great player and never got in each other's way. But it was to be a one time deal for us. That was the only time that we would ever play together as that band. That was Dave's only performance as a Domino because he decided to move on with his solo career in Los Angeles.

Before we went on to do our set we were backstage in the dressing room talking about what we should call ourselves as a band name. We had already been talking about it and had sort of arrived at Derek and the Dynamics. It wasn't going to be Eric Clapton and friends, though—Eric was certain about that. We called each other different names from time to time, terms of endearment, and Derek was Eric. Tony Ashton of Ashton, Gardner and Dyke was going to introduce us that evening, and he was the very person to change it all around, too. He was a really funny dude and a really great organ player as well. He and his band went on the road with us and they were always up to something, pulling pranks on everyone. So it didn't surprise me one bit when he went out there and introduced us as Derek and the Dominos. The first image that came to my mind was of all four of us dressed in matching zoot suits with two-inch cuffs, except Eric's, which would have been a different color. That was the first thing to come to mind. Other than that I thought that it was a great name. You have Domino matches and Domino sugar and Fats Domino. Why not Derek and the Dominos?

After the gig I offered Catherine James a ride back to Eric's with me in my new car. She accepted my offer and we were off. It always rains in England, and that day was no exception. It had just stopped and we were tearing down the A1. As we went through Esher the car aquaplaned and started to spin around. I just looked at Catherine and she was looking back at me. There was nothing that I could do except not panic and hold on. We were doing about ninety when this happened. I watched as the same scenery of trees and a little park land with a picnic table sitting on a knoll went by my front windshield three times before we hit the grassy knoll. I never turned the wheel. Instead, I slammed it into third gear and put the pedal to the metal and that car came off of that knoll and back onto the road and caught hold of it like a slot car. It came out of the hole like a rocket. Catherine was holding on with both hands, her eyes wide open so much that they looked like they were going to pop out. She was completely white-knuckling the whole ride. Just before you get to Eric's house there is a tunnel that goes down to a single lane. The stone walls on either side of it are about twenty-five feet tall, and it's a winding road where you have to stop and take turns letting the other car through. It is just a half-mile series of S-bends. It was a very good thing that no one was coming the other way that day because we drove straight through them at a very high rate of speed. I was going very fast, way too fast to be driving after the rain. We never stopped once and never slowed down at all, and not a word was said the whole way there. It must have had something to do with the combination of the output of the car and the intensity of that blow that I had taken before we left London. Either way you look at it, I should have never been behind the wheel that day. We made it to Eric's relatively unscathed, but Catherine was looking pretty shocked and kind of green around the gills, and there was grass and dirt caught up all under the front and rear of the car. We had just literally cut a path through that freshly rained-on wet grass and kept on going. She never rode with me again.

I went into London the very next day, after cleaning the Porsche up as best I could, and took it to a dealership. They weren't interested in it because of the little mishap I had with it. Fair enough, I thought, so I got back in it to go home. As I was turning sharply left into a very tiny mews my left front wheel got caught on a cornerstone. I was going very slowly as I was in the middle of London, but rather than back it off, I tried to gun it through and the left wheel popped out, and almost came completely off! It had broken the tie rod end. That was all the excuse that I needed. I left the car sitting there and called a hire car and had them take me towards Eric's place out on the A1, but not all the way there.

You see, there was a beautiful red 330 GTC Ferrari that I had been seeing and longing for every day that I drove into or out of London on that S-curve in that little village near Eric's. It was secondhand and two years old, but looked immaculate. It was still in the window when I had passed earlier on my drive into town to try to get rid of the Porsche, so I had the driver take me there and drop me off because I had a plan that I knew would work. I walked into the dealership and had my car registration in my hand. I told the salesman that I had a brand new Porsche 911S 2.2 sitting in a mews up in London and told him where and what had happened, including the spinout. I told him that I would swap him even for the Red Ferrari. He said, "It's a deal!" I gave him the registration and signed it over, and he did the same with the Ferrari, and I drove it away to Eric's. When I got there he couldn't believe that the salesman traded without even seeing the Porsche. I had wanted that car ever since I saw it and now it was mine. Eric knew that I had wanted it so he didn't mind that I had swapped the car that he had bought for me. He was happy that I got the Ferrari because he knew that I wanted one just like his. That car rocked!

Eric was sharing Hurtwood Edge with Alice Ormsby-Gore. She was his new girlfriend, although he did not love her and they would have a pretty tempestuous relationship over the

My 1968 red 330 GTC Ferrari.

following four years. The trouble was that he was still madly in love with Pattie, but she was not willing, or able, to leave George, which only made her even more attractive to Eric. It got him down on many occasions. In the meantime, the record label wanted some promo shots of the band but we didn't want to go anywhere to have our pictures taken because we were too busy doing what we were doing, which was playing and singing and writing songs and driving as fast as possible. We decided to have them done at Eric's house. Julian Lord, Alice's sister's boyfriend, was the photographer. What a lovely name. He had long blond hair and looked like he might have been Brian Jones' brother, kind of regal looking. We all got dressed up to have our pictures taken, but Jim had absolutely no sense of style at all. The number one drummer in the world—and from Hollywood—and he could not dress himself. I had him put on my leather shirt with fringe. I put on my patent leather boots and a purple velvet suit with brown leather inserts, very smart. Carl just wore a flowered shirt and Eric wore his Robin Hood outfit with some bananas on his belt. We looked fabulous. All we did was walk around the gardens at Eric's and stand here and there. We were really all about the music and taking pictures and doing a video was something that we weren't into at all. And that was the only photo session that we ever did. They were distributed as promo photos to the press and some ended up being used on our posthumous live album, *Derek and the Dominos in Concert*.

Our first tour started on August 1, 1970, at the Roundhouse in Dagenham, a suburb of London. We had rehearsed at Hurtwood Edge for several weeks, although when we first started the Dominos we had fewer songs in our repertoire. We decided to play some numbers off Eric's first solo record and some Cream songs on occasion. Later we would also played one Blind Faith song, "In the Presence of the Lord," on which I played piano. I was really happy that Eric pushed me into playing piano on it. He was the one who was so damn persistent on me playing piano and I am grateful to him. I really enjoyed playing that particular song and I loved the way it breaks into that real funky part and then back into those beautiful changes with Eric sailing away on his guitar. When we would start our set we would jam a couple of numbers first to get warmed up, and then Eric and I would start to sing all of our new songs together. Every time we'd write a new song we would eliminate an old number. The first to go was "Sunshine of Your Love." I was really happy about that one being first. And I think Eric was also, because he was still trying to get away from the whole Cream and Blind Faith superstar thing.

I do recall that first gig at the Roundhouse. It was a round building with a very high ceiling that went up to a point in the center. The ceiling looked like an upside down cone. I believe that it used to be where the trains would come in and would spin around to face the other direction, the end of the line, so to speak. This huge place had nine bars lined against the wall all the way around. We had a big stage, and the place was wall-to-wall skinheads and long-haired hippies. Not a good combination. We started the set with "Tell the Truth" and then into "Roll It Over" followed by "Presence of the Lord" and "Let It Rain." A fight broke out right in front of the stage between one of the skinheads and a hippie with hair that went down to his waist. The skinhead had the hippie's hair wound up with his left hand and was whipping his ass with his right. They were going around and around in a circle and the harder we played the bigger that fight got. The next thing you know everybody suddenly started beating the shit out of each other. Fights were breaking out all over this place until it was just one big brawl. The manager of the venue came up to the side of the stage and said for us to stop playing. Eric asked me "What did he say?" I replied, "He said to turn it up!" It was a hell of a night, I'll tell you. It started getting dangerous for us because it was all heading back around the room to where it had started, and that was right in the front of us. We just stopped haphazardly one by one and got the hell out of there. We had to jump off of the back of this five-foot-high stage because they were fighting on both sides of us and in the front. We were surrounded. There were emergency exit doors right behind this put-together stage, just behind the curtains. That was our only way out, and the doors had a chain on it. We couldn't believe it. We were all scared to death because it was getting very intense. Bruce and Bass Ward and Kevin, our other roadies, literally broke them down to get us out of there. I don't know how things like that happen but they do. What a way to start the tour! We talked about it all the way back to Hurtwood Edge that night.

After playing only a few shows on our U.K. tour we headed off to the south of France to a town called Biot. We were going to play the Popanalia festival which had been organized on the BYG record label on August 5, 1970. Pink Floyd and Soft Machine, among many others, were also on the bill. We arrived the day before and stayed at a farmhouse that belonged to some friends of the promoter. Unfortunately, the event was cancelled after a few hours when some radical revolutionaries, Les Companions de la Route, burned the stage and destroyed the equipment. We were walking out the door when we got the news about the fire. So we never did play in France. We just got high and played around in the farmhouse, a very old white stone building in the countryside which was owned by a French artist named Frandsen-de Schonberg, whose son was named Emile. There was an art studio out in the back of this place. It really wasn't a working farm with animals on it, there were only some chickens and ducks. Actually, the only animals there were us. With the gig cancelled we suddenly had all of this time on our hands and nothing to do until we left. So we were just hanging at the farmhouse getting high and drinking scotch. The next thing you know, Eric breaks out the Mandrax. The party was just beginning to take shape. There was only us and Bruce McCaskill, our road manager. Emile was in and out of there from time to time just to check and see if we needed anything. We had complete run of the house and were about to abuse the privilege to the max. When the Mandies started kicking in so did everything else that we had been doing. Nothing too crazy, just a little blow and some smoke, but those Mandrax were awesome when combined with alcohol.

Someone, I think it was Eric, threw the first egg, but after he did they started flying everywhere. There were a whole lot of eggs in a big basket on the kitchen table, fresh that morning from the chickens. They were trying to make the place as welcome for us as they possibly could. The egg fight went all through the house, inside and out. It was all-out war. It was mostly Eric and me, but Carl and Jim didn't walk away unscathed. Carl was the quiet type, but Jim was up for anything at any time. I remember walking into Carl's room when it started and he was just sitting there on the bed reading a book. I threw an egg at him and called his name. He looked up and it hit him right in the forehead and exploded all over his face. We were all completely covered with raw egg. It was everywhere. Not a room, wall or ceiling had escaped the eggs. After we settled down—and that was only because we ran out of eggs—we couldn't believe what we had just done to this man's lovely house. Eric and I were standing in the front entrance when Emile walked in. He looked at us and smiled as he shook his head, but didn't say a word. Not surprisingly, we were totally embarrassed at what we had just done. Actually it was not so much for what we had done, but more for the fact that we got caught red-handed with egg on our face and with the "smoking egg" in hand, so to speak. He was very polite and said nothing about what we had done, which made us feel that much worse. We started cleaning it up and he said to us, "I'll get the housekeeper to clean up this mess. Don't worry about it."

Then he asked us to follow him out to the studio, even though we were still covered with raw egg. I couldn't figure this guy out. Here we had just trashed his father's house and he is as calm as can be, as if nothing had happened at all. He said that his father had told him to let us have our pick of any of his artwork there in his studio. Eric walked straight to an oil painting that looked like Pattie and picked it up. We were all looking at it and were amazed at the resemblance. I got a small green statue of a man on his bended knees with the head of a praying mantis. I don't remember Carl or Jim choosing anything. Emile's father became a famous artist. And the likeness that he portrayed in his oil painting that looked so much like Pattie became the picture that millions of people have come to know as "Layla."

When we went out on our first tour we had no choice but to tune up in front of the audience. We didn't have the little tuners that we have now, which you can use to tune your guitar and no one hears you. And forget about having a guitar tech. Eric tuned his own guitar and changed his own strings then. I never saw anyone ever do it for him. When we finally kicked in, it was all over bar the shouting, and there was plenty of that. I remember we played the famous Speakeasy once. Hoyt Axton was at that gig. That was the first time that I ever met him. He came backstage, which was just behind a curtain that was the backdrop of this very small stage. That stage was so small that we could barely fit our four-piece band on it. I had to set my organ sideways and could just about reach out and hit Jim's cymbal with my left hand. It was so packed that it was sweating room only. I love playing in a close situation like that with great players. Hoyt had an ounce of coke in his pocket and broke it out and dumped it on the table and we all packed our noses with way to much of it and we hit the stage. People were standing right next to the front of the stage and we tuned up for what seemed like forever. Then Eric kicked in that wah-wah and we all fell into "Roll It Over" followed by "Tell the Truth" and everyone went wild. We tore that place down. People didn't know what to do because they had never heard a rock 'n' roll band like that before.

That was the very beginning, when we started our club tour. We played all over Great Britain and played only small clubs and the tickets were one pound each everywhere we played. It was largely through word of mouth that people knew we were coming to their town. We would sometimes use trains and occasionally Eric's car to get to our gigs. It really was great fun taking the train as well as riding in Eric's 6.3 Mercedes. Bruce McCaskill handled the driving. Eric would sit in the passenger seat and Jim, Carl and me in the back seat. It got uncomfortable on the long runs so we wound up drawing straws for the front seat and Eric didn't always win either.

The idea of playing all of those small venues was great and an inspiration to us. We learned our craft on the road and the band certainly would not have been as tight as it was had we not done it that way. One time I talked Eric into driving his Lilac 365 GTC Ferrari to one of the gigs. If my memory serves me well, he and I took it to the Black Prince in Bexley, Kent. (I understand that the building is still there today, but is now a Holiday Inn.) I remember pulling up right in front of the venue, where there were loads of people hanging around waiting to go in. Everyone surrounded the car as we pulled up, welcoming us as if we were their long-lost friends. The gig took place upstairs at the venue and was quite small. It was a long, narrow room with a low ceiling and jam-packed with people. There was sweating room only. I looked across the stage at Carl and his glasses had com-

Bobby and Eric Clapton at the Marquee Club in London, August 11, 1970 (photograph by Stefan Wallgren).

pletely steamed up. He had to play the whole set like that. It was incredibly hot and sweaty in that room, just perfect for a great show. After it was over we were in the dressing room and a dude starts knocking on the window. We were two stories up and he is staring and smiling through the window and wanting to come in so I went over and opened it up for him and let him crawl on in. His mates had made a pyramid up against the wall by standing on each other's shoulders and he was the one at the pinnacle. He came in and was treated by all of us like the special person that he was. He really, really wanted to meet us and shake all of our hands. He had a drink and went back out the window. On the way home I kept egging Eric to drive faster and faster, but he was reluctant to go more than 110 mph as he had just gotten his driver's license.

I drove myself to one gig, or at least part of the way. I had my red 1968 330 GTC Ferrari, which was almost like Eric's. The color was different, that was all. I still own it but it had been misplaced for thirty-something years due to my moving so often, but it has been tracked down, and it's getting time for it to come back home to me. Well, I was running just a little late so I was going a little too fast trying to get there on time when all of a sudden, it seemed like the faster I was going, the slower I went. Finally the engine was roaring and I was going about sixty and it kept getting slower and slower until it stopped on the side of the road and would not go any further. The engine was working but it was not going forward at all. I'm no mechanic, but I got out and looked under the car and the universal joint on the driveshaft had come loose in the back. So there I was, stuck on the side of the road with a broken down Ferrari and a gig to get to. I stopped a car. I told him who I was and where I was headed and how late I was. We were about fifty miles from the gig and I was about forty-five minutes behind everyone else. He was on his way to visit his mother, but he took me all the way there and pulled up at the front of this concert hall. I could hear that the band had started. They were playing "Sunshine of Your Love" and I thought, "Boy, that was quick! Broke down and late just one time and they're playing Cream songs!" I walked in through the front double doors of the hall and pushed them both open like I was going into a saloon and walked right down the middle aisle and everyone started applauding as I crawled up onto the front of the stage. We

Derek and the Dominos (me, Eric Clapton, Jim Gordon on drums, and Carl Radle on bass) at the Marquee Club in London, August 11, 1970 (photograph by Stefan Wallgren).

kicked into "Let It Rain," and the crowd started shouting and screaming and that never stopped until the end of the show.

Derek and the Dominos was the best band that I have ever played with in my life. I never looked at myself as being as accomplished a musician as Eric or any of the people around me. I could sing and had no reservation about that at all. Even though it was my forte, I did not think much about my prowess on the B3 because it was something that I didn't have to work at. I just played it. At first, nobody really knew for sure who we were until we started performing, and then they never forgot. It was pretty much word-of-mouth advertising. Stiggy came up with the "Derek is Eric" buttons to try to help. He was very upset with Eric and his reluctance to step out front with his name, even though he was already there physically. But for the most part we were faceless. We were billed, one time as "Eric Clapton presents his new band Derek and the Dominos featuring Eric Clapton, Bobby Whitlock, Carl Radle and Jim Gordon." But we were simply Derek and the Dominos. That was what Eric preferred and he always made a stink when it was any other way. He really did not want his name on any of our advertisements, period.

Eric and I had written several numbers together and after perfecting them live on our U.K. tour it was time to record them for our first album. Eric wanted Tom Dowd to produce the sessions. He had worked with him on an Aretha Franklin session in 1967 and respected him. Robert Stigwood made the call to Tom in Miami. Although he was producing the Allman Brothers' second album *Idlewild South*, at the time and had his hands full, he said he would love to produce us.

We flew off to Miami and headed to Criteria studios. When we were in the studio running over our material, trying to decide what we wanted to start with, Tom came walking in, smoking his pipe, with a stack of paper in his hand. He handed everyone a sheet with a bunch of numbers on it. I asked Eric, "What the hell is this?" He told me that it was a chord sheet done in numbers. I didn't have a clue what he meant and I still don't. Anyway, I told Tom that I didn't understand these numbers, so a few minutes later he came back in with charts written out with letters like E, A, B, back to E. I told Eric that he and I needed to have a talk about Tom's involvement and his position in it. We decided that he should stay behind the glass and make sure that the tape is always running and get everything. He was to not come back out into the studio while we were doing our thing. We had already been playing these songs on the road for a long time and didn't need him coming in and trying to re-arrange them. We were the producers and he was to be called the "executive producer" and I was the one who was to tell him. Tom was a hands-on engineer/producer who had worked with Eric before and was well aware that things could change at a moment's notice so he understood and was not offended.

When you walked through the front door of Criteria, the door to Studio A was to the left and the smaller Studio B was farther back on the right. As you entered the studio, a row of airplane seats was against the wall on the right and there were also beanbags for us to sit on. In Studio A the drums were on an open carousel against the far back wall facing the control room glass, across this very large studio room. The Steinway grand piano and Hammond B3 organ were facing the drums from the opposite end and on the far left wall, the one you saw as you walked in. Eric was facing the control room singing on an overhead mike hanging from a boom-stand. And I was to his right facing him, playing and singing as well. Eric's amps were on the right side of the middle of the room, and Carl was on the opposite side to Jim's right. Eric's guitar amps were set up on a straight-back wooden chair, and he used a little battery powered Pignose amp. It was the very first one ever made. The guy who made them brought the first two prototypes by for Eric and Duane Allman. It had one control knob that was a rubber pig nose, that's all. The only other amp he used was a small Fender Champ amp. You could talk over the Pignose, so we had to be particularly quiet when he did guitar overdub. If you made any noise at all, even out in the entrance, it would be picked up. Tom told us he had warned everybody in the studio that we would be very loud with huge Marshall stacks. That was because he remembered when Eric was in Cream. So he was very pleased that we recorded at low levels. Criteria still had hopsack hanging on the walls, and the control room had egg cartons for sound baffling. It took us only two weeks to record that album there. It was pretty primitive. There was a James Brown gold record hanging on the hallway wall, you can see it on the fold-out of the record. I'm walking by it with my yellow pants.

Eric was familiar with Duane Allman's work and particularly loved his playing on Wilson Pickett's version of "Hey Jude." They had never met. A couple of days into the sessions, Tom arranged for us to go and see the Allman Brothers Band play. The concert was at an open-air venue and the stage was a flat-bed trailer surrounded by bales of hay that were used as a protective barricade. We crawled on our hands and knees under the trailer to get in the front of the bales of hay and turned around and sat on the ground looking up at them. When Duane looked down he looked straight into the eyes of Eric Clapton and he stopped playing. His mouth fell open. Then Dickey looked down and did the same thing. After the show we invited them back to the studio and spent the night just jamming away. Eric asked Duane to sit in for the rest of the sessions. I knew Duane from the Delaney and Bonnie days, so we spent some time together when he joined us in Miami. He and I were in his room and he was playing his Dobro. He had been playing "Little Martha" for me. He had just written it shortly before he came down to be with us. We were sitting there and I asked him, "How do you do that so effortlessly?" He said, "You can do it Little Brother, just get a fishing pole and a bottle of Jack Black and an eight-ball and your Dobro and that slide I gave you and go down to the pond and do what I showed you. It'll come to you, just be patient." He had showed me how to tune to an open E and had given me some real cool advice about where to put my thumb on the back of the neck, keeping it there as an anchor or a home to come back to. Then when you went to the second position it was the same thing, very good advice. It just takes being born to do it and do it well. It is something that you can either do with style or you just end up making so much noise. Duane could make it sing for you. Eric told me once that he sings through his guitar. His guitar sings a song to you. It touches you with that unspoken melody. Duane also said that you don't have to go all over the neck to stay in the game. He could play every song in one position without moving to the second or third position. He was one of the very first to step up to the plate with an electric slide guitar and hit a grand slam every time he put that Gibson on and stuck that Coricidin bottle on his finger. Needless to say, it didn't work for me. The fishing pole, whiskey and the blow thing, I just wound up drunk and way too high for a couple of days, which took me another two to get over those two. I didn't hit the first note right and I didn't catch one damn fish. I loved Duane, he meant well. He surely was here to give, and when he did, he gave it his all. I'm proud to have been his friend and to have been affectionately known to him as Little Brother.

For the album cover shots, I took all of the pictures that I'm not in and Robin Turner took all of the rest. He is the guy with the twisted smile and cocked head on the right of the inside cover in the photo with two guys smiling with their eyes closed. The photo of Duane on the phone is of him scoring some blow. There is a shot in one book that has a picture of Eric and Duane standing in a room at the Thunderbird Beach Hotel in Miami. Duane is holding Eric's Dobro. I took that shot. It was in Eric's room and shortly afterward we all three did way too much blow and got very paranoid and decided that it would be best if we were to get rid of what we had left and clean our act up. We talked about getting rid of it but couldn't figure out how. It was an ounce of pure Peruvian flake. We decided that we should flush it down the toilet. Before we did, we dumped a huge farewell pile and lined it out and did it all before getting rid of the rest of it. So we went into the bathroom and Eric held one corner, Duane held the other and I held the middle of the bag and we poured it out and it shined like falling stars until it hit the water. Then we looked at each other and said, "Oh no! What did we just do?" Eric walked over to his night table and pulled out another ounce bag. Duane and I started thinking that this bag was going to meet the same fate as the other one. But Eric said, "This one, we keep for the road."

Layla *Album Song by Song*

"I Looked Away": This was the first song that Eric and I wrote together. We didn't plan for it to be the first one to be on the record, it just happened that way. As a matter of fact most of the songs on the record are in the order in which they were recorded. If the first three songs were any indication of what the rest of the record was going to sound like had it been just the four of us, it would have been just as great a record had Eric done all of the guitar himself. What brilliant guitar he played on these first three songs. We let it flow at all times during the recording process, just the same as we did when we were performing live. We made no distinction between the two. The vocals are live. I was completely free to sing when and where and what I wanted to. Eric and I did a Sam and Dave thing when we sang together. He would sing a verse and then I'd sing one and then we would sing together. The only overdubs were Jim's percussion and Eric's lead guitars. Eric's and my voices sound so young and perfect for each other. Everyone complements each other. Truly remarkable, especially as this was the first song that we recorded in Miami. We set the bar very high right from the start. All of the overdubs were done right after we recorded each song.

"Bell Bottom Blues": I remember Jim had been given some tabla drums by Ravi Shankar's drummer. He played a backwards snare on that one, then he used the tablas for the fills on the bridge. It was beautiful percussion work. I love the background vocals. That's Eric and me doubled. It sounds very lush and smooth. I love his dueling guitars throughout this song, absolutely brilliant. Eric's solo with that harmonic playing was a touch of class and sensitivity. I love my second part vocal on the bridge of this song. It really sets it off in my opinion. This song was about Pattie Boyd. I remember he walked into the TV room at Hurtwood Edge and asked me to listen to a new song he had been working on and played "Bell Bottom Blues." He had been secretly working on it and had written it for Pattie. She wanted some bell-bottom jeans that were only available at a little shop in Miami. She knew we were off to Florida to record and she wanted him to bring her a pair back. They were called Landlubbers. I had some and so did he. They were hip-huggers.

"Keep On Growing": This song started out as a great jam. I can't remember how many guitars Eric put on it. I think it was four, and they all played off of each other so beautifully. I'll never forget watching as Eric layered them, one by one. It was a case of next, second guitar, next, third guitar, next, fourth guitar. It was an incredible experience watching the master at work. Tom Dowd said that there wasn't room for a jam on this record because it was initially slated to be a single album. We really didn't have enough songs for one record, much less two. They were going to can this song and not use it. I asked for twenty minutes and took a yellow paper pad and a pencil out into the foyer and started to open myself for it to flow and it did, like a waterfall. The words and their meaning just poured out of me. It was about my life and its changes and being young and free and innocent. It is a song of hope. I went back in the studio and tried to put the vocal on with me singing it by myself and stopped in the middle of the first verse. I told Eric that we should do our Sam and Dave thing with it. We sing together and then I sing a verse, and then we sing together again and then I do another verse. That was our thing. We did it first take. The guitar work on the fade is awesome.

"Nobody Knows You When You're Down and Out": Sam the Sham was recording in studio B across the hall from us at Criteria Studios when we were doing the *Layla* session. Sam is from Memphis like me and he has been a family friend for as long as I can remember. His real name is Domingo Samudio. He knew that we didn't have all of the material that we needed and he suggested that we do "Nobody Knows You When You're Down and Out." It seemed a good idea and went right along with the theme of the record, even though at that time we weren't thinking about a theme. We were just trying to get our feet on the ground and get the recording process flowing. Sam had a huge hit with the song "Wooly Bully," but he never got to repeat the success he had with that song.

This was Duane Allman's first song with us. I believe that it was a song that he and Eric both had in common. Eric could really relate to it because he had lived that song and was to live it time and time again. Duane could relate to it because of where he came from and his musical heritage. This song was recorded live, vocals and all, with no overdubs. It was the first take, but of course it was all worked out before we went into it. This was a getting-to-know-each-other song. Duane was set up to the left of Eric and they would face each other while they played. And they looked each other right in the eyes. Eric is playing through his Champ amp. Duane is on a Fender Twin that was set back a ways on the right. Both Duane and Eric were very good leaders and made it easy to follow everything that was going down. Duane would let you know when it was coming and so would Eric.

"I Am Yours": This song is a poem written by the mystical Persian poet Nizami. Eric put a melody to it and I did the background vocals. There's a third part harmony I put on which gives it warmth as well as a certain mystique. Over the years and with the development of my own spiritual growth, I have come to the conclusion that there is a far deeper meaning and message behind this song. It's something other than that of just being a love poem, it is a letter to God. Jim is playing tablas and I am playing a lyrical-sounding organ, almost like a pan flute. Eric is playing that orange acoustic guitar that you see in the fold-out of the album. He bought it originally just to play at the end of "Layla" when the acoustic is playing along with the melody. Duane's slide on this is simply beautiful. Eric's vocal is live and the only overdubs are the two vocals that I did. Everything else is live. This is a lovely electric/acoustic song. Eric handed all of the lead over to Duane.

"Anyday": Eric and I were at Hurtwood Edge in the TV room just playing around with different tunings. Open D became the hot one for the evening. He and I had both been searching for different positions and chords. "Anyday" is a song that came through that search. We set the stage for the playing to begin. And begin it did. It's a song about two people fighting and going through what every couple goes through, wanting to leave and wanting to stay with the world closing in on you. But then a ray of hope shines through. She'll always be there for him. All he's got to do is call. I remember when Eric came up with the line, "To break the glass and twist the knife into yourself, you've gotta be a fool to understand." It gave me chills and it still does. I told him, "Man that's agony!" He said, "I know." I understood.

When we first played it, I thought that it sounded quite majestic. This song was live as well, although we redid our vocals. Duane plays the straight guitar solo on this. Eric and I sang the vocals. We worked very well together and it all came so naturally with us. The whole time that Duane was with us, Eric was always very respectful of his presence and abilities. He stepped aside and didn't mind sharing the spotlight with Duane. It says a lot about Eric. When we did "Anyday" live with the Dominos Eric played a Les Paul that was tuned to an open D, and played both slide and straight guitar at the same time. All he did was alternate between the two. He really was the quintessential guitar player.

"Key to the Highway": This is another of those jams that again happened because of Sam the Sham while he was recording *Hard and Heavy*. Eric had heard him recording a version for his own album and we decided to try it also. And that's what we were doing when Tom had to excuse himself, and when he left we just started playing spontaneously together. This is the unfolding of a song that was captured only after Tom had run down the hallway screaming, "Push up the faders!" That's why it fades in and there are absolutely no overdubs. The piano had a top for it that was a foot tall. It encased the entire top of it and prevented any leakage from the room. Eric and I are really in tune with each other and are feeling each other's movements. So is everyone. This song has a lot of emotion. You can hear Eric mess up at the beginning of his first solo after he starts singing and you can hear him yell "Phew" when he messes up. Real live stuff.

"Tell the Truth": We did this song in a lot of different tempos. I like this laid-back version. Sometimes Eric would get it a little too laid back. Live, I could always tell how long it was going to be by how long it took him to get through the guitar intro. On some nights, my fingers would be killing me. When we would leave the stage there would be blood on the piano keyboard. My thumbs and little fingers were beat to death. This song is live and also happens to be my favorite rock 'n' roll song that Eric and I ever wrote together. It's a huge sound and that has to do with the structure of the chords. The music is as big as the song and I'm singing my John Lennon low harmony.

"Why Does Love Got to Be So Sad": This was another live song, vocals and all. The parts between Eric and Duane were worked out as to just who was going to play when and where. It features some of Eric's finest playing ever. It was still very structured, but in a loose sort of way.

"Have You Ever Loved a Woman": The title says it all. Eric lamenting over his *Layla* and the precarious predicament he had gotten himself into. He took it all out on his guitar. This is all live with no overdubs. Some mighty fine intro guitar and some of the most anguished vocals he ever sang.

"Little Wing": This was done because Eric was friends with Jimi Hendrix and wanted to pay tribute to him. He was still alive when we recorded it, but sadly, Jimi never got to hear it because he died before the album was released. The world lost a truly unique talent. Duane came up with the intro. I thought that it sounded like the Roman army coming, very powerful. It was every bit as live as it gets. I had never heard the song and had the lyrics laid out in the front of me on top of my organ. I had to learn the song in an instant and sing it in the next. I did need to have the lyrics because we were singing live and there were no overdubs at all.

"It's Too Late": The only reason we did this song was because they needed a country song for the auditions to get us on the *Johnny Cash Show*. That was the only variety show on at that time that had musical guests, but they had to be country. This song was as close as we would get. We didn't tell them that we were a rock 'n' roll act. I do believe that Johnny wanted us regardless. I had to learn this on the spot and record it then as well.

"Layla": Those seven notes that Eric brought to the session were from the song that Albert King song "As the Years Go Passing By." They were the vocal melody of that blues song sped up and done on the guitar. It was not a guitar lick at all in the beginning. The piano solo is something that I was against from the very first time that I ever heard it. It has nothing to do with this song and never did. The nature of its origin taints the integrity of this beautiful song that Eric wrote all by himself. This single received a Grammy in 1998.

"Thorn Tree in the Garden": We were in the foyer of Criteria and a guy came in with several guitars to show us. He had the orange acoustic guitar that you see Eric holding in the centerfold of the album. He bought that guitar just to play the acoustic part at the end of "Layla" and "Thorn Tree in the Garden." There was also a Martin D35 there as well. Eric picked it up and played it then handed it to me and said, "It's yours." And then I handed it to Duane and asked him to play it before I did. Then we went into the studio and used it to record "Thorn Tree in the Garden."

The Thorn Tree Martin guitar (photograph by CoCo Carmel).

Eric asked me to close the record with this song. It is about my little dog that went missing from the Plantation. We did it on the last day after the recording and mixing was over. We were all strategically gathered around one omnidirectional microphone. I was sitting on a wooden stool and Eric was to my left and Jim was to his left standing back a little and played a bell. Duane was sitting directly across from me, a little to the right and was playing his Dobro. Carl was standing between Jim and Duane and played a pedal note. We ran through it twice to get everyone positioned in just the right place and then it was roll tape and one take did it. Tom Dowd said that this was the most perfect stereo recording he ever made. We were all sitting in a circle around one microphone, simply perfect. Just like the whole record, which won a Grammy in 2000.

At first, I didn't think we needed another guitar player on our *Layla and Other Assorted Love Songs* record. Eric was more than capable of taking care of that department himself. The first three songs give evidence of that. Eric is a great slide player and was quite capable of handling it all on his own. But then it would have been a very different sounding album without Duane Allman. I remember when he came out and played with us live for a few shows on our U.S. tour and how full and complete the sound was. Then, when he left, how that completeness went with him. Because the album had two guitarists, when performed live there was a void that we tried to fill and it didn't always work. I believe that if Duane had continued with us, we would have had more structure and longevity. He was a born leader. He had a command of his ability to lead so the respect for him was an added thing that came naturally.

The Domino Flat

When Derek and the Dominos got back to England from recording we had a party at the Domino flat in London. Robert Stigwood had rented a place for Carl, Jim and me, to get us out of Eric's house. The flat was at number 33 Thurloe Street, right across from the South Kensington tube station and more or less around the corner from Buckingham Palace and Hyde Park. Located in the center of town and a very, very expensive place to hand over to three wild rock 'n' rollers. This beautiful place was four stories tall, white, and had pillars out front with black iron fencing around it. It looked identical to Robert's office building. I've never seen it but I have been told that there is a brass plate on one of the columns that says "The Domino Flat—Derek and the Dominos 1970." I would imagine that it is because we sure left a lasting impression on the local community.

As soon as we had moved in, the first thing that Jim did was to get pissed off at me because I made the dining room my bedroom. He threw the TV out of the third-story window onto the sidewalk to show me how annoyed he was. He was one crazy dude. Real volatile. Out of the three bedrooms only one was sizeable; the others were real small. We drew straws and Carl won the big bedroom and Jim got the next size down, the third one was the size of a closet and on the very top floor, so I took the dining room and there was nothing anybody could do about it. When I was living at Hurtwood Edge I had bought a beautiful brass bed, but didn't have a house to put it in. I had seen it in an antiques store on the Kings Road, Chelsea, where Eric had got his bed. I bought it and left it there until I had a place to put it in and now I did. So I took over the dining room. It had a big fireplace with a lovely mantlepiece with a large gold gilt mirror on it, louvered French doors and a chandelier hanging from the twelve-foot high ceiling. It was without a doubt the nicest room in the place. We weren't drawing straws for the dining room! I hung all of my clothes on the louvers of the doors that could open up to the living room and you could see all of the hangers from in there. You could count how many shirts I had hanging there from the living room. It was too funny!

Eric would often come round to the flat, often in a depressed mood because of Pattie. We all ended up getting high and I seem to recall that things got out of hand one night with many glasses and plates getting smashed. I am sure that Robert Stigwood paid for all our damages to the landlord when we vacated the property. Jim was always griping about everything. Nothing was good enough and nothing pleased him and I was glad to get my own house when I did. He was hell to live with, and it caused bad feeling between all of us.

Eric would often tell me how much he admired and liked Jimi Hendrix. He really loved the guy. He used to talk about Jimi's amazing ability to use the wah wah. He said that Jimi made it talk. And he did. I think that's why Eric became so enthralled with the use of it and played it at most of our shows. Eric had heard that Jimi was staying in London after playing at the Isle of Wight Festival and a short European tour. He had made plans to go and see him on September 17, and he and I were supposed to have been with Jimi that night. Eric had bought a beautiful left-handed Fender Stratocaster that he was going to give him. We were at Hurtwood Edge and had been having a couple of drinks, nothing big or special, but as usual we were taking our time, and it slipped away from us. The next thing you know we had been playing and messing around with something or other and looked at the clock and it was too late to go. We would not have made it there on time and, besides, we had too much to drink, so we stayed home. We figured we would see him the next day. The next morning someone called Eric and told him the news that Jimi had died during the night. Eric was devastated. We had the chance to be with Jimi and blew it in a big way. I would imagine that Eric still has that guitar.

Another guitarist that Eric admired and loved was Buddy Guy. When he heard he would be playing in Paris on September 22, 1970, he flew out to see him. Buddy, along with Junior Wells, was supporting the Rolling Stones there. Eric ended up jamming with Buddy and Junior that night. Atlantic's Ahmet Ertegun was backstage and Eric suggested to him that he sign the two bluesmen up. Ahmet agreed on the condition Eric agreed to produce the album. Naturally he jumped at the chance. Bobby Keys was always calling for me to come somewhere with him and the Stones, so when he heard Eric was coming over, he asked me to come as well. The Stones were playing the Palais Des Sports arena. Everyone, including me, was staying at the George V Hotel, an old, elegant hotel, gilded and with brass and velvet everywhere, just my kind of place to stay. Mick and Bianca, who had just gotten together, and Keith and his wife, Anita, and myself, were sitting on the veranda having midafternoon drinks. Bobby came out and said that his mother had arrived from Lubbock, Texas, and would be down in a few minutes to join us all. He had flown her over to see her famous son play with the Rolling Stones. Of course the women there were all about high fashion and were dripping in jewels. Bianca had on a beige hat with a wide brim and looked like a movie star. Anita was a real hard woman, so no matter what she had on it wouldn't work. Mick was the only rock star I ever knew who was consistent when it came to good-looking women. Mrs. Keys came strolling through those big beautiful double doors and Bobby said, "Here she comes now!" He was very anxious to show off his mom to everyone and they were all very anxious to meet her. Those doors burst wide open and she made the grandest entrance you ever did see. She had on high heels and a light blue shoestring strap dress that was cut real low and shouldn't have been. A true Texas queen! Dark red lipstick and rouge with blue eye shadow and very long eyelashes. She was awesome. She completely outdid Bianca in the jewelry department with her three rows of graduating light blue, dark blue pop-beads. Topping off this magnificent display of courageous savoir-faire was a two foot tall red bee-hive hair-do! Man, this woman was confident. Everyone was speechless. I still don't remember her name other than Mrs. Keys and Bobby's mom. Mick leaned back and smiled and started applauding her. He is a class act. He stood up and put his arms around her as if he had always known her. Bianca and Anita said nothing. Keith was in stitches. And Bobby was just as proud of his mother as she was of her son. And well she should be, too.

Eric and I flew home the next day and went back out on the road in England. This time we played larger venues than on our first U.K. tour. I recall an incident on a train coming back home to London from somewhere up North. I'm pretty sure it was Scarborough in North Yorkshire. It was the last show before heading to London. Anyway, I guess that Eric had just about had enough of Jim for some reason. We had a private room in the first-class section that was big enough for all of us to stretch out a bit. It had two plush bench seats and fold-down tables that were burl wood, shiny and beautiful, and a huge window to look out at the countryside as we flew through it at 120 mph. There were racks overhead for storage and a private bathroom. This was a very nice coach. Carl and Jim were facing each other by the door and Eric and I were facing each other by the window watching the passing countryside and talking. I do remember that while we were talking he seemed a bit distant. He was really thinking something over very intensely. All of a sudden he stood up and reached to the overhead compartment and grabbed Jim's only bag and opened the window and threw it out. When it hit the wind outside it exploded and everything went everywhere. He sat back down and started reading a book like nothing had happened. It didn't really hit Jim at first, but when it did he freaked. He jumped up and started screaming, "What the fuck did you just do?!" Eric never said a word. He just looked up at him like, "What are you going to do about it?" and continued on with his book. Clearly, Jim had annoyed Eric and he just flipped out for a moment.

I'm convinced Jim wasn't cut out to be a rock 'n' roll drummer. In the beginning, like his contemporaries Carol Kay and Hal Blaine, he was real straight and nothing but business. A studio cat, in other words. He could not handle the realities of being on the road and being in the spotlight very well. Then the drugs started, and it was a downhill run that never stopped until that fateful evening in 1983 in L.A. when he killed his mother. Unbeknownst to us, and his family, he was a schizophrenic. So the drugs only exacerbated the situation. I really felt bad for his family. That's who crosses my mind when I think of all of that. He may have crossed the line, but he didn't mean to do what he did. He was a victim of his own circumstance. Self-perpetuated and motivated by the drug-induced demons that were in his head. I'm sure that those drugs opened doors in his mind that never existed before. I've been down that road. He was not mentally fit enough to keep up with any of us, yet he took massive amounts of everything. Every time that he and I happened to be sitting next to each other when we were on the road, he would take out his wallet and show me the same two pictures again and again and he'd say, "Would you like to see the picture of my little girl?" One was of his wife, and the other was of his lovely young daughter. That happened every time that we sat together, and that was a lot of times. It seemed to me that he knew that he was doing wrong but that there was nothing he could do about it. There was no turning back for him no matter what the price or the cost or to whom. I can still see her face, a real pretty little girl with long brown curls hanging down over her light blue dress with ruffled short sleeves. She looked to be about four years of age. I know that he loved his family, especially his little girl. But he was totally out of control as well as being out of his depth. Whatever I may have felt about his personality, I can honestly say that he was the best session drummer in the world and he made one hell of a mark as a live one as well. He raised the bar so high that no one will ever be able to reach it. I feel fortunate that I got to play with him at the pinnacle of his drumming prowess. What a drummer!

Playing Back Home

Our last date in the U.K. was at the stylish Lyceum Ballroom in London on the October 11, 1970, the same place we played our first show in June. Eric was still in the same somber mood that he had been on the train. Looking back, I think he was tired. We all were. But on top of that he still had the heartache of not having Pattie and losing his friend Jimi Hendrix. These events really hit him hard. Despite Eric being subdued, I remember it was a good show and we played several numbers from the "Layla" sessions. We desperately needed a break, but there was to be no rest for us as we flew out to the United States the next day for our first tour there. I was looking forward to that, and I was real proud to be playing in my own country. When we arrived in America, for what turned out to be the only tour that we would do of the States, we were driving from the airport to our hotel for our second show when Eric saw a huge billboard on the side of the road which read, "Eric Clapton and his band." It said where we would be playing, the Electric Factory, and he immediately had Bruce McCaskill stop the car at a gas station pay phone on the side of the road. Eric told him to call the office in London to tell them that we would not be playing that venue unless the sign was changed and his name taken off. This was in Philadelphia, and it was freezing. It was a sold-out show that he was threatening to cancel. That sign was changed within the hour, although everyone who had tickets knew it was Eric so it kind of defeated the point, really. From then on the adverts always read Derek and the Dominos. Robert Stigwood continued to be upset that Eric didn't want his name used in the press and in the ads because a lot of folks had no real idea who we were. If they had, we would have been playing larger venues. Eric really did embrace his anonymity as a band member and that made the three of us feel somewhat special that Eric would choose to remain in the shadows to just be one of us, one of the band. In Derek and the Dominos we split everything four ways. That was Eric's way of making us all equal.

When the Dominos played in New York City at the Fillmore East for what would ultimately be our only shows in that city, Eric had a little spare time on his hands and a pocket full of money. We played two nights. The second one was a miracle in itself. We were so wasted that it was pretty touch-and-go there for a while, especially "Crossroads." A little too much smack had been done, and I didn't know if Eric was going to make it back in on the verses in time to get out of them. When we were going into the second change he was just starting the first. We just kept on playing as if he did. It turned out to be a real interesting performance. I just listened to it the other day. We were all completely done in, but somehow the drugs never stopped us at all. They were just something that we did, not something that we were doing all of the time.

I think that it was Ahmet Ertegun who introduced Eric to this beautiful black chick at a party that was thrown for us by Atlantic Records during our stay in New York. We were there for the better part of a week and Eric got hooked up with her somehow. He was completely smitten with her and had taken her out for a couple of shopping sprees and spent thousands of dollars on her. He bought her a fur coat and a complete wardrobe. It looked like they were getting real thick and it was working out just fine. He was in love again—or was it in lust—again? She was way too wild for him. Eric called me to his room and said that he wanted to talk to me about something private. I went up to his room. We didn't get suites and have limos every time we went out: It was a rock 'n' roll tour, not a luxury trip. He asked me, "What do you think about me bringing her back to Hurtwood after we're finished the tour?" Alarm bells went off in my head and I told him that I thought that she was a beautiful woman, but I didn't see how she was going to fit in out there in the English countryside and doing her shopping in Cranleigh. Eric was determined to ask her, so I told him just to do it. She was one fine looking woman and she would sure dress up the place. I went on back to my room and a couple of hours later Bruce McCaskill called me about getting some money for her. Turns out that when Eric had asked her to go back to Hurtwood Edge she simply said that he owed her $5000 for her services. Eric had laid his heart on the line and she just stepped on it. Bruce and I took the money up and he gave it to Eric. It wasn't too much longer before she knocked on the door. Eric opened it up and threw a double handful of loose notes in her face and slammed the door. It went everywhere. I went out into the hall and watched her down on her hands and knees gathering it all together. It was mostly tens and twenties and I just stood there in amazement and watched her as she picked it all up off of the floor. I told her, "Didn't you know that he was really crazy about you and wanted to take you home with him?" and, "Don't you know or care about what you have just done and who you did it to?" She never said a word. She just kept picking up her money and when she had it all she left. What a beautiful tramp!

When we were on the road with Derek and the Dominos we really weren't a hotel-trashing band. There were a few that we partied a little heavy in, but we never tore any place up. We had other people on the road with us who were giving us a bad name. People like Elton John, who was real bad about tearing a hotel room up. We were declined hotel rooms in some of the places that we played because of Elton's bad behavior. He was our support band, which meant he always arrived at the hotel well before we did and was raising all manner of hell, so they wouldn't let us have rooms there. This happened several times, so we finally had to let him go from the tour. He was great but was a real handful. This was around the time that *Tumbleweed Connection* had come out. I would go out every night and stand there and watch and listen to that guy play and sing. At that time it was just him with Nigel Olsen on drums and Dee Murray playing bass. What a great trio. I thought that he was great then and still do think of him as a classic performer. I'm sure that there was a time or two when we had to let it all out, but that was mostly Jim's department. He did throw a television out of a hotel window once. I saw him when he did it, but he didn't tear the room up, he just tossed the television out of the window to see it fall. It was about twenty stories and it landed on the roof of the building down below and hit with a thunderous noise. I thought too much of those nice rooms that we were staying in to destroy them.

After our show in Jacksonville, Florida, we had a listening party at Criteria during a short break in the tour, a few days before playing the *Johnny Cash Show*. We were all sort of partying because the album was finished and ready for release. Jerry Wexler was there also and everybody in the room loved the album. Tom even said that is was the best album he had worked on since *The Genius of Ray Charles*. Jerry had just come by to check it all out, but he also had plans for me. He took me outside and presented me with an Atlantic solo contract along with a $9000 check. It was a complete surprise—I had not foreseen this at all. I had always wanted to be with Atlantic and here was Jerry, one of the co-founders, wanting to sign me up. I jumped at the chance. Don't get me wrong, I was committed to the band, but the thought of doing a solo album at some point was a thrilling proposition. When I went back in with the check for nine thousand dollars in my hand and told Eric, he was shocked that I had been so reckless in signing something without any legal representation and advice. But I thought that it was a very big deal being signed to Atlantic and that nine grand in my hand was the most money I had seen in my life at that point. Unfortunately, as Eric said, I signed that contract with nobody else there due to me being slightly worse for wear and it was something that would cost me dearly later.

The Johnny Cash Show

After our listening party in Miami we prepared ourselves for our first and only television appearance. We needed a vehicle to let everyone know who we were. That was the only television show that was a variety show that could accommodate us. The only drawback was that they didn't allow rock 'n' roll bands on it. They mainly only let country artists and acoustic acts like Neil Young, James Taylor and Neil Diamond on the show. Rock acts were not permitted. When we recorded our album, a country song was not anywhere near entering, must less crossing our minds to put on our record. The news came that they would prefer country or acoustic music on the show, so that's when we decided to play "It's Too Late." I think that it was Eric who came up with the idea of doing that particular song. It was country blues, and we were accepted on the show. We were very excited to be doing Johnny Cash's show, especially as he was just about as big a country artist as there was at that time and his show was hugely popular. It was filmed at the beautiful Ryman Auditorium on November 5, 1970, a 2,362-seat venue perhaps best known as the home of the Grand Ole Opry, the weekly country music radio show. *The Johnny Cash Show* was live but was delayed airing, which meant that if something went wrong they had an opportunity to correct the mistake and get on with the show live on the air. In the dressing room, which was stage right behind where I was sitting on the piano, was a long table. We had some blow that we had brought with us to Nashville and right before we went on Eric dumped a big pile of it out on the table and we each did two lines about a foot long. The crowd had arrived and the place was full. I had flown my family in, Granny Whitlock, my mom, my sister, Aunt Ginger and Uncle Tommy, and they were all sitting in the front row. My dad had no interest in coming and stayed away. The place was packed. And so were we. Here I am in front of my family all wired up, and I felt a terrible guilt. Then Johnny Cash came walking out, they were rolling tape, everybody was applauding, he gets up to the microphone, "Errrm ... who's on speed?" He was all wired up as well. Then he introduces us: "Ladies and Gentlemen, from London, England, Eric Clapton, Jim Gordon, Carl Radle and Bobby Whitlock." And as he's getting ready to say Derek and the Dominos, I held my hand up like I was in school, and said, "Wait a minute! I'm from Memphis, and my whole family is sitting in the front row, and he's from Tulsa and he's from Hollywood." Then the director says "Cut!" The place was in an uproar. Johnny was laughing. So they had to do a retake. Johnny walks off, comes back on and starts over, "Ladies and gentlemen, Bobby Whitlock, Jim Gordon, Carl Radle and Eric Clapton. Derek and the Dominos." This crowd wasn't there to see us, they were there for Johnny Cash, but they loved us anyway. There was a line two deep that went all the way around the block that was the rock 'n' roll crowd waiting for us to play when the country acts finished. They emptied the house of the country music fans and filled it right back up again with the waiting rock 'n'

On The Johnny Cash Show, *1970: Carl Perkins, left, me, Eric Clapton and Johnny Cash.*

rollers. We had already done "It's Too Late" and then "Matchbox" with Johnny and Carl Perkins. It's a pretty hard task to play a classic rock 'n' roll song standing and playing it right next to the person who wrote it. If Eric was burning that night it was because Carl Perkins lit the fire. He was smoking! There was no way to top what Carl was playing and Eric was intimidated by just being in the presence of Johnny Cash and Carl Perkins. You can see his shyness as he is being interviewed by Johnny as well as when Eric introduces Carl. Some time later I was on a plane waiting to go somewhere and Johnny and June Carter Cash and their son walked on and Johnny immediately recognized me. He said to his boy, "Say hello to Mr. Whitlock, son. He did my show some time back."

We were on the road with the Dominos and had to go through the airport in New York City to change planes for wherever it was that we were headed. It may have been Wisconsin but that's not important to the story. Bruce McCaskill was forced into carrying the dope for Eric and me, and he did not like it at all. It was cocaine and probably a little something else. There was at least an ounce of blow. It was enough to get us all in a world of trouble if we got caught. We told him that if he got caught that we would call the office and they would get him out of whatever trouble it was that he was in. But if we were to carry our own drugs and got caught, the show would be over for us and for him. There wouldn't be a concert and the tour would be disrupted. And to top it all off, he would have to answer to Robert Stigwood as to why we got busted when he could have prevented it by carrying the drugs for us. He couldn't come back with an argument and was carrying over an ounce of pure cocaine for Eric and me. He had it in his briefcase in case he needed to get rid of it in a hurry. And it was handy for us as well if we need a little on the flight. We were standing in line waiting to board the plane when two guys in suits started walking our way and I saw Bruce start turning grey. Jim was standing next to me holding his briefcase and he said, "Oh shit! I've got the works on me!" They walked right up to us and showed us their badges and took Jim away with them. They were the FBI and they took his briefcase from him and told us to wait right where we were, and then they took him into a room. Bruce was about to go into meltdown. We were all pretty nervous because we knew what Bruce was carrying and could go nowhere to get rid of it because we were being watched. I don't know how long it was, but it seemed forever. They eventually came back out and handed Jim his briefcase and walked away without ever saying a word to us. We were stunned. They had pulled Jim for unknowingly passing a counterfeit twenty-dollar bill. When they opened Jim's case they found his heroin and needles, spoons and syringes and surgical tubing and all. They took it all from him but could do nothing about it because it was an illegal search. They were looking for counterfeit money, not drugs. Jim was very lucky that day and so were we.

Duane Allman came out to join us in Tampa, Florida, at the Curtis Hixon Hall on December 1. I recently listened to a tape of this show and it brought back vivid memories of the evening. Duane was up there on stage with us standing right in front of me. My organ faced in towards the center so that I could watch Eric's mouth as we sang together. That's how I would get my cues as to what and when to sing. It came naturally to me especially when I was singing with Eric. But I was watching Duane as well. I couldn't help but see him. They traded off being the support guitar when the other would go off. Eric was playing the rhythm while Duane played the lead and then they would switch roles. Eric was very gracious when it came to letting the other guy have his lead. Our vocals worked great as usual, and the whole band was really excited on that night. A big part of that was because Duane was with us and we felt complete. That was the balancing factor with our record, a combination of Duane and Eric's unique styles with a combination that was respectful and worked as one. On "Layla," which was the opening number that night, we rocked the house. It kept going and going, and at one point I had my doubts that we were ever going to stop until Eric and I started singing the fade again as if we had rehearsed it, which we hadn't. We sang so very naturally together that we instinctively knew what the other was getting ready to do. We were locked tight. When the ending did finally come it ended on the upbeat chord. I remember thinking, "Are we going to come back to the first chord, the root note?" We didn't, it just ended suspended in space and time. The second song was "Got to Get Better in a Little While," a favorite of the band's, but Duane's playing was not very creative, just big chords and rhythm. The third song was "Key to the Highway" and is a real good example of what I'm talking about in relation to Duane being a structured player. The song sounds nothing like what we had recorded a few months before at Criteria. Duane played a pattern that Carl then Jim had to lock into. Eric and I were the only ones who were anywhere near the song and its essence. Duane was just not as fluid a player as Eric, so the songs and his part in them became a bit repetitious. The last song was "Why Does Love Got to Be So Sad," and we rocked. Duane and Eric were trading off towards the end but there was no way that Duane could keep up with Eric.

As a whole Duane was not used to being around such players as Eric and Jim Gordon and Carl Radle. I was, and am still, a rhythm player and I become the B3 when I play it. My approach is completely different to Gregg Allman's approach to playing it. It is never the same when I play the organ. The sound and dynamics are constantly changing. Gregg's organ always sounds the same as it did on record. Duane was great for our record but he would have not been good for our band in the long run because of his approach to what a band should be. *Layla* record was structured. Each song was gone through and worked out so we were sure. Even though it was live when we recorded it, we didn't just walk in and start playing and that was all there was to it. It wasn't that way at all. "Nobody Knows You When You're Down and Out" was a song that the Hour Glass did and Duane played the same licks on *Layla* record as he did with them. Eric was and is a fluid player. Duane couldn't keep up no matter how he tried. He was from a structured situation and was not used to creative flow and formless freedom. You can hear it when you listen to Allman Brothers records. Everything was and still is parts. Everyone had and still has a part to play rather than letting their role define them and the song.

The next number played was "Blues Power," and Eric was smoking on the intro. When we started to fade he was playing the "keep on keeping on" line, he wasn't singing it right away, he was playing it. It was very cool. Our voices together create a whole different atmosphere to a song. Next up was "Have You Ever Loved a Woman." Eric and Duane are sometimes indistinguishable from each other on this number. Even I had to really listen at times to tell, especially in a couple of different places. Of course you can tell the different guitar tones but it was just the way that they were playing together and off of each other.

They were already seasoned veterans of the rock 'n' roll world and were blues purists in their mid-twenties. There are times during the song that they play one right into the other and come across as one guitar. It's like a different player has taken over. Eric's playing flows so that it seems like each note leads right into the next one. That's really what it does as well but it goes much deeper than that. He is in the moment at all times. Sometimes more so than others but it is always flowing forth. He plays with a heavy pick and there is a certain way he angles it when he is going for different inflections of a harmonic sound. I still remember him showing me how he holds his pick and how he does it. He holds a pick the way that it is supposed to be held, with two fingers and a thumb. I didn't start out that way so it doesn't come naturally to me. I'm better at finger picking my guitar. It is a very precise movement that Eric does.

Next up were "Bottle of Red Wine" and "Let It Rain," which are great examples of Eric and me singing together. "Bottle of Red Wine" rocked for the shuffle it is, all except for Duane's part in it. He was so used to playing one-four-five that he got the song turned around during the solo. The first round went the right way but the second time he went into the traditional blues changes and it screwed the song up. We all recovered but his influence live was not a positive one on everything that we did. He was great for the record because it was a structured situation. But live he was not the guitar player for our band. We were not a southern rock band. We were a very sophisticated rock 'n' roll band with a lot more going on than playing the same old lick over and over in different keys. Even though there were mistakes, it is still a gig I remember with fond memories because of Duane joining us.

December saw the release of our debut double album. I would imagine that a lot of people have wondered at some point where the full title of the *Layla* album came from. Eric had the painting that he had been given in August in Biot, France, from Emile's father. Eric felt that it looked like Pattie and he wanted to use it for the front cover and call our album "Derek and the Dominos—Layla." That was absolutely cool with me. He and I made all of the decisions concerning the creative side of things. I remember that when Eric was telling me how he wanted to call the album *Layla*, I was busy eating my way through a box of assorted chocolates. And then it just came to me in a flash. Because we had all of those other assorted love songs I suggested, "How about calling it 'Layla and Other Assorted Love Songs?'" He loved it and it stuck. For the foldout design of the sleeve, Robin Turner and I arranged all the Kodak Instamatic shots on a piece of cardboard and Robin got it to the office in London. Robin and I also set the back sleeve up and a photographer from New York took the shot. He did it on the floor of the studio after we had finished recording and had it all set up looking very nice and orderly until I came along and dumped a very large ashtray full of cigarette butts on his arrangement. He got pissed and cleaned up as much as he could. As for Eric's shoes, well, they wouldn't listen to me and left them in.

The Last Show

I remember our last U.S. show, at Suffolk Community College in New York, on December 6, 1970. It turned out to be our last ever show, not that any of us knew it at the time. The concert started with me banging around on the piano and Eric plugging in and starting to tune up. We were tight but very loose and very casual at the same time. "Keep on Growing" was the first number of the evening, and Eric's wah-wah was great. The audience responded well. I remember it being quite roomy sounding. But all of our shows were roomy. We were playing in big halls and theaters. I'm on organ on this one and we're off and running. Our voices and the way that we used them defined the sound of Derek and the Dominos. We were very excited about this show because it was the end of the tour. Eric's guitar went out at the end of the song, but we just kept right on and it eventually came back on. It was a bad cord or something. He was really playing all out that night. It was one scorching lead after another. The college students liked it but didn't go crazy the way that they do today. At the end of the first song Eric started tuning up again and Carl was tuning his bass again and we were very casual about going into the next number. Some people were yelling for us to "stop fucking around and get on with it!" It was pretty amazing what I was hearing. I guess they thought that we couldn't hear them or maybe they just didn't care. Then all of a sudden Eric started to go into "Tell the Truth" with the slow intro and changes right in midstride to the fast version, real fast. He just lit up. It was as fast as the version that we did during George's session for *All Things Must Pass*. The only saving grace for me was the fact that I wasn't playing the piano or my fingers would have been bloodier than they already were. Carl Radle was on form and Jim Gordon was kicking. He rocked during this and every song. Eric's playing was incredible on this number, it was just pouring out of him like water. Carl was as steady as they come and Eric played some of my favorite solo guitar work. He was real creative using his full extension of range. It was a feel more than the notes. The atmosphere really was indescribable. He sounded like two different guitar players at times. It really was the most creative work that I have ever heard. And the crowd was in tune as well during all of this. We played "Stormy Monday" with me singing. I still had my young man's blues voice. Eric's playing was amazing. After his solo everybody applauded and I started the last verse and I remember thinking I sounded like a young man with an old man's blues. At the end everyone applauded and I still remember how it felt to be there with Jim Gordon and Carl Radle and Eric Clapton. It was an honor and I felt privileged then and still do to this very day. It amazes me still but doesn't surprise me how much everyone still loves that band.

Back in England and Christmas at Hurtwood Edge

After the U.S. tour, we all took a well-deserved break. Eric invited us all to stay at Hurtwood Edge for that Christmas. As usual I stayed in my favorite bedroom with the balcony overlooking the rolling hills. Jim and Carl had arrived earlier. It was still really cold in there but that didn't seem to matter because it was Christmas. And when I woke up with the sunrise there was a silence that I recognized. It had snowed. I looked out from my balcony in a state of wonderment across the rolling landscape all covered with a beautiful white blanket. It was Christmas morning and I really was there, looking out across a beautiful countryside that I would call home for many years to come. It was a wonderful experience, but I never once forgot my roots. As a matter of fact they tripped me up many times. My life in England was so alien to the one that I had lived when I was growing up. As alien as this one now is to the old me. You could hear Mrs. Eggby down in the kitchen getting everything ready for our breakfast, and she was to start preparing for Christmas dinner soon as well. It was going to be a big turkey with a ham, Yorkshire pudding, roast potatoes, cranberry sauce, fresh warm bread and a lovely hot brandy wine followed by Christmas pudding with cream on top for dessert. We all sat around the long table that is probably still there in the dining room. It had a bench that was on one side and big armchairs at either end with two normal chairs on the side facing out overlooking the gardens. I just loved that place and I have nothing but fond memories of it and the time spent there.

As you go down the drive at Hurtwood Edge you have twenty-foot high rhododendron of every color there on both sides. All were covered with snow. The house itself sits with the back of it as the entrance. There is a statue of a lady with a vase standing in the center of a round flower garden that is in the middle of the drive area. The Ferraris were backed up to the house and facing out and were ready to go at all times. The front of the house overlooked the hills and valley and had a stone and marble patio with steps leading down to the very bottom of the garden. The beautiful garden had very old mature trees and a swimming pool that Eric had just put in with a guitar mosaic in the bottom of it. It was very Eric. From the bottom of the garden you can see the house standing majestically

Christmastime at Hurtwood Edge, Eric Clapton's house, and the Safari Land Rover.

up on the top of the hill. It was quite an impressive place from down there. There are guest quarters where I kept my two dogs Sam and Dave for a while. It is a beautiful three-roomed apartment with arched doorways and a huge fireplace. That was my favorite part of the house, in the very bottom of it. It was a very long walk and climb back and the steps were covered with ice and snow and it was really cold there but that didn't seem to matter because it was Christmas at Hurtwood Edge. It was not so much the house, because that's just stone and wood, but it was what I felt there. That place was Eric, and you could feel his presence there even when he wasn't there.

Eric had arranged for a seven-foot tall Christmas tree to be erected in the front room, and it was adorned with all sorts of decorations that we had put on it. The mantle had stockings for everyone. They were filled with all sorts of things, like candy canes, party hats, a little car, a bag of marbles and some poppers. What fun we had with those silly hats and pulling those poppers and generally having the time of our lives. Eric has always been real big on Christmas. I think it has to do with that family thing. I wouldn't know because that is something I never had, so I didn't know about it. It just seemed to me that everyone that I could see around me had a family that loved them. After dinner we all got in the Safari Land Rover and went out for a drive to the village at night. Bruce was driving and we just went everywhere around there for a couple of hours. We were the only people out there. Not another car in sight. What fun we had, just driving on the snow-covered roads and drinking Bells Scotch and Green Ginger wine and having a few smokes, laughing and enjoying just all being there together. It was always great fun being with Eric. We never had a cross word, probably because he knew just how innocent I was then. He was always looking out after me like he was my big brother. He was always happy and laughing. Everyone else came first with Eric and he always made sure that everyone was always looked after. No one was overlooked at Christmas. After we got home it was time to open the presents. Eric had gone out and gotten everyone something special. He gave me a professional aluminum crossbow with sights. I would have a lot of fun with that during my time at Sunny Heights, which I will tell you about later. I got Eric a very old sitar that I found in the Chelsea Antiques market in the Kings Road. I thought for sure that he could play it. I never realized how complex an instrument it was, but what else would you get for a rock star guitar player who had everything?

I don't remember what he gave Carl, but it would have been something nice. He gave Jim a very old red wooden marching drum with a pair of hand carved sticks and a mallet. The drum had leatherheads that were strung together with gold rope. It had a sash with tassels hanging from one side that were gold braid. It was a beautiful piece and very old. As soon as he unwrapped it, Jim snapped, "What the hell is this?" Talk about ruining the atmosphere! I could not believe what I had just heard come out of his mouth. Eric was taken aback and didn't know what to say except "I'll take it back if you like Jim, I thought that you would like it." That guy was all about himself. Eric had gone out to London and got something very special for each of us only to be rudely rejected by that dude. It wasn't good enough for him and to top it off, Jim didn't get Eric anything. Most of the time Eric took everything that Jim dished out in his stride. Eric was a class act and relatively unshakeable. He took what Jim would say and seemed to store it away. That's just what he was doing, whether or not he knew it. Like everything else, it had to come out some way or another. It would just be a matter of time.

The End of the Dominos

In early 1971 the office was telling us that we wouldn't live six more months the way that we were going. They were right. Now, looking back on it with clear eyes, the band didn't live another six months. It was to be over just like Robert Stigwood had said. Even though we were still walking around, we really were dead, the living dead. The heart and soul of our band had died but we were just unaware of it at the time. I think that Eric knew it, though. He was a very perceptive individual, even then. I believe Carl knew because he was already making plans to work with Leon Russell. I knew about that because he told me so. I figured that Carl could do whatever he wanted to because he was a pretty levelheaded guy. Jim was oblivious to the world around him and I could not wait for the day when he was going to be replaced. I talked a lot about Jim Keltner again with Eric, hoping he would want to get him over for our next album.

After the Dominos came back from our American tour I was living in Chertsey. We had to let the London flat go because we were out on tour. Jim had gotten himself a flat in Chelsea and was driving an old two-door Bristol to get around. Carl stayed in a hotel or out at Eric's. My house in Chertsey was an old English farmhouse that was on the edge of a cliff overlooking the countryside. It belonged to a ship's captain who had gone out to sea. I never did get to meet him. The house was vine-covered white stone, two stories, with a slate roof and a detached stone garage and garden house that had slate roofs as well. There were five bedrooms and a sitting room and a kitchen. The front room had a huge fireplace that you could sit in. It was very large and the fire was at the back of it, and there were very old benches made of split logs painted black that had been built in there on each side of it. There was an iron arm attached to the wall with a big black pot that could swing over the fire, originally used for cooking. I don't know how many years ago that was, but it was a very old house. The fireplace seemed uncharacteristically large for a house with such small rooms, but I soon understood why when the first signs of winter set in. Those little radiators on the wall were merely decor. Eric let me borrow a couple of carpets from a closet in one of his small upstairs bedrooms. They were very old and worn, so I asked him if I could use them, and he said sure without even looking at what I was talking about. My two Dalmatians, Sam and Dave, messed the rugs up within minutes on the first day, just as soon as I put them down on the floor. These rugs were beautiful. They looked like they belonged in a tent out in the desert. So I took them outside and put them on the roof of my garden house and hosed them down real good. It was cold and the weather hadn't let up at all. The sun hadn't shined for a while so those rugs stayed up there for a couple of weeks longer than they should have. I checked on them every day or so to see if they were anywhere near dry but they weren't, so I'd turn them over and wash the other side and wait some more. At that particular time of the year the sun was a rarity, but finally

My house in Chertsey.

the day came after about three or four weeks that I checked on them and they were dry. When I took them off of the garden house roof they fell apart in my hands. They just crumbled like dried leaves. I gathered up all of the pieces and went to Eric's to take his rugs back and explained what had happened. They were in a sack. He looked at me and told me that they were not rugs meant for the floor. They were tapestries meant for hanging on the walls and were museum pieces. They were very old and rare and very, very expensive. Incredibly, Eric forgave me yet again for my ignorance. He was very tolerant and patient with me. He knew that I didn't know any better, I had never lived in a nice house or had a place called home in all of my life.

George and Pattie would drive through the snow and come visit quite often. Paula was living with me there also. George and I would sometimes play guitar and he showed me a few things. He and I would sit in the fireplace and have a drink. We would talk about what was happening to me and what was happening to him, how I grew up

With my Dalmatians Sam and Dave.

and my whole background. And he would tell me of his family and upbringing, just two friends sitting there talking about their every daylives and their bands. He would tell me about how the Beatles were formed and stories about them on the road and not being able to go out and play because they were too famous. He was doing his best to guide me in the right direction but I had a tendency to go a little astray. I had never had anything before, so I wanted to try it all. I wanted to take a big bite out of life. He and I would partake of various substances from time to time but nothing serious, a little smoke and a little blow now and then. He was a pretty straight dude, all things considered. We had many great talks and walks through my smallish gardens and his very extensive gardens at Friar Park. His grounds had underground tunnels and a huge cave under the house. Pretty amazing to go down in a hole between a couple of large rocks in George's garden and suddenly you're in an underground tunnel that's a cave with stalagmites and stalactites and a stream flowing through it. I remember one time when Leon Russell was out there with us, we three put on our Wellingtons and took a couple of torches and went down there in the dark and walked through the tunnel and out on to a pond. Leon had some kind of an experience then, I don't know what it was, he wouldn't say. But I think it had something to do with walking out of that tunnel and onto the top of the water. You had a sensation of walking on the water. Then we went back underground through another tunnel and eventually we would walk into this enormous cave with an entry that led secretly into the main house. It was a whole lot of fun exploring that big old place.

The Dominos sound guy, Ron Nevison, moved into my house because my lease was running out and he was taking it over. In fact I was still there after the lease ran out and Ron was hassling me all the time to find another place. Unfortunately the house burned down before I'd had a chance to find a new home. It happened while Paula and I were out with George and Pattie at Friar Park one day. We got back home and it was up in flames. My red Ferrari was in the garage that was detached from the house so it was fine, but the house was burning down real fast. I really didn't have anything but a couch, a table and a couple of rugs at the time. All of it was destroyed along with my clothes. People thought that I had something to do with it. I didn't. It was faulty wiring under the kitchen floor and it was a good thing that nobody was there when it happened. Ron was always going on about how I was a rock star and how much I had in the way of things, cars and a house. He was always having a go at me about my new lodgings when I moved, but it was just a matter of circumstance that a new house came my way. It was to be mine no matter if my house went up in flames or not. Unfortunately for Ron, he had finally moved into my house as I was moving out. He had just moved all of his things in and wasn't there either when it burned. But he was the first to point a finger my way. Then all the rest had a direction in which to look. It wasn't me, though, and the fire brigade revealed that in their report. It wasn't until about a year ago that Ron and I were talking on the phone and I told him that after all of these years had passed and the air was clear that I still had nothing to do with burning up his stuff. He lost all of his equipment and clothes—everything. He was pissed at me for years for no reason—or so I had thought. He told me that he didn't think that I had done it at all, and never had. That's not what he said at the time, though. I suppose that it was in the heat of the moment. So I went for years defending myself to myself and everyone else over nothing. After the fire he went to stay with Eric and Alice at Hurtwood Edge and stayed there quite a while.

Paula and I didn't have a place to move to, so we got in my Ferrari and drove back to Friar Park to stay a while with George and Pattie. It was great fun to be there with them while they were putting that place together. Pattie was lovely and took to me, I believe, because she had come from a similar abusive background. One day they said, "Come with us, we have something to show you." We got in their car and went to Weybridge, a town just outside of London. When we drove through the town centre, George said, "There's your bakery and there's your grocery store. Here's the train station and you can get a great breakfast there and a good strong cup of tea." We drove down the road a bit and pulled into this private estate that looked like a huge parkland. It was called St. George's Hill. That's a very exclusive estate where Tom Jones and, at that time, John Lennon lived. It has a fascinating history. In the seventeenth century it was the first place in the country where radical peasants known as Diggers and Levellers tried growing corn and other crops on common land at St. George's Hill. Their aim was to use the earth as a way of reclaiming the freedom that they felt they had lost through the Norman Conquest. They were able to defy the landlords as well as the army and the law for over a year, only to be driven off by rich landowners. It is ironic that by the late twentieth century it had become the richest and most exclusive residential area in the country.

We pulled up to some open gates and the sign said, Sunny Heights. The gates had writing all over them, "We Love You Beatles," and everything else Beatle-related that you could imagine. At the end of the drive there was a huge English manor house. George handed me the keys and said, "Welcome home!" Turns out it was Ringo Starr's old house and he had moved out when he and wife Maureen had split. It had 28 rooms and five bathrooms and a cinema and a pub, a real one. It was beautiful and was going to be my home for quite some time to come. There was a breakfast table that was built in and the kitchen had a stove with twelve burners. I guess they did a whole lot of partying. My bedroom had a built-in bed that John and Yoko had been warming up only weeks before I moved in. It's a good thing, too, because I didn't have a stick of furniture. What little I did have went up in flames with my house in Chertsey. John and Yoko were there for a while after Ringo and Maureen moved out. The house was really an Apple Corps property. All of their houses were bought and maintained through Apple. That's just good business. Neil Aspinall, a lovely man, ran their Apple Corps offices. The main bathroom was black marble and had a lilac tub. I had this really cool place and I was a rock star with all of the trappings, the keyword being trappings. That place was beautiful, on nine terraced acres. There was a greenhouse

At Sunny Heights after the Dominos split.

that I promptly filled with marijuana. The vegetable garden was full of it as well. I didn't think that it would really grow there so well but boy was I surprised. There was a very tall fence that surrounded the place and it was very private, gates behind gates. It had a waterfall with a koi pond as well as a one-acre rhododendron secret garden. You walked through tunnels cut through giant tree-sized rhododendron to little different areas within the maze and suddenly there's a place to have tea or just to sit and rest and look.

It was now January 1971 and Carl had gone off to do some work with Leon Russell in California and would be away for a couple of months. The Dominos' second album sessions were booked for April and May, so I thought it was a good time to start recording my first solo album. I knew that the studio was available and I had my

In the living room with Bear at Sunny Heights.

deal with Atlantic. My idea was to get all the people I had played with on it, including Delaney and Bonnie. The first person that I called was Eric and asked him if he would play on my album and he said yes straight away. The next person I was to call was George and he said that he would love to come and play on my record. I called Carl next, and he said that he would be there as soon as he was finished. Unfortunately that turned out to be longer than he had expected, so I eventually had to call Klaus Voorman. Jim Gordon was in no matter what, as were Bobby Keys and Jim Price. I called Andy Johns to engineer

and co-produce it for me. I liked the sound that he and his brother Glyn got. Plus he was used to working with big stars and knew these guys. For the most part the album was recorded with just Jim and Klaus and me, except for the live recordings with George and Eric on them. Then it was the full band with no overdubs. We recorded "Where There's a Will There's a Way," "A Day Without Jesus" and "Back in My Life Again," which I made up on the spot and we recorded words and all as they just came out. George had turned to me after we did "A Day Without Jesus" and said, "What's next?" I hadn't planned on doing another number and didn't have one in my head, so I told him that I didn't

The front of Sunny Heights.

know what was next. I drew a blank. Here I had Eric Clapton and George Harrison in my first session and I'm drawing a complete blank! I guess that's the best thing that could have happened because I had opened myself up for that creative influence to come into play. George said, "Why don't you just make something up?" I was sitting at the organ and said "OK, B minor." I gave Jim a tempo and he counted it off and we all started playing and it fell together as if it had already been written. Andy had a mike set up for me to sing through and the words came out at the same time as we were recording it. The story and the melody and all just fell out together at the same time. It was truly an amazing moment.

I had a couple of beautiful ballads that Eric played on. I didn't have a guitar that sounded like his big twelve-string did. He named it "Ivan the Terrible" and that was the guitar that I sat around and played all of the time while I was living at Eric's house in Surrey. What a beautiful sounding guitar it was. It had been co-designed by Eric and guitar maker Tony Zemaitis in early 1969. It had rosewood back and sides with a mahogany top that was decorated with a wood inlay shaped in a heart motif. The ebony bridge and fingerboard were bound and inlaid with silver. It looked as beautiful as it sounded. I remember Eric telling me that he had used it on the Blind Faith album. A lot of people would borrow it, including George, who used it during the *All Things Must Pass* sessions. I think it may have been for "My Sweet Lord." Dave Mason also borrowed Ivan for his only appearance with the Dominos at the Lyceum Dr. Spock concert. I knew it was just the perfect guitar for a couple of songs I had in mind for my album. I had to have that guitar on my record as well as Eric's Martin D45. I went to find him and asked if that would be OK. So I just simply asked him if I could use his two acoustics and he said yes.

A portrait of me from my first solo album, by CoCo Carmel (who at that time was Kim Carmel Bramlett).

He was sitting in the TV room and said it was not problem. I took the guitars and headed off to the studio to record a couple of ballads, "A Game Called Life" and "The Scenery Has Slowly Changed" with Jim Gordon. He and Eric had another falling-out, so Eric wasn't going anywhere near Jim. So it was just Jim and me in the studio that day recording those two songs. Eric came in the next day and overdubbed his part. I also wrote and recorded a nice love song for my girlfriend, "A Song for Paula." Paula and I were together for two years. We met when I first went to England and got together after she came to Miami when we were recording *Layla*. Eric sent for her to come and cut his hair—that's the truth. He didn't want anybody else to cut his hair but Paula for some reason. I don't know why—you've got to check out the *Johnny Cash Show* performance to see what I mean. I never let her touch my hair. We took to each other I guess because we were both so young and lost. She was a teenager and I had just turned twenty-one. I talked to Eric about it first because I didn't want to make any waves or get in his way if she was his girlfriend. I told him that I had feelings for her and she did for me. He gave us his blessings and said it was not a problem because it was Pattie that he was in love with. So Paula and I became this cute item. She went on the road with me for the better part of the Domino tour.

On my twenty-third birthday, March 18, 1971, I was on the way to Olympic Studios to meet Eric, George, Klaus and Jim. I was in my red 330 GTC Ferrari and had come to a roundabout and was waiting my turn. It had just stopped raining when I heard a car coming up from behind. The driver locked his brakes and smashed right into the rear end of my Ferrari. I got out to see if they were all right and check on my car. They were OK and my car wasn't badly damaged. He wasn't going that fast, he just panicked. They lived just up the street so we drove to their house to talk. I could see that they couldn't afford to repair a Ferrari so we never even went there with the discussion. They were devastated that they had wrecked my beautiful car. I told them not to worry that it wouldn't be much to repair and I would take care of it. We had a cup of tea and I left to go the studio where Eric had just pulled up in his Red Daytona. First thing he said was, "What the hell happened to the rear end of your car?" After I told him the story, he handed me a bundle of paper that was a very good attempt at wrapping my birthday present. It was more like rolling sheets wrapped around something. It made no difference, though, because when I unrolled it I found an incredibly beautiful turquoise necklace that was clearly very old. There was also a thick leather guitar strap with a long purple tail. It was very wide and had a brass ring on the front. There are pictures of Eric with it on. He told me that the necklace was a museum piece that he had bought for me. It was beautiful with several strands of turquoise stones that were so exact and precise that it made me wonder what tools they had used to do that. It was all put together with a thick hand-twisted string and it was very fragile and dear. It was not meant to be worn but to be appreciated and I really cherished it. After the session everybody came back to Sunny Heights to celebrate my birthday in style. Pattie, Paula, George and myself were all Pisces, so we decided that we were going to have a Pisces birthday party for all of us. Eric, Ronnie Wood and his wife, Andy Johns, Bobby Keys and his wife, Judy, Jim Price and his girlfriend and Klaus Voorman were all there. And of course Bruce and his wife, whose name just happened to be Paula as well. Then there were all of everyone's personal assistants like Terry Doran and Mal Evans. It was my twenty-third birthday, and it was pretty heavy and pretty heady for me at the same time. It was as if I were in a whirlwind of activity. There was so much going on around me that I could hardly distinguish reality from fantasy. It was like being in a dream, but there was no meaning or purpose to my life, it seemed, even with all that was happening in it. I got very wasted and went upstairs and crashed just after midnight. I still remember Pattie coming up to see me, as I lay on my bed upstairs. She put a cool damp hand towel on my forehead and said to me, "Dear Bobby, dear sweet Bobby, you will be just fine." I'll never forget her kindness in coming up there to comfort me. Truth be told, I felt totally out of place with all of them. I still thought of myself as the Bobby I had always known, the boy who chopped and picked cotton and was not that long from having been playing in honky-tonks in the South and in Memphis.

My first solo album sessions were great, and I will remember them for the rest of my life. There was one sour note, however. I thought it would be nice to have Delaney and Bonnie singing backing vocals on "A Day Without Jesus" for old times' sake. I had taken my tapes over to L.A. to put them on singing background. They invited me to stay at their house while I was over there. The next morning I got up late because of jet lag. Delaney was already at the studio and by the time Bonnie and I got there he was putting on a bass part on "Hello L.A. Bye-Bye Birmingham." Eric had played bass on that track. It was just Eric, Jim and me, and Delaney had erased Eric's bass. He said that Eric was no bass player and neither was Klaus for that matter. I couldn't believe it. On top of that he had added his bass on just about every one of the songs that Klaus had played on. That man had erased all of the bass that Klaus Voorman and Eric Clapton had played on my first record and put himself on playing his Dan-Electro instead. I was devastated. Maybe he was trying to be helpful, but it was my album and I felt he had sabotaged my first record.

When I left and was on my way to the airport to go back home to England, I noticed that I had forgotten my necklace that Eric had given me a few days before at my birthday. I had brought it over to show it to them. I remembered having left it on the night table by the bed in the room where I slept, so I had my driver turn around and head back to their house in the valley. When I arrived back, only about forty-five minutes after leaving, they had already gotten into a fight over the necklace and it was strewn from one end of that house to the other. It had been torn apart and thrown everywhere. I just turned and walked away without saying a word. I hadn't even walked in and closed the front door. As I was walking away to the limo they were blaming each other, but really, the only one whose fault it was was mine for always turning a blind eye and a deaf ear to them and their transgressions. I always forgave them because I thought that I knew them.

I took my tapes back to England and played what Delaney had done to them for Eric. He was very upset at what had happened. He asked, "Didn't you and Andy make safety copies?" I called Andy and he said that we had, so all wasn't lost after all. So we just made sure that we erased all of Delaney's parts first. There was no track sheet for the rest of them, so we didn't really know just who was doing what on what. But that was all right, we were back to the originals. I called Atlantic to say my album was ready for release and they flatly rejected my first record. They had no idea that I had been in the studio recording it at all because I hadn't asked them for anything. I saw nothing wrong with doing what came naturally. Had I not done what I did, my first record would have been just another generic record out of Atlantic. The studio was available and so were the players. Everyone was totally into it, except for Jerry Wexler. He had plans that I didn't know about. I had not heard from Atlantic since he had me sign that recording contract and handed me $9,000 under a street lamp at 10 at night on the hood of a limo out in front of Criteria. He told me that they didn't want to use any of my songs and had planned on Tom Dowd and him producing me with studio musicians in New York. It sounded to me like I was not going to have a say about my music or whom I could use. I asked Jerry if I could buy back my contract from them and he said "Yes, but it'll cost you." It did—$48,000, to be precise. I paid immediately. I spoke with Jerry about all of this a few weeks before he died. He was aware of everything that he had done and still didn't take the opportunity to correct the error of his ways. He died bearing a grudge against me. I talked to him about it and he told me that he could carry a grudge forever. That's a hell of a way to go through life. In the meantime, I was left with an album that could not be released because I had no label. But at least I did my album the way I wanted and I was sure I could get another deal by myself.

Unbeknownst to me, my co-producer and friend, Andy Johns, had been having an affair with Paula and she got pregnant. All this had been going on during the sessions for my first album. She was just a silly teenager really and I was even more so for getting hooked up with her in the first place. I wasn't really surprised to find out about her and Andy when I did. I should have seen it coming. So after my first recording sessions were finished, so was our relationship. I just turned around one day and she was gone. I had been surprised and jilted by my girlfriend of two years right after my twenty-third birthday. It was OK though, because I was pretty resilient and still am. I bounced back and took it all in my stride. I was happy for them, but was hurt by the rejection and deception of both of them. But she was pregnant with their son and we remained friends throughout it all. I was there when their son Will was born and was the first to see him. After they took him home we all sort of drifted apart and went our separate ways. I do know that the Boyd sisters played a more important role that I ever thought about before, in that they were the link between a lot of great players that would not have been brought together had it not been for one sister being with Mick Fleetwood and another being with George Harrison and the other being with Eric Clapton and then myself. The ties of musicians through just those four names is endless!

Even though I had Bruce McCaskill and his wife living at the other end of the house, I felt very alone in that big place with Paula gone. I couldn't take being there and being alone doing nothing with my life except pissing Tom Jones off because I played my Fender Twin at full volume at 3 in the morning. He was my neighbor. On top of that, I never once got the alarm figured out, which meant the police were coming and going all the time at Sunny Heights. The house was on the eighteenth hole of a golf course. That whole place and those folks who lived there were a little too stuffy for my tastes. The veranda off my bedroom had a panoramic view that overlooked the green. And the whole place was covered in very old cedar and huge oak trees that belonged to the queen. I had heard that the people at the country club wouldn't let anyone they didn't approve of, which included John Lennon, Ringo Starr, Tom Jones and Engelbert Humperdinck, join. And me, and I didn't even play golf. I just wanted to get at their snooty selves with something that would have a long-lasting effect, but I couldn't think of how to go about it. Then it came to me. At Christmas Eric had given me the aluminum crossbow. When you pulled the trigger you never saw the shaft until it hit the mark. You could shoot it into the sky and you couldn't even see it anywhere in the blue. It was very powerful, and it took two hands and all of my strength just to load it. All you had to do was to get the red dot on the target and pull the trigger and it was hit. All of the shafts that I had were made of the same metal and were painted very bright colors that glowed in the dark. There were red ones, green and blue neon ones and yellow neon with very brightly colored feathers. I had been thinking this over for quite some time before I went through with it. One very calm afternoon I went out on my veranda with about a dozen or so shafts and a bottle of Dom and started shooting the tops of every tree within reach of my crossbow. I had already shot a hole-in-one hole on the eighteenth green several times. I put every shaft that I had directly into the tops where they would never be able to get at them. Some of those big oaks looked like lit up Christmas trees when the sun hit them just right as it was setting. It really did look quite unique. There were just enough to notice. Each one had been precisely placed, like a live art display. I went back there many years after I had left. I had quite frankly forgotten about them until one day when I ran across my crossbow again as I was unpacking. I wanted to see if they were still there, so I drove by and they were, shining brightly in the tops of those trees. I've often wondered since then if they ever figured out who had done it.

The Dominos regrouped and we started talking about recording our second album.

We had written a few songs during the U.S. tour, although nowhere near enough for an album. As we were all living in different places now it made sense to gather at Eric's house in the Surrey countryside to rehearse and jam and try to come up with some new material. Looking back it's clear that our attempt to record a second Domino album was futile. There was a war of egos going down between Eric and Jim, and Jim and myself. Carl was indifferent. Jim was all on his own because he was in his own world. He cared less about any of us and was going through the whole experience with blinders on. He really couldn't appreciate what we had anymore and whom we were with. He wanted more than just being the best drummer there was playing in one of the best bands around. He wanted to be a big star like Eric and would do anything to achieve his goal. It didn't work out the way that he had planned. He wanted to sing and play not only piano but guitar as well. He was totally consumed with himself. He sang like he was lost. He was. He certainly didn't need to be trying to play guitar either—we had Eric Clapton as our guitar player. We entered the studio with all of this anxiety and anger going down.

When we first started recording, we were based in the small studio B at Olympic. It was pretty much like the last time we were in the studio. We didn't have any songs really, except for "High" and "Got to Get Better in a Little While," both of which we had played on the US tour. I remember Eric telling me in the doorway of the control room that for him, *Layla* was the epitome of his career and he could not see how we were going to top that. I told him that all we needed to do was what we did in the first place, write some more songs and keep recording. That's what we were doing anyway. But now Jim wanted in on our writing, and he couldn't write a song. That was not what he was good at. You have got to have that special place open for a song to flow through. He certainly was not open to anything else other than himself. He thought that it was all coming from him. He didn't have a clue about melodic and lyrical creativity. He was the drummer and I told him so many times. Eric and I wrote the songs and sang them and he should do what he did best, play drums and leave the singing and songwriting to us. So the sessions really never got off the ground because it was just one clever thing after the next playing wise. What few songs that we had were lacking in substance. Eric had already poured his heart out with *Layla*, so his inspirational well was dry. At first, we tried to just make up things like "Snake Lake Blues" but the lyrics were never written. It came about right after Eric had bought a full sized upright grand piano for the front room at Hurtwood. That was the first thing that happened after it was delivered. I had no piano to write on at my house so he bought this one for me to use. It was beautiful and had a huge sound. This was when he and I were writing songs for the second studio record. I was just sitting at the new piano and Eric walked in and said, "Let's write something. What shall it be about?" We were running out of inspirational subject matter because the girl thing had sort of diminished. I said, "The only thing that I know about is a lake where I used to go and catch snakes, we called it snake-lake." It was actually Reelfoot Lake in Tennessee, where I lived as a boy. I started playing the whole thing with Eric right then and there. The whole progression just came forth, even though neither Eric or myself planned for it to come out the way that it did. It just did. He and I had a way about writing that worked effortlessly. We then started on a song called "Dear Veronica" there in Eric's front room. He and I took what we did very seriously and were very protective of our relationship as a songwriting team. But even we couldn't get blood from a turnip. We couldn't force the songs out. The fact was that the drugs and alcohol had taken their toll on us in every way. I didn't finish and record "Dear Veronica" until a few years ago. Now it's on CoCo's and my *Lovers* CD.

So you see, Derek and the Dominos never really had any business going back in the studio at all. We had just come from recording our first record and went straight into a tour and were fresh off of it and straight into the studio to start another record. We should have taken a longer rest and given ourselves a chance, but we didn't.

Jim had nothing to do with any of the songs as far as writing them was concerned so he made up for it by getting very technical with his playing. Eric could keep up but I couldn't and didn't want to even try to get in that race. Jim would do something clever and Eric would top it. That was the way the whole thing was going down. Carl was sort of just there. He kept real quiet during those sessions and so did I. It was as if there was some sort of rivalry going down between Eric and Jim. Jim and Eric's musical battle was one that I wasn't prepared for, either emotionally or with ability. My musical prowess could not match theirs, except when I was on the B3 or singing. But Eric had me playing piano more and more and at that time I was not what I thought to be an accomplished piano player, I was an organ player. Now don't get me wrong, I'm real glad that Eric insisted that I play the piano because I play it more than I do organ now. And it is my primary instrument for my songwriting today. But back then it was a challenge for me. Here I was with the best guitar player and drummer in the world and me banging away on the piano thinking about Memphis Slim and Jerry Lee Lewis and my mama playing piano. Those were the only influences that I had to draw from and as it would turn out they were pretty good ones from a very deep well. I heard Memphis Slim recently and was astounded at how much we are alike in our simple approach to the piano. I didn't know that what I was doing on the piano was good. It took me several years and listening to all of my records one time to realize that I was an integral part of everything that I was involved with. I thought that I was just getting by. I still play the same way that I did when I first sat down during George's session and played on "Beware of Darkness." That was really me learning to play piano. I was just doing the best that I could with what limited experience that I had. I hadn't been out in the world very long and was just getting my feet wet. There were times that it was all that I could do to keep up.

Everyone was very high during those sessions. Our drug intake was at its maximum, and our tolerance level was way down. So by the end of each session tension was in the air. I wasn't as excited about us going back into the studio as I thought I was going to be because there seemed to be a real sense of paranoia among us that was brought on by the drugs. Heroin and cocaine will do that to you eventually. So we were doing what turned out to be not that many sessions in the small room and when Jim got a new set of drums we moved into the big room. But we never hit a lick in there because that was when it would be all over.

Some of the songs that we were doing were good, like "High," which is one of my very favorite songs. The movement that slows down in the middle is beautiful. What a great song, but a shame we never finished it. Eric had the engineer take the two-inch tape off of the machine and run it backwards. Eric then played a very high pattern and recorded to the tape playing backwards. Then they took the tape off and put it back right and when it was played back there was this very cool continuous indistinguishable something laying down in the track. What you are hearing is Eric's guitar backwards, very innovative and creative for the time. "Evil," "Got to Get Better in a Little While" and "Snake Lake Blues" are the only tracks that I really like from those sessions, even though they were not really finished. They had real potential to be great songs. You don't hear any keyboards on quite a few numbers. That's because I wasn't going to play on a bunch of material that I felt was not as good as it could be and have that left as a part of my legacy. I felt very strongly about that.

On top of that, Jim Gordon was going into the studio without any of us knowing it and doing things on his own, and even brought in Renée Armand in for one song called "Devil Road." He was basically trying to record a solo album using our studio time, and he got to the point where he was acting like he really did know how to sing and write songs, and play guitar and piano. He was doing way too much heroin and coke mixed together and shooting it so he was thinking up all sorts of rubbish. Actually, we were all in a pretty strange place because of the drugs. There was a lot of anger and paranoia amongst us, especially in matters to do with money. I don't know how he went about it, but Jim had worked something out at the office, and had bought a new set of drums and a new car. We couldn't figure how he suddenly appeared to have this large amount of money to spend. Everything was supposed to have been equal. Eric and I were both on fixed incomes from the office, and the tour money was just an added extra. But we had spent ours. Maybe Jim didn't spend all of his money like Eric and I did. Come to think of it, I don't remember Jim ever buying anything. Jim and Carl had their own arrangements with the office. As far as I was concerned, we all ate it on that tour and here he is getting a new car. It wasn't just a money thing, because that car wasn't a whole lot of money back then, not like it would be now. It was more a matter of principle. It didn't sit well with any of us. Jim asked for Eric, Carl, and me to meet him in front of his flat because he was going to pull up in his new car that he was so damn proud of. We didn't know what it was all about because he wouldn't tell us. It was supposed to have been some kind of big surprise. He didn't have to tell us because when we heard it we knew. We were standing out on the street as he came around the corner in a solid white Ferrari Daytona Spyder. It was white inside and out and was drop-dead gorgeous. Eric and I were both thinking, "What the hell is all this about?" This guy doesn't even know anything about cars.

We never did find out how he did it, because that night would be the last time that all four of us would ever play together. That evening was our last time to ever be in the same room at the same time. It was pretty damn cold in that studio that night, and I'm not talking about the temperature. The atmosphere was so thick that you could have cut it with a knife. Jim Gordon carried that with him anyway. He was sort of chilling to be around. Along with his new white car, he had gotten a brand new set of drums with twelve toms on it. It had two kicks and a row of toms that spanned from the smallest to the largest right across the front of the kit and right around to the two big floor toms in a spiral. A great kit of drums, but they each had to be tuned separately to a certain note on the piano. He was a very musical drummer and would play a melody on them. "A Game Called Life" on my first album is a good example of that. So we had to sit through him tuning twelve drums for hours on end. My job was easy, just monotonous. All I did was hit the same damn note over and over and over. It took hours. Eric was just sitting up against the wall all of this time with his guitar in his lap waiting patiently, smoking about a half pack of cigarettes while he waited. He had put on a new set of strings and stretched them out and was trying to get in tune as well. All of this taking place while Jim is banging away and I am hitting the same note again and again. It was maddening. Carl just sat there with his back to the glass and never said a word. After several hours of Jim tuning all of those drums came the break-in warm up. He was a hell of a drummer but after two or three hours all we wanted to do was to get on with it. Finally he stopped his drum solo and Eric started to tune his guitar for the first time without drums banging.

He was simply tuning his guitar and had not said a word. Then Jim said sharply, "Do you want me to tune that damn thing for you?" I looked over at Carl and he looked at me at the same time, thinking, "Oh shit!" Eric stood up and shouted back to Jim, "I'll never play with you again!" And with that he set his guitar down and walked out the door and kept to his word. He had finally had enough of Jim Gordon. When Eric walked out Jim looked puzzled, as if he had no idea what had happened. He didn't even know what he had done because he was so wrapped up in himself because of his drug intake. He had crossed the line big time and did not even realize it.

I had been drinking and doing blow while all of this was going down. When it had finally sunk in we left the studio and went back to Jim's flat, the place where it all got started. I was sitting on the couch and got up to go to the restroom and, when I did, I started to fall because I had real bad vertigo. I was falling forward and as I fell I was trying to catch myself but couldn't and fell headfirst right onto the radiator on the wall. Bruce took me to the hospital and they put some butterfly tape on my forehead to keep me from scarring. It didn't work and I still have a three-inch scar in my forehead that is just now fading after all of these years. The next day I went out to Eric's to see how he was and what we should do next, but he did not want to talk about what had happened. I could not help but notice that Jim's picture was down off the window ledge. It was in the trash. Carl's was next to go, and mine never did come down off of the window ledge while I was still around. It had started with just Eric and me and after all of this time, it seems that it ended with just Eric and me.

Going Solo

Derek and the Dominos just dissolved without anything further being considered or discussed. The fact is that band would not have been together very much longer anyway because of Jim Gordon, even if the argument in the studio had not happened. I was not going to continue to play with Jim any longer myself. I had my fill of him. Eric just beat me to the punch. We could have called Jim Keltner in as a replacement and gotten the problem solved easily enough. There were a lot of bands that continued to perform when they were all on junk and we were one of them. Jim was going to have to go no matter what. I'm sure we would have all fared much better with a solid man like Jim Keltner to rely on, in more ways than one. But that drug thing seems to give everyone an excuse to do nothing. They take no responsibility for their actions or their lives. I'm speaking with a voice of authority here because I'm talking about me, too. I had a hell of a time growing out of myself and realizing what I had become. For years I went to counselors, shrinks, psychologists, making myself promises that I couldn't keep and operating on fear and guilt. I went to different therapists and groups like AA and NA but I just kept right on wrecking my ship every time I thought that it was clear sailing. I just went into a downward spiral and kept right on falling deeper and deeper into the nothingness that had filled my mind until it finally exploded. I completely fell apart in 2001. I had a complete mental, physical, and emotional breakdown.

After the Dominos split, Eric went home to Hurtwood Edge and locked himself away from the public and music world. He felt that he had nothing more to give. He had gambled everything by pouring his emotions out on our record and it failed to get him Pattie. He basically went into a self-imposed exile and at the time I had no idea when, or even if, he would ever make it back. The hardest part of it was that it affected everyone around him, but he was unaware of it. When you are doing heroin you feel isolated and insulated from everything and everyone, and especially from the physical and emotional pain that you're going through. Trouble was, we had a band and there were more people involved in his world than just him and Alice. And she wasn't a part of anything except his nightmare. They would have really bad arguments, especially when they became desperate for heroin. I heard that Eric got so angry once that he smashed his beautiful Zemaitis 12-string acoustic against the wall until there was nothing left but the neck.

The tapes for my first solo album were just sitting on a shelf in the front room at Sunny Heights gathering dust. It's not that I wasn't interested in doing anything with them, it was that my priority was getting Eric to change his mind and to come out and play Dominos with me. But that was clearly not going to happen anytime soon, so I decided I needed to try and get a new solo deal and make sure my album got released. Fate gave me a helping hand because Bobby Keys rang me and asked me to come over to

France and hang out with him and the Stones while they were recording their new album. It was summer and it sounded like a good idea at the time so I packed my bag and did just that. I flew over to Nice and headed off to the Villa Nellcote, a beautiful 16-room waterfront mansion that once served as the local Gestapo headquarters for the Nazis during World War II. The basement was turned into a makeshift studio for the band. When I arrived one of the first people that I met was Jimmy Miller, who was producing the sessions. As I wandered around the large rooms, I couldn't help noticing a large sugar bowl full of coke with a butter knife in it, sitting on a table. You could just help yourself and I did. Gram Parsons, who was a friend of Keith Richards, was staying at the villa during the time when I was over there and he stayed pretty close to the sugar bowl. He was a country music purist and I believe Keith revered that in Gram. He stayed true to his school and never ventured away from that. He had a song that comes to mind that he played for me one time at the Plantation and it was called "She." It was just Gram and his guitar and myself sitting in the kitchen in the middle of a summer afternoon and he was singing to me, "Oh, she sure could sing!" What a great moment that was.

I had been there for several days in and out of the villa and all over the countryside. The villa was set high on a cliff that overlooked a bay and just below was Aristotle Onassis's yacht. It had a helicopter pad and was rather long and was solid white. I was impressed. I thought I wouldn't mind having one just like it as well as the lifestyle that went with it. Jimmy and I had started a dialogue that included the possibility of us doing a deal. He wanted me to sign with Jimmy Miller Productions and asked me if I had a manager or someone representing me. I told him that I didn't. He introduced me to George Greif, his manager. George had discovered Jose Feliciano and other acts and was a familiar figure in the record industry. We all got on really well. After hanging out with Bobby and the Stones I felt I needed to go back home. I couldn't keep up with those guys. I don't mean to insinuate that everyone there was wasted, because that was not the case at all. Charlie is a class act as are Bill and Mick Taylor. Nicky Hopkins was there and he was doing what I wanted to do on that record and that was to play piano on a couple of rock 'n' roll songs. He was a great player and I had nothing but respect for him. Actually the only people who were hovering around the sugar bowl that was full of cocaine, not sugar, were Gram and me. I never did see anybody else taking any drugs at all. That includes Keith. Now how they looked was a different story completely. You can tell when someone is high on cocaine or heroin. Or both. I remember one evening being asked by Bianca if I would sing a song for her and Anita and a couple of other girls who were there at the chateau. I said that I would be very happy to. There was a small grand piano. The setting was perfect. It was facing out the window overlooking the harbor. I had some really beautiful ballads that I had written and they were my choice to sing. I did "Thorn Tree" on the piano and I can't remember the rest. I was sitting with my back to them and they were all decked out and looking like the fine women they were. Or at least thought that they were. When I got finished playing "Thorn Tree in the Garden" I got up to leave the room. As I was walking out I heard Anita laughingly say to Bianca, "He had his shirt tucked in his underwear." I was totally embarrassed. I always tucked my shirt in my underwear if I was wearing any. It keeps the shirt from coming out. I still do it when I need to.

Before heading back to England I went to St. Tropez with Jimmy Miller and George Greif and stayed at Zsa Zsa Gabor's house for a couple of days. I met Salvador Dalí at a party that she threw at her home. More importantly, I met a girl there who really took a liking to me. Her name was Yvelyne. She was from Tahiti and was fabulously wealthy and owned houses all over the world including one in Paris. She and I got on really well and she kept saying, "Je t'aime, mon cheri" to me all the time, especially in private moments. I'm sure you know what I'm talking about. Our lives consisted of being up for an early breakfast and into the launch and off to a little island for bouillabaisse and Cold Duck, a very tasty drink indeed. After about a week of staying on different boats and lying in the sun and generally doing nothing but going from one place to another drinking and eating all day long, it was time for me to go home. Jimmy and George decided that they were going to drive back to Paris and see the countryside and invited me along. I took them up on their offer and we were on our way. I said goodbye to my new friends and left with Jimmy and George. We were about an hour into our journey back to Paris when they started talking about how Yvelyne and I were getting on. They asked me what I thought of her and I told them that she was really nice but she kept saying "Je t'aime, je t'aime" to me all the time and I didn't know what it meant. They said that she was telling me that she loved me. I thought that they had set me up with her, but I just didn't know for sure. Either way, Yvelyne and I kept seeing each other for quite some time after our initial meeting.

One of the last times Eric and I actually went out to socialize was when we went to London to see Leon Russell at the Rainbow Theatre on December 2, 1971. It was the opening show of a three-night run. We went to the gig in Eric's lilac Ferrari and we sat in the balcony to the left of the stage. Unfortunately the sound there was really terrible so I could not enjoy the show. Denny Cordell, who was Leon's partner in Shelter Records, was there that night. There were a ton of hangers-on as well. After their performance everyone came up to see us in our balcony seats. We didn't go down to the backstage area, which was the usual protocol, because Eric was not up to seeing a lot of people and answering too many questions. They all came up to see us instead. Leon asked me how the sound was and I told him the truth. Eric did not get up and play that night, but I heard that he joined the band on stage on the last night, although he stayed in the shadows at the back so he would not be recognized. He really was not in great shape.

Bobby Keys called me to say that he and the Stones were in Olympic Studios in Barnes, and that Jimmy had asked if I would come down because he wanted to carry on the conversation we started in Nice. Jimmy had plenty of time to talk with me because it was a session where they didn't really know what they were going to do. Mick was just running down ideas and everyone was just sitting around waiting on Keith to show. Mick and I got to talking about my background as a preacher's son, and that's when he came up with the song, "I Just Want to See His Face." Jimmy was great in the studio and had a way of hearing things that I could relate to. He heard things really raw, and with the Stones it doesn't get any more raw than that! He did an incredible job of capturing the moment. Kind of like a great photographer has a way of capturing the moment when his subject is in just the right position and the light is just right. *Exile on Main Street* was recorded over a period of a couple of years. They didn't keep very good records back then and just a few years ago I had one of Mick's guys calling me to confirm Mick's accounting of it all for a book trying to set the record straight on those sessions. They did a couple of tracks while they were waiting on Keith to show. When he finally did show up at about 3 in the morning he added his parts and started recording. At one point in a solo he nodded out. He just stopped playing and the rest of the band kept on and finished the take and came inside the control to listen back. Keith was out cold! Jimmy rolled the tape and when it got to that place in the song he hit record and Keith picked up the solo right where he left off. I had never seen anything like it. Jimmy somehow knew that Keith would fire back up at the right moment. That's how in tune he was. He was a good man and I always considered him a good friend. He certainly left his mark in the music world with his wonderful productions.

Jimmy told me that he was getting ready to leave for L.A. in a few days and that he had talked with his manager. George said that he was interested in managing my career. I had never had anybody interested in being my manager, even though Robert Stigwood was technically, because he was the Dominos' manager as well as Eric's. At last it seemed like something positive was happening for me. I had a party at Sunny Heights to celebrate the fact that I was going to be signing a new solo contract and flying off to Los Angeles. The day after the party Bruce was cleaning up and I told him that I would be going to the States in a few weeks' time, probably for a few months, and for him to watch after the place while I was gone. Right about that time the phone rang and it was my dad calling from America telling me that they had all gotten tickets and passports and were on their way to England to see me in about a week's time. I didn't expect it or even see it coming because I hadn't seen my family in several years. We rarely even spoke. My dad, the Baptist preacher, was against what I did for a living. He was also a captain and chaplain with the Memphis Sheriff's Department and would have had no problem making an example of me if he was to find out about the drugs and alcohol and my way of life. He would have had no problem having me busted and sent to jail to set an example for someone else who might think of choosing this path. I went into panic mode. I called the travel agent and had a ticket arranged for me to leave for L.A. two days later. I called and told my dad that I had to go on the road and that we would have to make it another time. Two days later I left Sunny Heights and would never live there again. After me not coming back there for several months the Apple offices thought that I wasn't going to come back there to live. They didn't want someone other than me living there, even if he did work for me, so Apple took the house back and sent Bruce packing. He moved everything out for me and put everything in storage and would soon be joining me in the United States.

I flew over with my first solo album tapes and met with Jimmy, George and Sid Garris, George's partner and a lovely man who loved my singing. We all met in George's office in the Greif-Garris Building on Beverly Boulevard. The first thing George did was to put a production deal together with him, Jimmy and myself. George also became my manager. As soon as I signed on the dotted line we walked down the street to the office of Jay Lasker, the head of ABC Dunhill in Los Angeles, and presented him *Bobby Whitlock*, my first recording. They worked out a deal and we took the tapes to Sunset Sound in Hollywood to make final mixes and overdubs where needed. ABC decided I should start recording my second album as soon as possible. As we were in the studio anyway it made sense to start straight away, so I put a band together for the sessions that included Rick Vito on guitar. Mick Jagger and Keith Richards came to hang out with us at both the demo and the recording sessions. I remember they were impressed with Rick and kept asking who this guitarist was. Hoyt Axton heard I was in town recording a new album. I had known him since the Dominos days and he came by George Greif's office one day and said that he had written a song for me called "Ease Your Pain," a ballad that talked about Jesus. He sang it for me. I really loved the song but decided that I would do it up-tempo. George also got the Edwin Hawkins Singers to sing background on the record, a very big deal at that time because they were still riding high with "Oh Happy Day." I also had the L.A. Symphony play on "Back Home in England." It was all done pretty much live and very quickly. I literally had two records going at the same time. They could have released it as a double album because tracks from both sessions were on both albums. Jimmy Miller did an incredible job of capturing the moment. George started putting together a tour to support my two new records. He was used to dealing with another side of the industry, the Vegas and Hollywood side. He had no knowledge of and had never been around rock 'n' rollers before. He didn't respect us at all. He just tolerated us because he managed Jimmy Miller. George was very good friends with Jimmy's dad, a very powerful man in Las Vegas, hence the connection. I put together a very good little rock 'n' roll band with Rick Vito on guitar, Eddie Tuduri on drums and Keith Ellis on bass. We rehearsed in L.A. and by the time we started our tour we were more than ready to go. As soon as I knew the tour was taking place, I called Bruce McCaskill to come over and join me as road manager. It was great having him with me, especially as we had been working together ever since the Delaney and Bonnie days.

The band was tight and everyone was very excited about going out on the road. Our first gig was at some hole in the wall, just where I do not remember, but it was a complete letdown for everyone. A more worthwhile gig was the one we did at the notorious Max's Kansas City at 213 Park Avenue South, New York. It was a great show and it was also great fun being in New York. Another not-so-pleasant show was in Columbus, Ohio, at a club called Dr. Brown's Descent. There was a bullet hole in the life-sized poster of me that was hanging out in the front window of the club, and it went downhill from there. Someone let off a smoke bomb during our set and the fire sprinkler system went off and the place had to be evacuated. The show was over barely two songs into the set. Despite some low points the band was really rocking and we went ahead and played every hole that George had booked for us. He got us the wrong agent, and that was just his error in judgment. The worst event happened after a show at a club in Minneapolis. Afterwards I was talking with a few friends and Bruce came to me and said that we should be going since we were walking and it was quite a way back to the hotel. We had been paid cash for the show and Bruce put it in the same aluminum briefcase that he used on the last Dominos U.S. tour. This time it held our night's payroll as well as the previous gigs, our passports and airline tickets to the next venue. It was very late and just as we turned the corner across the street from our hotel, we walked right into the business end of a .44 caliber Smith and Wesson, fully loaded and cocked back, and it was being held by a very nervous black dude. He demanded the briefcase and our wallets. I told Bruce to give him

Left: *Performing at Max's Kansas City with my new band (courtesy Eddie Tuduri).* **Right:** *At Max's: Rick Vito (left, background), me, Eddie Tuduri and Keith Ellis (courtesy Eddie Tuduri).*

everything and he did. He took it all and turned and ran away into the dark of night. We stood there sort of stunned. As soon as Bruce and I got back to our room we called the club owner who just happened to be the chief of police. He said that we would have everything back by morning, which was only a few hours away. Sure enough, after a late breakfast, our things were returned to us by the police. They said that it was easy to figure out. That guy was trying to use my ticket to get on an airplane with the briefcase full of everything that he would need for his very long vacation. I never heard anything about whatever happened to that dude either. I was just glad to have our property back, especially my passport, otherwise it would have taken weeks to get a new one issued before being able to get back to England.

While I was on tour in the United States George had made a deal for my albums to be released by CBS in England. "Ease Your Pain" was on the U.K. edition of *Bobby Whitlock* and also came out there as a single. The two albums were released a few months apart. *Bobby Whitlock* came out in June 1972 with *Raw Velvet* coming out later in the year. The press advertising could not mention Eric Clapton and George Harrison due to contractual reasons, but word soon got out anyway. The label organized a few shows for the press in London for me to promote the albums. I used the same band as the US tour and played at the Speakeasy on July 26, the Kings Cross Cinema on July 28 and back to the Speakeasy on July 29.

Fun and Games with Keith Moon

Keith Moon and I were very good friends. He would always greet me with a cheery "Bobby, dear boy!" He lived down the road from me when I lived in Chertsey and we spent a great deal of time together. I loved Moonie! We had the same likes and dislikes. We loved being completely free to be whatever we wanted to be. If it came to mind it was done. Our lives then were fantasies played out on the stage of life. They were made up as we went along with no rules and no boundaries. He lived in a beautiful four-towered cuboidal construction called Tara. The original owner had named it after the house in the classic *Gone with the Wind*. It was a stark white place inside and out, just beautiful and very modern looking. Not unlike something you would see in a futuristic episode of Doctor Who. Keith had bought it in early 1971 and The Who had a huge party there to launch *Who's Next*. There was a pub right at the end of his drive. We would spend every Sunday at the pub and on the front lawn of Tara. A rave-up was always in the making. After a few brandies and some Dom and a few Pimm's No. 1 cups, out came the blue meanies and mayhem would ensue.

He had some beautiful cars parked on the grounds along with some very hot hot rods—an AC Cobra and a T-Bucket with straight pipes. It was so powerful that it would stand on end. He had a beautiful Rolls-Royce Corniche and my favorite, a Morgan with a wooden frame and a V8. It was awesome. He never drove any of them farther than the end of his drive because he didn't have a license and couldn't get one, especially in the shape he stayed in with a brandy in one hand. Not to mention the fact that he had accidentally run over a guy that worked for him and dragged him down the road a ways without knowing it. He didn't make it either. I know that it hit Keith real hard and he never really got over it. Keith and his wife, Kim, told me all about the incident one day. It was an accident, of course, but Keith lived with the guilt for the rest of his days. When he needed to be somewhere, he had his personal assistant, Dougal, drive him. But when he was home and fancied a drive he would just get very loose and drive all over the grounds at Tara with me right there with him. It was way too much fun, grown men playing cars in the yard, doing donuts on the front lawn in an AC Cobra. He finally flew it over the fence and totaled that one. I'm smiling and laughing as I reflect on this lovely man. He was a dear friend and one of the most generous people that I ever knew. He was completely selfless.

He had a swimming pool in the back of the house with an underwater sound system. He also had a deep-sea diver's suit with a big round head on it—you've seen them in the movies, I'm sure. He would put it on, turn up the music and jump in to the bottom of the pool and stay there like Forrest Gump. Too funny! When I left England and Sunny Heights to go play in America I had no place to stay when I came back after my brief tour. Moonie said that he had a couple of houses and that I could have my choice. One was in London and was modern with a moat around it, the other was on the River Thames and had four large round rooms and came with a beautiful mahogany Chris-Craft boat, and a private dock with a boat house. The main house had round windows and large curved windows that looked out over the Thames. It was white and very nautical looking and was the one that I moved into until I got my place in Ascot some time later. It was perfect for me at that time—I was running around in circles, so it seemed very appropriate. The only thing that I had to remember to do was to go down to the boat every now and then and turn on a bilge pump that emptied the water that would get in through rain and just from sitting still in the water. I had my friend and driver Dave Long driving me everywhere to get things for the house. Weeks went by and I hadn't checked on the boat but a couple of times. I never really went out in it, I mainly just looked at it because it was so beautiful. It looked great floating there at the end of the dock. I would sometimes go down and sit in it and drink champagne and watch the other boats pass by and wave at them all. It seemed like the thing to do. Anyway, one day I happened to look down there and it was gone. I thought, "Oh no! Someone's stolen the *Mayflower!*" I ran outside and down to the dock and I saw the rope stretched real tight downwards and I could see that it was still attached to something. I just couldn't see the boat. I could just make out the chrome ring that was on the front of it that it was attached to. It had sunk, it was my fault and I felt really bad. I had to tell Keith and he said, "Not to worry, dear boy!" What a guy!

C'est la Vie!

I had not seen my French girlfriend in a while. She wasn't interested in coming to England because she thought that it was very boring. In fact, she had never been over to see me and had no interest in doing so. So I would travel to and from France on a regular basis to see her. Yvelyne had her house there on Avenue Foch. It was a beautiful four-story place that had a cobblestone courtyard and a carriage house. Her parents had a huge place six blocks away on the same street. It used to be the Nazi headquarters during the war. That place was beautiful, as was hers, but her parents' place was full of Louis XIV furniture—the real thing. It looked like a live-in museum. There were oil paintings on the walls and on every ceiling in the place. I have never seen anything like it to this day. Those folks were loaded! I flew over and arrived at Yvelyne's house one day and she told me that her car had just been stolen from right in front of her place. I said that she should contact the police and she said that by the time her car would be found it would be stripped and worth nothing and it was just entirely too much trouble. She said that she would just go buy another one. It turned out to be a brand new Porsche Targa. Way too much money! All those folks did was go out to eat and drink wine and party then go somewhere else and do the same thing. Actually, now that I stop to think about it, that's exactly what I did when I was home. She hung out with Bianca Jagger as well as Eddie Barclay, the owner of Barclay Records in Paris. They were the very elite set and everyone that they ran with was incredibly wealthy. I would become friends with Eddie Barclay as well in time. His record company owner would be my label in France for my first two records.

Once I met and dined with Baron Philippe de Rothschild in Paris. We all went into his wine cellar and had some vintage wines, a pretty incredible experience for me at such a young age. At the dinner was an older woman named Madame Patino, who was having a coming-out party for one of her four daughters, and I was asked to play for the event. I went back home and got it all together to come back over for the big event. I had just done those shows in London, so I had my band with Rick Vito on guitar, Eddie Tuduri on drums and Keith Ellis on bass guitar. We were a loud rock 'n' roll band, for sure. This was a black tie event and was very formal. I had my tailor in London make me a special suit just for it. It was a burgundy crushed velvet jacket with short tails and had two large gold buttons with a gold chain draped from one to the other. The lapels and the stripe going down the sides of my legs were silk. There I was, in solid burgundy and looking fabulous with my silk Deborah and Clare shirt along with my silk scarf. The party was held in an elegant old palace in Paris that had a very long room that backed onto a wall of glass and spectacular gardens and fountains like I had never seen before. There were about five very long tables set up, stacks of plates and bowls and about three or four different glasses for each person. There were at least three different forks and three or four different knives and spoons for each person as well. I had never seen anything like it in my life. This room had eight chandeliers made of orchids. They were about ten feet across and full of candles and were absolutely beautiful, and were going to last only that evening. I was told that each chandelier cost $250,000. Such decadence! This was some kind of a do. The folks back home would not have believed this one for sure. They had invited only the most influential and wealthy people that they knew for her daughter's party. There was a prince from somewhere with his wife and a lot of different people from all over the world. A lot of different accents were in the room.

When we arrived, Madame Patino was at the front of the line to greet everyone as they walked in. Next in line were her four daughters all standing in accordance with their ages, the youngest being last in line and standing next to their secretary, the woman who looked after the needs of the family. The plan was supposed to be that when I entered I was supposed to bow and take her hand and kiss it. Then I was to do the same right down the line. This was really my kind of thing and I was already dressed for the occasion. I walked up to Madame and took her hand and shook it and said, "How ya doin'!" I did the same to each of the daughters all the way down to the youngest then I bowed to her and kissed her hand and shook the secretary's hand and went on in.

We had assigned seats. Yvelyne was seated directly across from me at a very wide and very long table. I didn't know where to start and what to do with all the silverware in front of me. She said to me very politely, "Just start from the outside, darling, and work your way in." Easier said than done for me. There were about seven courses in this meal and three wines. It takes a very long time to eat a meal of such planning and proportions. All the while Yvelyne was playing with my feet under the table and generally trying to get me to do something funny or mess up in some way. I was always the first to knock over the wine glasses or walk away from the table with the tablecloth caught on my belt buckle or something ridiculous like that. Those sorts of things were always befalling me. But I was just getting broken in on hanging with the incredibly rich and boring. I was the only life to the party as far as I could see. They were all very quiet eaters—I mean, not a sound was made, and everyone sort of talked without making any noise. There was a murmur in the room that was annoying the hell out of me. Finally I tapped on the side of my glass with my knife several times and the place went deafeningly quiet all at once and every eye was on me. I said very loudly, "By now I guess that you are all wondering why I called you all to be here for dinner." No one thought that it was very funny at all. They all spoke French or Dutch or Iranian or something other than English so communicating was not so easy. This was a full-blown all-night affair that was going on and I had not even got to play yet. I was to play after the meal, which had started with some wine and soup followed by another wine and a salad. Then came some other something all around the table that everyone took tiny bites of, including me. Then came a different wine, and a huge lobster tail was set in front of each of us. After a couple of glasses more of that very fine wine I was starting to get a bit loopy as was everyone else in a quiet sort of way. Next came an aperitif. I didn't know what it was and it didn't matter at this point, but it tasted awful. Yvelyne told me this was to cleanse my palate, but it was already washed clean with all of the wine I'd been drinking. This was the halfway point, or so I was told. All the while she kept playing with my feet, trying to get me to do something. She was a rebel rich girl and I was the rebel rock star. They brought round a very fine little crystal dish that sat up on a stem and it was full of water with a lemon floating in it. The room was incredibly quiet. I took the lemon out of mine and got Yvelyne's lemon as well and squeezed them in the water and took some sugar and put it in and stirred it all together and turned it up and drank it all. When I put it down on the table I looked to my left and they all looked like fanned cards with the person at the end of the table with his head on it. They were all looking and had been watching me during this whole time making lemonade from my finger bowl. No one but Yvelyne and my band appreciated my humorous ways. Those people in Paris that she hung out with were the most boring people I ever was to be around, then or since. It seemed to me that there was no substance to their lives. I had my fill of them as well and went back to England as quickly as I could.

Yvelyne and I saw each other only once after that. I went to Nice to see her. But the days before I headed to Heathrow, I had been slamming pretty hard with Keith Moon. Even though I hadn't done any hard drugs in a few days I still had them in my system. When I say hard drugs I am referring to Valium, cocaine and Mandrax. I had stuck an ounce of compressed pot in the crotch of my underwear so that I would have some smoke when I got there. A compressed ounce of pot is about as big as small box of matches. It was pretty easy to conceal. I boarded the plane for Nice and I was in the first class section in the second row by the aisle. Once we were in the air I ordered a large brandy and dry ginger. Within minutes, that one drink had knocked me out. I was told that I was lying across the aisle and the stewardess thought that I had died at first. They could not wake me up at all. It must have been the combination of drugs still in my system. The next thing I remember was sitting in a straight-back chair in the middle of the French customs office at the Nice airport in my underwear. They had taken off all of my clothes. As soon as I realized where I was and what had happened I said in a real southern accent, "What the hell's going on here?" The customs official said, "He's a bloody American!" Actually he said something in French that preceded American but I didn't know what it was. I knew what he meant though. They threw my clothes at me and told me to get out of there and that I had better not cause any trouble while I was there in France. I was very fortunate that they didn't look in my underwear. I had a car waiting outside for me and I got in and was taken to my hotel on the Riviera. It was right on the beach and looked just like it does in the movies.

Yvelyne had her brother with her and he was a lovely guy. I figured she brought him along it was because she was going to tell me au revoir and she may have been a little concerned about how I was going to react. We three were on the beach, and she told me that her father had me checked out and that the people that I was running with were not to his liking and that she would have to end the relationship. I had no problem with it at all and simply got up and walked to my room, packed my bag and called my car to take me to the airport. A few hours later I was home with my feet up playing my guitar and pondering my next adventure. My French girlfriend was no more. Oh, well, c'est la vie!

Going Gold

Eric's name had been in constant motion, even when he was standing still for those two years that he was in hiding, thanks to a sustained public relations campaign by his management. Robert Stigwood released *The History of Eric Clapton*, a double album compilation, in March 1972. This was when Eric had started getting serious about staying at home and doing heroin. Robert knew how important it was to keep Eric's name alive, even if it meant releasing old material. I remember at the time that people thought that Eric had retired and this career retrospective did nothing do dissuade the record buying public of thinking otherwise. And that was exactly what Robert wanted the public and press to believe, because it was better than admitting Eric was a drug addict. The biggest selling point of the album was the inclusion of two previously unreleased versions of Derek and the Dominos' "Tell the Truth." One was the fast Phil Spector version, which was going to be our first single until we cancelled it, and the other was a long slow instrumental jam based on the main riff of the song. Luckily, "Layla" was also included, on side four of this compilation, which ended up giving our album's title song a massive new lease on life, particularly on the radio. It turned "Layla" into a huge hit when it was released as a single in July 1972, which in turn, sparked a huge revival in our original album and sent it soaring up the charts a year and a half after its original release. It was the album that everybody would have at parties both in the United Kingdom and the United States that summer. It was amazing, especially as I had not realized all this had been going on. When I found out I was pulling up to Eric's house in what would have no doubt been another futile attempt at getting him to come out and play. I was sitting in the back of a Gold Pullman Mercedes limo that used to be Pete Townshend's, with my man Dave behind the wheel. I had a copy of *Rolling Stone*, which I had yet to open, and when I did, it landed right on the announcement "Derek and the Dominos ships gold!" *Layla* had been a slow burner, but it exploded in 1972 with the title track being a top ten hit single both in England and the United States. So the big money started to roll in at last. I had Dave turn around and take me straight away to the office and I got twenty thousand pounds cash from David Shaw. He was the financial comptroller there and handled all of the money for Robert Stigwood. I walked into his office without calling first and said, "I just found out about our record shipping gold and I need some money!" This lovely man in his tailor-made suit says to me "How much?" I didn't have a figure in mind, so I just said, "Twenty thousand pounds!" I should have said fifty. "No problem, Bobby," he said, "but you'll have to wait a few minutes." It took all of fifteen minutes for his runner to arrive back at the office with a sack full of cash from Barclay's Bank. Then David called me back in and handed over the cash, bag and all! I kept that sack for many years.

I had Dave drive me straight to Maranello's Concessionaires in Egham, the Ferrari people who to this day handle all of Eric's needs associated with his passion for Ferraris. I had just returned from France and was still living in that four round-roomed house with the sunken boat, the *Mayflower*, that belonged to Keith Moon. He and I had been up for a day or so slamming. So there I am with twenty grand and some blow still left in my pocket and looking pretty rough with a two-day beard, jeans and a western fringed jacket, and long hair that hadn't been brushed. I must have looked like anything but a well-to-do rock star. As we arrived at Maranello's I had Dave pull up past the front window because I didn't want them to see me getting out of that limo. I was thinking that I didn't want them to think that I had any money. Hell, if I didn't have money what would I be doing there in the first place? All of those cars are expensive! I walked into the showroom and there was a guy down the hall talking on the phone. I signaled him to let him know that I was there. He just nodded and even after he had put the phone down he didn't come over to help me. So I got his attention a few minutes later, and still no response from him. He finally came into the showroom where I had been looking at a little red Dino and a beautiful blue Daytona just like Eric's red one in front of a huge front window. His name was Mike Salmon, and he was a retired race car driver. I was to find out some time later that he was talking about racing on the phone that day to another race car driver. Anyway, I asked him about the price on the Dino and he said, "You can't afford it, son." Then I asked about the Daytona, and he said, "You can't afford that one either!"

I could see where this was going. I leaned out the front door and motioned for Dave to back the limo up in the front of the glass, and I walked out without saying a word and got in the back and told Dave, "Take me to London to H.R. Owens!" It was under a building in the basement of an exclusive store. I can't remember the name of it—it wasn't Harrods but some place like it—but that's not important to this story. We pulled down into this place which had literally dozens of fine rare classic automobiles. I had never seen anything like it. They had vintage Rolls-Royces, Ferraris, Porsches, Mercedes, and right in the middle sat a blue Daytona, just like the one at Maranello's. I asked for the youngest salesman and asked him to bring a bottle of Bell's scotch whiskey when he came. His name was Derek Kindler, and he turned out to be a friend for many years. He walked up and asked what he could do to be of assistance. I told him, "I want that blue Daytona and I'll pay you cash if you will have it insured for me before I leave the building." Insurance in the United Kingdom is a must if you want to drive on their roads. He did and we had a drink to seal the deal and I laid out 10,750 pounds cash. No questions asked, no quibbling over the price, nothing but a clean cash transaction. I didn't even drive it out at first. I just got in it and cranked it up to listen to it. When I did drive away the first place that I went to was Maranello's. I pulled up in the front of the place and Mike was in the showroom with some very distinguished gentleman engaged in a deep conversation. I honked the horn and he looked my way. I gave him the middle-finger high sign and laid two strips of rubber as I smoked the tires out of there. It was immature, I know, but boy, it felt very satisfying. Some time later I was to see him and his wife sitting across the room at the Bailiwick restaurant in Virginia Water. They didn't see me, but I had the waiter take a bottle of Dom Perignon to them. He looked up at me and smiled and nodded his head with hello and thanks. I went over and he introduced me to his wife, who was a lovely lady who had already been filled in on the cocky young rock star. We talked for a while and he told me of his racing days and how he had been burned very badly in a crash and had retired to sell Ferraris rather than race them. We remained friends until I moved away and we lost touch. That blue Daytona was the car in which I would later have a spectacular crash.

I kept on trying to get to Eric on a regular basis, but it seemed impossible to reach him on any level. I was completely pissed off with him. We had written all of these great songs, had a great hit record and had a band without a drummer who could have easily been replaced, and Eric decided to take a heroin hiatus. I was furious with him. After I bought my new Daytona, I went to his house to show it to him and to celebrate our album going gold. But he wouldn't come out. I had brought two bottles of Dom, one for him and one for me. I drank mine while I roamed the gardens while he was deciding whether he was going to come out. I left one bottle on the stairs that led down to the garden. I guess he must have found it eventually. I really thought that with our album finally getting the recognition it deserved he would be willing to get the band back together. I went back to the car and I raced my engine and blew my horn and screamed for him to "Come out of that house!" I had to talk to him myself and get it straight from him what he thought that he was doing. But he had seen his decision through and he was completely alienated from himself. He was not making his own decisions anymore, the heroin was making them all for him. And none of them were good.

He eventually did come to the front door and opened it wide and stood there in the doorway. He was in a tattered tan bathrobe that came down to his knees. He had no shoes on and his hair looked as if it hadn't been washed in weeks. He looked like I imagined Howard Hughes to look when he was laid up in the bed doing drugs, long stringy hair and not very clean. Eric's fingernails had gotten very long and were yellow. He was an absolute mess, and I was really shocked to see my friend in such bad shape. I asked, "What do you think you're doing to us?" He just looked at me in a vacant way and simply said, "Nice car." After a few minutes of staring he asked angrily, "Where did you get the money for that car?" He hadn't even heard about our album going gold. He wasn't reading the newspaper, he was doing heroin. After I had said my piece he turned around and slammed the door and I got back in my car and did a donut around the statue in the front of that beautiful place, slinging gravel everywhere as I tore out of the drive and through the gate and didn't see him after that for a very long time. Eric was angry that I could walk into the office with no money and then walk back out with 20,000 pounds in my pocket because Robert Stigwood had cut him off financially. He did not appreciate the fact that Robert was doing what he thought best and that by cutting off the financial assistance to Eric he would have no money to buy drugs. If you are an addict, that kind of rationale does not register, and it didn't work because Eric and Alice just started selling guitars, rugs and jewelry to get cash for their drug needs. Ron Nevison, who had moved into Eric's house when my old house burned down, was asked by him to sell his guitars on his behalf. Eric may have been a heroin addict, but he realized it would not have looked good for him to do it himself. Not only that, he was in no shape to do it anyway. It put Ron in an awkward position, but he was only following Eric's instructions. He would take whichever guitar it was to be sold to London and sell it and come back home and give the money to Alice. She would then go back to town and score the dope for Eric and herself. She was very strung out most of the time and sadly that would eventually be the cause of her demise. She died in 1995 after a heroin overdose.

New Home, New Girlfriend, New Adventures

After living at one of Keith Moon's houses for many months, I finally found a place of my own in Ascot called Oaklands and had it completely renovated once I had moved in. I'll always remember Keith fondly as a good heart who was full of life and a most generous man, and most importantly, a very, very good friend. When I got my house in Ascot I still had no girlfriend or companion. One of the main reasons I had bought the Daytona, aside from the fact that I wanted what Eric had, was to pick up girls, and I was hoping for a woman! I thought, "Maybe this will work, nothing else has!" I could not find a girlfriend no matter what I did. The first thing was that I couldn't get anybody to get in there with me. They'd all say, "I'm not getting in that car with you." I just looked like trouble, twenty-three, rock star, fast car and a pocket full of dope, drinking Dom. I couldn't blame them, really, because I would not have gotten in there with me either. If you've ever driven, or ridden in, a high-performance automobile like that Daytona Ferrari, you'll know how much power it has. I could pin your head to the back of the seat and you couldn't raise it forward if you tried because it has so much torque. It would go as fast as you wanted to go, and as quick as you wanted it to, and get you there sooner than you needed to be. It was so intense that I broke a tooth once just from the exhilaration.

Oaklands was a lovely two-story brick English Tudor house on several acres with literally thousands of little lead-edged diamond-shaped pieces of glass in all of the windows. It was quite beautiful but very hard to clean. I was lucky because I had a woman who came three times a week to do the house and I hired window cleaners to come every month. The house was set back off the road probably a hundred yards and was very secluded. It had a huge oak tree in the middle of the garden that belonged to the Queen. All of the deer, swans and a lot of special trees belong to her and this was one of them. I wasn't allowed to hang a hammock from it or trim it without special permission. I thought to myself, this is perfect! So I got a long rope and a very secure waterproof sack and hooked the rope to the highest limb. I kept all of my dope in that sack in the top of the Queen's tree. It was protected by the Queen of England! The house had not been lived in since 1928, which was probably why I got it at such a low price. I gutted it and had it painted. Each room was color coordinated. The main room had light gold cloth hopsack walls with long gold velvet drapes that bunched up on the floor. My upstairs bedroom was the same with a beautiful antique brass bed. There was a green bedroom and a royal blue room and the dining room was my music room and that was burgundy. One bedroom was nothing but a large closet with clothes everywhere and each of the room's curtains matched the walls. Then I had the whole house carpeted with long white, deep pile carpet

Oaklands Ascot.

about two inches thick. The kitchen had grass mat flooring. That place was beautiful and it was mine.

One time I had to call some office in London about something or other and this girl answered with the nicest voice. You see where I'm going already, I'm sure, and you're right. I called back just to talk to her. I thought myself to be a good judge of character and I believed and trusted everybody. We made a date for me to pick her up after her work one day. My driver, Dave Long, was my friend as well. I helped him get his start with a limo service. Seemed like a good idea, and it would help keep me from behind the wheel. I wasn't completely irresponsible. We went to London and Dave, as usual, parked the Mercedes Pullman up on the sidewalk next to Harrods. It was not long before a policeman came up to the car and signaled for Dave to roll down the window before telling him to move. Dave just told him to piss off and rolled up the window. The cop got angry and wrote a ticket and stuck it on the window. Dave rolled down the window again and got it, and tore it up and threw it on the ground right in front of the policeman. All of this is going on while I'm in the back getting high while I'm waiting for my date to come out of the building. I had never seen this woman. I had only talked to her. It was a blind date and very exciting! Out she came and Dave opened the door of that beautiful gold Pullman and in stepped this gorgeous blond. Let's call her Julianne. She spoke five languages and was a descendant of a very famous man.

Anyway, we arrived at my home and that was the start of our relationship. Before I knew it, she sort of started leaving things behind. The more she left, the more she returned until she had step by step and very methodically moved herself in! This woman had moved herself in and was telling me that she loved me and I'm telling her that I was in lust, not love. I was in a quandary and didn't know what to do. I asked her to leave and she wouldn't go and it didn't get better. I wanted this woman out of my house and out of my life and straight away. It was a hopeless situation. One night, about three months into this, I was kicking back on my couch watching TV with no sound and playing my guitar, stretched out and comfortable with my feet crossed on the coffee table. She walked into the room wearing a white negligee and had her hands behind her back. She had a strange look on her face, and I asked her, "What are you doing? What are you up to?" Before I knew it she threw a handful of Amplex breath mints at me to distract me and with the other hand and in one motion drew a butcher knife from behind her back with a ten-inch blade and slammed herself in the stomach with it. It sounded like somebody stabbing a sack full of beans. The knife slowly fell out of her stomach and she collapsed onto the floor. I was horrified. I don't know why but the first thing I did after I realized what had happened was to pick up the knife and take it to the kitchen and put it in the sink. I was in shock and clearly not thinking straight. I went back in and picked her up and doubled her knees into her chest and held her like a ball. I held her in my lap as I dialed for the ambulance. Her intestines had come out and I put them back in and held the wound. She was slowly dying in my arms. I heard the ambulance speed past my front gates, sirens screaming. They missed the house twice so I called again and told them that I would meet them on the road. I picked her up and took her out towards the road. She was a small person and I had her doubled up and was carrying her like a big ball. But she was so heavy as she became dead weight that I dropped her in the middle of the front garden. So I picked her back up and carried her; her legs were across my right arm and her shoulders and head were across my left arm. We made it to the road and I sat there on the curb with her in my arms and she with her guts in her lap, and then the ambulance pulled up. The ambulance men arrived and put her in the back and the driver and the other dude immediately started yelling at me and accusing me of stabbing this girl. They shoved me around a bit because they really thought that I had done this. I rode to the hospital in the back of the ambulance with them. There were no police involved at this time.

But when we got to the hospital they were there and they grabbed me and threw me in a car and took me to the interrogation room at the CID headquarters in Windsor. It was a blank room with a table in the middle with a round gooseneck lamp on it, just like in the movies. There were two chairs on one side and one on the other. They came in with some tea for me and brought a wool army blanket for me to wrap up with and the questioning began. I was still covered from head to foot with her dried blood. It was all over my hands and face, and my shirt and pants were completely soaked. She nearly bled to death in my arms. There were two interrogation officers at a time, a nice guy and a not-so-nice guy. I was asked over and over to tell the story of what happened and every time it changed slightly because I kept remembering more and more. I had no attorney as I felt I didn't need one because I didn't do anything. And that's what I kept telling them and telling them over and over and over. But they thought for sure that I had stabbed that girl. I went through sixteen hours of four different pairs of good-guy, bad-guy officers trying to get me to confess, and I wouldn't. Finally, in walked Detective Sergeant John Clements and Sergeant Ken Punter. They said that the surgeon's report had come back and it stated that it was a self-inflicted wound. When she woke up after surgery she said that she did it to herself.

John and Ken said, "Let's take you home. We'll clean the place up for you." When we walked out of the interrogation room everyone applauded on the way out the front door to my freedom. I got in the car with them and we went back home to Oaklands. When we arrived the door was wide open and the whole front entrance was covered with blood. Ken started to clean up the floor and John went out to follow the trail of blood. He came back in and asked me if I knew that she was pregnant. I didn't. He had just found the

The Queen's mighty oak (photograph by Lindsey Bennett).

fetus. It was a boy about three months old and fully formed. She had aborted herself by trying to kill herself and the baby. She succeeded with the child. It aborted in my lap while I was calling the ambulance and I had not realized it. I remember that moment all too well. Sometimes, I wish that I didn't. The nightmare didn't stop there, though. After she was released from the hospital where she had been kept for psychiatric evaluation she showed up one night at my house and in my bedroom. I was sleeping and I woke up to find Julianne standing there in the dark by the side of my bed. When I awakened and saw her standing there by my bedside, she opened her blouse and exposed her wound in the moonlight. It was horrifying. The image that I recall makes me weak even now. It freaked me out and I started screaming in terror. It was a nightmare that had come true! I didn't know if this was really happening or not! I was screaming for her to get out of my bedroom and out of my house! My bodyguard Bob Miller had been there since the night after she stabbed herself. He used to be a bodyguard for Frank Sinatra and Aretha Franklin. I had called my friend Robert Fitzpatrick in the States and told him what had happened and he sent Bob over. Bob heard my screams and came running down the hallway and into my bedroom. He grabbed Julianne and took her out of the house. Then he called Detective Sergeant John Clements straight away and told him what had happened. The police managed to get hold of her and where to this day I do not know, but there was a peace bond put on her and she could not come within fifty yards of me anywhere that I went. That was the beginning of my rapid decline into the drugs and alcohol. And soon I would total my Daytona with Bob in there with me. John Clements and Ken Punter remain my very good friends to this day. Julianne stalked me for years. The last time she called was when

I was still in Mississippi. I told her everything. She said that she didn't know about the baby. That was a lie and I will have to live with the memory of her doing it to herself and the baby. I never heard from her again.

    I was alone again in Ascot and would often go drive on my private racing track to clear my mind. My private racing track was actually how I viewed the drive home through the Great Park in Windsor. There was never any traffic late at night, and that was the road to stretch out on, that, and the M4. I loved driving on that at about 3 in the morning. It was lit up with amber lights and looks like a tunnel when you're flying down it doing about a hundred and twenty. My hours were exactly the opposite of everyone in England. I was up all night playing and singing and whatever else I was doing at the moment. Just like most folks would conduct their day, I would conduct my night. Like going out for a midnight ride, then coming back home to party for a while. And then I'd be sleeping in till noon or 1 in the afternoon. So when I was out driving there was never anyone on the road because they were all at home asleep. From one side of the park, gate to gate, to the next, could be quite an exhilarating ride in that Daytona. One night I was coming back from London and had a clear road ahead so I kicked it down and let it rock a bit. I was really motoring but I didn't know how fast I was going, because I was busy going through the gears without taking my foot up off the floor. I was speed shifting. It's awesome when that thing gets wound up. It screams. Twelve cylinders and six dual Webers and five speeds! It was a race car with a street car body. All of a sudden in my rearview mirror I spotted some lights coming up on me real fast. I was sure that it must be the police in one of their supercars. As it got closer, I could clearly see that it was Rod Stewart in his Maserati Bora just eating my lunch. He took me by surprise and flew by me like a rocket. So I slammed it down even harder but could not catch up with him. Good old Rod was gone into the night, and I left him to it because I knew that I would never forget the night that I chased Rod Stewart through the Great Park in Windsor, and he didn't even know who I was.

    Another time when I was returning from an overnight stay in London it was a lovely Sunday summer's day and the air was fresh and clear. I got to the entrance of the Great Park and was doing my typical thing of tearing through it. About the time that I got to really rocking, the traffic seemed to just stop. Everyone was just crawling along. There was a line of traffic a mile long and I was at the tail end of it. I couldn't even see the other end at all. That Daytona has a powerful engine and a very strong clutch to be pushing in and letting out every two or three seconds. The car was beginning to overheat, and so was I. I was getting worn out pushing the clutch in so many times. There wasn't a car coming from the other direction and the coast seemed to me to be clear. So I got on the other side of the road in what would be the passing lane and kicked it down. I was passing everybody in that very long line of crawling cars. I was shifting out of third and into fourth at about ninety miles per hour and the line of traffic was just a blur to my left as I sped past them all. I couldn't figure out why they were staying in that line and just barely moving. The English have this thing about queues, so I thought this must have something to do with that. All this is going through my head as I'm doing well over a hundred miles per hour when all of a sudden I see in the very front of that line a carriage with two guys wearing feathered hats. It was a black carriage trimmed with gold and was being pulled by six white horses who were about to come unglued as I sped past. They were rearing in the air and about to break loose. I couldn't see anything but what flashed by as I tore past, and it seemed to be someone I recognized but I couldn't be sure. I kept going and didn't bother to look back for fear of what I might see. About ten minutes later I was home, and when

I walked through the front door the phone began to ring. It was Detective Sergeant John Clements telling me that I had just passed the Queen of England and she was not too happy about it. I told him that if I had known it was the Queen that I would have honked. He went on to say that if I was to pull another stunt like that I would be deported! I guess a few hundred years ago it would have been, "Off with his head!"

I decided to get on with my life and kept myself busy bouncing back and forth between the United States and Great Britain. I was just biding my time, waiting in vain for Eric to come out of his house, but he never did except to see his family who lived locally. So I had nothing else to do but go driving or shopping or go out into the countryside looking for antiques. I would go to the pub or out to London to eat, or go to the Bailiwick restaurant in Virginia Water, a very nice old place with lovely food and beautiful wine. It is still there, but is now known as Edwinns. I would normally go there with Bobby Keys, and every time that we would go out to eat, which was at least three times a month, he would always get the check. I would say, "I'll get the next one." Every time it was the same thing, he'd call and we'd go out to the Bailiwick, the check would come and I'd say, "I got it," he'd say, "No, I've got it" and I'd say, "OK." He'd get the check and he'd be pissed about it and wouldn't call for a few weeks.

Anyway, after a week or two he would call and say "Hey, BW, let's call Donovan and Ronnie Wood and go out to the Bailiwick, and this time you're buying!" I'd say, "Great, I'll meet you there." I'd jump in my Daytona and was there in about ten minutes. We would have a full five- or six-course meal with fine wine and champagne, not an inexpensive evening. The check would come and I'd say, "I've got it!" but Bobby could not contain himself in front of his rock star friends and said, "No, I've got it," I said, "No, I've got it!" He then said more emphatically, "No! I said that I've got it!" What else could I say except, "OK!" He was pissed again and had been beat again at his own game. I don't know what it was, but he was always playing it and losing every time. This went on for a very long time and I don't remember ever paying when we went out to eat.

There was another time he came over to my place in Ascot. He was kinda out of it and asked to use the phone upstairs and took it into the bathroom to use it in private. He was calling somebody in Brazil. He was in there for a very long time and I began to be concerned because I couldn't hear any talking. This was after telling him to hurry up and get off of the phone and not to run up my bill. I went back up there and banged on the door and there was no answer. I couldn't open the door because he had his back against it. I finally managed to push him out of the way enough that I could squeeze through and check on him. He had completely passed out and the phone was off the hook. I poured some water on his head and he came around and was pissed that I had dumped water on his head. He didn't realize that I had been out there for over an hour trying to get to him. When the phone bill arrived, I was shocked. His call came to over 600 pounds, which was an awful lot of money back then. Looks like I ended up paying for all our meals after all!

Caribou Ranch

I recently looked at a picture from the early Domino era of Eric and his grandmother, Rose, in her dining room. It was a photo shoot for *Life* magazine, which was doing a feature on rock stars and their parents. He is standing behind her on her left and she is seated at her dining room table in front of the fireplace. She's smiling, as always, because she is so proud of her Eric. The table has a silver service and the candles are lit and it is set for tea for two. He's wearing a purple shirt with white buttons and a light colored vest and jeans with a rope belt. And right around his neck hanging from a gold chain as plain as day was a coke spoon shaped like a snake. I had one just like it. We had matching coke spoons and were proud of them too! I have a picture of me wearing mine as well. My other coke spoon eventually wound up on one of Keith Richards' chains and there is a famous picture of him wearing it. It's a silver forearm with the fingers folded in on an upturned hand with a very large palm. You could pretty much wipe out half a gram of someone's bottle with two scoops with it. He also had a brass belt buckle of mine as well. It was two interlocking roses. It's in a famous shot of Keith. It's funny how even the smallest of things come back to you when you see an old photo. Anyway, the point of the story is that I was going to America for a visit and was leaving from Heathrow heading to Los Angeles. I had been up for a couple of days drinking wine and snorting cocaine and playing my guitar. Just doing what I pretty much did all of the time. I'd go outside and just get in my Daytona and start it up and rev the engine. That was awesome enough and safe enough provided I didn't go tearing out the drive, which of course I usually did! Life back then was just one big party at Oaklands. I was pretty shattered when Conway dropped me off at the airport. He was my guy, and his wife, Maureen, was the cook and housekeeper. They both lived at my house in Ascot and looked after things for me. Conway dropped me off outside the terminal, and I looked a mess, I'm sure. I was wearing jeans, cowboy boots and my fringe leather jacket. It had very long fringes and looked very cool. I wore a Deborah and Clare silk painted shirt that was open in the front and my gold snake coke spoon hanging from a gold chain around my neck. My hair was down past my shoulders and hadn't been washed in two or three days. I had to have been a sight to look at. I also had on a wide leather belt with a great big brass buckle, and the customs official said, "Where's your horse?" I was in no shape to realize he was joking with me because of my attire. Instead, I panicked inside. I thought he meant heroin, and I was as high as a kite! I told him that I quit doing it six months ago and he said, "Come with me!" I knew that I was a goner because I had my favorite Barclay's Bank bag with the name of the bank on the side that I had got from the Robert Stigwood Organisation office a few months before. I had put 15,000 pounds in English currency in it, which was worth over double that at the time in the United States because of the rate of exchange. It was $2.45 to the pound if I remember correctly.

I never thought of exchanging it at the airport and didn't do it for years after just because I didn't know that I could. Also, there was a sign that plainly read that you could not take more than a certain amount of pounds out of the country. I think it was £50 or so at the time. I needed more than that. The customs official asked, "What's in the bank bag?" I told him, "Fifteen thousand pounds." He said, "Yeah, right," and never opened it up. Then they did the old strip search as I mentally sang "Moon River." Of course the only drugs that I had were in me so they gave me my bag full of money without even opening it and let me get on the plane. I got the feeling they had far more important things to do than deal with this doped-up American rock 'n' roller who is going back to where he came from anyway. They were more than happy to be rid of me, I'm sure! When I got to L.A. the customs guy said, "What's in the bag?" I said, "Fifteen thousand pounds." He opened it up and dumped it all out on the table and started laughing. He asked me, "How the hell did you get out of the country with all that money?" I told him that I just told them what it was and they didn't seem to believe me and never even opened it. So I just walked on through with it. He put it back in the bag and was laughing all the while and said to me, "You're one lucky dude!" He handed me the bag and said, "Welcome to L.A.!"

In 1972 in England, rock stars played only every now and then. Ever since I had been in bands I was used to playing all of the time. It seemed strange to me that these guys had all of that success and were not going out to perform their songs. I used to come to Los Angeles out of boredom as there was absolutely nothing going on for me in England. I would stay at the Continental on Sunset and get a white limo to drive me around. I'd get some Dom and a little blow from a photographer I knew there and go visiting all of my friends that didn't take the plunge. On this particular trip I met a conga player named Ghia Guermo. He was from Cuba, and his dad was way up there in Castro's government. He had run away to L.A. to pursue his dream of becoming a famous conga player. He knew Stephen Stills through Joe Lala, a well respected percussionist friend of mine. Joe had played with Stephen, and Ghia was to meet Stephen at the Beverly Hilton about a recording gig for his next album and asked me to come along. He was supposed to play on the forthcoming Manassas sessions in Colorado. We went over to Stephen's room and Ghia introduced me to him. He seemed nice enough and we hit it off right away. Before you knew it Stephen asked me if I wanted to play on the new record and told me they were leaving in the morning to go to Colorado. I said yes, and we left the next morning and wound up waist deep in snow when we arrived. Ghia was from Cuba and had never seen snow. That for me was worth it all, just being there to see him in that snow. We were invited to stay at Stephen's house up in the mountains. I know it's all mountains there but he was very high up, quite beautiful. He had a huge snowcat but I don't think that he did much driving in the snow and I was told that it was used for emergencies only.

On the second day, Stephen, Ghia, and I went skiing near Rollinsville. We all got our ski gear and put it on like we knew what we were doing. Stephen could ski, but Ghia had never seen snow until the day before and I had never skied before either. We got on a ski lift and went to the top. The beginner slope was to the left and the advanced slope was to the right. There was nothing straight ahead but woods. No turning around for me now. I could stand up and go forward but I couldn't stop, and that's real important! Stephen had taken off and was nowhere to be seen and I was kind of sliding around with the children. I was trying to figure out how to stop when suddenly Ghia came at me from over a hill and turned sideways and sprayed snow all over me like he had been doing it all of his life. He was a natural! He said, "Come with me, man! Come with me!" I took off behind him, not really knowing where I was headed, and then through the trees and over a hump out onto the very top of the advanced slope! I fell immediately and stopped as I watched one of my skis take off down the mountain. It was so high that the ski lodge at the bottom looked the size of a matchbox. It was frightening! And Ghia was skiing like a professional! I didn't know what to do, so I positioned myself on the one ski I had left and was going to sit on it and ride it down the mountain. But when I tried to sit down the ski shot out from under me like a rocket. My feet went up in the air and I landed on my back and spun around head first down the mountain and was right behind the ski! I was going so fast that all I could see were trees to the right of me and trees to the left of me and the sky up above full of clouds. I was on my back tearing down that mountain in a bright blue nylon suit and going how fast I don't know! Then, whummp! And darkness. I had stopped in the middle of a snowdrift in the front of the lodge where everyone was standing, watching this comedy of errors go down. Someone pulled me out by my feet. That's all that was sticking out of the snow. When I stood up my eyebrows and my hair were icicles. I was totally embarrassed. Not cool at all. To top it off, Ghia came sliding up for a spectacular spraying stop and said, "Are you all right, man?" I've never skied since.

The album we were recording was to be the second Manassas album, *Down the Road*. We went into Caribou, a beautiful studio near Nederland. It belonged to a famous dude named Jim Guercio. We started to record and things were going fairly well except that Stephen thought he could play everything including the Hammond B3. It's no secret that Stephen had his drug demons at the time. It would seem that everybody did back then. It was very clear to me that I was being used, but to what extent I did not know yet. He would come in after I got finished with my parts and would try to take over. Stephen's really not an organ player. The Hammond B3 is my thing. But despite all of this, everything was real cool between us. When we were recording at Caribou we had Dallas Taylor on drums, Joe Lala on congas, Fuzzy Samuels on bass, Chris Hillman, Joe Walsh and Stephen on guitars, Paul Harris on piano and me on the organ, when I could keep Stephen off of it, that is! For some reason, right in the middle of recording at Caribou he decided that he wanted to go to Miami to finish the album. When we got there we went into Criteria Studios, a place I knew very well. Nothing had changed since we did the *Layla* record. The hopsack was still on the walls and the piano and the Hammond were still in the place they were when I last played them. We had Ronnie and Howie Albert as engineers as well on the sessions for Stephen. Dallas Taylor had come along and was hanging out, banging away on his drums. We had the tracks from Caribou and all that they needed was to be tidied up. That would include putting background vocals and organ and some piano on them. Not a big deal at all. Then we were to mix it and head on back to Colorado with the tapes in hand. That was not to be the case, though. Stephen was not in the best of shape in the studio and was not really focusing on the project at hand. Nothing was getting accomplished and the studio was costing a lot of money. I eventually wandered out into the studio and Dallas and I started playing around on a rhythm and some changes that I was playing on the guitar. He was on the drums and I was just playing and singing away. We were not paying any attention to Ronnie and Howie and Stephen at all. They were not listening to Stephen either, they were listening to, and recording, what Dallas and I were playing. I had the vocal melody and the changes all down and we asked the guys to record it for us. They told us that they already did. They knew when to hit record. Ronnie and Howie were in tune with how I operated, at least. Fortunately they got it before we had a chance to ruin it by overdoing it. When Dallas and I were finished we went outside for some air and when we came back in Stephen had gone into the studio and put a bass part on our song and then he put another guitar part on it. Then he put some keyboards on it and then he sang the melody and put his words to it and turned it into "City Junkies." Stephen went back to Colorado the next day and left the tapes for Ronnie and Howie and me to finish. What luck! We did some great background vocals and some Hammond and mixed it for him. I took the tapes back to Colorado the next day and gave them to Stephen's guy, who was a go-for guy as far as I could tell. It was always, "go for this or go for that or go for some cheeseburgers and be quick about it!" or something like that. He just did whatever he was told to do and when to do it by Stephen. I'll never forget that guy because he never paid me for playing, singing and helping to produce and mix the record. It was his responsibility to do so as well. He was the road manager-cum-business manager of sorts and did a little of everything. It's hard to tell just who's who when the crew act like it's their star. Everybody's the boss when he's not looking. He said that I got to stay at Stephen's house and play on his record and that was payment enough for me and then proceeded to run me out of town. Turns out they were pissed off at me because a girlfriend of a photographer friend of theirs had flown there to see me without their, or my, knowledge. I had moved out of Stephen's house and was staying in this beautiful huge log house that had the original small log cabin in the middle of it. They had built the big house right around the little one. It was nestled in between two very tall mountains with another one behind it. It really was a magical setting.

I had met this girl in Los Angeles during the many times that I darkened her boyfriend photographer's threshold. You see, as well as taking photos, he would also supply me with drugs, and he became my dealer for some time. I guess his girlfriend had her sights on me even though she was with him. She lived with him in L.A. I didn't have a clue that she was going to show up. Her name was Linda, and she was Danish, very beautiful and a model. One day I looked out the front window and there was a car pulling up at the bottom of the drive. I couldn't make out just who it was that was getting out but it was a girl with long blonde hair. She closed the car door and it drove away and left her standing there. She started walking towards the house and I could see my destiny walking straight for the house I was staying in. It was my dealer's girlfriend and everyone there knew that she was there and had come out to the ranch where I was staying. It is a very closed community in the mountains and everyone knows everything about everyone else's business. Suddenly there was an uprising against me even though I had nothing to do with this set-up. That's what it was, too, a set-up, and she was the one who was behind it. She stayed the night and I was run out of the Rollinsville area the next day. I was told that I was not welcome anymore. They were all very close to the drug dealer and had a sense of loyalty to the man who supplied them with photos and dope. I left her at the ranch and flew back to England to my place in Ascot. I didn't need that kind of trouble in my life. It wouldn't be too much longer before my phone would ring there and she would be on the other end of it asking if she and her older sister could stay for a few days on their way to Denmark to visit family.

The Daytona Crash

After getting home from Colorado I was seeing a lot of Keith Moon because we would have so much fun together. I was leaving his house early one morning after one of our rave-ups and shortly after tearing out of the drive at Tara in Chertsey, I crashed my Daytona. That Daytona had a big cockpit and I had trouble shifting the gears even with the seat pulled all the way up, so I had it sent in to the garage to have it adjusted. They raised it one inch and moved it forward two inches. The trouble was that every time I shifted the transmission my leg tapped the seat catch slowly downward, because they had used long bolts and stacks of washers to do this and it was not in line with Ferrari specs. So by the time I hit third gear the seat would fly back. This happened twice near the house, but I was going very slowly through Ascot and it was not a major problem. I had told my big Samoan bodyguard, Bob Miller, that the next day I would be taking it back to the shop for repair. Right about that time Mooney called and asked me to come on over. Without thinking Bob and I jumped in the Ferrari and tore out to Keith's house. Nothing happened with the seat on the way there, but when we left at about 5 in the morning it was a different story altogether. As was usual with me, the pedal was to the metal. I knew how to speed-shift so the accelerator pedal never came up when I shifted. That car has twelve cylinders, six dual Webers and a five-speed transmission and would go 190 mph. It only showed 180 mph on the face of it, but I have buried it and left my foot to the floor until it wouldn't go any faster and just left it there many times. Everything seems to be slower than it really is when you're going that fast. I wasn't responsible to anyone, not even to myself back then. I thought, "What have I got to lose, my life?" I was out of control and didn't know it. I thought that I could be any way I wanted to be and that was all right.

When I hit third gear that morning I was shifting out at about ninety and the seat flew back and the accelerator pedal went to the floor. The wheel pulled to the right and my right arm got wrenched because my elbow was jammed into the door pull and I still had a grip on the steering wheel. The right front tire caught the curb across from the Rose and Crown Pub and it spun the car around in the road three times. I had just shifted out of third at 90 mph into fourth. It hit a lamp pole and tore it down then mowed down a brick wall and hit a forty-foot pine tree at the end of the wall. It cut the tree in two and uprooted it. The car nose-dived and took to the air and did one and a half flips with a half twist and landed upside down with the top of the door panel buried a foot into the ground. After flying completely over the second flat's front garden, I hit the end of the brick wall at flat number one and landed in flat number three's front garden. The roof was below the steering wheel column and the speedometer was stuck on 155. There were twenty-eight gallons of fuel in the tank because it was never empty. It felt like I had plenty of time to think about my life as we were flying through the air. I knew in my heart that what I was doing and the way I was living was wrong. I said to myself, "If I live through this I'll go play every honky-tonk from Memphis to Los Angeles. All I want to do is walk away from this. I'm not supposed to go this way!" Everything had become super-animated in slow motion, the bricks were coming through the windshield one at a time in chunks, then, "WHAM!" Bob had reached up and pulled me under himself because I was suspended up in the top of the roof. I had come out of my seatbelt and was in the top of the car as it flipped through the air. All of this took place less than fifty yards in front of some council flats. As soon as we came to a standstill it was eerily calm, and you could smell blood, gas and oil. Incredibly we weren't knocked out. I told Bob, "I'm sorry," as we lay folded up in there. He said, "You didn't mean to crash, it wasn't your fault. Are you OK?"

Then someone grabbed my foot and started pulling me out. The man whose garden we had landed in had run out with a shovel and dug a hole and yanked the door open enough to pull me out. I stood up and said that there was someone else in there. He got Bob out. Bob had received two cracked ribs. I had seventeen shattered teeth and a piece of chrome trim that went straight through my left arm like an arrow. I just pulled it out. We weren't in pain, just shock. I also had a chunk of glass that tore into my right wrist and another piece just under my left eye on my cheekbone. The impact was so tremendous that there wasn't an entry hole for either piece. When the front windshield broke it flew into a million tiny quarter-inch square chunks with the rubber shatterproof center still holding them together. The doctor had to cut my wrist and under my left eye to remove them. I still have the scars. I was lucky because had it been just a little up and to the right I would have been made blind in that eye.

When that guy pulled us out there were ten- and twenty-pound notes floating down to the ground and the wheels were still spinning. I used to carry a lot of cash in the back of my seat because I didn't have any cards and I was always on the lookout for antiques. We went into his house and had some tea while we waited for the ambulance to arrive. They took us to the Royal Hospital in Windsor. They had us take off all our clothes and put on these backless hospital gowns and stuck us in a room to ourselves. In walks a policeman who says to me, "Blow in this tube." I said, "I just totaled my Ferrari and you want me to blow into some tube? Go get a doctor and tell him to bring us some Mandrax!" He looked like Terry-Thomas, the English comedian with a split between his front teeth, and was very upset at my arrogance. Nonetheless, he went for the doctor.

As soon as he did I threw Bob a little piece of hash that I had in my underwear and told him to

My Daytona.

give it to the orderly and tell him to call a hire car and have him meet us out in the front of the hospital. I jumped out of the window and ran across the lawn in that green gown and as it always goes in my world, up pulled the car. I jumped in and told the driver to wait because here comes Big Bob running across the lawn in his green gown and socks. He jumped in the car and the driver took us home, where I immediately called my policeman friend, Detective Sergeant John Clements, and told him what had happened and that I was pouring some brandy as we spoke and had taken some Mandrax for the pain, so if the police come over I'll already be wasted! He told me that he had already heard about it and said, "Bobby, why didn't you just call me? I would have come and taken care of everything." The next morning I got a call from a friend in Rome and he asked if I was all right and said that it was in the morning paper there. Eric read all about it that following morning, as did Pete Townshend. The question is not how I survived, rather why I survived. I always knew that I was here for a special purpose. Even when I was young it was something that I felt.

A man dug this hole to pull us out on the driver's side.

The car, righted.

It was a hell of a wreck to walk away from. My mouth was very painful after the crash. I didn't remember the wreck all at once. It came to me in rushes and flashes just like you see when one of the astronauts was returning to the womb in *2001 Space Odyssey*, one flash and one moment at a time. This recalling and recollecting was to last for years. I went to the doctor just to be checked out, and I was put on a regime of drugs for the aftershock. But the effect of the drugs would in the end have a longer-lasting effect than the shock of the wreck. I took a black beauty in the morning and a Librium at lunch and

> 1-7-73
>
> Mrs M Hodges
> 1 Sandhills Lane
> Virginia Water
> Surrey.
>
> Dear Mr. Byatt,
>
> With reference of Bobby Whitlock & Jimmy Miller,
>
> How are the lads after there flying bit?, you know I reckon they put the film "Bullit" in the shade Although I joke and perhaps I shouldn't there's no one more pleased than me to see them walk out of that wreck all in one piece they achieved what I would think to be a miracle.
>
> Why I've wrote is to ask a favour and that is could you send

Above and opposite: *Letter from the man who dug the hole and pulled us out. It was his garden we landed in.*

> 2
>
> me a few posters of the lado signed if poss for the kids I've got three. And would you ask them if they would like a piece of the pine tree that changed there course and I think perhaps helped to save there lives, they might like it as a good luck piece.
>
> Sincerely
>
> [signature]

a blue Valium in the afternoon and then a Mandrax at night. The pill intake naturally doubled within weeks. All I had to do was call the doctor and a driver would pick up the prescription and go get it filled and bring it to the house. The package was always wrapped like a brown present from the pharmacy. Of course I was still doing my cocaine and smoking a little opium-hash and drinking alcohol. The drugs were sending me out of control and my behavior was out there as well.

The Daytona wreckage was in my garage and I tried to get back in it many times but couldn't fit in. My bodyguard did his job very well that fateful morning. I could not even fit myself back in there and just could not imagine how we ever just walked away with the wheels still spinning. That's when I started heading towards leaving that life behind and going back to America. I had made myself a promise and I was going to keep it. I went to a dentist in Harley Street in London, in a very old building with tall ceilings and stark white rooms with a fireplace in each one. There was only one chair and it was right in the middle of the front room. It looked like the poster ad for the movie *Sweeney Todd*. It was a very old chair that resembled a barber chair more than a dentist chair. They had prepared for my arrival. There was a nurse, who was to give me something to knock me out, but it didn't work, and I woke up during the surgery. They said that I had the constitution of a horse. It took quite a bit to keep me out and under. I guess that's because I had so many drugs in my body already.

When it was finally over and I awakened the dentist told me to not drink any hot liquid. I'm wiped out and he's giving me instructions. They had given me temporary teeth that were made of plaster. It was not the state-of-the-art dentistry that we have in America. I don't know why, but I left there thinking that I was never going to have to go back again. I didn't realize that they had to make my permanent ones. I had my driver take me back to Ascot to my home and packed my bags to go and visit my friend Donovan in Scotland on the Isle of Skye. When I got there the first thing that I did was have a cup of hot tea and a bowl of soup. All of the plaster fell out of my mouth and every nerve in seventeen teeth was exposed. I was on the Isle of Skye and things there weren't much different than they were a thousand years ago. The weather changes there every five minutes! It is freezing cold one moment and the next it is pouring freezing cold rain and then the sun would shine for a second, and then it would do something else to freeze my face! With every breath I took that touched my teeth I would just about go to my knees. I finally got up in the morning and just got a mouth full of water and got the worst pain that you can imagine. Everything for the rest of the day couldn't match my morning wake-up. I had to stay a week longer because I was just too weak to travel. I should have never left my house, that's for sure. The pain that I was in was incredible. I can't even write about it because there are no words to describe that much physical pain! There was a Dustin Hoffman movie called *Marathon Man* and that is probably pretty close. It's about a Nazi war criminal who would strap his patients down in the chair and do dental work on them without any Novocaine. I could really relate to the pain the character Dustin Hoffman was playing in that scene. It was simply torture! About three weeks later I got my new teeth in London. The pain that I was in was horrible and nothing I took would stop it. None of the drugs that I was on would even dent it. The dentist put the new teeth in and sent me out the door. It felt like they must have put someone else's teeth in because I could not put my front teeth together. The back teeth were not much better because they were so big that I couldn't close my mouth all the way. I could literally put my finger in the front of my mouth and bite down and I could not even bite my own finger. That's how bad a job that dentist did. My mouth wouldn't close properly and I refused to go back to the same dentist or any other dentist in England for that matter. So I didn't have it seen to until several years later when I went to a dentist in America just to have my teeth cleaned. I was on a little gas and there was a picture on the ceiling of a giraffe chewing. His bottom jaw was on one side and the top of his mouth was on the other. He looked just like I felt. I started laughing and couldn't stop! I have a funny laugh, like Desi Arnaz, and the whole place started laughing with me. The dentist asked me why I was laughing so much. I told him about my bite problem and he checked it out for me. He adjusted and filed my back teeth until my bite had been corrected. He couldn't believe that I had gone that long without having my bite adjusted. I told him that I would not go back to a dentist in England if every tooth in my head went bad all at once and my life depended on it. I had to have it all redone again, and this time it was done by the number one dentist in Nashville in 2005. It cost a lot of money to have seventeen teeth done all at once, but I now have a beautiful mouth full of ivories.

Wakey, Wakey!

When my parents were getting their divorce they called and asked if they could send my brother over to stay with me for a while. Things were getting pretty hairy there and Nate was just fourteen, so they needed him out of the way. That was not a problem for me, since there was plenty of room at my place in Ascot so, of course, I told my Mom that I would be happy to have him come over to stay with me. I was looking forward to seeing my little brother. He is ten years my junior and we never had a close relationship because I was up and gone from there by the time he was five. I thought that this would be a great opportunity to get a bit closer to him.

I picked him up at Heathrow in John Lennon's solid white Rolls-Royce limousine. I had access to it through my driver Dave Long. I figured that Nate would appreciate a ride with his big brother in the back seat of a Beatle's limousine. Dave was dressed in his finest with tall black boots and a black cap and leather gloves with tan driver's pants. He looked very dashing. My brother was grinning from ear to ear, sitting there in the back seat of that beautiful car with burlwood, leather, zip windows and a stocked bar. I had a lot of fun watching him and the scenery go by. We arrived at Oaklands and pulled up to that beautiful English Tudor place, all covered with very old live oaks and huge rhododendron in full bloom. My garden was lovely. It was two and a half acres and everything was lush and beautiful. I had the whole place surrounded with a nine-foot wooden fence, so it was very private and secluded. I got him settled in and put him in the green room.

After I got my brother settled in we tried to have a conversation, but that wasn't so easy to do because we didn't have but one thing in common and that was that we came from the same womb. I also found out that another reason that he was sent over to me was because he had been busted for selling drugs. He had been sneaking up in the attic where my dad had been keeping display cases full of every kind of drug there was, and my little brother had been going up there for two years and doing everything that was in those two cases. He told me so himself. The Drug Enforcement Agency used them for talking about the dangers of dope ("And here's what it looks like kids!"). I had seen them years before and questioned my dad about having all of that around the house. He was a captain and a chaplain in the sheriff's department in Memphis, Tennessee, and was not to be fooled with. Unbeknownst to me, my parents had asked him to call them after he arrived. I took the telephone off the hook because I wanted to spend quality time with my brother and try to establish something, but there was nothing. We just could not connect on any level. He was just a little kid from Diaz, Arkansas, and it wasn't his fault. That night my parents tried to call and couldn't get through. At about 2 in the morning I heard some noise outside my window followed by a loud sarcastic shout, "Wakey, wakey!" It was the police! They were everywhere. My parents had called and told them that they feared for their youngest son because they believed that there were drugs in the house. I went downstairs and let the police in. There were a dozen of them swarming all over the place looking for drugs. They asked, "All right now, Mr. Whitlock, where is it?" The only thing that I had there except for prescription drugs was a little chunk of hash about as big as the end of your little finger. They asked again, "Where is it, Mr. Whitlock?" I reached into the drawer of a Welsh dresser and gave it to them. It was in a plastic guitar string case. They took both of us into custody and had my brother bring his bag, which had never been unpacked. He was in one car and I was in the other. He never said a word, he just looked at me in a state of bewilderment as he went one way, and I went another. He didn't know what had happened. I think to this day he still carries that with him. Neither he nor my parents knew what their actions would cost me in the end. The police put him on the first flight home and then took me back to my home. He went back on the very same plane with the exact same crew that had brought him over except that now he was being escorted by the police onto the plane. I had to go to court and it cost me a fine of 50 pounds. I thought that would be the end of it. In fact, it was be an event that would cost me dearly, as I would find out later.

Leaving England and Eric

Unbeknownst to me RSO had released *Derek and the Dominos in Concert*, a double album recorded at our Fillmore East shows in New York in October 1970. It was released in January 1973. Eric probably knew that we were being recorded because I can't imagine anything slipping by him like that. But it was never mentioned to me; we had never even discussed it. I didn't find out about it until I had picked up a copy of *Rolling Stone* magazine. It was another step by RSO to keep Eric's name in the music press. And it worked. The album sold very well and made us a lot of money on top of what we were still getting from the *Layla* album and single. Eric and I had been great friends and then after the drugs took hold, Eric's management made it all about Eric and not a band with a problematic drummer and an inexperienced kid from Memphis. There were a lot of drugs and alcohol to be sure, so I don't blame them one bit! Robert Stigwood offered to be my manager and I very smartly told him that I didn't need him to be a star. That's probably my one regret. Then he offered me a gig with RSO when he first started it but it didn't make any sense to me. I told him that I sing and play. That's what I do. My career with Eric was over then and I'm sure that Robert saw to it. He could step back and see it all very clearly. All he had to do when it came to me was just to wait as I was bound to self-destruct sooner rather than later. I really had no control over the situation. Robert was trying his best to keep me away from Eric and help me at the same time. I just couldn't see it because I was too inexperienced. I was out there completely on my own, in a world that I had only dreamed about. It really was a case of turn around and there I am and I'm playing rock 'n' roll and I'm a star and didn't even know it.

Robert was trying to keep me away from Eric, as was everybody else, and I didn't know why, I didn't give Eric the heroin and make him take it. That was all his idea. The idea of taking heroin scared the hell out of me because I had never been around anything like that ever. But what was I to do? Not do it with him? We had talked about going down that road together but that is a one-man ride. That drug was way too big for me and the first time I did it my whole life changed that instant and has remained that way ever since. But I think now that looking back, Robert was just trying to help me. I always held him in high regard and still do. It was just that I had never been out in the world. I was just spreading my wings. We had this great band that wasn't really real because Eric was hiding behind the name. The whole experience was a like being in a dream to me. So I turned my back and walked out of my pretend life. Then the reality set in, gone were the cars, the money, the houses, and everything that went along with being who I thought I was, Bobby Whitlock, "Rock Star!" You see, for a long, long time I thought that it was a title or something that could be taken away from me. I didn't know that it is who I really am forever.

When I was flying through the air in the Daytona I had made myself a promise to get out of England and go do what I was put here on this earth to do if I walked away from that. I did just that, too. I walked relatively unscathed out of that twisted steel. It was all so surrealistic, with that money floating down from the sky and the wheels still spinning and that car upside down and buried in the ground like that. Looking back, it seems very eerie to me. I guess that I didn't move fast enough because the air suspension on my 6.3 Mercedes came unglued two weeks later as a big reminder. I walked away from that one also, but I can tell you it wasn't going to take another mishap for me to make my mind up. I steadily started making plans to get out as soon as I could figure it all out. It wasn't easy, though, because I was in a state of confusion, and I was the only one there, running around in circles inside and out. The next thing you know the phone rings and it is Moonie asking if I could put up James Bond for a week or two. Yes, that's what I said, Bond, James Bond. Turns out Keith was very good friends with George Lazenby, who had played James Bond in *On Her Majesty's Secret Service*. He had been out at sea with some billionaire heiress floating around the world on a boat. Anyway, Keith didn't have room to put George and his then-wife Chrissie up at the time, so he asked me if I could help him out. It put a wrinkle in my plan to leave, but Keith had been so generous to me I felt that this was the least I could do for him. They showed up at my door about three days later with a suitcase and a guitar. As it would turn out Chrissie was about to give birth very soon. They had been floating around the planet for two years and pulled into London on the Thames on an Oriental junk. I thought that all rather romantic. George and Chrissie came to stay for a while and we would sit out on the lawn and have drinks together, just me, and "James." I thought that it was very cool. We got along really well. He was a pleasure to be around and had a lot of class and style and Chrissie was a lovely

James Bond (George Lazenby) and a friend.

woman. Being pregnant suited her beautifully. I told her she looked as if she were carrying a girl. Some time later George would send me a photograph of his little girl in that open guitar case all smiling and happy in her little pink booties. I sure did enjoy having them around. It was a pleasure and it was all mine. I really hated to see them go because they were great company. They stayed a couple of weeks and just as they were leaving a call came from Linda, the girl that I had last seen in Colorado at the Stephen Stills session. She said that she and her sister were on their way to Denmark and wanted to stop by and stay a few days and visit England on their way there. I did not think it would be a problem. They arrived and I went off to Scotland to the Isle of Skye the next day to get away from them. I just wanted to be alone for a while after everything I had been through. I told them they were welcome to stay and to make themselves at home, but I needed to be alone for a while. Donovan had an island there with a little village on it that he was resurrecting and I went there to stay with him again. At least my teeth didn't hurt this time though. When I returned from Scotland a week or so later, I was shocked to find that the two Danes had re-arranged my whole house! I couldn't believe it! Everything was where it wasn't supposed to be. What was upstairs was downstairs and vise versa. I guess that they thought they were helping, but they left the following day. About a week later, Linda called and asked if she could drop by on her way back to America and visit for a few days. Her older sister had got hooked up with a doctor in Denmark and was going to stay with him forever. Little did I know that after Linda returned, she and I would eventually get married and she would be staying with me for seventeen years!

Fall from Grace in Peach Country

I was in a state of limbo. I really didn't know what to do. I just knew that I could not stay in England and continue that way of life with all of the people with whom I had surrounded myself. I was surely going to lose my physical sense of life were I to stay there. Linda had just arrived at Oaklands for the second time only days before and had no idea that I had planned on moving back to the United States. I had made arrangements with the travel agent to get me two one-way tickets for America via Jamaica after a one-month stay there. I asked her what her favorite pieces of furniture were and she told me. They were the ones that I had put into storage. She had only just come back after she and her sister stayed with me and rearranged my house while I was away. I should have known better from her first visit what she was up to. Perhaps I did and didn't want to admit it to myself. I just didn't want to take responsibility for myself. That was more than likely the case. My life was falling apart and I just knew in my heart that what I was doing was wrong and not the way that I should be conducting myself. I could see no other option than to go to the land of opportunity. America. That was the only place where I knew that I could be the captain of my own ship no matter what the weather was like. At least I stood a chance there.

One day I told Linda to pack her things because we were moving back to the States for a while. I was going to go and play rock 'n' roll in every honky-tonk and rock 'n' roll club that was there. I was worn out with doing nothing but drinking and drugging each and every day. After the wrecks and that stabbing incident, the wake-up calls were just too big to ignore and it was time to go. She was surprised, but there was nothing that she could do about it because I had made my mind up. Everything was in motion. We left several days later for Montego Bay and then on to Negril, where we stayed in a thatched hut on the top of a cliff overlooking the ocean. It had no electricity. I was smoking great big spliffs and eating fresh lobster and playing my guitar every day. That was all that I needed to be doing at that moment in time. Exploring the island and eating mangos was a daily ritual. Killing time, that's what I was doing. Putting off living my life and taking responsibility for it. I just wasn't ready yet. The time finally came, after about a month or so of doing nothing, for us to be getting on with it. I was ready and eager to get started by this time. I can take only just so much of doing nothing because I start to get stagnant. We flew to California and stayed there a while. I wanted to get a band together as soon as possible so we set up shop, or house, more like. I had the grandest of intentions. And you know what is said about good intentions, the road to hell is paved with them. I never did get started with a band or anything even close. Nobody wanted to just play. It seemed like everybody wanted to be a star but didn't want to do anything to become one. And to me it was more important at the time for some reason to try and keep

Linda happy. That was a full-time job in and of itself and it was to be mine for many years to come.

I woke up very ill one morning and could hardly get out of bed. My stomach was killing me and I was sweating and throwing up and I didn't know what was happening to me. I didn't know if I had ingested something or just what was wrong with me. I was sweating like nobody's business and was having hot and cold flashes. It was getting pretty hairy so I figured that I had better get to the nearest hospital, Tarzana Medical Emergency Hospital. I was living in Calabasas at the time. It was a pretty short drive but it seemed to take forever getting there. I pulled into the unloading area and just fell out of my car. I was really sick by this time. It was very scary for me and I was completely alone. They took me into the hospital and into a room and I was asked to sit on a table that was used to examine women. I knew what it was because it had stirrups on either side for their feet. I sat on the end of it and rested my elbows in each one of them to hold myself up with my head in my hands and sweat dripping on to the floor and waited for the doctor to come and examine me. There was a chart or two hanging on the wall and there was a shadowbox display hanging on the wall as well. In it was every different size of needle and syringe that there was. The doctor finally came in and asked for me to stand and drop my pants. That I did. And then he put his two fingers behind my scrotum and said cough. I did as he asked and when I did I started to black out and fell straight back. I remember seeing the light on the ceiling go from the top of my vision to the bottom as I fell straight backwards like a tree. I hit the marble floor and I still remember my head slamming into it. I found myself in a tunnel of light so bright that it was blinding, but in a beautiful way. There was a feeling of peace and exhilaration like I had never felt before or since. This was not a physical thing that was happening to me. There was no sense of body whatsoever. Colors, like great splashes of oil paint, were flashing past me as I was catapulted through this tunnel that was so beautiful and bright. There was a feeling of freedom and I didn't want to return to this world. I knew what was happening and could see the end of it approaching fast and did not want to go back, but I knew that it was not my time and was told so by the presence standing in the light at the end, or should I say beginning, of that tunnel that said, "It is not your time yet." The next thing that I remember was being on my back with the doctor's fist withdrawing from my chest. As it turned out my heart had stopped. It got caught in between beats for some reason and stopped. He had to punch me in the chest to start my heart back up. He had rolled me back up with my knees in front of my face and had his left hand on my right inner thigh where there is a big vein. This whole episode only took seconds. Time is irrelevant in a situation like that anyway. A moment can be like a thousand years when it comes to the passing experience. There was a look of terror in his eyes when I opened mine. He was young and inexperienced and said that he wished that he had me hooked up to an EKG machine because my heart had stopped. He was totally freaked out. The very first thing that I thought was that I wanted to punch him in the face for bringing me back into this world. I did not want to come back at all. I mean that, I really, really didn't want to come back here and finish what I am here for. Even knowing that I was leaving behind family and friends and my future didn't matter at all because I didn't want to come back. That was my freedom from this world and all of its illusion. I still remember it and the feeling of it. It wasn't death and dying. It was being born again and living.

California had proved a waste of time, so I decided that there could be no better place to start over than where it all started for me in the first place, my hometown of Memphis,

Tennessee. We went straight to Memphis from Los Angeles and got an apartment on the outskirts of town. We had nothing to speak of and were traveling light. Then Linda told me she was pregnant, which was a shock to say the least. To be honest it took me a few days to be cool with the news. I had no other choice. I was really in over my head, and now I was soon to be a daddy as well. My life, as I used to know it, as an independent single rock star was over for good and I knew it. Here I was, twenty-four years old and about to shoot my career right down the tubes while being completely dominated emotionally by this woman. She knew the right buttons to push to get her way with me. "I'm pregnant" worked every time. It stopped me leaving her many times before and after that. This time it was true, though. She really was pregnant with our daughter. I was and still am a committed and dedicated man when it comes to my family. They always come first with me. I was basically just floundering. I didn't know what to do, period. I didn't have a manager and I didn't have a record company either. Unfortunately, it was just me making all of my own decisions, and I had no one to trust or rely on who wouldn't be self serving.

I was really taking stock of what was happening in my world and wasn't too pleased with what I found. I had gotten myself into another corner. Only this time I had a pregnant girlfriend with me in it. I thought that I would call Robert Stigwood and tell him the mess that I had gotten myself into and see if he would help me get out of it and help with my career. He immediately got on the telephone when he heard that I was calling. I told him where I was and what was going down and that I wanted to come back and talk with him about my career and life. This was on a Monday. Robert told me that he wanted for me to come back but that he was in the middle of a lot of meetings at that very moment and could not talk. He said for me to call him back on Wednesday because he had something to discuss with me. Just what that was, though, I was never to find out. After I was finished with my conversation with Robert I turned around and there stood Linda looking very upset. She had a scornful look on her face because she had been listening to my conversation and knew that I had leaving on my mind. And that it would not include her! She immediately started in with the most despicable and vile language that one could possibly imagine. You would have thought that I was doing something other than trying to further myself, and in turn make her life fruitful and happy as well. She started attacking my persona and soft places and gentle demeanor and I felt I was a beaten little boy again.

I was sitting at the kitchen table, drinking a Coke and smoking a cigarette, and picked up *Rolling Stone*. There was a picture of the Allman Brothers Band on it and there was a big article. I already knew them via Duane's association with Delaney and Bonnie and Derek and the Dominos. In fact, when we were on the road with Derek and the Dominos the only thing that we listened to was the Allman Brothers Band. I loved them back then and still do now. "Whipping Post" and "One Way Out" are my favorites. I read the article and in it there was a piece that mentioned Phil Walden. I had forgotten that I knew him from when I went to Macon, Georgia, with Booker T and the MGs and sang out in the front of them back in 1966. He was the owner of Capricorn Records and managed and discovered Otis Redding and the Allman Brothers Band. I was already familiar with southern rock 'n' roll and saw it as the only real music that I could relate to at all that was happening anywhere in the world at that time. I still wasn't sure what Robert Stigwood had had in mind for me. I do know that it was right about the time when Eric started to resurface. Perhaps he wanted to get Eric and me back together. But I certainly wasn't prepared for a solo career and superstardom at that point in time in my life. So I think that it was probably to get us back together again. Eric and I were very productive when we were together and not doing drugs. But it didn't matter because I decided to give Phil Walden a call instead. I got him on the phone and he asked me to come to Macon. I loaded the truck and was Georgia bound. I never returned the call to Robert Stigwood. That call could have been the one that would have changed my destiny. That would have been the call to make and I didn't do it. For sure that was my one true regret. I should have given Linda a ticket back to where she came from and called Robert and gotten on with my career and life as that was all happening so very naturally. But no, I had to start running things. And I very nearly ran my life and career into the ground. I'm only just now getting back on my feet after my fall from grace.

We got a hotel room in Macon and I called Phil and told him that we were in town. He said, "We?" I explained to him that I had gone ahead and moved on down with my girlfriend and my dog. That was the only place in the world where any music worth listening to was and I wanted to be a part of it. He took me as being very serious and we signed a record contract and a publishing/management deal, but all he ever managed to do was not to do a very good job of it. He did, however, give me an opportunity when no one else would. My hands had been completely tied and I didn't even know it. We lived there for a few years then moved and then moved back. It was a geographical thing and I was dragging my problem around with me. It's a wonder that Linda didn't have scars all over her from being dragged all over the world.

That two-year period during the Capricorn years (1974 to 1976) was a monumental time for me. It was the beginning of growth and change in my life. I went from being a single rock 'n' roll star to being a dad. My daughter was born the same day as my first record with Capricorn, *One of a Kind*, came out. I was changing in every possible direction

Me with Father Patrick Shinnick, left, at Frank Fenter's house in Macon, Georgia, circa 1976 (photograph by Kiki Fenter, courtesy of Rob Duner-Fenter).

that one could imagine. Being me was a comedy of errors, or so it seemed at the time, especially now that I am able to reflect on it from a safe distance. During our time there, we lived on a farm just outside of Macon. That is one beautiful little town. It has cherry blossom trees everywhere and is one beautiful sight to behold when it is in full bloom. The town dates to before the Civil War. All of the Allman Brothers Band lived in and around there. In fact their farm was a few miles outside of town, and I stayed at the cabin there many a night, drinking whiskey and shooting guns and playing guitar with Dickey Betts. He is a good friend, as is Gregg Allman. Gregg was the only person who came to sit with me when my daughter was born. He just showed up and sat with me in the lobby drinking beer and waiting on Ashley. He had fallen in the shower and had broken his arm and was in a cast. He sat with me and we talked for hours and drank probably way too many beers. Then we heard a very loud groan from down the hall and there was the crying of a newborn baby girl. Her name is Ashley Faye Whitlock. Greg and I saw her for the first time together. He would be Ashley's godfather.

After a few weeks we flew to Los Angeles to show Ashley to Linda's family before coming back to England to sell Oaklands and organize what things we would take back to Macon. Unfortunately, our trip would prove to be disastrous. When I was busted in England I was fined fifty pounds and had thought that was the end of it. Unfortunately, it wasn't. As soon as Linda and I, along with baby Ashley, arrived at Heathrow Airport, immigration told me that I couldn't enter the country again as a foreign visitor with a conviction because of my drug bust. We were put into the detention center at the airport and our passports were taken away until the following day. They had in the meantime called the Stigwood office because I had given them their number as a contact. We were told by immigration that, usually, whoever it was who got caught in our particular situation would be sent back to the point of embarkation. In our case, that would have meant Los Angeles.

Ashley Faye Whitlock all dressed up.

We had just gotten off a very long flight and really had no other plans other than to go back to Oaklands and relax for a few days before sorting out our furniture and things. That was not to happen, though. The customs office had called Stigwood's office and I guess that they were told that they knew me but that they didn't represent me anymore. I'm not sure that Robert could have helped anyway, but I hoped that he would be able to do something. But because he said he knew me they told us we would not be sent back to California and that we could go anywhere on this planet that we wanted to go, except for Great Britain. I turned to an out-of-control and distraught Linda, who had been sleeping in the detention center with our baby girl and said, "Where would you like to go? Pick a place. You just name it." She said, "Denmark." I could have nearly died when I heard that word, but that is where we would wind up that evening. We ended up staying in Aarhus, freezing and watching the tankers pass by our picture window in the summer house that we had rented. The irony was not lost on me: a summer house in the winter in Denmark! Go figure! That would be the end of me being able to return to England for ten years because of the minor drug bust that was still on my record. Everything that I owned was there and it also signaled the end of any chances of me doing anything with Eric anytime soon. I would imagine that the English government had had just about enough of me disrespecting their monarchy. I had my home, my kitties, my beautiful cars and all of my clothes, antiques and equipment taken from me by people that I knew, or thought I did. It was as if a bunch of vultures had descended on my life and took whatever they wanted. All that was left was the table, chairs, sideboard and a dragon mirror. My life was wrecked over $5/8$ gram of cannabis resin. That was

My little girl, now a woman, Ashley Faye Whitlock.

all there was, barely enough to roll a joint with, but enough to keep me from coming back into the country for ten long years, the next time I was to try to re-enter.

After a few weeks in Denmark, we decided to go back to America and resume my Capricorn career. Phil Walden had given me free rein as to whom I wanted to play on my records and what songs I wanted to do. This would turn out to be for me a huge growing experience. I still was going in every direction with my voice. No one but me knew it, though. I've been doing that up until just recently. I have finally matured. Chuck Leavell is a good friend to this day, and he naturally accepted my invitation to be on my records. If I could play like anyone other than myself it would be Chuck. I love the way he plays. He tells me that he wishes that he could play with my feeling. He and I together really work well. It's a good combination. Dickey came by and played a haunting slide part on a song titled "You Don't Have to Be Alone." He's a great player and has a unique style. I'm still a better shot with a 30-30 than he is, though. We used to have shooting contests out at the farm. I am a very good shot and can quick-draw a pistol and use a bullwhip and throw a knife and hit a moving target. He didn't stand much of a chance at those types of contests with me. But mind you, I never got into any guitar challenges with him either. He's a hell of a guitar player. He didn't have to worry about filling anybody's shoes when Duane left the scene. Dickey had already established himself as the guitar player he is today. I am of the mind that no one can fill anybody's shoes. We have got to fill our own and walk in them ourselves. Different members of different bands who were signed to the label were asked to be a part of my records. I became friends with everyone who was on the label and who lived in the Macon area. Phil's brother Alan Walden is still a good friend after all of these years. He still lives there as does Chuck and his wife, Rose Lane. We are all still in touch with each other. I call Chuck my friend who is a tree-hugging Rolling Stone. Dru Lombar and Larry Howard, the guitar players from Grinderswitch, were very good friends and played on my records in Macon. Their band opened a lot for the Allman Brothers shows. They got to do what I was promised but never got to do. It doesn't matter though because it all worked out for the best for everyone. My first album for them had not done very well, and when it came to my second record with Capricorn, *Rock Your Sox Off*, I had gotten disheartened. It did not help that Phil told me that if this didn't work that he would give me my walking papers, which he did. But the last thing that he did just before that was to surprise me with a new album cover that was a drawing of some socks that was done by Martin Mull. What a stupid album cover! I had no say and it was being pressed when I got to see the revised version. It is a downright embarrassment. I had nothing to do with it. Had it been his record I am sure that it would have looked different. By this point, Phil was more interested in helping to get Jimmy Carter elected as president of the United States. He told me that he wanted to be the governor of Georgia. He'd probably have made a good one too. I have never received a dime or even a royalty statement from Capricorn Records to this day. He had all of the publishing as well. Nothing ever came my way. As it would turn out, my life and career have been one big struggle. It's all history now. Phil left the scene in 2006. We returned to Memphis before deciding what our next step should be.

It was now the summer of 1977 and Linda was pregnant again. Nothing was happening in Memphis so we left with three-year-old Ashley and headed to California. I have lost count of how many times I have left Memphis. We went to Los Angeles and stayed at her folks' place at first. We didn't really know what we were going to do. As usual, I was just winging it. The only two people I was close to in L.A. at that time were Duck Dunn and Steve Cropper. Shortly after we arrived I went to visit Duck and his wife, June, and Duck and I got to talking about what I was up to. I told him that I really didn't have any plans and he asked me if I knew who Cosmo (Doug Clifford) was and I told him I didn't. He said Cosmo was the drummer for Creedence Clearwater Revival and that we would probably get along well together and that we ought to hook up and form a band. He gave me Doug's number and later that evening I gave him a call. He said to come on up and I did. I stayed at his house for a few days and we got on well and decided to form a band. He had a house for rent in Pinole on the Bay side and I moved my family into that. Doug and I started to rehearse at the old Creedence warehouse called Cosmo's Factory. I really liked Doug and thought him a good friend and a great drummer. He is a straight-ahead drummer and we worked really well together. We decided right away that Duck would be perfect for bass. I called him and told him what we had in mind and asked him if he would like to play with us, and he said that he would. I started having guitar player tryouts and there was a long line. We were a pretty credible little unit, Duck, Doug and me. I was doing all of the singing although Cosmo would join in and sing backgrounds every now and then. Duck would come up to the Bay area every week to rehearse with us and we actually went in and recorded about thirteen tracks with Michael O'Neil from Wichita Falls, Texas, on guitar. He was the guy that I finally settled on. We were a really good rock 'n' roll band. Doug and I had written some songs together and we had decided to call ourselves California Gold. It was the time of bands naming themselves after states and the like.

Linda gave birth to our son, Beau, in Berkeley on June 13, 1978. It was a full moon and was on a Friday. I was there when he was born and saw him make his appearance into this world at the hands of Dr. Nishamini at the hospital. It was a very beautiful experience watching him as he entered my life and became a part of my world, my son, Beau Elijah Whitlock.

Meanwhile Doug had gone out one night to a Holiday Inn and befriended the bass player and the guitar player in the band playing there and gave them a gig that very night! I don't know what got into him or what it was that was to ever possess him to call my friend Duck Dunn, who had been flying in every week to rehearse with us on his own dime, and fire him! I could not believe it, my old friend Duck was fired by my new friend and band

Ashley and Beau in Pinole, California.

mate Cosmo. And so was Michael. He fired Michael and hired a new guitarist, David Vega, and a bass player, Tom Miller, to replace Duck. Both were lovely guys, especially Tom. I understand that he went on to play with Carlos Santana and some other people. As soon as I heard about Doug firing Duck there was an immediate separation between us. I guess he felt he didn't need to ask me about his decision to fire Duck and Michael because he was financing the whole thing and outranked me in that department. Nonetheless, we were a band and we should have talked about it first. Doug paid everyone a salary, including me. All were advances against what we were to make when this thing would eventually get off of the ground. But all that we ever did was to rehearse and then rehearse some more. We ended up playing only one gig, and I remember it well. David was one loud-ass guitar player, I can tell you. His amp was on my side and he played on eleven. I told him that I couldn't hear and to turn it down, but he didn't hold me in the regard that I thought he should. He went all night long at that gig and kept his volume where I at least could hear to sing. Then on the very last note of the evening he turned his guitar wide open and hit a note that was so loud that it shut my right ear down. It was completely closed and as a result I have

Ashley and Beau in 1998.

had permanent ear damage in that ear ever since. That was the start of my awareness of my hearing and the decline of it. Now I live in a sea of noise in my head.

Out of the blue Doug decided that he was going to take a vacation and go to twelve countries and go to all of their breweries and tour them all. In the meantime, here I was stuck with a wife and two kids and no money as usual and no friend named Duck Dunn anymore. Luckily, I had a royalty check arrive in the mail at the right time for once. So we decided to get the hell out of there and away from being controlled by anyone and go back to Memphis and figure things out. Doug had left for his trip and the whole thing had already fallen apart, and I really didn't want to be there for the aftermath. I still like Cosmo though, and I am grateful to him for having helped me, and my family back then. He had no idea I was living with a woman who had complete control over my situation. I pretty much had to do whatever she said to keep the peace in my home. She was the one who was so disgruntled at living in Pinole and me having a band with Cosmo. Once again I had let myself be manipulated. Sometimes I look back and wonder if there was any backbone there at all. I would do just about anything not to rock the boat. Cosmo paid for my son's birth and the doctor who gave me my vasectomy. He had had a vasectomy and said that if I got one that he would pay for it. I don't know what compelled him to make such an offer but I took him up on it. That would be the end of Linda using "I'm pregnant" as emotional blackmail. Thanks, Cosmo!

Elvis' Caddy

In the early '80s I lived in Nashville, Tennessee. It was my first time living there and I hadn't been exposed to that aspect of the industry before. I was the new kid in town and everyone wanted to write a song with me or get me to play on their record. At least, that is until they all found out that I couldn't read the number system or chord chart and didn't care to learn it either. Not only that, I had views about writing songs as well as everything else that was going on in that city, and they didn't like them. The new kid tag wore off in two weeks flat—except with the songwriters. Everywhere I went they were there, pen in hand and pad in lap. Even when I was hanging out at the local watering hole with a fledgling songwriter who really wanted to be, and thought that he could be, a star, he would be grabbing napkins and writing down what I had just said. I remember the day, the bar, the weather outside and what I said and to whom and when and why I said it. It came out of a conversation about me being a rock star and having friends in high places. I told him that I've friends in high and in low places. I could see it happening then and it still does happen there that way. You can be just having a casual conversation over drinks and say something and out comes a pen and someone is writing down what you just said and putting it in their pocket. The next thing you know you hear your everyday common phrase being used in the hook line for a hit song. It would turn out in the end that he would only wind up spending all of the money that he made on dope and would be forever struggling like all of the rest who have fallen by the wayside in that place. And it would appear that he is still no wiser from the lessons that he should have learned.

I did get to know and become friends with John Prine and Roger Cook in Nashville. They both are the finest songwriters that I know. Roger co-wrote "I'd Like to Teach the World to Sing in Perfect Harmony" and "You've Got Your Troubles" and about another hundred number one worldwide hits. And we all know about John Prine and "Sam Stone." What a great song! I have written with both of them and learned a lot about writing songs from just being around them and other people who write songs. One day in the early spring I was daydreaming as usual. I came up with some Oriental-sounding chords and changes and the thought came to me of being on a slow boat to China with Linda and what that would be like. It was scary! But it made me think about what if it was with someone who you really loved, just floating around the world in a Chinese junk like George and Chrissie Lazenby did. I figured the person I should call to write it with me would be John Prine. I gave him a call and told him that I had this idea about a guy and a girl being together on a Chinese junk and floating around the world. It was to be called "Slow Boat to China." He asked me if I had ever heard the Hoagy Carmichael–Frank Loesser song "On a Slow Boat to China." I said I hadn't and he said, "Good, come on over!" I went straight over to John's house there in Nashville and we sat out back and wrote well into the evening. We were bouncing around ideas and watching the stars and finished it before I left. That concluded our evening's songwriting and "Slow Boat to China" came out great when we recorded it. It can be found on his *Aimless Love* album. Linda sang background on it. I had hoped that it would help her feel better about herself, at least that was my intention. It didn't work, though. The biggest mistake that I made with her other than being with her and staying so damn long was to get her to sing with me. It was to try to make her happy, if only for an hour at a time. Next thing you know it's, "If it wasn't for me you wouldn't be where you are today!" She was right in that had it not been for her working herself into my life, my life would have been a lot more harmonious.

In Nashville they are always trying to make something out of nothing when it already is something. There are very few who step aside and let it come through. There are a few who know what the hell I'm talking about in the first place. They all had their ears open and pen in hand when I was around and they still do when I am. I was playing a beautiful concert grand piano at a session. Every top player was on this particular session including Larry Byrom, who was the guitar player with Steppenwolf. The producer had handed out the customary number charts and gave me a chord sheet with the chords written out. I still can't follow something like that because I can't read something and play it. It just doesn't compute with me. When I hear a song I immediately know my part. A song is to me like a painting is to someone else. I see it as a picture and a story in my mind's eye and I hear it with my mind's inner ear. It's like a watercolor and my organ is the framed picture, and I am the artist and the drawbars are my colors and my hands and fingers are my brushes and the Leslie is the flow of it all. It is the rise and fall of emotion. I am but the instrument through which the part that is supposed to be me is flowing.

It would seem to me that the only thing that should matter is whether or not you can play and sing. On that particular session Larry was sitting in a chair at the end of the keyboard to my right. The engineer hit record and when it got to a certain place in the song the producer stopped it and said, "Put a diamond on that Bobby!" I said, "OK!" Then I turned to Larry and asked, "What's a diamond?" He told me just to stop where I did. I still don't get it because I didn't do anything any differently that I had done already, but it was perfect for him the second time around. I guess that it was going too smoothly and he wasn't really needed so he had to say something. I could go on and on about Nashville.

I stayed away from home for several days for my peace of mind and sanity. On one of those days, I was invited out to a bass player's log cabin on the lake. There was a piano and it looked as if a songwriting session was about to begin, Nashville-style. I had just been through an awful experience and knew that this time it was over. I had let her slip away. I sat down at the piano and just like that the whole song fell out of me, melody and all. There is a line in the song where it says, "And now that it's over and there's nothing more I can say." I could hear Ray Charles singing in my mind and sang that line the way that I imagined that he would sing it. The song is called "Slip Away" and was about my experience of what was happening to me at that very moment. I was singing and playing the piano and this was all just pouring out and was going down on a cassette tape recorder. One run through and that was it. It just fell out like water pouring over a rock.

After several days of serious thinking, I reconciled with Linda and we decided to move to California for what I hoped would be a fresh start. Before we left Nashville I bought a 1976 white two-door Cadillac Eldorado for $1000. Elvis had bought it and given it to one of his producers as a gift. It was beautiful and very powerful, with a 6.6-liter engine with front wheel drive (it would smoke the front tires) and a blue velour interior.

It was a very long car, and I took down my mailbox a half a dozen times with it! I had the seat all laid back and was stylin' in Elvis' Caddy. I had it all fixed up and took it to Los Angeles when we moved in early 1983. On our way out of town I stopped by CBS Records and dropped a tape of my new song, "Slip Away," at the office of Margie Ulrich, the head of A&R. When I put it on her desk I told her that this song was for Ray Charles. Now, you have got to imagine the odds on just getting a song to Ray Charles, much less getting him to record it. I thought nothing more about it, and we moved to a place in Westlake Village outside Los Angeles. There was a knock on our door several months later and it was the UPS man with a package for me. In it was a tape of "Slip Away" recorded by Ray Charles and a note that was written by Margie but dictated by Ray Charles. He said he was planning to release his definitive country album and that he would do the world a favor and go back in the studio and record "Slip Away" for it. That's just what he did as well. He recorded his album and had it mixed and ready and then he went back into the studio and recorded my song, "Slip Away." He sang it exactly the way that I did. What an honor. Ray Charles singing me singing him can be heard on his *From the Pages of My Life* album.

We had only been in Westlake Village for six or so months when I got the opportunity to go to England to the wedding of a friend, Stuart Laurence, and his fiancée, Lisa. He is Donovan's brother-in-law and my good friend since 1969. I loved being back in England so much that I decided to stay and look for work because I was allowed back into the U.K. now that ten years had passed since my drug bust. I rented a car and after looking around for a few weeks found myself a lovely typical English cottage with a slate roof. It was on the edge of Wargrave, a small village not far from George Harrison's place. I called Linda and told her the news and asked her to come over. She wasn't thrilled about uprooting and leaving all of her family but she packed a couple of suitcases and came on over with the kids. I picked them up and as we headed to our new home we got to talking about where everything was—our horses, our furniture and my Elvis Caddy. The horses were being boarded and the furniture was on its way, but she had given my Cadillac to her sister. I wasn't surprised somehow. Six or seven months went by and I asked her sister what had become of my Caddy. She told me that she had sold it to some Mexicans for $700 and that they had driven it into the ground before parking it out in the back of their place where it was being used as a chicken coop. I couldn't believe it, my Elvis Presley Cadillac was somewhere in the valley and had chickens roosting in it!

My Old Pal

I was really enjoying being back in England. It had been way too long since I was able to come back to a place I called home. It didn't matter what had gone down in the past because I felt that this was a fresh start for us. I had signed a deal with Rondor Music, a very well-known music publisher in London. It basically afforded us the move over to set up house. I arranged all of this on my own and Linda was actually pleased. I had completely furnished the cottage and had bought her a classic 1970 Mercedes 280 sedan. I had bought myself a 1972 Mercedes 300SEL 3.5, which rocked, to say the least. One day I had to go into the publisher's office in Parson's Green. They were always wanting me to meet with a songwriter or I was there recording something. It was a pretty good set-up for me, and it sure made things a little easier having a steady income. Anyway, I had to take Linda's car because mine was in the shop being tuned up from one of my little excursions. Her car was a six-cylinder automatic and was slow at best—beautiful, but slow. It was in the middle of summer and the traffic was backed up. I was just getting ready to cross over the Hammersmith Bridge on the Hammersmith Bridge Road and the car was beginning to heat up. There was traffic as far as the eye could see and I didn't have any water for it. There was no gas station nearby and the car was about to boil over, stuck in the middle of London traffic. After a few more feet, the gauge was in the red. There was absolutely nothing that I could do about my situation except hope for the best. I looked up and there was a black Berlinetta Boxer headed my way. I thought, "That looks like something that Eric would drive." It kept getting closer and closer and as it came by me I could see that it was Eric. He looked up and saw me and we locked eyes and smiled at each other with boyish glee and surprise while pointing at each other. His line sped up and he was in the flow as was I, and neither of us could stop. It had been ten years since I had last seen Eric and I hadn't spoken with him. Ten years with no communication with each other. He was headed in the direction of his house and I could see his car getting smaller in my rear view mirror. On impulse I whipped my car around into the oncoming lane and was headed the wrong way on the wrong side of the street, driving head-on into traffic until I could get myself right. You can just imagine the commotion. I could just about see Eric way up ahead, but he was getting farther and farther away. By now my car was completely buried in the red and steam was boiling out from under the hood and I was doing about sixty. Finally I caught up enough that he could see my flashing lights. I saw him hesitate and hit his brakes and pull into a little rest area on the side of the road. He got out of his car and was standing there as I came in with steam boiling out from underneath the hood. It looked like it was on fire. I was embarrassed but that didn't matter because I was so pleased to see him. We hugged and said hello and asked how we had been doing and what was going on in each other's lives. He was telling me about an Italian

Me and my toys at Witherly Cottage, England.

woman at Hurtwood and I was telling him about my family and that I was writing a lot of songs and building up my catalog. Cars were starting to slow down and stop because they recognized us. It was time to split before we caused a traffic accident. I knew that it would probably be another ten years until I would see him again. We gave each other a hug goodbye. Then Eric got back in his car and drove away very slowly. It meant a lot to me to see and speak with him again and I went home and wrote a song about him called "My Old Pal." I recorded it a few years ago and it is now on my *Vintage* CD.

Pool of Tears

I was sound asleep in my bed when I heard my dad's voice calling me. It was as clear as a bell and he said, "Bob, where are you son? I need you!" The phone rang and it was 4:30 in the morning. My sister was on the other end and she said that daddy had died. I told her, "I already know." She was surprised and asked if Mama had called me with the news, but I told her, "No, Daddy came to me in the night and told me that he needed me and asked me where I was," so I knew then. They all thought I was crazy but it didn't matter to me because I knew something they didn't.

I had only just returned from seeing my dad in the hospital in Memphis two weeks earlier. He had had a stroke and was in and out of a coma. The doctors told my sister and my dad's second wife that he might pull through but if he did, he would be pretty much a vegetable and would require a lot of care. I told them that they were fooling themselves because the only way he would be leaving that place was in a plastic bag. I was proved right, too. They kept him in there, poking him full of drugs to keep his body functioning, but it was useless. I couldn't stay and be a part of all of that. He wound up passing from a bleeding ulcer in his stomach. All that he could say was "wah, wah, wah," and he could only move his left arm and leg. There was nobody home when you looked into his eyes. My dad and I had discussed "pulling the plug" if it was time to one day. I told him that I would and I told his wife the same thing as he lay there with tubes coming out everywhere. The day that I was due to go back home I went to see my dad for the last time. My brother was sitting in a chair at the foot of the bed. My dad would come in and out in brief intervals and I went and stood next to him on his left side and held his hand in mine. I told him that I had to go back home to my family and that I couldn't stay with him any longer. I told him that I would see him again one day in a far better place than he was in right now. I kissed his forehead and said goodbye. He squeezed my hand real hard and opened his eyes and looked directly into mine and said, "Wah, wah, wah." I knew that he was saying that he loved me and that he was sorry for all the pain he had caused me as a child. I looked over and my brother's face was in his hands and on the floor was a pool of tears between his feet. I said goodbye and walked out of the room. As I wandered down the corridor, I could still hear my Dad saying, "Wah, wah, wah! Wah, wah, wah!" I didn't turn around and go back to him. I couldn't. Perhaps I should have but I didn't. I went back home to England feeling like I had made my peace with him.

Magical Ireland

One day I went to the Home Office in London to have my visa extended and they said that they would be happy to help me out—out of the country, that is! My visa had expired and I had not renewed it. So once again I was in trouble with British immigration. As far as I was concerned I was a resident. I had my house in Wargrave, two Mercedes, two dogs, two children and a wife. On top of that I was paying taxes so I thought that I was just as entitled to be there as much as anyone else. I had made friends with Detective Sergeant John Clements, so I gave him a call to see if he had any advice on how to deal with my dilemma. He said that I should go to Ireland and try to work things out from there. It just so happens I had just returned from there after doing a guest appearance on the show "Sessions" for RTE One. No sooner had I hung up than the phone started ringing. It was David Heffernan, who was one of the Heffernan twins, David and Gerald. They were the show's producers. "Sessions" was a rock 'n' roll show with a great house band and their last guest was due to be Rory Gallagher. But he had taken a fall in the studio and hurt his back and couldn't make it, so they were wondering if I would be interested in coming right back over and having my own one-hour show on their special when it aired. Of course I agreed. It seemed that once again fate had worked its magic as I would be going to Ireland anyway to avoid getting kicked out of England. They took care of all the expenses. I rented Barberstown Castle outside of Dublin and put my guests up there as well. I had flown Steve Cropper over from L.A. and had John Parr come over from England, as well as my sister-in-law. Barberstown Castle belonged to Eric for a while, but not then. His one-time manager Roger Forrester was part-owner with him. I talked to him once about possibly buying it from them, but it never happened. I ended up staying there with my family for a month after the show was taped. There was no one there except for us and the people who cooked and cleaned. It was a ball for the kids. You could go out on the top of the tower and see the whole countryside. I have several friends, including Donovan, who have castles in Ireland. It's an experience to live there with everyone knowing who you are and every one of them so polite and respectful. That whole country has a spiritual feel that you can sense all around you as soon as you touch down.

During that time when we had the castle to ourselves, we started looking around the country to see where we might possibly want to live. A place came up on the lake at Loch Derg in County Tipperary near Nenagh. It was part of a thirteenth century castle ruin and was quite beautiful, with a huge stone wall surrounding this very old estate of twenty beautiful acres of meticulously manicured, very old gardens. We lived in the cottage behind the manor house at the castle. There was a huge cobblestone courtyard that we shared with the horses. The kitchen used to be the smoke house part of the building, which was very large as it held the livestock in one part and us in the other part. It was a two-story building, L-shaped, and had three-foot thick walls and a slate roof. Our side had twelve rooms. A door in the upstairs bedroom opened into the attic, where our resident bats lived. Yes, there was a belfry, and they lived in it. At night you could look up through the roof and see the stars. It never did leak once. There was a very large yard in the back with a few apple trees and an old stable. Also part of the estate was an old tower, Castle Loch, that was on a small island where, centuries ago, they would throw their valuables into the water when they were invaded. The children enjoyed the three years that they spent there, and Christmas was exactly as you would imagine it to be, all covered with snow and the land so still and quiet. There was always a magical, mystical feel in the air that made you feel at peace, whole and full. I moved there to put my brakes on and to figure what it was that I was supposed to be doing in this life.

There was a warm band of air that ran through that part of Ireland due to the Gulf Stream. It created an amazing microclimate. There was a palm tree growing in the garden, as well as the largest rhododendron in Ireland—it must have been fifty feet tall. Little plaques carried a description of all the plants along with their Latin names. The garden was very well kept. It also had one of the oldest trees in the world in it: It was full of gnarls and branches with no leaves and was right in the middle of this beautiful garden. There were pine trees, at least a dozen of them in a circle, that grew from one huge main tree in the center. And then there was a row of trees around that circle of trees as well as two dozen others that were extensions of those around them. I remember on a midsummer's night we stayed up until midnight and went with the children out to that magical fairy ring of trees to go leprechaun hunting. Beau had a little fishing net, which I told him was for catching leprechauns, and that if he caught one, he would grant him his wish no matter what it was. I had a pocket full of small pebbles that I had collected during our walk through the garden. We sat on a log and it was very, very quiet, and Beau would be listening for any movement in the trees. As he did, I would secretly flip a pebble through the trees with my thumb. He would say, "I hear one, Dad! I hear one for sure this time!" And I would wait for a few more minutes then I would flick a couple of larger ones and he would get excited. He never caught on. I had such a great time with my children when they were growing up. I was determined to give them the childhood I never had. They were always loved and protected by their dad. One of my fondest memories from Ireland is when I heard Beau playing my Stratocaster at the top of the stairs. He was only seven at the time. My guitar was tuned to an open E and I had been showing him how to make the different barré chord changes such as E to the A then to the B. All in open tuning. He was singing as he was playing, "I love you. I love the way you always make me feel. I love you, I love you." I couldn't wait to get it on tape, so I called up the stairs to Beau and asked him to come down and let me record him. He was shy and didn't want to. I really wanted to recapture that moment. So I had an idea that I knew would work. I had him put on his Wellingtons and we went out under the apple tree in the back yard and sat in the swing. I put the cassette recorder in the side of his boot and turned it on. He wouldn't play it while I was standing there so I walked back into the house and grabbed my camera. He had my white Strat and had his leg crossed, sitting in that swing, and was serious. I stood in the doorway and watched and started taking pictures as he started playing and singing about love and how it made him feel and about loving someone and wanting someone. It was pretty amazing to be a witness to the creative principle at work through a child. I went back out after he had finished, which was quite a while, because when he got started he was letting it all out. He took the tape deck out of his boot and handed it to me and said with a voice so sweet, "I hope that you're satisfied!" I finished it and recorded it and put it on my *My Time* album in 2009. The song is called "I Love You."

When Beau turned eight we had a birthday party and he invited all of his classmates. There were about a dozen children, all his age. They played games, and we had set up a very large table full of sandwiches, cake and soda. It was a very memorable occasion for Beau, and for me. I gave him his first real knife with a bone handle and a sheath. I hoped it would be something that he could keep forever. The games were over, and it was time for the children to go back home to Portroe up on the top of the mountain from us. They were all laughing and still having the time of their lives singing and playing as they left. We started cleaning up and noticed that Beau's new knife was nowhere to be found. We searched high and low but gave up the search after two days. Early one morning I was up making breakfast for the children and was getting them ready to take them to their bus stop. I was having a cup of tea while I was waiting for them to come down the stairs when Beau's dog, Daisy, who was lying by the door, looked up at me. I could see that she had something on her mind. She was an English Spaniel and a very smart dog. It suddenly hit me: She probably took the knife because it had a bone handle! I opened the back door and we went outside and I asked her, "Did you take Beau's knife? Where's the bone?" She took off and came back in about thirty seconds with Beau's knife in her mouth.

Beau under the apple tree writing "I Love You."

One day I was driving home from Dublin, which was about two and a half hours away. You had to go through some very narrow, twisted lanes. I was driving very slowly around a sharp bend and I saw a buck deer and his doe mate up ahead. They were about the size of a real small greyhound, and he had a rack of antlers about the size of your hand. He flicked his tail up and with two leaps they were through the thickets and briars that were on either side of the road. My friend Philip Donelly was visiting and had arrived at Castle Loch several hours before me. Philip and I go way back. He used to play with John Prine and the Everly Brothers and was on numerous hits recorded in Nashville. When I got down to the bottom and through the pasture to the house I went in and said hello to everyone and started telling them about the miniature deer. Philip said that they were wiped out in the Ice Age, when the glacier came across Ireland and made the peat fields.

I told him that a couple were missed because I had just seen them on the side of the road. A few weeks later I took an artifact that I had found to the Museum of Art and Natural History in Dublin. It was an old broach that I had found in a dry lakebed. About three hundred years ago it held a sash. My Irish friends were always on at me about how I was always finding things. While I was there in the museum I had a look around, and there stood two giant deer skeletons from before the Ice Age. They were about nine feet tall at the shoulder and right next to them stood two miniature deer skeletons, two feet tall, from the same time. I do believe that was all I needed to confirm that there is another dimension that we don't see, hear, taste, touch or smell.

I appeared on television quite a lot when we lived in Ireland. I was a very public and recognizable figure in that amazing country. The whole country isn't much bigger than the state of Arkansas. You can arrive at Shannon airport and drive all the way across the country to Dublin in a matter of a few hours. Even quicker than that if you catch a train. I used to do that all of the time. I would drive myself to Nenagh train station and ride the train to Dublin and back when I had to take care of some business or do another television show. The people on the train always seemed to know who I was and could not believe that I would ride the train with them, me being on the telly and all. I did a Christmas special and sang "Silent Night." I did a very soulful rendition of that song and those people didn't expect it at all. That Christmas Eve, there were 3.5 million people watching the live broadcast. Back in Portroe, everyone at Dan Larkin's pub down on the lake had gathered round the box to watch their favorite resident rock star doing his thing. I used to go to Dan's place every Thursday evening to have a little play with him and the rest of his very talented family. There were always other people who would show up and bring their fiddles and guitars and drums. They were very serious about their music and still are, I would imagine. Dan was a member of the Scottish National Fiddle Orchestra and could really play that thing. We would all be playing with the fire roaring and outside the snow would be a foot deep. It was warm and cozy in that little room. The guy that played the bodhrán would hold it in front of the fire before we started playing. That was how he tuned it up. The heat from the fire tightened the skin to the exact tone that he was looking for. I remember a man playing some bones one time. He could really play those things. I could never quite get the hang of it. We would all be playing away on some jig and then like birds in the sky and fish in the sea they would all move

Beau and Daisy—what a smart dog!

at once and everyone would go into the minor at the exact same time. I could never figure out how they all knew when to go to it. Dan would say that it was the Morris Minor coming. It was just that everyone was in tune with their source and each other. It was a solid unit and the songs played themselves. Dan Larkin became my friend and still is to this day. He is a fine man and makes some excellent mead wine. I learned a lot from Dan and the rest of the musicians I was exposed to. I really got into their music and revered their abilities. Everyone was as accomplished at their instrument as I am with my voice and organ playing. Celtic music is akin to bluegrass music, which I love also.

Being a public figure has its pluses and minuses. There is definitely a down side to being famous. Your privacy is invaded. Our house was on a walled-in twenty-acre estate and we were pretty locked in there and you really had to know how to get to it. Nonetheless, I would receive mail addressed to Bobby Whitlock, Ireland. It would arrive no matter if it had an address or not.

Not everyone in Ireland approved of me being there, in spite of the fact that I was there to give, not to receive. I wanted nothing from that country, just to live there in peace. I loved that country and all of its people. I understood everyone's plight and in order for me to live there I had to remain apolitical: meaning that I rode the fence when it came to their parties and their religious concerns. I was not to get involved in anything concerning their differences no matter how I felt. I had to keep it to myself. I applied for an artist tax exemption and was amongst the last to be approved by the government before the program was ended. I was and am considered a guest in that beautiful country and can come and go as I please. I accepted their terms and was living quite a comfortable life. One day Ashley answered the phone and she had a frightened look as she handed it to me. She was only eleven at the time. An Irish man with a very thick brogue was saying, "Get out of town; you're not wanted around!" That was all that he said, over and over. And he called back several more times with the same message. It got quite unnerving as there were guns being run up the Shannon and people would go up the lake with them. They were taking them up north for the Irish Republican Army. One night I looked across the field and saw dozens of little lights coming down the mountainside. It was a

Dan Larkin's Pub in Portroe, Ireland.

search party, and the Garda were looking for weapons. They searched every building, including ours, and every barn and haystack around the countryside. They did find a cache of arms under a slurry heap on a nearby farm, and the farmer was arrested.

The second time our anonymous caller rang I went to the local Garda and told the chief what was happening. They could do nothing and had no way of tracking the call. The calls kept coming from this man, so I asked a friend to put the word out that I was being harassed by someone and it was looking like it was the IRA behind it. That got their immediate attention. My friend was contacted by them, and one evening he took me way back in the mountains into a very remote part of the county to a four room cottage for a meeting with one of the heads of the IRA. This was a very scary deal for me. There was a lot of unrest then, and bombs were going off just about every other day. A load of musicians had just been killed not long before my meeting. It was a very heavy deal, and this guy was a wanted man. I was sitting across the table from one of the most powerful people in that country. He was just a man with a cause and he was on a mission, and part of it was to exonerate the IRA from having anything to do with what was going down in my world. He said for me to not contact the Garda again and that it would be taken care of. The calls stopped. I was pretty shaken up by the whole episode and was very concerned for the safety of my family despite the reassurances from the IRA that there was nothing to concern myself about. It didn't matter by that time. I had had enough of being in their limelight and felt that it was time to pack up and go back to America. We told no one that we were leaving. I had a huge shipping crate brought to the house and some men loaded everything but the dogs into it and it was sealed up and put on a ship headed for America. We flew back home to the heart of more trouble than Ireland ever thought about. Yep, it was Memphis, Tennessee.

Back in Memphis

Shortly after arriving back in States in 1989 I bought a little log house in the woods outside of Memphis. This was the area I grew up in, so I was very familiar with every nook and cranny. It wasn't far from the Mississippi River and the Shelby Forest State Park. That's a beautiful place and was even more so when I was a boy. There was a church where my dad preached for many years and a general store that had a bench on the front porch where my dad carved his name with a pocketknife. He had a thing for carving his initials on trees, poles, benches, tables and chairs and would leave his mark everywhere. His name was James Edgar Whitlock, so his initials spelled JEW. So he was going all over the countryside and him a Southern Baptist preacher carving "JEW" on every post there was! Way too funny! I did the same thing when I was about twelve, but my initials are RSW. That actually looks good. I was named after two baseball players, Bob Feller and Stan Musial. My middle name is Stanley and I was going to be a professional baseball player until I got that idea knocked out of me. Thank goodness for small miracles. When I was last there our initials were still there on that bench. My dad's name is on the cornerstone of that Baptist church. They fired him for sitting in as an interim pastor for the local black church's minister who had fallen ill. They were God-fearing racists. It has really changed there now and is really a beautiful place to see. There are big beautiful houses where there used to be old shacks and barns. Beau lives in the area with my grandchildren. His house is not that far from his mother's, and it's good for the children to live in a place that is familiar to them and that they are near family they have always known.

A few weeks after we settled into our new home we heard it was carnival time. It was also the hottest part of the summer. When the weather turns hot in Memphis, Tennessee, it is unbearable, even at night. The Cotton Carnival had made its annual stop and had set up camp, as it always had done, on the edge of the Mississippi. There were rides, a haunted house and a guy riding a motorcycle in a steel ball cage, all of the usual carnival games and attractions that I had enjoyed ever since I was a little boy when I went there with my grandmother and Uncle Jimbo. There was something new there, though. It was a chicken behind glass that played tic-tac-toe for money. How could I resist? I laid down my $5 bill and then the game started. I hit an X, he hit an O. Then out of a chute came a kernel of corn that landed right at his feet. I hit another X and he hit another O and out came another kernel of corn. I hit another X and he hit an O and struck a line across the board and beat me! I was sure that this was a fluke so I put down another $5 bill and the game began again. This time I hit the O and he immediately hit an X. A kernel rolled out, and I hit an O and he hit the X and then I blocked him with my next O and he hit an X and striped a line across the board and beat me again! This damn chicken had beat me at tic-tac-toe two times! I laid another $5 bill down and I made the chicken start first this time.

He hit an O and then kernels of corn rolled out for him. I thought that this didn't look good for me—I was about to be shut down by a chicken. I hit the X and then he hit an O then I hit another X and he hit an O and immediately struck the line across the board and struck it again for good measure, I guess, but it pissed me off. I stood there and lost $80 of the $90 that I had brought. I didn't win one game! I guess the moral of this story is don't ever play tic-tac-toe with a chicken because they are a whole lot smarter than you think. To top my day off I went to throw the speed baseball game in front of my kids. There were a couple of real tall guys, throwing like they did when they were young and impressing even me. I was a catcher and had a pretty good arm and could just about knock you down with a baseball, but it had been quite some time since I threw a baseball. Beau played hurley in Ireland and wasn't into American games yet. I got the ball and everyone was standing around just waiting for me to fire it down the line and scorch one in. I readied myself and squatted down into the catcher position so that I could get the full effect of the motion of the throw. And, if I'm honest, to grandstand a little in front of my kids and the tall guys. I came up out of the catcher squat position and fired the ball as hard as I could right out from under my chin, where I had thrown from all of my life. Unfortunately, this time I didn't let go of the ball and it hit squarely between my two feet. I just about buried it in the soft ground. I felt humiliated. Even more so when everyone applauded and my children laughed. Everyone thought that it was funny except me. They all had a good time and everyone had a good laugh at my expense. That was OK, though, because I had had it out with that damn chicken and all that I wanted to do was stop by Colonel Sanders' place on the way home and eat his cousin. He tasted fine!

I really felt I had stepped back in time by coming back to where I grew up. I also knew it was probably a big mistake. It just took a bit of time for me to realize it. Nothing had really changed for the most part in a state-of-consciousness sort of way. The people who were there, and still are, have not changed on the inside even though appearances tend to lead you to believe otherwise. Never judge by appearances. I had bought myself another vintage Mercedes 300 SEL 4.5 and one day I pulled into the full service area of a gas station. A good ol' boy came walking out with an oily red rag in his hand, chewing gum, and he had his baseball cap cocked back on his head. I told him to fill the tank and check the oil, and that if he didn't mind, would he be so kind as to wipe the windscreen as well. He stuck the nozzle in the tank and was checking the oil and then he started looking at the front of the car and under the front of it. Then he started walking around it looking at the edge all the way to the back. Then he looked all across it and dropped out of sight. Up he popped and made his way round to the front again. He stood back a bit as to assess the whole situation and started scratching his head and looking more confused than he was already. He walked up to my window and said, "I have looked all the way around your car and up under the front and back and I can't find that windscreen anywhere!" I told him, "That's all right, just clean the window for me."

By now things between Linda and me had reached rock bottom. We had had a raging argument only days before Mother's Day. We had only been back in the country for two months, and Mother's Day was fast approaching, so I booked a table at Chez Philippe, at the Peabody Hotel, a very exclusive French restaurant, in Memphis. I was always doing whatever it took to keep the peace, but there was never a day that went by in the whole seventeen years that we didn't argue or have a big fight. Usually it was about money and how much of it that I didn't have or the fact that I didn't have a real man's job or a real man's body. Anyway, this Mother's Day was one day that I wanted to have go by without an uproar. I had it all set up with a special table in a particular area of the restaurant. It was in the middle at the top of this very lovely three-tiered room with columns, velvet drapes, chandeliers, stained glass and brass. I knew the chef quite well and was always requesting special things that he was happy to make for me. I was and still am very good friends with Gary Belz, whose family owns the Peabody. He also owns the House of Blues and Ocean Way Studios in Memphis, Nashville and in Los Angeles. The stage had been set for the perfect romantic evening with Chateaubriand and Lobster Thermidor. I had picked out a lovely white chardonnay, a beautiful red wine along with champagne and a special dessert. I was very happy that the day had been going rather smoothly but I knew that something would make her unhappy. On our way to the hotel there had been a lot of talk about nothing as usual because our relationship was one of little or no communication at best.

But this time I was set up for a fall and took it hook line and sinker. On the way to the Peabody we were talking and right in the middle of the conversation she casually said, "I think that we should get a divorce." I acted like I didn't hear her and kept right on driving and talking about the mindless nothings that she understood so well. I did not want this day and meal to be spoiled. We arrived at the hotel and settled down to our meal. Before long the conversation started heading south.

We went back home and pretty much straight to bed. It was a king size bed that felt way too small the way I was feeling. Before we went to sleep and were lying in the dark, I told her, "I think that you're right," she said, "About what?" I told her that I agreed with her about getting a divorce. She told me that I was crazy and that I did not know what I was talking about. She denied ever having said she wanted a divorce. A huge argument ensued after which I got up and put my clothes back on, got in my car and took off. It was 3 o'clock in the morning, and I tore down that country road in my Mercedes. There was thick fog everywhere. I was going too fast and came to a T-junction and didn't see the stop sign because of the fog and my speed and I ran straight through it and straddled a row of bushes that ran from the road all the way up the driveway and between two houses. Had I not kept going straight and gone to the left or right a few feet I would have run right through either one of their front doors at about sixty miles an hour. The car would not move off of the top of the bushes. I knew the guy who lived in the house on the right so I knocked on his door and he answered, "What the hell are you doing here at this hour, Bobby?" He hadn't heard all the commotion because I didn't hit my brakes. I didn't have to. I apologized about damaging the bushes and told him what was going on and he said that he would give me a ride back home and I could get the car later. He did just that, and I had a tow truck come for my car that morning. I had to replace the shrubs and the flower garden had to be redone, but other than that I was just fortunate to have kept going straight. That day was a terrible Mother's Day.

Sadly my relationship with Linda was largely a question-and-answer relationship, just answering each other by simply saying yes and no. It was, yes I did or no I didn't, or yes I will or no I won't. It was one screwed up relationship from the very start.

By now you are probably thinking, "Why didn't he just leave her?" I knew I was going to leave her but just didn't know when or how, but there was one thing I knew for sure and that's that I wasn't going to leave a house full of fatherless children when I did. I had been abandoned many times and wanted to be the father that I never had. I put my children first in my life and my career suffered because of it, but I was happy to do it.

After the Mother's Day episode, I went to a little country store in Shake Rag in the forest later that afternoon and met two of my favorite aunts, Aunt Ruby and Aunt Mertis, both sisters of my dad. We sat outside on the porch and had a few beers and talked about my situation. I called home to see if Linda would like to join us and clear the air, but my invitation fell on deaf ears. We talked and listened to the jukebox for a while. I can still remember what song was playing, "Diggin' Up Bones," sung by Randy Travis. I said goodbye to my aunts and went back to the cabin that I would only be calling home for about fifteen more minutes. When I got there Linda had thrown all of my clothes and gold and platinum records and guitars in a great big mud hole about a foot deep at the end of the drive. I had some beautiful suits and shirts that I had collected over the years and they were all floating in that mud bath. I just backed my car up to that muddy pile of what little I owned and filled up the trunk with the mud-soaked clothes and picked my guitars and records up and put them in the back seat. The front seat was full of shoes and boots and my car was packed to the max with muddy everything. The log cabin in the woods where we lived is right around the corner from where she lives right now as she married a neighbor.

As for me, I went straight to the Peabody Hotel and got a suite. I had the bellboy get two large hanging carts just for the clothes alone. They were full of my dirty shirts and suits with mud slowly dripping onto the beautiful lobby floor. We took it all up to my room and I was going to have the clothes taken to the cleaners but it came to me to ask the housekeeper how big her husband was. She said that he was my height and build and asked me why I wanted to know. I just gave her everything that I had except what was on my back. Then I went shopping for new things to wear in my new life. I was starting all over again and it felt great. Well, for a short while at least.

Building My Barn

I could not stay in the Peabody forever, so I found myself a nice apartment up on Union and Front streets. When I moved there I was feeling quite alone and I would sit up at night and watch the changing of the guards down in the alley below. After midnight there was a whole different world that came to life downtown. There was a black midget pimp who was really something to see. This little guy had it all going on, complete with a purple zoot suit, big rings, a hat with a plume and his coat dragging on the ground. He was doing the best that he could with what he had to work with. I would sit up in my window and look at the world go by from the second floor of this very cool period building that had been renovated and had about twelve very nice apartments in it. They all had wood floors that were there when the building was a cotton warehouse when Memphis was first growing. The boards were oak and each one was about two feet wide. There was a free-standing potbellied wood-burning stove that was in the middle of the front room. It was a loft apartment and was set up for one person only. It was a great little place and when I looked to the right I could see the river from my window and to the left I could see downtown. Before long I wound up with a crazy nutcase from east Memphis and ended up sharing her house for about two months. I had been manipulated one more time but there was nothing that I could do but make the best of the situation. At least I had my own room and bathroom. It started getting weird pretty fast as soon as I found out about her using and dealing cocaine. I got on a two-month bender with her and had to flee for my own sanity. I was really crazy getting back into that scene, but it was just the way it was for that moment. That was the end of it for me, and I got a nice little brick place in Lucy, Tennessee. It was just across the railroad tracks from my Granny Whitlock's house. Lucy is a little community that consists mostly of my kinfolk. Granny's house was on the corner with Uncle Aubrey and Aunt Wilma's next door. Then next to theirs was Uncle Gene and Aunt Mary's house. My cousins Virgil, Linda and Gloria were there too. We all had fun growing up together, especially Virgil and me. He's a retired cop now.

Ashley had been unceremoniously kicked out of the house at midnight by her mom and was living with me. We had a great time for those seven months. I used to cook for her every day. Her mother didn't see or speak to her for nearly all of that time. Ashley was only twelve and I'm sure it hit her hard. It's hard enough just being twelve under normal circumstances and here she was in the middle of our turmoil. It saddens me that she had to be witness to all of that terrible behavior from her parents.

One day there was a barbeque that we read about on the wall of the local grocery store. Ashley said that I should go to it and that I needed to get out and see some of my family. She said that I needed to get out of the house, which was pretty insightful for a twelve-year-old. I went to the affair, which was down on the Mississippi River. My Uncle

Tommy had a booth set up and was cooking, as were about fifty other people. It was a big do, and there were a lot of people there. Some I knew from my past and some whom I didn't know. I was walking past this table full of folks and someone said, "Bobby Whitlock, aren't you even going to say hello?" I turned around and immediately recognized the grown-up woman as a childhood friend of mine, Vivian. That was the beginning of the end of my old life. She and I started dating and eventually we got married. Ashley and I moved to her farm in Mississippi after we were wed. It was a huge horse farm with a French style country mansion in the middle of it. Shortly after we moved in the IRS came along and started looking over her books. Things were not good and she ended up having to sell the farm to pay the IRS the money she owed them.

Her farm had a big barn and some fencing, and she decided to tear it all down and take it to her father's farm near Oxford. It was still hers to tear down because the papers weren't signed yet on the sale of the house that went for virtually nothing. I was there when the deal went down. She never touched a dime of the money she got for the property. It went straight across the table to the taxman. It was a family affair for about two days, complete with picnic baskets and beer. After it was all torn down she had her oldest son pull the tractor and wagon up between the trees to block the view of where the barn used to be so that when they came up the drive to look at the house the last time before she moved out they wouldn't see a vacant lot. I guess that's when the manipulation of the scene came into play. She thought that I had money because I was a rock star and my songs were often played on the radio. Never judge by appearances. I had just paid out a huge sum and half of my royalties to my ex-wife and then another half of what was left went in a palimony suit to that nutcase back in Memphis at the same time. It felt like I was having two divorces at once, and as a result I was living off of a fourth of my income, so it was a pretty hard time financially for me. Anyway, this barn—wood and tin and fencing and all—was moved onto the place in Mississippi and was just stacked in a pile until it was re-assembled. At best it was to be a weekend retreat and was to be quite small. Once I got started building though, it started getting bigger and bigger. I dug at least a thousand two-and-a-half-foot deep holes with a hand-held post-hole digger for the cedar fence. I did this pretty much by myself. Vivian's sons were going to help, but as soon as the sun got too hot, they decided the work was too hard for them. Other times, as soon as their mama finished helping and was out of sight, so were they, and I was happy about it, too, because they weren't as passionate about life as I was. One day I was tired and decided to stop for a while and was just looking at what I had done. That hard fresh cut white oak board and cedar post fence that I had built was beautiful. The boards were fourteen feet long and one foot across and two inches thick. The fence was three boards high and seven foot centers with two rows of barbed wire. Each board had to be cut with a handsaw—no electricity involved in any of this work. This was one stout fence. You might go over or under it, but nothing was going to go through it. I strung the barbed wire all by myself as well. That's an art unto itself. When I string a piece of barbed wire it stays strung. Both of my forearms are covered with scars from stringing that barbed wire. I started adding on to the barn with plans that were just pictures in my mind as I had never built a house before, or a barn. I would just draw it out on a piece of paper and get whichever carpenter who was there at the time to get it done. I did a lot of hands-on work myself because there was no other way. I learned about building by following every carpenter and finishing his work for him, or having to redo it and get it right myself. Finally this place started taking shape and was finished enough for me to move into. I say me because nobody else wanted to live out there in the

The Ark, the house I built in Mississippi.

middle of the woods. But living in an unfinished barn seemed like a real good idea to me. The building itself was one hundred feet wide and eighty feet deep with a tin roof and a screened-in porch halfway around it. The bedroom and sitting room area upstairs was fifty-eight feet by twenty-seven feet with a seven foot vaulted ceiling. The whole building was about fourteen thousand square feet and sat in the middle of a five-acre lawn on a hill overlooking a wooded valley and rolling hills. It was very isolated and remote, not to mention very, very beautiful.

Empty Fruit Basket

I was having a very difficult time dealing with life in general. On top of that I had a family that was completely using me up in every way, and I got seriously depressed. I went to a doctor who put me on some very powerful anti-depressants. I was taking 1000 milligrams of Depekote and 150 milligrams of Effexor every day. Not to mention the Valium and other meds that I was taking. If you're not already really depressed, those drugs will get you there in a big way and will very quickly have you thinking about all sorts of things that ordinarily wouldn't enter your mind. Life for me was bleak. It was a wonder I could function at all. I was told that I would have to be on those drugs for the rest of my life. Also, I had a ringing in my right ear and it was diagnosed to be TMJ. The doctor I was seeing for the treatment had prescribed Flexeril, a muscle relaxant, every night. It works by blocking nerve impulses or pain sensations that are sent to your brain, and will kick your ass, especially when combined with a little alcohol.

I had bought an old building in Holly Springs, Mississippi, that was half a block off the town square. This beautiful little town is straight out of the not-so Civil War, with sixty-five antebellum homes. The building that I bought to renovate used to be the newspaper office during the Civil War and before that it was the Marshall County jailhouse. More recently, it had been a doctor's office, which hadn't been in operation for many years, and there was a wino living there whom I had to move out before I could fix the place up. Sort of exchanging one wino for another. We had already torn down the barn on the old farm and had moved it out to the land where I would eventually build my house. Or barn, I should say. But this little building downtown, right behind the City Café, turned out to be beautiful. The funeral parlor was directly across the street and the pharmacy was on the corner. That turned out to be way too handy. Every night when I went to bed about 1 in the morning I would hear someone playing a cello. Not playing a song, but playing two notes, doo do, doo do, doo do. I couldn't figure it out because there wasn't anybody around. I mean at night that place was dead quiet. I would get out of bed and go outside in my underwear, checking the flower shop next door to see if someone was messing with me. I think that those pills were getting me a little paranoid as well because I could never find a soul playing anything at all. It's a wonder that I didn't go to jail because I was out there one block from the courthouse running around at 2 in the morning just about every night in my underwear and cowboy boots listening to the flower shop walls. I had no idea what was wrong with me.

It wasn't too very long after the honeymoon was over that I started getting edged out of the way. What was going down in my life was no different than it had always been: Don't lie, cheat or steal and pay your taxes. Mine had gotten out of hand what with the divorce and the palimony suit, then to top it all off after the palimony thing, I married

Vivian. It was a marriage of convenience that turned out to be not so convenient for her or me. She had thought that I had money. I did, it was just that someone else was hanging on to it at the time and would be for quite some time to come. It's only just recently that I have developed an understanding and respect for money. Not so much it, but what's behind it, the nature of it and the understanding that it is the fruit from the tree of life. Unfortunately, back then my fruit basket was pretty much empty. It seemed like everyone else had their fingers in my financial pie, including the IRS. They wanted what I didn't have. Money. They wanted their share and didn't really care where it came from. And they wanted it right then. I was completely broke and Vivian thought that it would be best if I went to Ireland where I have a few friends and chill out there while she and my attorney got my tax mess sorted out. She had me convinced that I was in jeopardy and could be looking at a little time for not filing my taxes. I had been living out of the country for a while and my tax situation was and still is complicated. I still don't understand it all. I just pay them each month. I'm good with them now but that was not the case then.

I flew to Shannon airport and my friend Philip Donnelly picked me up and took me to our friend Jessica Roth's castle in Cashel to stay for a week or so. I started looking around and found a place in County Waterford in Tallow on the edge of the village. It was the dower house of the main house, Lisnabrin Lodge. It was Sir Walter Raleigh's house and was the place where he lodged his troops. It had an acre of walled gardens with every flower you could possibly imagine. The dower house is the house where the parents would be moved when they got older and the family grew. The main house was very large. The dower house had five bedrooms and was anything but small. I stayed there among friends for three months and really didn't have that much contact with anyone in the States except when it was convenient for them. I really love Ireland and when I left there I left the house full of Oriental rugs, furniture, some Levi's hanging in the closet next to my new wax jacket, and a Volvo. I had planned on returning but that was not to be the case for many years to come. When I finally did get back home to the States my tax situation was no different than when I had left. I still had to pay them what they wanted. But what had become very clear to me was that Vivian had just wanted me out of her sight for some reason. And to be quite honest I was more than happy to be away from them all. It was quiet and peaceful there in Ireland and it was a very soulful place to be. I imagine that I will eventually move back there for part of the time each year. Who knows? When I got my house there and was in there for the first night, I lay in bed and was looking out into the pasture at the sheep and the cows and all of a sudden I heard, doo do, doo do, doo do. I thought to myself that if the fat lady starts singing I'm done for! After three months of enduring that constant torture with the never ceasing ringing and cello playing I would go back to the States.

After being home for a week or so I remember walking down our very long drive at the farm with Vivian, and as we were stopping and feeling the afternoon breeze, she asked, "Do you hear all of those birds?" I replied, "What birds?" The situation was far worse than it had been in Ireland, and I was so sure that the noises in my head could be heard outside of my own left ear that I had Beau put his ear next to mine, because I knew that he had to be able to hear it, it was and still is so loud. I went to five different specialists and they did an MRI and all sorts of tests and put me on a whole load of drugs. I was started on a regimen of all sorts of pills, and that would turn out to be my undoing. They told me I had lost 95 percent of the lows in my hearing on my left side and 75 percent of my highs on my right side. I have no problem with the headphones in the studio, I just have to trust someone to hear certain frequencies for me because it is like hearing through a veil for me. I had an operation that was supposed to help me. The surgeon drilled a hole in my skull behind my left ear the size of a quarter. He cut through my ear from the front to the bottom of the back and then through my ear canal and peeled it all back, exposing my skull which had $2/3$ of the mastoid bone eaten away by a blood clot from a baseball bat blow during a long-ago argument. It looks like coral even now, and when the surgeon was finished he just sewed it up and my bass player, Handgun, came and took me home to the couch in my building in Holly Springs. Vivian only dropped me off, and she had Handgun pick me up and take me home! She could not even be bothered to come and pick me up. This was a major operation and they treated it like I just had a root canal or something.

My whole life was about to change because of this and I felt pretty alone. The operation took care of some of the noise but was replaced by the sound of my pounding heartbeat and the whole Amazon jungle. Sometimes there are even whistles and chirping. I took a further test and I was told that I had catastrophic tinnitus. I was suicidal and had contemplated many times a way out of this nightmare other than old age. I finally, after a very long time of suffering alone, found a doctor who heard my cry. I went to a doctor in Memphis as a last resort to have my whole left inner ear's workings removed because I was so miserable. He did several days of testing and concluded that I had Meniere's disease and that he could help me. I had been experiencing debilitating vertigo along with the entire Amazon jungle and the entire Democratic Convention all at once, and it was weighing pretty heavily on me. The fluid in the endolymphatic sac wouldn't drain so he put in a permanent shunt. I still had problems, though, but rather than find a way out of this I elected to turn it around and learn to live with this malady and to take back my dominion over this body. I hear through these ears, not with them, I see through these eyes, not with them and I sing through this voice, not with it. I have forgotten complete silence. I don't remember what silence sounded like. It gets very hard to deal with at times but at least I don't have to deal with the effects of the drugs that I was given. In fact the noise was still there but even more so because of those drugs. If I have to suffer with this I want to be aware of my suffering. I'm certain that there is purpose to everything that happens to us all.

I had bought some cutover land from a banker friend in Holly Springs while all of this had been going on and I had built this massive barn of a house with an aviary that looked like one at the zoo. I had also built a house and a barn for my mother-in-law and father-in law. I never do anything in a small way. The property was a very old plantation that went back in the family since before the Civil War. It was several hundred acres and had been select cut. That means basically that they came in and raped the land of its hardwoods. I could see through all of that. I saw my place in my mind. It was three and a half miles up a gravel road and my nearest neighbor lived a couple of miles away.

My New Deal

There were not a lot of musical opportunities for me at this time so I concentrated my energies on my building projects. Then out of the blue the phone rang and it was my friend Jack Tempchin, best known for writing the Eagles classic "Peaceful Easy Feeling." He was calling to ask me if I would like to do a "famous songwriter in the round" concert at The Bottom Line in New York. I agreed and did my part of the show, which had an arm's length of famous songwriters. I closed the show with an a cappella version of "Will the Circle Be Unbroken," which brought the house down. As the evening came to a close there was a line that went all the way out the door of people wanting to have me sign some albums or talk to me about something. Then there were three guys who asked me to go out at that late hour and talk about doing a record deal with a new label they were starting in England. It seemed a pretty good deal to me, so we shook hands and I went back to my hotel and then back home the next day. I couldn't help thinking that my little break to the Big Apple had turned out far better than I ever could have hoped for. Back at the farm nothing had changed in the two days I'd been gone. Everything still needed doing, and there was nobody but me to do it. My horses had to be looked after each day as well as my birds and dogs.

The record company I had signed with was called Grapevine, and they were hooked up with the Ritz Music Group in London. They were a reputable firm and at the time, a solid company. I flew over to London to look at different studios that I would use to record my new studio album. While I was there I ended up having dinner with Emmylou Harris and Mary Black and the record company executive. We were all three on the same label. Also with us was a producer who was filming a show for the BBC with Emmylou. Her keyboard player had become ill and couldn't do the show and I was asked to fill in. I said that I would be happy to. We had our dinner and talked a while, then I went back to my hotel room and off to bed. The next day we did the show. I wasn't expecting it, but I was asked if I would sing "Bell Bottom Blues" while they were getting their lighting and camera angles down. I did and they filmed me doing it. He said that when my record was finished that he would get me on another show. He just didn't know what it was at that time. It would turn out to be *Later with Jools Holland*.

The label was dragging their feet with financing so I flew home and waited to hear when I could go into the studio and record my new album. I was going crazy and had to do something to express myself. I was crumbling inside day by day. Finally I could stand it no longer and turned what had started out to be a big open three-sided shed for my tractor and cars into a recording studio of the highest caliber. I took my experience of building the barn and just drew a plan out on a piece of paper and stuck a stick in the ground and started walking until I thought that would be about how wide I wanted it.

My control room at Dead Horse in Mississippi.

Then I turned to the left and started walking again until it was as deep as I thought that it should be. Turns out that it was sixty feet wide and thirty-eight feet deep. I put three covered porches around it, one at each entrance. It was lovely to sit on any one of those porches and play guitar at night listening to the tree frogs and all of the nightlife. Two of the entrances were French doors, and a big heavy front door which I had made myself. The doors inside were from Pepper Tanner Studios, an old recording facility in Memphis.

My main room, with a 1956 Hammond B3 and a Yamaha C3 Concert Grand.

They did a lot of demos in the '60s and the place, sadly, was being demolished—such is the way of history sometimes. My studio was made like the barn but with ten different kinds of fresh cut timber. The inside had forty-five-degree-cut boards for the walls with beamed ceilings. The walls looked like a great big "W" all made out of ten kinds of wood. It really was absolutely beautiful inside and out, and I built it with my own money. I paid cash for everything. I paid for every load of lumber that was brought and for every yard of gravel that was brought and for every person ever to work there. As soon as it was built I recorded my *It's About Time* album while the record company were still trying to get their paperwork

My 1956 Hammond B3. I was the first ever to play this organ because it had been in storage ever since it was new.

together. They were just taking too long to get everything organized, and I didn't want to wait. It turned out to be a good thing, because that beautiful place would never have been built had I waited. The band consisted of Brady Blade on drums, Daryll Johnson on bass and Buddy Miller on guitar. Steve Cropper did his parts at his studio in Nashville without me even being there. He's Steve Cropper; I would have just been in the way. Jim Horn drove from Nashville and brought his wife when he came to play his parts. Everyone stayed at the farm and at a nice place in Oxford. When the album was finished and everyone had gone home it was as if it had never happened at all. Things were exactly the same on the farm, not to mention a complete and utter disrespect for me, and what I did for a living. It seemed everyone I had been involved with romantically wanted me to be anything but a musician. I was just waiting for the day to come when I would be liberated from that place.

In the end I recorded just that one record there and then let everyone in Oxford who wanted to record come and do it for free. The North Mississippi Allstars were the first, and then there was a steady procession of bands, from my son's friends to locals, just trying to get their feet wet in my studio. It became a state-of-the-art recording facility against all manner of objections from Vivian. She just saw it as a complete waste of time and money. But as I had done it all on my own money I didn't have to ask anyone for their permission to do anything. I still don't, for that matter, as I am not governed by a corporate suit or any corporation, and that is exactly what the record company was. The only good to come of it was that through circumstances arising from that last trip to London and that meeting with Emmylou Harris I was invited to be on the popular *Later with Jools*

Holland television show to promote my new CD. The call came through from the producer. It was only a couple of days later that they called again and asked if it would be all right with me if Eric Clapton did the show with me. I told them that I would have to think it over. I wanted to do the show, but I didn't want to ride on Eric's star power to do it. Unfortunately I was having a very difficult time with my meds then and was drinking wine to kick them all in. I have done some serious drugs in my past and nothing even comes close to those anti-depressants. The producer called back after me not getting back to them right away and he was in a bit of a panic. Something about Eric's plans and I don't know what else it all was, but I agreed to do it.

I flew over on April 24, 2000, and nearly got thrown off of the plane because of my physical condition and my impatience. My mouth always preceded my good judgment, but it was always too late by then. I really could not help myself at that time. I was taking what was given to me by the various doctors to try to make everyone else happy about my mental condition. Which was perfectly fine. It was just covered up with all of those prescribed drugs. I had to spiral down even more before I hit bottom. I was put up at the Inn on the Park, which was very nice and very near Princess Diana's palace in Kensington.

I went to the studio the following day for rehearsals and a run-through. When I walked in I had just come in from the sun and was focusing on finding the piano and had walked right past Eric, who was sitting on his guitar amp. He was wearing a baseball cap and a sweatshirt and looked just like I imagined he would. I went over and apologized for ignoring him and had a little talk. He had driven himself and his then-girlfriend, and now wife, Melia, and carried his own guitar in. We rehearsed the songs that we were to do, "Bell Bottom Blues" being one of them. I never played an E major on the organ so I didn't play it on the piano. I didn't have to play it because Eric and Carl Radle already were. The organ is a different kind of instrument. You can bridge gaps in sound without moving around a lot. Anyway, we elected to leave it out completely. Eric had done it some time earlier at Royal Albert Hall with a full orchestra and played an E major every time it came around. That's the way it should go. He ought to know, he wrote it. After we finished the rehearsal he asked me what I was wearing for the main show and I told him just a blue shirt. That's about all that I could fit into because I was so bloated from taking all of those drugs. My neurotransmitters were shorting out, and I was convulsing sporadically. My hands shook uncontrollably and didn't stop until my fingers touched the keys. As a direct result of all of those prescription drugs given to me by three doctors, I was about to come unglued in front of the world with Eric Clapton and Jools Holland and his band and everyone in the whole room watching it all unfold. It was all that I could do to hold myself together the whole time that I was there, on and off camera. My insides were trembling so much that my stomach ached from the contractions, and I was wringing wet. I remember looking across the room and seeing Eric sitting so calm and serene and I knew right then what had to happen. Eric told me that he thought that I was just nervous. In reality I felt like the bug in *Men in Black*. I couldn't fit into my skin. It was way too small. I just couldn't wait for it all to be over and for me to be back safe at home in my isolated world. The Grapevine label and the Ritz Music group eventually went belly up and the president of the company gave me back my masters and told me that I could do with them as I pleased. "It's About Time" was released only in Great Britain and was a limited release at best. It morphed into *My Time* after all these years: We remastered it and added two new songs and released it properly in 2009.

The Spiritual Void

The *Jools Holland* show was the final wake-up call. I had to free myself of those pharmaceuticals because I knew that they were about to be the end of me. I was afraid that I was going to be like the walking dead. I didn't know where to turn, so I tried a psychologist in Oxford, Mississippi. That didn't turn out too well because when I arrived he had all of my records in his office for me to sign. I was losing my mind and this idiot wanted me to give him my autograph. I felt I couldn't turn to anyone.

Then I had a thought. I had been talking with Delaney Bramlett and his wife, CoCo, over the last few years and knew that he had also been fighting his own demons with drugs and alcohol. CoCo and I had always gotten on well on the phone and I thought that she might be able to give me some advice. It seemed that neither of us had anyone we could talk to or who could see us for who we were. CoCo was the only intelligent person that I knew. It was always a joy to hear her lovely voice at the end of the phone. By the time I was to make this call to CoCo, Delaney had been in rehab nineteen times and had just returned from one more time and was doing well for the moment. I asked her for information on the place where Delaney had just been. She was surprised that I had asked her that because from the outside it looked like things were OK with me and my family. CoCo had a friend who was married to the guy that shod my horses, and she had been keeping her up to date with what was going on with me. I told CoCo that I wanted to go into treatment to get off of these pills that I had been taking. I had been told that I would have to take them the rest of my life and I wasn't going for it. I wanted to be off all of them straight away. She said that the facility was Discovery Place, near Nashville, Tennessee. She sent me the brochure that read on the front, "Discovery Place, A Spiritual Retreat."

When I saw that word, "spiritual," I knew what it was that was missing and had been all of my life, God. I felt I was spiritually bankrupt and had been filling a void that I didn't even know existed with alcohol, drugs, sex and everything else imaginable. But at least I had seen a glimpse of light at the end of the tunnel, and one that wasn't a freight train this time. I had all of the answers. Now I was going to have to find the questions to them. I just had to get those drugs out of my system. Vivian was totally against it, as was most everybody else, except for one doctor, Dr. Radwyn Hyckle, a psychiatrist who was the head of Charter Lakeside in Memphis. He was the only doctor who told me that I was an artist and that all of those drugs were robbing me of my creativity. He wanted to see me off everything. So thank you, Dr. Hyckle.

When I checked in I lied and said I didn't need to detox so that I could get in quicker. The staff are not doctors but recovered alcoholics and addicts. It was a big antebellum mansion on a lake in the country and was very serene. Vivian dropped me off on the road out front and didn't even get out of her truck. She just drove off and didn't look back. That was soon to be the same thing that I would do to her. I went through withdrawal symptoms for three solid days and nights, throwing up purple bile the whole time, and I very nearly died because I had I stopped taking the drugs the day that I checked in. They confiscated all of them. It didn't matter to me because I would rather have died than to live the rest of my life like that. I went into convulsions within hours and it got real hairy and very, very scary very quickly. Things leveled out after several days of agony, and then I wanted to find out what had happened to me. Why did all of that happen? When I was at my lowest ebb about three days into the sweats and the shakes, I was slumped in a chair when a voice came to me and said, "Fear not!" It told me that all of my fears had been relieved, and they had been. The voice was as clear to me now as it is to me then. I knew whose voice it was, too: It was the voice of my own consciousness. I went through the whole month just to get an education. And that month was made easier with the support of CoCo, who would send a constant stream of cards and candy from Los Angeles. I did not get one card from home, but my daughter sent a couple of cards of encouragement. When the time came for me to leave I asked my childhood friend Danny Abbott if he would pick me up and take me back to Mississippi. And he, like the very good friend he was, agreed to do just that. He has since passed and I think of him often. When I got home, I was sober, and the circus was just beginning to start. I remember the date very well; it was October 13, 2000. It was the day I came off the meds. When I came off those powerful drugs I came off of everything else as a consequence. I had taken to drugs very easily, but after years of abuse, I luckily grew away from it all. If I hadn't, I have no doubt I would not be around today.

Meeting CoCo for the First Time

CoCo and Delaney came to Mississippi to visit some of his relatives. My farm wasn't too far away, so I drove over to see them and got to finally meet CoCo in person. We had been talking on the phone ever since she and Delaney got together and had become friends after many conversations throughout the years for many different reasons. He was twenty years her senior and she was his slave. The first thing I heard when she opened the door was "Get me my shoes!" I could see it in her eyes and tell by the way that she responded to him that he was controlling her. And it saddened me yet again because I could see that nothing with Delaney had changed over the years.

I went to see his family for a visit and there was all of the usual southern Mississippi hospitality going on. Lots of sweet ice tea and barbecue and Delaney, the star of the show as always, singing and looking up with his hand held to the sky. This was all taking place in the living room and I was standing in the dining room looking around the corner at CoCo. I couldn't keep my eyes off of her because I was falling in love with her. She had no idea, of course, and we were both married so nothing was going to happen. She was my best friend and here he was old enough to be her daddy and she was this beautiful light that no one saw but me. I couldn't take it anymore so I just left without saying goodbye. I went back home to my isolated self-imposed prison on that hill out in the middle of nowhere. All I kept thinking about was the fact that he had her and did not appreciate her. He did not see or hear the light that I could so plainly see with a voice that shined through a wall of sound. Night was closing in and it was getting dark. The next morning I collected myself and got on with my daily chores of feeding all of my birds and horses and tried to get some normality back in my life.

CoCo called me up a few weeks after they got back to California to tell me Delaney was throwing up blood and a lot of it. He wouldn't let her call anybody but me. I told her to take him to the hospital straight away. She told me that he didn't want to go, so I got him on the phone and told him that Eric Clapton had nearly bled to death from a bleeding ulcer in the '80s. When he heard that Eric had gone into the hospital for the same thing, he suddenly agreed to go. CoCo said that they didn't have any money. I told her to take him to the nearest emergency hospital because they cannot refuse a dying man. He had not been able to stop drinking alcohol and doing drugs, and it was literally killing him. She took him to the hospital and they took him straight into ICU where he stayed for nearly twenty days.

A few days after the phone call, I flew out to help CoCo with the family and to help get him moved to another hospital. The Bramlett family were giving CoCo a hard time, as if it were her fault Delaney was ill. She was the one bit of sanity in that whole family. He was doing drugs and drinking the first day that I met him forty-three years ago and he still was. It was really sad to witness. When I arrived at the hospital he was in restraints and going through very bad delirium tremens, which are a severe reaction to withdrawal from alcohol and can be deadly. They usually start between 24 to 72 hours after a chronic alcoholic either stops or limits his drinking. Delaney was hooked up to an Ativan drip and was going in and out of consciousness as he was detoxing. When they loosened his restraints he would become violent and delusional. As a result of his violent outbursts, he was asked to leave, and we had no choice but to move him out of the V.A. Hospital to Michael's House, a chemical dependency treatment center in Palm Springs. I helped them move him off of his bed onto the gurney for the ride.

Delaney had been planning on organizing a benefit show for the various rehabs he had been in. Unfortunately, he had fallen off the wagon again and was not in good shape. I'm pretty sure that he did not remember a thing about me being there and talking about a band for the show, and him giving Bobby Keys the finger at the mention of his name for some reason. I stayed only two nights there at Delaney's house, with his mother and CoCo. I stayed in the pool house both nights and the second day I took CoCo out for a nice Italian lunch. I thought that I'd give her a little pampering because, heaven knows, she needed it. Jack Tempchin heard I was in town and asked me to come and sing and play a few numbers with him at The Joint, a club in Hollywood where he was playing. I asked CoCo to go and then I asked Mamaw if she would like to go with us. She said no, she was going to stay at home. We went to the club and I played, then we came back home and I went to bed in the pool house and CoCo went to her room. The next morning I left California and flew back home to Mississippi to start organizing the benefit show. I took over the responsibility from Delaney and decided to hold it at the famous Ryman Theater in Nashville because it was a convenient location for all the musicians. Bonnie called and said that I should ask CoCo if she would like to sing with her, Bekka Bramlett and me for the show. I had rounded up the best of the best to do this show. I had contacted Chuck Leavell, Bobby Keys, Jim Horn, Steve Cropper, Levon Helm and my friend Peter Young, who was going to play guitar with us as well. I have no doubt that had it all happened—which it didn't—it would have been an amazing night as well as the first time that all three of the Bramlett women had sung together. Everyone wanted to be a part of it, and I was really looking forward to it. I called CoCo out in L.A. to tell her what Bonnie had said and that I would like for her to come and play with us. I also told her that it would do her good to get away since Delaney was in the Palm Springs facility. She said that she would be happy to do it. I was very, very excited about it and so was everyone else I told. CoCo had sent some recordings of some of her songs and they were in every player on the farm and in everybody's car, including Vivian's. As a matter of fact she said to me once that she thought that CoCo and I would make a very good singing duo. I would sing along with CoCo's songs and it did sound good. Everyone started showing up at the farm for rehearsals, and I had to put some of them in one of the other houses on the other side of the place, and at my sister-in-law's house, which was right next door. Anyway, CoCo was going to drive to Mississippi in her lovely old blue Mercedes along with her dog Queenie. I emptied the tool room in the barn and turned it into a space for CoCo ready for her arrival in a couple of weeks. It was on the corner and had a little porch as well. I was real big on porches, as you have probably figured out. Seemed like the thing to do. Every porch needs some stairs and a swing on it. I did this room out myself, decorating it with an African motif, and I put a closet in it. It also had its own separate bathroom with a very large shower. I put in a beautiful iron bed with end tables and a big leopard picture on the wall. It turned out really well. I was proud of my work, and Vivian actually came out and helped with the decorating. I loved doing this room for CoCo—she meant the world to me and I wanted only the best for her and this room would be big in her world. I knew because I had just left her world and had seen how she had been living. She was the servant to all of them and they all treated her like she was their personal slave. No one there appreciated her. Not only had she been looking after Delaney and going through all of that, she had to look after his mother as well, and that woman could be a handful.

The plan was for CoCo to do the show in Nashville and then go back home to California after it was over. Some of the proceeds were to go to Discovery Place, where Delaney had been, and to Michael's House, where he was staying. We also had a silent auction set up at the Ryman with several very cool hot rods as well as several guitars donated by Fender and Gibson. All of the money was to go to charity. Delaney's daughter Susanne and I worked very hard to get him into Michael's House. No other place would take him because of his history and the financial aspect. It wasn't that easy to accomplish what we did by getting him in there. It took a lot of calls and pleading with strangers for assistance in every way possible.

Then disaster struck. Someone had called Delaney at Michael's House and told him about CoCo coming to Mississippi for the show

Me on our first day in Mississippi (photograph by CoCo Carmel).

CoCo on our first day in Mississippi (photograph by Bobby Whitlock).

and that she was having an affair with me, which wasn't true. Delaney called her and told her that she better leave the keys and the credit cards where they were, and he would see her when he got home. He was furious and demanded to know about her relationship with me. He seemed to have come out of his dementia and to have sobered up immediately and was on his way home to stop her from leaving. He did not believe she was simply coming to sing at the show that would have benefited several rehab facilities. CoCo was terrified and feared the worst from him. She knew that this was the end of her marriage and that she had no other option but to move away for her own sanity and safety. She had been planning her escape for years, but the opportunity had never presented itself like this before. She had been methodically putting things in her car very secretly so Mamaw would not get any more suspicious than she already was. The car was loaded and he was now on his way home, so she locked his precious guitars in the closet. She put Queenie in the car and the house keys in the freezer outside and put that place high and behind her. She would never look back and hasn't since.

Her mother, Sheryl, drove with her to Dallas and caught a plane back to San Diego. She went to keep her company and to spend some time with her daughter, because neither knew how long it would be before they were to see each other again. CoCo was calling me all along the way to find out how close she was. I kept telling her that it's not that far from Dallas to Mississippi. It didn't look that far on the map to me. It was that same day that she called and told me that she was in Memphis. She had driven ten hours straight. I was so excited that I could hardly contain myself! She would be there in an hour! I couldn't believe she was almost there! I went to meet her at the turnoff at the Holly Springs exit. When she turned off she went left onto another place down below. I was on my phone and she was on hers. I said, "I'm up here!" She had turned into a lot just below where I was standing. I said again, "I'm up here!" I went down the hill to be with CoCo and to welcome her to my home and to my world. She had left, never to return to that old way of life. We did not know at that time just who it was that made the call that would ultimately be the one that would so drastically change all of our lives forever. That person had started a false rumor that CoCo and I were having an affair, which we weren't, but it didn't matter anyhow because folks had already made their minds up and there would be no changing them. Later, Delaney relapsed from what was to be his last chance at sobriety. He would eventually pass on December 27, 2008, never knowing the truth about CoCo leaving and the relationship between us. At home, all hell was breaking loose because everybody thought that CoCo and I had had an adulterous affair, and nothing could have been further from the truth. I still considered Delaney my friend, so was she, and we were both married. The air was so thick that you could cut it with a knife. Both sides of our families had lost control of us, and they in turn lost control of themselves. CoCo and I stayed clean and sober.

In the meantime I received a telephone call from a guy who said that he was a big fan and had both Eric's and my autographs on the *Layla* album when the Dominos were on the road in America. His name was Tim Wilson and he told me that he had done a report about the Dominos for his school graduation. He said that he had a dream about making a record with me and some other people for an all-star session. Unfortunately, my life was out of control and I was going through a very rough patch with my marital problems. I couldn't even count on myself for anything, so I told him I would not be able to help him. I hung up and went on about my daily business of looking after my horses and birds on my farm. A couple of days later Jerry Wexler called me. I could hardly believe that he was calling me, and I couldn't wait to hear what it was about. He told me that an aspiring record producer with whom he had been in contact really needed me to be a part of his project and that he, Jerry, highly recommended that I do it. Even though I was not thinking straight, I decided to at least find out about the session. It wasn't thirty minutes after I hung up the phone with Jerry that Tim called me again. He asked if I had talked to Jerry Wexler and I told him that I had and I asked what the project entailed. It was going to be called the *All Night All Stars* and was the brainchild of Steve Melton, the other producer, and Tim. They both shared a huge respect for the music from the South. Tim is also a Southern comedian, and many legendary Southern musicians have graced his comedy albums. Steve has been behind the mixing desk for albums by artists as diverse as the Amazing Rhythm Aces, Etta James, Bob Seger, Lynyrd Skynyrd and Levon Helm, to name but a few. Their idea for the *All Night All Stars* was a simple one, to share the magic of Southern R&B music of the late '60s and early '70s with a new generation of listeners. What a great idea!

I remember Tim telling me that he had a dream of me driving in my Oldsmobile 98 with him, Levon Helm and Gregg Allman and we were on our way to the studio to cut a record, and he was the producer. He didn't at that time know that I had a 1971 Oldsmobile 98 sitting outside the window and was looking at it as he was telling me this. He said that he had always wanted to put a band together with Levon, Gregg, and me and go into the studio with him producing "A Day Without Jesus." He said that it was his favorite song and that he was supposed to be doing this. I told him that I was looking at my Olds right then and that I would be happy to do it, just let me know when and where. He said he would be back in touch after he got it all put together. At this point it was unclear just where the sessions were to be held. It was either going to be in Nashville or Muscle Shoals. I was hoping for Nashville. Another call from Steve confirmed that it would be there. He also told me that there would be a lot of other well known players who were going to be on it as well and the album would be released by Capitol Records. Tim and Steve got members of the Atlanta Rhythm Section, the Allman Brothers Band, Lynyrd Skynyrd, Steppenwolf, Traffic, Wet Willie and The Band, along with some amazing vocalists and session musicians synonymous with blue-eyed soul to play on the album.

The only problem was that all of this was going down while everything in my world was falling apart. I had also been rehearsing my band for the Ryman gig, and CoCo was still making plans to come and be on the show at this time. And now I had this record going down. So there was a lot of activity in my life all at once, but it was all very well organized, which was surprising because I didn't have anyone helping me. I was basically running the show from my end quite well. Or so it would seem for a while. When CoCo finally arrived we were pretty much ignored by everyone because of the drama that was starting up. As a result, the Delaney benefit show was stopped by me because everything was crashing down around me at the farm. On top of that the promoter wanted me to sign a completely unreasonable deal that would have meant that the rehab centers would not have seen a dime. It was an impossible situation, and my stress levels were off the scale! I went to a doctor and was prescribed some powerful anti-depressants. I did not want to go down that road again, but I needed something to see me through the mess I found myself in. Unfortunately, I had a very bad reaction.

I walked up on my porch one evening and when I walked through the double French doors my front room had a family of Mexicans in it. There was a woman and three nasty little children with runny noses sitting on my couch not saying a word. And there was a man standing by the big front door and another standing right behind my blue leather chair. And another one was sitting in it. They were dressed like banditos complete with bullet belts, chaps, six shooters at their sides, large hats with well-worn brims and boots with Mexican spurs with big rowels on them. They never said a word but just looked at me in a sinister way while grinning and nodding their heads with those large mustaches and beards. Strangers in my home and I'm all alone with them and outnumbered! Like a flash I drew my gun with the hammer cocked and said, "Get the hell out of my house!" They just stood there. "Get out of my house!" I said again. Same thing, just nodding and grinning, and then I pulled the trigger! Bam!" I shot right next to my chair and hit my rifle holster that was hanging on the end post of the cedar railing behind the chair. Then they all vanished! They were just an illusion. It was a hallucination, and it was because of the combination of those powerful drugs and the wine I had been drinking.

I got my rifle out of the holster that was full of holes and a huge silver throwing knife that was perfectly balanced. I can hit a moving target with it and throw it underhanded or from behind my back and it sticks! I stuck the knife in the back of my belt and walked out into the night. Chance, who was always with me, was 155 pounds of pure badass dog! That dog loved me and I loved him. We walked out in the front yard and I could see a motor home pulling through the gate to my pasture down into my woods and then disappearing into the dark. Chance and I ran after them. But it was just underbrush everywhere and it was pitch black down in those woods. I got caught up in the thickets and briars and thorns. I didn't realize that I was still hallucinating. Then I saw some headlights through the trees up on the road. They turned into the drive and pulled partway up and stopped and got out. Vivian was coming home from work with her sister and her boyfriend. I came walking up out of the woods with that big ol' dog and all scratched up with a knife in my left hand and a 30-30 Winchester long rifle in the right. It had been a hell of a night, and it wasn't over yet! I walked up and she and her sister were standing there like they suspected that something might have been going down that may have been a little unusual. She asked, "What's going on here? What the hell have you been doing?" So I told her about the Mexicans and what had gone down. She said that I was crazy. And then she said, "What are you doing with that rifle?" All of this time I was crying out for help. She should have been calling the medics to come and help me.

There was a time I was staring down the barrel of a loaded and cocked .44 Ruger Bearcat! I called 911 and asked for the suicide hotline, and they didn't have one. And the woman on the other end of the line thought that I had just had too much to drink and should sleep it off. I couldn't even get the police to come and take me away. I would have rather been in a jailhouse in town than sitting in that self-imposed prison on that hill, locked away in the one that was my mind. At least I would be safe from myself. That's who I was afraid of. I stopped taking those meds the next day. Cold turkey.

I took CoCo and a guitar player friend of ours to a meal at the City Cafe in Oxford. I didn't live far away and was always alone out there, so going to Oxford was a daily treat for me. Sometimes I would go to different places in town and sit at the bar and socialize with folks. I was just lonely. Vivian went to work in Memphis sixty miles away every day at 11 in the morning and didn't come home until 2 or 3 every night. She wouldn't quit the job that she had when we got married and it really bothered me because she didn't need the money. What I did not realize was that she was stashing away every dime that she made and making plans. I got up to go to the restroom, and when I came walking back CoCo and our friend were in a very deep conversation, and she had a shocked expression. I sat down and she told me that he had just told her that all of my family on both sides, except for Beau and my brother, Nate, had signed legal papers and were going to have me put away in the state mental institution in Oxford. They said that I was incapable of handling my personal affairs and that I was delusional and out of control. It seemed that there would be nothing that CoCo or I could do about it. Had it happened I'm certain that I would still be in there.

I dropped CoCo off at her room at the farm. It was very dark with no moon, but the sky was full of stars. It looked absolutely astounding, and a sense of peace came over me. I got back in my '71 Oldsmobile and drove to the other side of my place and sat on the a hill looking out across the valley at my home on the other side, saying to myself out loud, "Bobby, how much longer are you going to put up with all of this?" I knew then that it wouldn't be much longer.

The next day I brought CoCo back to the farm after having had lunch in Oxford. There were cars that I had never seen before. I recognized my daughter's but none of the rest. Something was definitely happening. When I walked in the door my wife went upstairs. I followed, trying to get her to tell me what was going on. She told me that they all wanted me to see another doctor, a shrink, and have me put on some more medication. I had taken enough of that to last ten lifetimes and that was not going to be happening to me again. To be honest, I would rather be dead than to be on all of that again. It very nearly killed me coming off all of that stuff only months before.

Suddenly, in the middle of all this, she asked, "Do you want a divorce?" I told her that she didn't want me to answer when there was so much turmoil going down. She asked again. She wasn't asking, she was really telling me that she was the one who wanted it, so I said, "Yes!"

She told me to get that woman out of her house and pack my clothes and get the hell out of there. All the time she was saying this, I was packing. I knew that something was going to be going down, I just didn't know when. I went downstairs and told CoCo that I was going to get us some rooms at a hotel in Oxford until I could figure out what to do. We had two rooms, one for CoCo and Queenie and one for me. The next day we went to Holly Springs to the bank to see my friend Dick. I paid the six-month note of $30,000 and kept $5,000 for us to get started with our new life, whatever it was to be. I told Dick that I wanted to sign everything over in my wife's name. He asked why.

I told him that Vivian wanted a divorce and that she would be wanting it all and she could have it. I took CoCo back to her room and went to the farm against CoCo's advice. The sheriff wasn't there yet. I walked up to the porch and she was sitting there waiting. I asked her what she thought she deserved out of our union and she screamed, "Everything!" I told her that that's what I thought that she would say and handed her the deeds and the paid tax receipt and turned and walked away. I have seen her only one time since, by accident and very briefly. Friends thought that I was crazy for walking away and not putting up a fight for my home and all of my things, including everything in the studio. I said, "Why would I fight for something that I really don't want?" I left that place in the pouring rain and have never looked back.

No one cried except me when I had my breakdown after I realized the magnitude of what had happened and that I had lost everything, as well every one of my family members. My daughter had said, "Daddy why don't you just go ahead and tell them that you did have an affair, even if it's not true!" I told her, "At the risk of losing my entire family and all that I have, I will not tell a lie and degrade this beautiful friendship that I have with CoCo just to appease all of your insatiable appetites for control over something of which you have none." I was so sad because I couldn't believe that my family would believe such a thing. I thought that they knew me better than that. They all turned their backs on me, all that is, except Beau. He said to me, "Hell, Dad, you divorced my own mother and I stayed out of it, why should I get upset over you divorcing this woman?" His sister didn't see it that way, though. To this day I have yet to see my daughter Ashley, and it has been nine years. This all took place in May 2001. After all of this time we are just now re-establishing our relationship from afar. CoCo was my good friend and she was the only intelligent person that I knew. The rest were a bunch of hayseeds who couldn't carry on a conversation, and I haven't heard from or seen one of them since I left.

Safe at Last

There's nothing quite like a setback to get you started all over again. CoCo and I were holed up in a hotel with her old dog Queenie. We were stunned by the events that were happening all around us. Outside it was a black sky and it was pouring. I was to leave anyway to go to Nashville to be on the *All Night All Stars* session. It was my intention to take CoCo there to meet everyone and help her get her a new start in life. I loved her so deeply that I would have been her manservant for the rest of my life just to be with her. We were just the very best of friends, and I wanted only the best for CoCo. Even though we were close enough to touch, we were out of each other's reach, because we were both still married. I went to her room to call Steve Melton, the co-producer, who lived in Muscle Shoals, to ask if I could leave my guitars in his studio on the way to Nashville for the session. This all happened in front of CoCo. I dialed his number and there was no tone, no ring, no nothing. I said, "Hello?" He said, "Hello?" I said "Steve?" he said, "Bobby?" We had called each other at exactly the same time, and there was no ring on either end. He was calling to tell me that the session had been moved to Muscle Shoals. CoCo, Queenie and I headed to Muscle Shoals. At least we had someplace to go and something to do when we got there. As we were about to leave, our friend Peter Young called to tell us that there was a roadblock set up on the Marshall County line to stop me and that the sheriff was going to take me to the mental asylum in Oxford. Peter had called from my farm, where he was still staying and would continue to stay for quite some time after I left. The roadblock was east so we decided that we would head north through Batesville and then on to Memphis and east to Alabama. We did just that in the dead of night and in the pouring rain. When we got through Memphis we had to go through a short stretch of Mississippi right through Marshall County. It was raining so hard that I couldn't see CoCo behind me and had to keep slowing down for her to catch up. Her car was a diesel Mercedes and wasn't very fast. The worst part was that we had to stop for gas at this place in the middle of nowhere just a few miles from the Alabama state line, in Marshall County, no less! We pulled up under the awning and up to the pumps and I filled both cars. When I walked in to pay I saw there were three highway patrol officers and a couple of rednecks from Holly Springs whom I recognized. They knew me as "that musician feller." None of them said a word. When I was standing there paying for the gas they were sitting behind me and I could feel them staring holes through me. The atmosphere in there was so thick that you could cut through it with a knife. It made the hair on the back of my neck stand up, and I felt like turning around and running out of there as fast as I could. Instead, I casually turned and nodded to them as I passed their scornful frowns. My heart was pounding so hard that I thought for sure that they could hear it. We pulled out of there and took a right onto the highway and headed east toward the Alabama state line a few miles away. The rain had let up considerably and we could see a little better. In fact I could see clear enough to see blue lights coming up on us fast in the distance. They lit up the haze-filled night sky with a bright blue and red glow that signaled trouble. It was the sheriff! I kicked that Rocket 88 down and that big four-barrel opened up on that 455 engine, and those glass packs racked off. I tore down that highway with my foot to the floor and I was going so fast that I lost CoCo in the spray behind me. I finally slowed down and she caught up as we crossed the Alabama state line. Safe at last!

The first thing we did was to find an apartment. But after four months we did not have enough money to pay the rent, and it was only $300. I had spent what little I had brought with me, and the well had run dry. I had $9 in my pocket and was in the middle of a complete breakdown. I was sober but I still had the Democratic National Convention in my head. I was crying all of the time because I had lost everything and everyone that I ever knew in my life. They all had turned their backs on me when I needed them the most. Nobody believed me or in me. I felt totally alone and was in the bathtub crying like a little boy whose dog had just died. I didn't know what to do and CoCo was doing her best to console me. But she was going through her own personal turmoil at the time as well. We were both on the run from our respective families.

I didn't know what to do about the financial situation so I called Warner-Chappell and spoke with my contact there in royalties. He and I had a relationship that went back many years, and I thought that he would be able to give me an advance on my royalties because he was in charge of royalties. I told him of my dilemma and that I was going through hell and was suffering because of what had happened and was happening to me. I told him that I had stopped taking all of the medicine that I had been taking and was feeling the effects of it. I told him that all I had was $9 in my pocket and my world was coming apart. He said that they couldn't advance me any money but asked if I had ever thought of selling the income from my catalog. I told him that I didn't know that it was mine to sell. He told me that he was going to talk to his superior there and he felt sure that they would buy my share of the income from *Layla*. I owned a quarter of the income generated by the copyrights to it and was unaware of the fact that I could sell it. He hung up the phone and it wasn't ten minutes later that it rang again and they said that they would give me a lot of money for my share. Well, I had $9 in my pocket

CoCo and me on the road and on the run in my 1971 Olds Rocket 88 (photograph by Bobby Whitlock).

and was having a complete mental breakdown and they want to buy my copyright interest today! Hell yes, I'll sell it! I didn't realize that when I did that I would be selling my rights for Warner-Chappell in the United States as well. I thought that they were two different branches of the same tree. I thought that the European monies were one side of the company and that the American side was a different branch, like mechanicals and sales and airplay. I just didn't have a very clear understanding as to what was really taking place. I thought that I would still receive my money from United States sales. That was not to be the case as I would find out later. Turns out I sold my income rights for the world forever! I was ignorant, not stupid. Had I known then what I know now I would never have sold it, or at least not all of it. I could have sold only part of it but I wanted to rid myself of it. I thought that it was the root of my problem. But when I sold it nothing changed. Not really. But it did give us enough to get a fresh start.

We went to Muscle Shoals studios to play on the *All Night All Stars* sessions and they went really well, all things considered, and only took ten days to complete. It was also the first time that CoCo and I were recorded singing together. We did "A Day Without Jesus" and "Tell the Truth." When we went to Alabama we had not planned on staying. I never in my whole life planned on going, much less living, there. We were initially staying at the Holiday Inn in Muscle Shoals to be near the studio. Then I ended up renting a house on the Tennessee River and stayed there while CoCo and her old dog Queenie continued to stay at the hotel. After a while of seeing each other, what with me driving into town to visit her or CoCo coming out to my house to visit me on the river, we decided to move in together. Everyone had already crucified us and were calling us adulterers and thieves anyway. It was terrible what was being said about CoCo and me behind our backs. After the sessions we decided to stay and give it a go, so I bought a house that needed renovating in Tuscumbia, and we moved into the apartments across the street. We were, on a daily basis, tearing it apart and starting the renovation. In the meantime I had bought CoCo a 1956 356 Porsche, and we sent her old Mercedes back to Delaney. I had one of my workers drive it to California and then fly back. I had my 1955 Chevy hot rod pickup truck and my 1971 Oldsmobile Rocket 88 as well. We seemed to have accumulated quite a lot of things when we first started our lives over.

I was asked to participate on another all-star session when we were in Alabama. But before I tell you about it I need to

Shopping in Tuscumbia, Alabama, with the $4 suit that had been on the rack since 1965, a perfect fit (photograph by CoCo Carmel).

recount a story that Delaney told me. He said he had had a guitar that once belonged to Duane Allman that he sold for $10,000. It was a little red Gibson guitar. I have one just like it that I got from a pawn shop in Oxford, Mississippi, for $175. Delaney asked me for it once over the phone and I told him, "No way, man!" That's when he told me that he had had one just like mine that he had sold to a Japanese collector. He told the dude that he had found it in a pawn shop in Atlanta and that Duane had said that it was his first-ever guitar. Delaney then told me that Duane had asked for it back but Delaney refused. Delaney said that there was a thumbnail chip off the paint on the back and that's how he knew it was Duane's. The Japanese guy had another man drive down with the money from San Francisco to pick it up for him. Delaney started to get cold feet because he was really not sure that it was Duane's and this guy was coming straight to Delaney's house with the money. Delaney wanted to stop the transaction but it was all too late. The deal had been struck and this dude got stuck. As fate would have it I was to meet this Japanese collector in Alabama and play on his record. I then found out that he is a famous guitar player as well as a very wealthy collector of vintage guitars in Japan. His name is Kunio Kishida. I played on a session for his *Alabama Boy* and *Statesboro Blues* albums along with Chuck Leavell and a bunch of other famous people. Johnny Sandlin was his producer. When CoCo and I went to the session Kunio had all of his guitars lined up and was changing guitars in the middle of each song. He'd stop the tape and change guitars then roll tape and record. He wanted different tones as he went along. I had never seen anybody do that, but it makes sense in a way. He had a big book with pictures of all of his guitars, and one of them was that little red Gibson. He was the mysterious buyer. We told Johnny the story of Lil' Red in the control room and he said not to tell Kunio, that it would ruin the mystique.

Shortly after those sessions I got a call asking if CoCo and I would be interested in doing a concert at a college in New Jersey as well as some radio shows in New York and the surrounding area. We went on one of our walks and decided that we would give it a try and see what would become of it. We sold the house and left the Porsche and the truck with a friend in Tuscumbia and headed off to New Jersey. It seemed that we were supposed to be going there. We played our concert at the Centenary College in Hackettstown, New Jersey, and were offered a slot on their college radio. We ended up doing I don't know how many live radio shows there because after our first appearance there were a lot of requests for our return, and we fulfilled them all. With about sixteen disc jockeys on rotation and with all of them different asking us to be on their shows, we were kept very busy. We were offered a beautiful stone house on the mountainside overlooking the Raritan River there in Califon. New Jersey is the Garden State, and as far as we were concerned we were living in the flowerpot of it. It was the most beautiful countryside that we had ever seen. And so was our new home. We thought that it just might be the place for us, and it became our home for a year and a half.

Delaney and I hadn't spoken since CoCo and I had moved to New Jersey, until December 12, 2003. He had been calling and not saying anything for two years. Somehow he always managed to get our number until we figured out who it was that was giving it out, then we cut them off. We knew it was him because CoCo recognized the war shows that were always blaring and we heard his dog Elton's bark. We were just about to go to bed and the phone rang and CoCo answered it. She said, "It's Delaney. He wants to talk to you," and handed me the phone. He said that there were six biker dudes on their way over and that they were going to beat the crap out of me and that they should be pulling up about right now. I didn't believe a word of it and told him that if they couldn't find the place to give them my number and I would tell them how to get there. Then he warned me, "If anything happens to CoCo I'm going to cut your head off!" I told him that the only person who had ever hurt CoCo was him. He called me a nappy-headed motherfucker and slammed down the phone, and we never heard from him again. No bikers ever did show up. I remember telling Levon Helm this story sometime later when we were recording in Nashville. He said, "Bobby, that's just that old drunk talk." And that's what it was. I was completely sober and clean and I never did raise my voice to him ever, not even then. I knew that you couldn't meet the problem on the level of the problem. I was not going to get way down there with him. I have always known that he was acting out of fear and could not help himself.

We also were going back and forth to New York City doing just about every radio show that would have us along with a concert at Fordham University. One of the most memorable radio broadcasts was a one-hour live show at 5 o'clock in the afternoon on Sirius Radio. Part of that show is on our CD *Metamorphosis*, which came out in December 2009. We were fifty-two stories up the Rockefeller Center building looking out over the city and singing to the planet. It would turn out that CoCo and I did well over a hundred hours of live radio while we were living in that area. We just about oversaturated that place. When we had finished with our business in the New York area, we realized that we weren't cut out to be living in that climate. It was entirely too cold for way too long there. We both like the sunshine and the ocean nearby. So by the time the second winter started closing in we both decided to leave our lovely stone house in Califon and head to California because we were familiar with it and had what we thought were good connections there.

CoCo went to stay at her parents' house in San Diego and I stayed at a friend's house in the Valley. We weren't married yet and could not be sleeping together at her parents' house. It just wasn't right, and she and I felt uncomfortable. They're lovely people and they understood our plight. Her mother's name is Sheryl and she is a class act, to be sure. She is the epitome of grace and style and a very beautiful woman who looks remarkably like Jacqueline Kennedy. She was a model, a fashion columnist and a stewardess in her early days during her courtship with Gig, her husband of fifty-five years. They live in a beautiful two-story Mediterranean tiled roof mansion (that used to be the Jack Daniel's distillery laboratories) high atop the countryside. It is surrounded by a ten-foot tall, three-foot thick stone wall that is over a hundred years old

Gig Conaughton (U.S. Navy).

and is covered with vines that are as big as your leg. Their garden is very mature. The place is absolutely beautiful and you can see the ocean from their top floor. You have to be up there to see over the wall. Gig was an aerial photographer and Navy fighter pilot and was one of the elite who flew the last of the last of the F-8s during the Korean and Vietnam wars. Fast jet planes and fast cars, my kind of guy. He attended Annapolis and was among the few who worked their way up to the high rank of captain. He also was to be the ship's captain who would retire the famous aircraft carrier the *Oriskany*. Theirs was a romance straight out of the books. It was Camelot, U.S. Navy style! They not only were an outstanding couple and the center of attraction in their world, they were presented to the Queen of England and invited to the changing of the guards. That is something that doesn't happen to just anyone. Their life was one of color and constant change and was played out on the world stage. They had four children who stood like stair steps and even looked like the Kennedys. I can see it all. Captain R.G. Conaughton, a career officer and dashing young fighter pilot with the looks of a Kennedy, in his dress whites pulling up the circular drive with the Christmas tree that was planted the year before and now a foot taller. He was coming back after a tour of duty to his family and beautiful two-story brick home near Annapolis, Maryland, in his 1967 black Corvette Stingray. And Sheryl dressed, as always, in high heels and to the nines coming out to greet him with all of the children lined up in accordance to their ages to welcome their handsome father back home from the war. It paints a picture like no other. CoCo and I drove by the old house a few years ago and the tree is still standing and is now forty-five feet tall. They would raise their four children all over this planet, from Japan to Italy and Great Britain and finally back to the United States. They had two sons and two daughters, Gig, Gary, CoCo and Kelly. Gig, the oldest, is an award-winning writer and lives outside San Diego. Gary is a very successful photographer in San Diego and was the very person to take those rare photographs of the Rosewood Telecaster that belonged to George Harrison, which graced the cover of Bonhams auction catalogue. CoCo is my wife and partner, and her younger sister, Kelly, sings and is married to a famous trumpet player, John Fumo, who plays with Neil Diamond. They remind me of a white Sade and Miles Davis. Very cool music if I say so myself. They have two sons as well, Cosmo, eighteen, and Bix, five. They are my family as well and I love them all. I feel privileged to be a part of their world and am grateful that they were brought together in this lifetime. Without them ever getting together, there would be no CoCo. And without CoCo there would be no me.

Sheryl Conaughton.

Hard Times

When CoCo and I were in California the IRS had laid claim to all that I had. We were pretty broke but I had already put together a plan to get our cars back while I tried to sort out my tax situation. We had left her car and my truck with a friend back in Alabama when we went to New Jersey. I decided to take a bus to Alabama and bring them back to San Diego. I was real short on cash but managed to scrape up enough to get there and some money for the gas to get back. I had intended on pulling her Porsche with the truck, which wouldn't have been a problem. I got a Greyhound ticket that was supposed to stop only five times between San Diego and Florence, Alabama. Unfortunately it stopped seventeen different times! Yuma, Phoenix, Houck, Albuquerque, Tucumcari, Little Rock, Memphis, you name it, we stopped there. And that was only part of the list on the ticket. That bus stopped at every hog-wallow there was between each of the seventeen different scheduled stops! I left San Diego October 28, 2003, when California was burning, and you could see the fires from that bus. It was amazing. When we were about a hundred and fifty miles into the desert the western sky was purple because of the fire. We drove on, stopping and going and stopping and going until I thought that I was going to just take off running into the dark of the night out there in that desert.

After a while though, I realized that this was quite an amazing journey and settled down for the ride. After many hours of not being able to sleep I walked up and asked the driver if I could sit up front and talk with him. He said yes, and I started to really open my eyes. He asked me what I was doing riding the bus to Alabama. Turns out he knew who I was and had some of my recordings and had been a cook at Hazelden, the rehab place where Eric Clapton had been. He told me that when Eric first went to Hazelden nobody believed who he said that he was, at least not until he was able to play the guitar some weeks later. Then there was no doubt. I told him that I had to come on this incredible ride. Anyone can fly in a plane and I felt as though it was meant to be a part of my experience.

When I arrived in Florence I saw my truck pulling up out in the front of the bus depot. Behind the wheel was someone I had thought to be a friend—I'll call him Mike—who had been looking after it for me. Turns out, Mike was not a friend at all. I was just going to stay one night with him and have a hitch put on my truck and pick up CoCo's car and head back to California. Simple. He knew about the IRS and that I didn't have but a limited supply of cash for the moment. He told me that he loved both me and CoCo and went on to tell me that he had been given as a gift a building that was a part of a recording studio complex. He said we could stay there and all that I needed to do was to fix it up and we could live in it for free until we got our feet back on the ground. The building was a cement block machine shop about fifty yards from the studio. It was sixty by forty and had a very high ceiling. It had a stone divider wall halfway through it. The bathroom was very small and in the corner. I thought that the building was perfect. I could fix this up and turn it into what would look like a loft apartment, no problem. I called CoCo and told her the news but she was none too happy with it. She reluctantly submitted to my desire to build this place up and start our little record label, to be called Domino, from there and resurrect that studio.

We did the place up ourselves, and it was beautiful. I had built a huge stone fireplace with the same stones from the apartment. We had the drums and the Hammond and two Leslies set up and ready. I had built CoCo a studio room out of the old barn that I had torn down and moved and the cedar that was left from under our house downtown. She did the kitchen herself and it had a black and white French checked floor. I built a quite rustic looking sink counter for the kitchen. CoCo and I painted the floor and she did most of the walls herself. The bathroom was done out with a claw-foot tub and a toilet with the water up on the wall with a long chain to pull. I built a big closet out of what was left of the cedar. We had set up a beautiful Chinese opium bed and hung other Chinese pieces on the walls. It was really something to be proud of. That place looked awesome! Everyone around could not believe that we had done it all ourselves. The roof had a terrible leak, and rainwater would come pouring through. I finally managed to stop it on March 12, 2004, after spending every dime that I had at the time on the roof and then running electricity and plumbing for that place. We had also been paying Mike rent anyway because I did not want to be obliged to anyone.

Then out of the blue and on that morning there was an eviction notice hanging on our door. We could not believe it. Mike was evicting us with no warning! He started trying to have our cars towed away when we weren't there or when we were asleep. Then he started terrorizing us in various ways. I'm pretty sure he drained the brake fluid out of my truck because I saw him and another guy looking at the front of it that morning. I thought that he was just showing it off. Shortly after that, I got in and drove off in it. He didn't see me leaving, and I didn't know about the fluid being drained out. As fate would have it, he drove by just as I pulled out and was behind him. He saw me in his rear view

CoCo's 1956 356 Porsche.

My 1955 Chevy hot rod truck.

mirror and took off like a rocket as fast as he could and I didn't know why. I was trying to catch up and he hooked a hard right at the T-junction and his car bottomed out when he hit the drain by the curb. I hit my brakes and they were completely gone. I barely made it around the corner. If someone had been coming in the other direction it would have been curtains for sure. That idiot had drained the fluid out and knew that he was about to be rear-ended—and he almost was!

Mike ended up taking us to court. The first time was to have us evicted. We couldn't afford to be thrown out on the street. And that is exactly what happens when you are evicted. I saw a man on a Sunday morning right after church emptying out a small rental house. He was throwing everything in it, which wasn't that much, out in the street. I was driving by and as I passed I saw children's things in all of that mess and parts of a baby bed. I stopped my car and rolled down the window and asked, "What the hell are you doing? That's a child's chair and toys!" He said that they were being evicted because they were behind on their rent. That place has one of the highest unemployment rates in the whole country. It is so backward that it's hard to communicate with anyone at all. This is what Mike was going to do to us. Only he was going to keep everything. He was fighting for what was already his and he didn't know it. He took us to court and we all went before the judge. CoCo and I had our friend Robert Smith representing us. He is a lovely man and an incredible attorney. Mike had gone to Huntsville and gotten two attorneys to represent him. The judge heard what he had to say and then asked Robert up to speak for us. We had brought pictures of what we had done and the judge told me that I did beautiful work. We won that case and moved as quickly as possible.

We weren't moved a day until we were served with another summons. This time Mike was suing us for vandalizing his property. My improvements had added to the value of the property by at least $20,000. The man who lived next to the machine shop called and said that Mike had borrowed his tractor and was tearing down the walls on the inside with the blade on the tractor. We went over there with a camera. I got up on a barrel and took pictures of the tractor with the blade up in the air tearing down a wall. The tractor stopped in midair.

We didn't pay attention to the court system and didn't defend ourselves. We had done nothing and we had twenty-eight witnesses who all signed a document stating the condition of the place when we were there. These were all of his friends who had visited us since it caused quite a stir when we decided to move into that place and fix it up. Since we didn't defend ourselves we lost the case by default. He was awarded $30,000 according to the court papers, and his actions forced me into bankruptcy. As fate would have it, turns out that Robert's specialty was bankruptcy. He said that he would see to it and take care of it. I did and put Mike's name right at the top of the list.

The funny thing is that Mike wanted what we had planned on giving him anyway. CoCo and I had intended on leaving everything there for him, and I was going to give him the truck for taking us in. We really did think that he was our friend and really did love us, but all along he was using us for his own personal gain. I had already given him vintage amps and a 1950 Hammond organ and tone cabinet for his studio. Leaving everything behind makes moving a whole lot easier and is an adventure. Mike's actions did force me into bankruptcy, though. I didn't know that I could or even needed to as I had always paid cash for everything. I got my credit checked and it was not good. I didn't think that I owed anybody in the world. It would seem that I forgot about two ex-wives and their credit cards that I was still responsible for. And I owed everybody with initials. I mean, who the hell is GMAC? There were jewels and trucks and cars that had been put on my tab. Had our so-called friend known that his actions would eventually free me of over a $250,000 of debt he probably would not have sued me. In a funny sort of way he did me a great favor, but he does not get my thanks. I don't have anything for him except the song that CoCo and I wrote called the "Dice of God." It is about karmic law, and he was the inspiration behind it. I filed a Chapter Thirteen just hours before the law that had been changed went into effect, and it cleared my entire debt field forever. I had put our so-called friend's name right at the top of the list. He showed up at the hearing at bankruptcy court with a pile of papers as tall as he was. He was representing himself and looked really bad and completely stressed out. We never put up a defense any time we were taken to court. We were innocent and there was nothing to defend, so everything that he did, he did to himself.

By now we didn't have a dime. At one point things were so tough that we had to look around all over the house to find enough change for me to walk to the market and get a can of beans. This is the absolute truth. I had not planned on telling the depth of the gravity of our financial demise, but I had never had such a hard time in my whole life with money ever since CoCo and I left Mississippi. It would seem that when I sold my catalog and the money ran out so did everyone we knew. We were penniless and at one point were virtually on the streets in Muscle Shoals, Alabama. There were no gigs, and we didn't have gas money to get there even if there were. We wound up selling our furniture, which consisted of Chinese antiques, to our landlord and left that place with nothing but our clothes, guitars and our dogs and cats. It afforded us our move to Nashville to figure out what to do next.

Our Swiss Adventure

Shortly after we settled in Nashville the phone rang and it was some people from Japan wanting us to go to Switzerland to play shows for a corporate event. They requested just CoCo and me, and they were going to pay a lot of money. And I do mean a lot of money! For that reason we didn't believe it to be true and sort of shrugged it off and didn't respond. We didn't know these people at all and were weary of dealing with strangers. But they were very persistent and started sending us e-mails that were supposed to clarify what they were trying to say to us. This went on for several months. To us it all just seemed so incredible that we would suddenly be getting paid so much money and for it be true. We were so used to being walked on and talked about and not having anything that their proposal seemed like a dream that was not real at all. When the figures that they sent didn't compute it got even more unbelievable. When it was sent as yen it looked crazy. We still had a hard time believing it but relented in the end and said yes. After all, what did have we to lose? They sent a contract straight away and half of the money up front. We were stunned. All that we had to do was to pay our own way there three different times and do three forty-five minute shows. It was a very big deal for them to have us, it would seem. Sometimes I forget who I am. But this was about CoCo and me, not just me. We suddenly had enough money to start all over so we bought new everything there in Nashville. New guitars, furniture, and I got my new teeth finally after all of these years. We got new clothes and I got an old 1991 Mercedes 560 SEL and had it painted black with gold metal flake and had the windows blacked out, a Bobby standard. It was very cool and used to belong to a former Miss America. I think that she got it after she put on a little weight because the driver seat was pretty worn out.

We had gone back and forth to Switzerland three times and played for five thousand Japanese folks who were all dressed in formal attire. We were the stars of the show all three times. This was a big corporate gig for some very wealthy people. After the first set, they rushed the stage and were mobbing us. It was amazing. They absolutely loved CoCo! After the first performance security guards were posted at both sides of and in front of the stage and they still rushed it. One evening we had the opportunity to go to the Grand Théâtre de Genève to see the amazing solo violinist Olivier Charlier play. We were sitting in the balcony in the back of this 19th century opera house that was full of formally attired Japanese people. The stage was set and everyone was anxiously awaiting the night's performance when all of a sudden a woman looked behind her and locked eyes with CoCo. She pointed up at us and screamed, "CoCo! CoCo!" Everyone turned around and saw us and suddenly there was a sea of penguins coming up the stairs to surround my darling CoCo. They all wanted to touch her and to get our autographs and to get photos of us, and them all together. It was quite unexpected but very welcome, to be sure. We had been rejected by everyone that we both knew and here were these complete strangers welcoming us with open arms. We were deeply bowed to on the streets of Geneva every time one, or groups, of them saw or passed us. It was like a scene from *A Hard Day's Night* what with us ducking them at the airport. Everywhere we turned Japanese people were right around the corner wanting to touch us and have pictures taken with us. It was a wonderful experience. What a great experience for CoCo and me.

Lovers

CoCo and I are extensions of each other. We are two souls that were adrift in a sea of despair who found a harbor of peace in each other's arms. We are mirror images of each other, just in different bodies. When we sing together it becomes three voices. There's this third part that happens at certain times with our voices that is that third harmonic from an invisible singer. It's just CoCo and me, and we play guitar the same way as well, so we sound like one big guitar because we play so much alike. We call our band The Invisible Souls. You can't see them, but they're whatever you want them to be. Whether it's an orchestra or a rock 'n' roll band, it's up to your imagination, because we just set the stage for that to come into play. We are in tune with each other and are sensitive to what each of our strengths are and we let it flow at all times whether it's in or out of the studio, at home and in everything that we do. We have both cast our fate to the wind and do what is put before us every moment. Our life reflects that and our playing together reflects it as well. I leave it entirely up to her as to what she listens to and wants to sing or play. She is absolutely free to be who she is at all times.

Love is not a big enough word for how I feel about CoCo. How I feel and what I know can only be read in between the lines. She held my hand and stood by me when I was in my darkest hour and was my strength when I could not stand on my own. CoCo was my confidante and my confidence when I had none. When I thought that I had lost everything, she showed me that in actual fact I had been set free and had gained everything with that freedom. She was a light in my world that had never shone before. Thanks to her we started all over with a brand new life and I was liberated from that low state of consciousness that I had been living in. CoCo was right there beside me through all of my trials and tribulations, and still is. We dated each other and were engaged for five years and were married on December 24, 2005, in Nashville, Ten-

CoCo Carmel and Bobby Whitlock (photograph by Todd V. Wolfson).

Our wedding day, December 24, 2005. From left Paul Zamek, Yoshiko Iwabe, Takashi Inoue. On right, Robert Smith and Michael Hasty, Dez Zamek.

nessee. We had a very small wedding in a little chapel with only six guests. Our dear friend Yoshiko came from Japan and was CoCo's bridesmaid and flower girl. After the wedding ceremony we all went to Merchants Restaurant. It used to be a hotel right downtown on Broadway and was turned into a very nice restaurant. The place was decorated to the maximum for Christmas. A very large tree was in the foyer at the foot of the stairs and lights were everywhere. There wasn't a soul out that evening because of the snow and ice and because it was Christmas Eve and everyone was home with their families. So it would be that the whole of Nashville was shut down just for us. We were the only people out on the street that evening. CoCo looked so beautiful in her wedding dress. I will never forget how she glowed. Her father took her out and bought it for her. He even picked it out. When we left the valet pulled my Mercedes 560 up and we got in and drove away. The hood was adorned with a large white ribbon that stretched from the center where there was a huge white bow attached, and the ribbon went back to either side of it. I did it myself for CoCo. My car was black with solid gold metal flake and the windows were darkened. It was lighting up gold every time we passed under the street lamps all the way to our house in Belle Meade. We spent our wedding night there alone with our two dogs and our two kitties.

Our New Home in Austin

When we got back to Nashville after our third and final time in Switzerland we were in a quandary as to what to do next. One day we were taking our daily walk with Simone and Eddie, our two dogs, and were talking about what we thought might be in store for us next. L.A. was out of the question, and so was going back to anywhere we had already lived and played. The only place that I knew that I had never been where music was happening was Austin, Texas. I knew that Willie Nelson was in Austin but that was about it. I decided to call an old guitar player friend of mine, Dave Millsap in Fort Worth, and asked him what was going on musically in Texas. He had played with me once before when I lived outside of Fort Worth in the mid–'80s. He said that the only place where anything was happening in Texas was in Austin. He had two people's numbers for me to try. One was a piano player, who immediately tried to dissuade me from coming. He said that you could not make a living in Austin if you are a musician. I later found out he was right. Then again, I didn't want to go there to make a living, I wanted to go there to play music. The other guy I called was a guitar player, Stephen Bruton, and he and CoCo and I would become eternal friends. When I called, he was in the middle of a session in L.A. but stopped what he was doing and talked to me for quite a while. He told me about a club, the Saxon Pub, that would be the place for us to play and gave me a number. I called and couldn't get the promoter to call me back, so I called Stephen back, and he called the owner. He rang back and said that we could play a one-hour set. I booked the gig and we drove to Austin and felt right at home. We did the one show and decided that this was where we belonged, at least for the time being. We went back to Nashville and started looking for a house to lease in Austin via the internet. The very last one we saw was on a golf course and we were just about to take it when our agent called and said that she had found another house on a horse farm that sounded just right for us. It would turn out that she was right. Our landlady and friend Hazel has a horse farm and another one down the road a ways. The farm that we live on is a brood mare farm and the other is a stud farm. The mares come here to have their babies. They're beautiful running in the fields outside our windows front and back. We live in a Texas farmhouse that is about two hundred years old and it and the other house on the property that Hazel lives in were downtown in Austin before they were moved here. They have been renovated and are quite beautiful, sitting back off the road on the edge of town on this tree-covered estate of a farm. A big creek runs through the property, and we have a couple of large swimming holes. This place is what I call secluded but not remote. We have been here for over three years now. The house is in the country and the end of our drive is in the city.

Shortly after we arrived tragedy struck. I never in my life thought that I would have such a close bond with a cat. I have always been an animal lover, but that applied only to

Performing at the Austin Music Awards (photograph by Don "Winker" Emmons).

birds, horses and dogs. That is until CoCo captured, after a whole year of trying, a mama feral cat. She had been living under the building that we were living in. It took CoCo capturing a lot of very pissed off tomcats first. She had a live capture cage trap. I wouldn't go out there and let the last tom out. He was real mad about being in that cage all night long, so I had a couple of the workers who were working for me at the time release him. When the cage was opened that tom shot out of there like a rocket!

CoCo did finally capture Mama. And when she brought her into the house to let her out of the cage she ran under the kitchen sink somehow and got up under the framing of it. She wouldn't come out and was in a place where she couldn't be reached. CoCo decided to leave her there and continued to feed her and to just wait for her to come out. Mama used a bucket that was under the sink for her personal needs—very smart cat! It turned out that it would be quite some time before she eventually ventured out, about six weeks or so. When she did finally make her appearance it was just to run under the stairs and get

With my friend Stephen Bruton (photograph by CoCo Carmel).

inside the wall. I knocked a hole in the wall and we got her out, and I turned the hole into a kitty doorway. Mama was pregnant. She had three babies, and I wanted to keep them all. There was a female tortoise shell that we named Eartha Kitty and two males named T.C. and Romeo. They were tuxedo cats, black and white, and look like they are dressed for a formal dinner. T.C.'s name was going to be C.C., which stood for carbon copy, because he is perfectly balanced symmetrically. He looks like the mirror image of himself on either side. I changed it to T.C., Top Cat. Romeo was solid black and had a white chest and a white spot on his chin. When they were big enough to start walking they started getting their pecking order in place. Of course it was Mama first, then Eartha, then T.C. and last, Romeo. They couldn't have been two months old when T.C. and Romeo traded places. I saw it happen. Romeo became T.C. and T.C. became Romeo. It was strange to watch the transformation. Their personalities switched just like that.

Romeo took over the role of being my cat. At first T.C. was the alpha cat then it all turned around. Romeo was my constant shadow for seven years. T.C. kept his distance and would never let anyone touch him, not even when he was feeding. He would run at the first movement towards him. I really hated it, too, because I was smitten with him. He was the one to get close to me first. Then Romeo took his place. Everywhere I went and every time that I turned around there was Romeo looking up to me with those big beautiful loving eyes. I could be sitting in my chair and he would come up to me and reach up, and gently touch me with his paw and start talking to me. I didn't know what he was saying, but I always knew what he meant. We communicated with each other like I have never done with an animal before. He would just get in my face and we would just look deeply into each other's eyes. It was as if we were one. When he was little we were living in New Jersey, and he would climb up the side of the bedspread and get on my chest and start kneading my chest with his paws. Then he would lie down on me and go to sleep. This happened each and every day and night. When we moved to our new home in Austin we found a big creek, Walnut Creek, which runs through the property. It has a couple of swimming holes and is a quiet, beautiful place. Something that we didn't expect, however, were coyotes coming up close to the house.

I won't ever forget when Romeo came upstairs to me and started talking to me one day, and kept at it. I thought that it was our landlady's old barn cat Thomas wanting to fight it out with him again, and he was trying to tell me about it. Romeo and her old grey cat would get into it about every other night and Romeo would generally get the short end of the stick. He was a lover, not a fighter. So I just thought that he was telling me about Hazel's cat Thomas. He was just about annoying but he had something that he was trying his best to tell me. Everything that I did wasn't it. He just kept on coming up to me and talking away. Finally he ran downstairs

My Romeo (photograph by CoCo Carmel).

and out the cat door and I heard him howl like it was a cat fight. Then his howl abruptly cut off. I ran downstairs and out the back door and couldn't see him anywhere. Then I remembered that the next-door neighbor had just lost his cat only days before to the coyotes. That's what happened to my Romeo, September 2, 2007. But I couldn't believe it and thought that he had left me. I thought that he had run away from me and that he was saying goodbye and I didn't know it. I thought that he couldn't take that barn cat beating him up anymore and that he was leaving me. I was so sad that he was saying goodbye and I didn't know.

CoCo and I looked everywhere for him for over a year and I have mourned him like nothing that I can ever recall. Then we got an e-mail from someone whose address was private saying that they had him and were holding him for ransom. They said that they were going to do something horrible to him if they didn't get their money. I was prepared to do anything to get my Romeo back. At least I saw a ray of hope that he was still alive and we would be together again. We called the police and they sent a detective out and he took a report, and then we called for a follow-up. Meanwhile we found out through the newspaper that the scammers had been going through the paper and doing this to a lot of people. I couldn't stand the not knowing about Romeo and how he was doing, if he was being fed, and all of the natural concerns I could imagine. It was a difficult time. They never did call us back, and the police said that this was a criminal offense perpetrated by a cruel scam ring. These people were taking grief-stricken people like me and extorting money. They would go around and get the numbers off of the telephone poles and out of the paper where we, like other people, had put up missing kitty signs with our numbers on. They were never caught.

My heart aches because I still miss him. I'll never get over losing my Romeo. I don't want to. The tears are falling like rain in my heart right now because I miss him so. Sometimes I thought that I was being punished because of a sick black cat that I had to put down once. That's what I thought for a very long time. I thought that I was being punished, and I was, too. I was punishing myself instead of forgiving myself. CoCo told me, "Haven't you ever thought that Romeo had to leave in order for you to love T.C. so much?" And I do, too! I'm probably closer to him than I have ever been to any animal in my life. He has slowly become his brother. I know that he is his brother's keeper. As a matter of fact we were at the dinner table one evening and I had been crying about Romeo, right after it happened. T.C. has a very low voice and he came up and meowed, and his voice was Romeo's. We couldn't believe it! I said to him that he was his brother's keeper. He was his brother as well. Romeo never left me. He joined his brother T.C. because he knew how heartbroken I was and still am. T.C. has become my Romeo. He follows me around everywhere and loves for me to brush him, and he gets lots of special treats and lots and lots of love from CoCo and me. He still doesn't like to be picked up, but he is very big on staying right within reach so that he can rub up against me. He lies right down next to me everywhere and looks up at me and talks away. He's really smart and lets me know just what it is that he needs. Mostly it's just a stroke down his back and then he head-butts me. He loves me, too.

We landed a permanent residency at the Saxon Pub, one of the premier listening rooms in Texas. Every one of the acts gets their share of the door. By selling my catalogue in a state of mental confusion in 2001 I had completely cut my ties with my past, and that would include my dependence on them. Now I didn't have that financial cushion that I had had since 1970. CoCo and I started going out and playing acoustically together with no band because no one would play with us unless they were paid. Actually nobody wanted to have anything to do with us at first.

It's only just in the past few years that we have been together here in Austin that we have finally been accepted for being who we are, and for what we do. When we first came to Austin the people accepted us as the couple that we were and are. We're Bobby Whitlock and CoCo Carmel, and everybody is happy for us here. It is just now that we have finally found our niche in this business. It has come back to just CoCo and me yet one more time. That is the way that we started out and it has come back around that this is the way that it is now as well. In the end the truth will always prevail. And the truth is that I love my life and I love my wife, CoCo Carmel. We have a beautiful life and a brilliant future that is unfolding right in front of us each moment. In the end it would be that the money was a stumbling block and when it was removed the pathway was clear to walk. Now we have new monies coming from a different avenue, although coming from the same original source. We get digital downloading now that we didn't used to get. It wasn't even a term in 1970.

One day CoCo and I were in the club parking lot when the owner, Joe Ables, pulled up. He asked what we were up to and we told him that we were trying to get the sessions and the players organized for the time slot that we had booked at Pedernales Studio in Austin. It's Willie Nelson's place. He said that he was out at Willie's golf course and saw him drive by and waved at him. He didn't know Willie very well, although he had met him on occasion. He said to us, "Why don't you ask Willie to play on it?" We hadn't thought about it but I said, "Now that you mention it, it sounds like a good idea!" I had already called the studio to book it and found out that Freddie Fletcher was part-owner. He was also Willie's cousin and had been looking after him ever since I had known Freddie, whom I had met in 1981 in Nashville. I didn't know that he even lived here.

I called and asked him if he thought that Willie might consider playing on a song that I had written with Eric Clapton that had never been recorded, "Dear Veronica." He said that he'd ask. Next thing you know he called back and Willie had said, "Yes, and when?" We had not put anyone on our master demos yet. It was still me on drums and guitars and keyboards, and CoCo on bass, sax, flutes, background vocals and

My beautiful CoCo with her saxophone and her lovely black hat, in her favorite photo (photograph by Don "Winker" Emmons).

strings. We were to redo the drums and guitars and keyboards at his studio but hadn't done it yet.

The first day we got the tape up, in walks Willie. He was the first on the scene. What a lovely man. He asked, "What's the song you want me to do?" CoCo had asked me a few days before about getting him to play on her song "True Love," as he would have been perfect for it. But he had agreed to do one song and it was the Clapton/Whitlock song "Dear Veronica," a tribute to Veronica Lake. I told CoCo not to worry and to leave it with me. When Willie asked what song he was to play on I told him it was CoCo's "True Love." He asked me about the background of the song and I said, "She had written and recorded it while I was out shopping for groceries. It was one of those songs that just fell out of her." It is sometimes not appropriate to bring the "God" word in as it puts some folks off. Not Willie, though, as we would find out later. He went on out into the studio and started noodling around on Trigger—that's his guitar's name. CoCo was sitting on the couch and she looked up at me and said, "I think that I'm going to be sick. He's out there playing my song and I don't know if it's good or what. I really think that I'm going to throw up!" I tried to comfort her and told her that she should not worry so because "it's a great song." Roll tape. Willie sailed through it and then said, "Let's do another one." Roll tape for take two, which turned out as perfect as take one. Then he said, "Let's do one more just so you'll have it."

Steve Chadie, the engineer for Willie over the last twelve years, said, "He never does that unless he really likes something." It was fantastic! He came back in the control room and was listening back and the song sounded absolutely

Trigger, Willie Nelson's guitar (photograph by CoCo Carmel).

Willie Nelson listening to "Dear Veronica" (illustration by CoCo Carmel).

gorgeous. It was flawless work on his behalf. We didn't even have to edit any of his licks out of it.

I then said to him that I would like for him to play on a song that Eric Clapton and I had written long ago that was a tribute to Veronica Lake. Ol' Willie knew that I was pulling a fast one! He had brought five of his grade school friends with him to the session and he broke out a big fat "killer bud" Willie joint and asked everyone if they would like a hit. They all declined, but I must confess that I did have a toke with Willie. As a matter of fact I took several. All of his friends were talking about Veronica Lake and knew all of her movies and just about everything there was to know about her. He went out there and did the same thing with "Dear Veronica" as he had done with "True Love." When he came back in the control room he said, "You can keep the best and lose the rest." We kept everything. It was a pleasure and a joy mixing those two songs. We got to hear them over and over. I know every lick he played on both of them as well as the ones that didn't make it on to the CD. After the session, he left and took his friends to *Luck*, a movie set western town that he had built for his movie *Red Headed Stranger*. CoCo and I go every now and then as we have an open door there. Willie Nelson is one fine man!

The King of Luck

CoCo and I never really know what's going to happen next in our world. Every time we turn around everything changes in a big way. Like the time Billy Bob Thornton and his band the Boxmasters showed up at our gig in Austin. We were standing outside waiting for our turn to play when up pulled a black Cadillac Escalade with the windows all blacked out. The occupants got out and were all standing around in a group in the parking lot there in front of the club, and CoCo said to me, "Hey, Honey, that's Billy Bob Thornton standing there." That was the last person that I ever expected to be pulling up at one of our shows. I walked over towards him and he turned to me and smiled and without even saying a word opened his arms like I was his long lost friend. He gave me a big hug and said, "Hello there, Bobby, I thought that was you!" It was as if we had always known each other. He was no stranger to me at all. I think that has to do with being from the same part of the country and having similar backgrounds. What a lovely man he is. I introduced him to everyone and we started talking about people that we know from his neck of the woods. We talked about a guitar player friend of mine in Mississippi, Barry Swain, and his Dad, old Doc Swain, and Aunt Lavern. Barry played on my *My Time* record and his Aunt Lavern used to baby-sit Billy Bob when he lived in El Dorado, Arkansas.

He told me that he had tried several times to call my mother to talk to her but her number had been changed. Billy Bob has been carrying around a copy of my mother's manuscript, written about her life, and is talking about it as a movie idea. He really likes it and reckons that it is a very, very viable commodity. He has called me twice about it. Coming from Billy Bob Thornton the Oscar winning actor/writer/director/producer, I take that as being pretty serious. It's a lot of short stories about my mother growing up during the Depression. It reads like the *The Grapes of Wrath* and *The Color Purple*. I'm proud of my mom for writing her life story. Billy Bob has plans on doing something with it, just when, no one knows. Those things just have to come together on their own just like everything else worthwhile does.

He asked CoCo and me if we would like to be in a documentary that he and Willie were shooting out at Willie's town, Luck. Of course we said that we'd love to. This was all taking place outside in front of the little nightclub where we were playing. We went in and did a quick sound check. In they all walked and pulled up chairs and sat five feet in front of us the whole hour. It was a great set as well. It was just the two of us and we were really on that night. CoCo's guitar playing was blossoming, and we rocked their socks off! Some people were talking very loudly in the back of the club while I was telling a story between songs. Billy Bob told me later that he was going to get up and get in their faces and tell them to shut the fuck up. It made me feel real good, and I sort of chuckled inside. I told him that they would have never forgotten it. He said that they had quietened down about the time that he was going to get up. When we were finished with our set we packed our guitars and stood around talking about tomorrow. Billy Bob tried one more time to get me to go out and hang with him and his band but it was in vain. I told him that I would check with CoCo and see what she had in mind. I'm not a good hanger-outer. I used to be when I was drinking and drugging but that is of no interest to me anymore. More likely than not, he just wanted to talk about music and the documentary or my mom's manuscript and get to know me a little better. He asked me what we did after our shows and I told him that we stop and buy a piece of chocolate and go home and have some tea and talk about the gig. We did just that, too!

The next day, Billy Bob's assistant Lisa called to confirm the next day and night for the filming and to tell me how excited they all were about our show when they returned to the bus. I had given them all a copy of our *Lovers* CD and it was playing on the bus and on everyone's headset. This is that thing working away keeping us busy as usual. Lisa said that Billy Bob wanted us to ride to Luck in his bus so that we could all get to know each other and to discuss what he had in mind for the filming and our segment of it. We brought my Mercedes so that we had a way back home when we finished. We were so excited that we hardly slept. The next day we were feeling a little ragged but ready to go, and Lisa called and said that it had been postponed because of rain. We had spent the whole day before picking out our clothes and getting ready for this one and now we had the time to get ready for the next day. That was cool because we were exhausted from getting ready and we needed the rest.

Looking happy these days (photograph by CoCo Carmel).

We were to meet Billy Bob at the bus by the Four Seasons hotel right on the Colorado River that runs straight through downtown Austin. We pulled up in front of the bus and parked the Mercedes. We were just chilling in it waiting on Billy Bob. He was in the hotel doing his thing, getting ready to go to Luck. It felt like we were in scene in a movie. His assistant got out of the bus and CoCo spotted her. She said, "There's Lisa!" I got out of the car and introduced myself but she already knew who I was and told me that they were all very excited to have CoCo and me there. It would turn out that the bus departure was going to be another hour, so we decided to go for a coffee. When we returned everyone was on the bus. Larry had the car parked in front of the bus all ready to go. CoCo and I got on the bus, and it was packed with people. Everybody was smoking cigarettes and standing in the aisles. There was no place to sit. We went to the back of the bus, where Billy Bob introduced us to J.D., who played guitar in his band. We chatted a few minutes and then we went to the front because the smoke was getting pretty thick. When we got to the front there were even more people on it than before. Jimmy Vaughan walked on as did Joe Ely and Shelby Lynne, and the whole thing was getting too cramped. So I told CoCo let's get back in the Mercedes and drive there ourselves. We walked off the bus and as soon as we did it pulled away. We laughed as the bus went one way and we went the other. But we had been to Luck several times before so we knew the way. We went straight out of Lamar to the freeway and I got to kick my Mercedes down. What fun! That car rocks! It will go from zero to sixty in six and a half seconds, and a quarter of a mile in fifteen seconds, and 165 mph top end, and get you there real quick! That is more than fast enough for me. We got to the other side of town and were headed out toward hill country when we saw the bus at a red light with the turn signal on. It was turning left when it should have been turning right. We pulled up and told them to follow us, which they did. We rolled on out through the hill country and past Willie's golf course, Briarcliff, and then up the hill to the gates that led to his little town of Luck. Luck has a dirt road main street that runs through it, and on one end is the general store. That's where we did the filming. It is a big old two-story building that has a porch that goes around the front to the back. On the other end of the street is a little white church with a steeple that has a bell with a rope that you pull to ring it. When my mom came to visit we took her to Luck and when we went into Willie's church she sat on the right, second pew back next to the window. She said that was always her seat in their church. She didn't have far to go to get to the piano. I remember it to be true as well. CoCo took a picture of her sitting there. Along the wooden sidewalks are a bank building, a city hall, a justice of the peace and an opera house. There is a tailor's shop and a couple of falling down buildings that were lawyers' offices and some barns. There is a corral, a livery and stables with a wooden water tower. And then there's a saloon with swinging doors that don't swing so well anymore. It has an old upright piano with the ivory coming off the keys that CoCo used for the last shot in her "Layla" video. This town is surrounded by beautiful mature oak trees.

You could just imagine that something really did take place there many years ago. But there was a picnic table with a banquet all laid out for everyone under it today. And there was plenty of everything that you could possibly want to eat and drink. When the filming started everyone had to be very quiet. Billy Bob can hear a pin drop outside from in the building. I have never known anyone with such acute hearing. He heard camera noise from across the room that no one else heard. I guess that's a part of his gift of directing and producing. This was a full-blown movie set that we were in the middle of, and when the cameras started rolling it had to be perfectly quiet inside and out. It was sort of eerie out under that oak tree with eighty-five people eating fried chicken in the dark trying to not make any noise. Everyone was just chewing and nodding their heads. It reminded me of those rich folks in Paris long ago.

Back inside, one of the crew sat CoCo down and I was next to her, and we were facing Billy Bob and the Boxmasters as we all played and sang in sort of a broken circle in the middle of this huge room. Everyone did a few numbers and we all joined in. Joe Ely sat in and so did Jimmy Vaughan. When Willie came on with Ray Benson they did some old tunes together. This was all done with acoustic guitars, nothing electric, no drummers or bass players. Billy Bob would ask for another different song, and the musicians would just start playing whatever it was that he had asked. He is the consummate professional. He asked me to join Willie, Ray, Jimmy and Shelby for "Kansas City." It was way too cool singing and playing guitar with Willie. When I started to sing Willie started to smile. That's one thing that I can do, and that's sing. I didn't get in the way, or sing any hot licks. I just sang along with Willie and did some answering scats around what he was singing. I am very good at singing like that as well as singing lead. I learned a whole lot from Delaney that I never knew, and still don't realize until I have to draw on an influence. Then there it is. Strange, that. Come to think of it I have some really great influences to draw on as well. As soon as all of the singing was over, everyone went outside and I asked Billy Bob if he would talk to my mom if I called her. He said that he would be happy to. I called and handed the phone to Paula Nelson, Willie's daughter, whom she had met when she visited last year. They spoke for a few minutes and then I handed it over to Billy Bob. CoCo was filming the whole thing. They talked for probably five minutes as well. She was over the moon with the excitement of Billy Bob Thornton telling her how much he liked her manuscript and that he was going to do something with it. When he handed the phone back I told him that there would be some extra stars in his crown for what he just did.

 I thought we were finished and thanked him, and he said that he wanted us to have some still photographs and a group shot done down at the Opera House. They took pictures of CoCo and me then they took individual shots of everyone and then did a few group shots. They said that CoCo lights up the room, and she does, too! They did our photos first. They took my picture about twenty times and then took CoCo's. She knows how to work a camera and the photographers always love her because she makes their job fun and easy. She is on when the camera is. Everyone was at the top of his game, since it was a real Hollywood production. That Billy Bob Thornton doesn't mess around when it comes to doing a film. He is really good at being on that side of the camera, and he is a great producer and director. When we were getting ready to leave again, he took me aside and quietly said, "Hey, Bobby, I really would like for you and CoCo to stay because Willie is going to do three special songs with the room emptied out, and I want you and CoCo to be there and be a part of it. It will just be the three of us." I saw this as something very special getting ready to happen. We went back to the general store and there was only the camera, sound and lighting crew and seven or eight technicians.

 We were sitting in wooden chairs about eight feet in front of Willie, facing him, just Billy Bob, CoCo and me. It was quite some feeling sitting that close to Willie and us being the only ones there except for the crew. He had Trigger, his guitar, and was sitting in a wooden chair with his back to the bar across from the three of us and he started to sing. The room was absolutely silent while he sang. There was a feeling of a peaceful presence all about us, an aura of reverence about the whole room. When he finished a beautiful ballad there was absolute silence. No one said a word as he sat there tuning Trigger and stroking his beard, thinking about the next song. Still not one word was said by anyone and the cameras never stopped rolling the whole time. Willie started to play and he was taking us somewhere far away in his song. All of these songs were new and no one had ever heard them until now. He sang a beautiful song and there was again silence. Then he started to sing again and we all sat there transfixed on Willie Nelson singing the third song to the three of us. We were in a cocoon, a protective cloak that was filled with love and beauty and wonder with Willie Nelson singing to us. When he finished singing I thought that it was over, but everyone sat perfectly still. No one said a word during this whole time or moved a muscle. Not even Willie. The cameras just rolled and we watched and listened. Then he started to sing yet one more song. We all just sat there in a state of wonder as he sang the most beautiful song to us. Even when he finished no one talked. We all just sat there silent for a few minutes. It was a sacred moment for us all, including Willie.

We walked outside and I knew for sure that it was time to leave and started to say goodbye to Willie and Billy Bob. Then Billy Bob said, "Hey, man, I want you and CoCo to hang and let me interview you about how you feel about Willie." It was Willie's birthday and this was a very special documentary that Billy Bob was putting together, and I'm sure that he could have asked presidents and kings and queens and world leaders to be interviewed about their friend Willie Nelson, and here he is asking CoCo and me to do an interview that the whole planet is going to see. We had only ever been with Willie the one time he showed up and played on our record. We knew him in a personal way from then only. That was how close CoCo and I were to Willie. But we were closer than we thought or could ever imagine. He had played on our songs, and it doesn't get any more personal than that. He was and is a part of us forever through our songs. Willie's daughter Paula, Ray Benson, Kinky Friedman, Joe Ely, Jimmy Vaughan, and Shelby Lynne were interviewed one person at a time. Everyone was telling funny stories and about how much they loved Willie and how much he meant. Billy Bob waited until everyone else had been interviewed and then he called us in from outside and we were the last to be interviewed. Willie and everyone else was in the room while our interview was going down, and there were cameras everywhere. We sat in two chairs in the middle of the room. Willie was behind the bar just to our right and behind us. I could see him but CoCo couldn't. The bar is about twenty-five feet long, and there are pictures on all of the walls of Willie and his horses, and there were deer heads, too—just the way you would imagine an old western hotel and general store with a saloon would look. We could just make out Billy Bob through

Being interviewed by Billy Bob Thornton for Willie's Nelson's seventy-sixth birthday documentary, **The King of Luck** *(courtesy Billy Bob Thornton).*

the lights, sitting on a tall armchair directly across from us. I gestured for CoCo to go first and then Billy Bob asked CoCo what she thought about Willie's songwriting. "I'm glad that you asked me that question. I remember when I first heard 'Crazy,' it touched me in a way that I had never been touched before. That song came from a place deep down within him and I knew right then that that was where I wanted my songs to come from. From that special place deep within." I was completely surprised when she said, "When Mr. Nelson played on my song, 'True Love,' he asked the history of this song." Then she said, "I didn't know where he stood on the God word, so I said nothing and Willie just took it out into the studio and started playing it. It came when I had a God experience. So now he knows." I could see Willie's face from where I sat and there were tears in his eyes.

Then I just started talking without a break. Just like me to jump in at the appropriate moment. CoCo was doing a great job of holding herself together during a very special and an emotional moment. It was a holy moment. You could feel it in the room. I told the story about how I knew Willie's cousin Freddie and had asked him if he thought that Willie would play on a song on our record, how Willie was the first to show up at the sessions, did 'True Love,' and then 'Dear Veronica.'" Then Billy Bob said, "Bobby, in a stream of consciousness, tell us what kind of guitar player you think that Willie Nelson is." I closed my eyes a moment and it came through. "Willie is a fluid guitar player and his whole body is the vibrato." Billy Bob waved his arms and said, "Cut! That's a wrap!" I said, "Is that all you need?" He said that was just what he was looking for.

I turned and walked over to the bar where Willie was standing and he said that it was beautiful what we had said. There were still tears in his eyes. I thanked him and then we really did start getting ready to leave. Everyone was shaking our hands and telling us how much they enjoyed our singing and playing. We were an integral part of an important event that will go down forever in musical history.

The Flow

By June 2009 I was pretty bad off financially. We had just been invited to see Eric play a show that month in Houston and we probably were not going to be able to afford to go. There I was, Bobby Whitlock, and was having to call the phone company to keep them from turning my telephone off because I couldn't pay my bill that was less than $100. I have sold millions of records and everyone in the music world including the woman at the telephone company with whom I spoke knows who I am. It was an embarrassing state of affairs. I had to keep my phone on, at least until Eric left Texas.

CoCo and I played every Sunday night at our usual club for the door. One Sunday we made $133. That put food in our refrigerator and was gas money for the week. The week before that was not as lucrative. This was all about spiritual growth. My good is not dependent on anyone or anything outside of my own being. Our gig is what we were supposed to be doing at that point in time. We were not playing and singing in that place for the money. Oh no, not at all! It would be nice to be playing in huge arenas, but that is not what's happening at the moment. I am finishing this book that I never even meant to write in the first place, but I am glad I have. It is about my life and this story is a part of it.

In 2008 I had a cathartic experience, and I became this place for the writing to flow through, as well as my singing and songwriting and playing. I had to do this, not just because I wanted to, and I do, but because I could not, not do this. I know that everything will turn around in its own good time. It would seem that I have been living my whole life for this moment that I am in right now. I am not moved by these happenings in my material world, but they are disturbing at times while I am going through them. I sort of stand aside and let it take over and run the show. Just make the call and tell the truth, and that is exactly what I did, too.

I was behind in my rent, but everybody I talked to said that they would be very happy to give me two extra weeks, which was July 2. If I did not pay up by then they would have no other alternative than to shut me down. It's a hell of a deal being me sometimes. But it has always been this way with me in my world, no matter how much money I had or didn't have. If I had a lot of money it was never enough, or so it would seem. Somehow it was gone. I don't know where all of this is leading, but I for one am very happy to be a part of it. I do know that the higher you climb the farther you fall. And I fell a mighty long way. I knocked a hole in the bottom of the bottom. I went from working in the fields to being a rock star to walking away from that status to working the same fields again. I had no substance to my life. I felt that would get me back to reality. It did all right. A little too real, if you ask me.

But now I am over being ignorant to the world and the ways of it. I finally have what I never had and so desperately needed, and that was experience. When I was just starting out in this world I had all of this great talent but nothing to back it up. You really do have to live the blues to sing them. I had to live my life to sing and write about it. I have lived several lifetimes since then. Now I have an infinite well from which to draw. I am finally ready for whatever is to come my way. No matter what it is I am ready for it. I finally do have a song to sing to the world. I know that whatever it is that awaits me I will be able to handle it with grace and style, because it won't be me doing the handling of it. I have turned everything over and let that which created it take care of its own. Whatever level of success is to come my way will be because of me living to be a part of it. I am just going to be the instrument through which it operates. I will be very happy to fulfill whatever role it is that I am to play in whatever is to be. Eric and I may just do a couple of Derek and the Dominos shows next year. Who knows? It would be a lot of fun and would complete the circle. Or cycle. It seems that Eric may have just been saving the best for last. I'm the only person in his career that he has not gone back in time with. He has played with everyone who was in his past except for me. I was a part of one of the most important things to ever happen to him musically. I would have to be the one to play the role of me were he to want to play Dominos.

Eric and Steve Winwood were playing the Toyota Center in Houston on June 24, 2009, and CoCo and I were due to see him. There were tickets from Eric for us along with backstage passes, and we were supposed to be going to talk with him for a while. The last time we saw him was on October 18, 2006, at the BJCC Arena in Birmingham, Alabama, but we never got to say hello or anything. We couldn't get past his tour manager, Peter Jackson, who I don't think really believed that I was who I said I was. Eric did look our way and dedicated "Anyday" to me that night. He said, "This is for Bobby." I looked quite different then. I was still going through a lot of outward changes. I look like me now. There has been a lot of inner growth so that has made for a change in my appearance. I look better and am healthier than I ever have looked or been in my whole life. I work out every day and don't drink alcohol or take any drugs, and don't eat anything from the animal kingdom. The earth as a whole is safe from me. The birds and fish and all of God's creatures are safe from being on my plate at dinner. It's a funny world for me right now. There is a whole lot going down.

Two days before the show something happened—just like it always does—that enabled us to afford the trip and pay our rent as well. BMI royalties arrived unexpectedly. You just never know where your good might be coming from, or when. The songs that Eric and I wrote some forty-something years ago are still paying my bills. Although I tried to rid myself of what I then considered a financial crutch by selling my copyrights to the *Layla* catalog, they came in another form or avenue. We now receive digital downloading, something not even in thought back when we did that record. We were all set with our hotel and the Merc was shined up and full of gas for the trip. The end of the day was made even more complete when my coauthor Marc sent me the finished first four chapters, which I would be giving to Eric to read. I just wish that Michael Eaton, his manager, could have been there as well. He is a nice man and has helped us out from time to time with different issues. CoCo and I don't have anyone else in our experience at all. We don't have agents or managers or lawyers or any personal anyone. It's just CoCo and me. Ahead of the show I started listening to the Derek and the Dominos live tape again and it was awesome! What a band! Eric and I are a natural combination where our voices and playing together are concerned. I am to his singing and performance what CoCo is to mine. I placed a firm foundation there for him to work from. She does the same for me. It sort of takes the weight off singing and at the same time gives it a boost. It puts a fire under it. It was going to be a lot of fun seeing Eric again. CoCo even baked two loaves of bread, one for Eric and one for Steve Winwood.

So after several hours of resting our bodies we loaded the car and pulled out of the drive at 10 o'clock and headed towards Houston. It turned out that it took only two hours to get there. So we had plenty of time to find our hotel room. Hannah, who was the woman in charge of production for Eric, called and said that tickets and passes would be at the front office. Sure enough they were where they were supposed to be, and we stopped on the way to the hotel and picked them up. It was just a few miles from the Toyota Center. We got to our room and chilled out for a while then went to the venue at 6:30. When the doors finally did open everyone was about to faint because a record heat wave had hit the area. I had to show the bread to the guard at the gate, who took it from me. I would imagine that it was thrown away. It made sense to me, though: They didn't know me. We went into the hall and our seats were the third row back and the end two seats to the side that Steve was on, which was the opposite side from Eric. They were great seats for the show. People were filing in and the place started to fill up. We went to the hospitality suite for the guests. Then we went back to our seats and just waited and watched the place fill up. Finally I went back to try to get someone to get me to Eric or someone who would take some books to him. I could not get any assistance once again, and was beginning to get frustrated, so I went back to my seat. Mind you this is a pretty good walk and climb up and down those stairs. CoCo stayed right where she was.

When I got back to my seat CoCo said that they had called and that Eric wanted to see me and that we were running out of time. She handed me the phone and as soon as she did it rang and vibrated at the same time. Quite a shock, given the gravity of the situation, and I very nearly dropped the phone. It was Hannah and she asked where I was and I told her in front of the stage. She had me wait and told me that she and Peter Jackson were on their way to get me. That to me meant us, CoCo and me. Eric was looking forward to meeting her as well. Michael told us that he had told them all that we would be there. Suddenly everyone around is realizing that there is something special going on down where we were seated. The guy in front of us turned around and said "You're Bobby Whitlock, and you're a legend." Then up walks Eric's personal tour manager and Hannah. We followed them, walking right across the front of the stage. The whole place could see this all going down. We disappeared behind curtains and through some big doors to the area that I had just been asked to leave not ten minutes before.

The sea parted as we walked through with smiles from everyone. Then there was Eric standing in the hallway talking with someone. Suddenly that guy was gone and Eric smiled as I walked toward him and said hello and gave me a big hug, and I introduced him to CoCo. He asked how I had been and I told him that I was doing just fine and I asked how he was and he said just great. Then I told him that I had these two books for him. One was the first draft of the Domino chapters of my book. The other was *The Contemplative Life*, by Joel S. Goldsmith. I told him that my whole world had changed since the last time we were together. He asked, "How so?" I told him that I had a spiritual awakening six months after the *Jools Holland* show and the desire for everything was lifted from me. I told him that I was having a very difficult time in my life when we were doing that show. He said that he hadn't realized and thought that I was just nervous. The truth was that I had been strung out on prescription drugs and was drinking also. He said that he had no idea that was happening to me at the time.

I told Eric that I remembered a time when he and I were talking about God and spirituality and that he asked me to call my dad. Eric was asking me questions that I had no answer to. So we called my dad and we were so pissed that we didn't know what he was talking about. Eric didn't have a Bible in the house at that time either. I quoted John 3:16 and mixed another Bells and Coke. We started talking about his lovely home, Hurtwood Edge, and how I bet it is really a happy home when he returns from the road with shouts of "Daddy, Daddy, Daddy!" He said that the rooms upstairs were all children's rooms now. I told him that I was a grandfather now and my child-raising days were over. I said that CoCo and I had set ourselves free and started all over. Eric was very happy for us. He asked what we were doing and I told him about the new CD that CoCo had compiled and was having mastered and that it was called *Vintage*. He said that he couldn't wait to hear it. Then he said that he would put the books in his personal travel bag and read the manuscript on the plane later that day. When it was time for Eric to start getting ready for the show and we were saying goodbye he said, "We'll stay in touch." I told him that we were sitting just to his right about three rows up. He smiled and then he walked right past me and put his arms around CoCo and gave her a real hug. There is a big difference in one that is from the heart than one that has nothing behind it. We said goodbye, and then Peter Jackson escorted us back to our seats. They were all extremely generous and helpful. We went back and sat down and waited for the concert to start.

Eric and Steve walked out and the crowd went wild. They had Chris Stainton on keyboards. Steve is a great piano player and I guess Eric told him where I was sitting because he was looking all around the area where we were and at one point he looked right at me and we locked eyes. The show was very casual and Eric and Steve had a good time playing with each other—it came across in the music and their persona on stage.

I must confess that I heard Eric and me singing and playing in my mind while they were doing their thing. I have been listening a lot to us lately and we cast a pretty big shadow over the songs that we did together and on the music world as a whole. It would take Eric and me playing together again for them to sound like the record. Our voices defined the sound of Derek and the Dominos. Not Duane and Eric's guitars. That was two great guitar players working it out together. Our voices were the essence of it all. They were the expression of the song or poem. Everything else was added things.

Eric and Steve played an acoustic set. I had told Eric backstage that his acoustic performances were among my favorites that I have on my YouTube channel. I told him about my Bobby Whitlock channel with all of the videos on it. One favorite was "Groaning the Blues," and I told Eric that his solo on that one was just that thing flowing out of him. He said that it happens now and then. It certainly happened several times that night in Houston. Eric kept looking our way as well. But that locking eyes with Steve was something that I will not forget. The whole set was just great and as they kicked into "Cocaine" as their encore number, we made our way up the stairs and to a waiting cab that took us back to the hotel. We decided to come on back home and I'm glad that we did because it was lovely waking up in our own bed in the morning and having our first cup of coffee together and talking about the previous night's show, and Eric and Steve. What a great day we had. Thank you, Eric. The cream always rises to the top, and an oak tree takes many years to become mature. Perhaps Eric has saved the best for last, Derek and the Domino!

Full Circle

I know that we all put a significance to numbers and what they mean or represent to each one of us. Some numbers recall birth dates and others death dates and still others with the start or end of a world war. Most of the time they represent the beginning or end to something, or some sort of tragedy or other discontent in the world at large. I did get married on the same date to both Linda and Vivian, October 13. I didn't mean to, it just turned out that way. And I didn't really know about it until recently when I was talking to Beau about what day it was. It was that very date too, October 13. He and I were talking about the date and I said that there was something about October 13 that stood out in my mind. He told me that was when his mom and I got married. I told him that that was the date when Vivian and I got married, too! That's probably the reason my daughter and I have been so alienated. She probably thought that I did it on purpose, but I didn't. Turns out I also finished my song "My Life" on October 13, 2007.

Another date that stands out is December 18. For some reason everything that is of any significance in my life seems to have happened in September, October and December. When I joined Delaney and Bonnie he had me sign a band contract with them on that day. It was a work for hire agreement where they would basically get everything and I would receive what I have gotten from them all of these years. Nothing! I was just a member of their band and received $96.50 a week. When we went on the road I got an extra $12.50 a day for meals—even when we went on the road with Eric Clapton and George Harrison. I can hardly believe that I am writing this and that it is true. I really thought that they were my friends. Anyway, after the band was history, so was my contract with them—it had expired.

I moved on and got with Eric and lived with him at his house for six months. He and I started writing songs, and we put together Derek and the Dominos. We recorded the *Layla* record and went on tour and then went back to England where I eventually wound up living in Ringo's old house, Sunny Heights. This was in the winter of 1970. While I was living there I received a call from Delaney and his manager, Alan Pariser. They wanted me to sign with Delaney and Bonnie's DelBon publishing company. Delaney was my friend, or so I thought, and I trusted him. He said that DelBon would collect all of my money for me and make sure that I got it all and that they would get me movie scores and the like. He basically promised me that they would do all of the things that a good publisher would do. I believed him. And after reading the contract that had been sent over and discussed with him and Alan over the phone for about four hours, I signed it and returned it.

This was in the winter of 1970 and I was standing in my pub drinking scotch and snorting cocaine the whole time that they were reading this contract to me over the phone.

Bobby Whitlock in Austin, January 2009 (photograph by CoCo Carmel).

I didn't have an attorney and told Delaney that I should probably run this all by Robert Stigwood. He told me that he was my friend and that I could trust him with what he and Alan had put together. The contract had arrived a few days earlier and I thought that it was the old one and was just for me to keep as a piece of memorabilia, so I had just thrown it in a drawer in the front room. I hadn't even opened it. I told Delaney that everything that Eric and I had already written was assigned to Throat Music, Eric's publishing company. He said that it didn't matter and that they would collect my money for me and make sure that I got all that was coming to me. Of course I didn't know anything about publishing and thought that having a publishing company entailed having a building and a staff and that it was a very big deal to have one.

It would turn out that I would be the only person to ever sign with their DelBon publishing company. What they really wanted, unbeknownst to me, was my *Layla* money. They wanted to collect my royalties from the songs that Eric and I had written and recorded earlier. He knew that there would be a lot of money generated from the publishing end of that record and wanted it. I told them that the *Layla* songs were already with Eric's company but I was very happy to have them collecting money from the future songs that I would be writing. When the record finally did come out and had DelBon Publishing on it I told everyone at Stigwood's office that Delaney had backdated the contract but nobody believed me. They all thought that I was trying to pull a fast one on them. I didn't know how to do something like that. I knew absolutely nothing about business then. I was putting all of my trust in my so-called friends, Delaney and Bonnie.

The matter wouldn't be resolved until my writing partner and editor, Marc Roberty, discovered that I couldn't have been at Sunny Heights in 1969 because I was on the road with Delaney & Bonnie and Friends with Eric Clapton at that time. I had not even heard of Sunny Heights, much less lived there. I wasn't even living in England. I was living in L.A. and on the road with Delaney & Bonnie. But sure enough, I am sitting here with the contract in front of me, reading it as I write this story about a misguided sense of loyalty and love. It has the date December 18, 1969, at the very top. And at the end it has Delaney's signature as the publisher and mine as the writer and my address: Sunny Heights, South Road, St. George's Hill, Weybridge, Surrey, England. My best friend hoodwinked me into signing my publishing rights over to his and Bonnie's company and they never paid me a dime. Had it not been for Marc being so knowledgeable about dates this would have never surfaced and would have never seen the light of day. I had never had copies of any of my contracts until CoCo and I got together. The one thing that she did bring with her when she left Delaney was all of the paperwork from the office in the house. She didn't know that my paperwork was included, though. I had never had copies of my contract with Delaney and Bonnie, or Derek and the Dominos, or anything. One evening in Alabama she was going through her papers and asked me, "Does this belong to you?" It was my Derek and the Dominos contract. Then we looked deeper into the pile of papers and there was the DelBon document. I hadn't seen this since I left it all there some forty-odd years ago "for safe keeping." The backdated contract wasn't presented to the Stigwood organization until the record was about to come out. Then it was too late for me to do anything about it because nobody ever believed anything that I said. They thought that I was just young and immature, and didn't have a clue. They were probably right about that, but they misjudged the integrity factor. I have never lied, cheated or stolen anything in my life.

September 2, 2009, is another date that I will never forget. In September of 2001, I sold my future income generated from the copyrights for the six songs that I co-wrote with Eric on Derek and the Dominos *Layla and Other Assorted Love Songs* to Warner/Chappell. That money was the root of all of the discontent in my life up till then—or so it seemed to me at the time. My whole family and everyone associated with them made it their business to use me just as much as I would allow, which was pretty much do-as-you-please. "Here's the money, just leave me alone." That was all that anyone seemed to be interested in for all of those years. Up until I sold the fruit and its source I was hearing from everyone about his or her needs and wants and desires every time that I turned around. When the money was gone, so were they all. Family, so-called friends and associates were all gone, vanished. In fact, I unwittingly set it all up and allowed everything about it to happen for the very reason it did. I am completely responsible for everything that happened to me and to them all. They were all set up just as much as I was. I set them up to set me up for a fall that I knew would make us all grow whether we wanted to or not. I knew that from where I was sitting everything that went down was all a part of a much greater thing that was taking place in all of our lives. It was the creative principle in operation. Like being a beholder of my life in action. I was literally standing aside from myself and just being the instrument for it to function as my life. There is more to my life than song and rhyme. There is life itself to let take place.

That's what was and is still happening, and I know it to be a fact because it made itself evident September 2, 2009. My cell number had recently been changed and no one had it but Eric and his attorney/business manager, Michael Eaton, and my writing partner, Marc. The first time it rang was September 2, and it was Marc telling me that we had got our publisher confirmed. The second time it rang that same day it was Michael Eaton, who also had looked after the Bee Gees for over thirty years. Needless to say, Michael is someone important to be doing business with, or having look after something that has to do with Eric Clapton for you. I had been writing my book ever since September 2008. Funny this. All of these dates are in September. There must be something of significance that I'm missing here. There is! That's the same date that my Romeo went missing too, September 2, 2007.

Michael told me to sit down because he had something to say to me that would take quite a while. He asked me not to speak while he was telling me this. He didn't want me to break his flow, which I understood. He said that he and Eric were going over details about the *Layla and Other Assorted Love Songs* record and Eric asked him, "How does Bobby benefit from this?" Michael told him, "He doesn't, because he sold his entitlement to the income to Warner/Chappell in 2001." Michael told Eric the events leading up to my selling my income source, and Eric immediately said, "How can we make this right? No one should benefit but Bobby and me because we were the ones who wrote the songs!"

Eric and Michael went to Warner/Chappell and bought back my entitlement to the income. Warner/Chappell have been instructed to start paying me what they had been paying me before I had sold them. Eric bought the right to my income and gave it back to me. My good had been restored to me. I had to let it go in order to have it back. And I'm going to keep it this time. Now there is only CoCo and me to concern ourselves with and our lives have started all over yet once again. Eric Clapton gave me my freedom and start in this business in 1970. Now he has done it again forty years later. Thank you, Eric.

Selected Discography

Bobby Whitlock

"Where There's a Will There's a Way": This was recorded in the small room, or Studio B at Olympic Studios. Eric is playing slide guitar and is sitting about six feet from me in front of and to my right with his back to the drum booth. George is playing rhythm guitar and is standing three feet directly in front of me and is looking me in the eyes the whole time. Klaus Voorman is on bass and Jim Gordon is in the drum booth where he stayed the whole time. The horns were overdubbed. I just listened for the first time and counted how many times I said yeah in it. I said yeah thirty-eight times. I was just finding my way then.

"A Song for Paula": Jim played his tablas on this track. Delaney plays the bass and solo duet and he and Bonnie are singing background vocals. Jim Gordon's drumming on this whole record was astounding. He was at his very best at that time.

"A Game Called Life": I am playing "Ivan the Terrible," Eric's twelve-string guitar. Chris Wood is playing the flute. Delaney is playing bass. This was written when I first arrived at Eric's house. I was still thinking about my first wife, Cathy, and it was somewhat of a message to her.

"Country Life": This song has Carl Radle on bass and Jim Keltner on drums. Jerry McGee is playing guitar and Bonnie and Delaney are singing background vocals. It's a very candid look at the way I was raised and was a direct result of landing there in Hollywood with all of that circus going down. It was my first country song, and I wrote it all by myself. I was thinking about Tennessee and what I used to call home.

"Back in My Life Again": When we did this session I had no idea really what I was going to do. I was just playing it by ear. George and Eric were playing the guitars, Klaus Voorman was on bass, Jim Gordon was playing drums and the horns were overdubbed. We did two songs that evening and I thought that was going to be the end of it. After we were finished with "Where There's a Will," George said to me, "What's next?" I didn't have a clue. I was not prepared to do three songs that evening. At best we would only walk away with two tracks when we recorded. But here I am with George Harrison standing three feet in front of me asking what we were going to do next. I told him that I didn't have anything in mind. That was probably a good thing. Not having anything in mind. George said, "Why don't you just make something up?" I immediately said to Andy Johns, "Hit record." I told everyone that it would be in B minor and gave Jim a tempo and we just started playing it and the words and melody all came out at the same time. I had a story line running through my mind that was happening at the same time as the song was flowing forth

"The Scenery Has Slowly Changed": This originally had Klaus on it but Delaney put his bass on it when I wasn't looking. Jim Gordon was on drums. Eric came in and it was just Andy and me and Eric in the studio. He had already heard this song when I wrote it at his house. "The Scenery Has Slowly Changed" and "A Game Called Life" were written at about the same time, shortly after I arrived at Hurtwood Edge. This is the most beautiful guitar work that I have ever heard Eric play. What he played was for me, I'm sure, because he was playing how I felt. I wish that I hadn't rocked this at the end, though.

"Straight Life": I got the inspiration for this

song when I was in a hotel room one evening with Patsy Camp and some other people. Someone was in the bathroom shooting up and Patsy turned to me and said, "I'd rather be a good girl in Atlanta than to be a junkie in L.A." A song was born! Jerry McGee is playing guitar and Carl is on bass and Jim Keltner is playing drums. Delaney and Bonnie are singing background vocals.

"Dreams of a Hobo": This was the second song that I ever wrote, and I was fourteen when I did it. Jim Keltner is playing his kit with his fingers. Jerry hit a funky little note that should have been replaced but it was left in to make it seem all the more real. Looking back, I should have had him redo it. This song was a fantasy that I pictured very clearly in my mind's eye and ear. It still plays back to me like it was a movie or a visual book being played out for me to witness time and again. The hobo was really me.

"Back Home in England": This whole song was a dream. I woke up and wrote it all down in the middle of the night while I was in a hotel in L.A. Jim Price is playing the trombone. Jim Gordon is playing drums and Delaney is on bass. I'm playing the Leslie guitar. This also has the Los Angeles symphony on it.

Raw Velvet

"Tell the Truth": Rick Vito is playing lead guitar and I am playing the rhythm guitar. Keith Ellis is on bass and Don Poncher is playing drums.

"Bustin' My Ass": This song has the Edwin Hawkins Singers on it. We had to keep the word ass muted every time it came around. It was a matter of respect for them and their attempt to keep it all way up there.

"Write You a Letter": Eric was yet again the premise of a song. I was thinking that if things didn't start getting better that I just might be knocking on his door again. My little rock band really cooked. Rick Vito is one of the finest guitar players that I have ever worked with.

"Ease Your Pain": This song was written for me by Hoyt Axton. It was originally a ballad that had Jesus and sweet moonshine in it and I liked it. I just heard it up-tempo and with the Edwin Hawkins Singers on it.

"If You Ever": This song is almost out of my vocal range. I don't know why I just didn't change the key. It was probably because that I wrote it in this key on the guitar. I'm playing rhythm and Rick is on lead guitar.

"Hello L.A., Bye-Bye Birmingham": This has Jim Gordon on drums, and Eric is on bass and slide. And I'm playing rhythm guitar.

"You Came Along": Just me on the piano with the Los Angeles Symphony.

"Think About It": This song was pretty much live. I don't know how a xylophone got on there. That was a Jimmy Miller addition. I really like the melody and the words. I just don't know why I wanted to rock every ballad that I wrote. This song would have been beautiful as a simple ballad. Same thing with "The Scenery Has Slowly Changed."

"Satisfied": I'm playing acoustic and electric rhythm guitars.

"Dearest I Wonder": Rick Vito plays a beautiful slide part on this. This song also was to be telling a story that I didn't know was to come true very shortly after I wrote it.

"Start All Over": I love this song. I am playing the Leslie guitar. Rick plays beautifully on this. Seems that these songs were telling me what I didn't know until it was over.

Lovers

Initially when CoCo and I went into Pedernales Studio in Austin it was *The Master Demos*, the tracks that we had been recording ever since we had gotten together. It was me on drums and guitar for the most part, and CoCo played the bass, sax, flutes and strings. She produced and engineered the master demos—that is, until we booked time at Willie's studio, and then we had Steve Chadie as engineer as well. The first person to show up was Willie. We hadn't even gotten Brannen Temple on drums yet. It was still my drums, which were not that bad, if I say so myself. That's what I originally did, play drums.

We had done a show that our dear friend Stephen Bruton was heading up with Kris Kristofferson, Bonnie Raitt and others. There was a ten piece band that included Eric Johnson and David Grissom on guitars along with Stephen. Brannen was playing drums and that evening we rocked all twenty-three thousand people right out of their socks! We did "Why Does Love Got to Be So Sad," and our version of *Layla* and completely blew everyone away! What a band. When we booked the time to record I decided to get Brannen, Stephen, Eric and David to come in and overdub guitars on *Layla*. Brannen came in after Willie was finished and put his drums on everything. He used my drumming and the click track as a guide. We kept CoCo's bass parts because they were the best! That is another one of her many talents or gifts. Eric, Stephen and David came two days later and set up in the same way that they had on the show. David was on one end of the room and Eric was on the other and Stephen was in the middle facing the control room glass and me. We were going to do *Layla* only, but after they were finished it was so good that they suggested themselves that they do the rest of the record. Stephen said, "Hey Bobby, why don't we just do the whole thing?" They recorded live and there were no overdubs with the exception of Stephen's slide on "Dice of God."

"Lovers": It sounds as if everyone is in the room all at the same time playing together. That's because all three guitars are live and creating their own nuance, or feel, or layer, in the song. I wrote this for CoCo and it depicts our life and love. She plays the tastiest sax ever. CoCo does for me what I did for Eric. She is my support vocal and that takes weight off of me as the lead singer. We are a great singing duo.

"Dice of God": I gave Stephen a little amp that was very old and had never before worked for me. The speaker hole was shaped like a guitar. I figured that he could put it on a shelf in his studio at home and it would look good sitting there. But he plugged it in and the tubes lit up and he played his slide part through it, and it sounded incredible! He did one take only and just as soon as he was finished so was the amplifier. It burned out at the end of the song. This song is about karmic law. I have the guitars placed in the mix as they were placed in the room.

"True Love": This is one of my favorite CoCo Carmel songs. I am sure that this song and version of it is destined to be a classic. The guitar that Willie played was absolute and there were no edits that had to be made. It is flawless.

"You Don't Know": This is a happy song about love and the wonder of it. This song is what CoCo does for me.

"Best Days of Our Lives": David Grissom kicks this song off with some scorching guitar. There was a time back when we were living in that machine shop in Alabama when I told CoCo, "One day we will look back on all of this as the best days of our lives." We were having extremely hard times and were literally locking ourselves away from the world outside. It was crazy out there. All that we had was each other to hold on to. It's still that way, and I'm glad of it. I'm a better man for having lived through those hard times.

"Power of Love": This is a real soul song. Homer Banks could have written this—but he didn't. CoCo does the best background vocals ever. She has a way of doing them that is completely unique. Her style is more like Pop Staples than anything else I can think of.

"Ain't No Other Baby": This is a very cool song. It was started many years ago and the premise of it was the birth of my daughter, Ashley Faye. When I first saw her I said, "You are the most beautiful child that I have ever seen. There ain't no other baby in this world like you." I would carry that line and this melody and chord structure for nearly three decades before CoCo helped me finish it.

"One Voice": This song came to me and I knew that I had to have my dear friend Roger Cook as the one to finish it with. He wrote many worldwide hit records and one of them is, "I'd Like to Teach the World to Sing (in Perfect Harmony)." This song is right there with the oneness of us all. This is one world and we're all living in it under the same sky with all the birds in it. We are one soul with one voice. We are all that voice. That one voice.

"Dear Veronica": This is a song that Eric and I started at the end of the Dominos. I didn't finish it until several years ago. I had been carrying it around in my head for all of those years and never sat down and did anything with it. I guess that it wasn't time yet. It has come to fruition as have I. Willie is playing beautifully on this tribute to Veronica Lake.

"Layla": Eric's song as it should be. No piano part. Just seven minutes of scorching guitars done as live as it gets!

My Time

I built a recording studio in the hill country down in Mississippi just to record this record. I sure am glad that I did too.

"Sold Me Down the River": Brady Blade counts off this straight ahead rock 'n' roll opener. Darryl Johnson is on bass and Buddy Miller is playing rhythm guitar. I'm playing the slide guitar and the piano and organ. My son, Beau, and daughter, Ashley, are singing background vocals on this whole record. Ashley has a lovely, innocent-sounding voice and Beau sounds exactly like me when I was his age and was with the Dominos. Our timbres are the same. I knew this would be the only opportunity I would ever have to sing with both of my children. Now it's there forever.

"Bell Bottom Blues": I couldn't resist doing this song. I am playing a 1956 Hammond B3 through four Leslie speakers all set differently. It is very lush sounding. Beau is singing my old part on this.

"It's Only Midnight": Steve Cropper and I wrote this song. After I finished recording it, I sent it to him in Nashville and he put his signature guitar on it. Jim Horn came down to Mississippi and played sax and all of the horn section parts on everything.

"A Wing and a Prayer": The piano that I'm playing is a new Yamaha C3. Along with the Hammond B3 and a couple of Leslies and my children's choir, it sounds like the little church in the woods.

"Home": I did an acoustic radio tour across America in the mid-'70s. During a live interview in Red River, New Mexico, a woman called the station on the request line and was on the air with us. She said that she had a request. She said that she needed help finding her son who had been missing for some time. She said that no one would help her because it was a domestic dispute. This conversation was live on the airwaves. I said that I didn't know what I could do but to write a song about it and sing it. She said that she tried to get some people in Nashville to help her by doing just that but no one would. I told her that I would do whatever I could do. After that during each and every interview that I did—and that was a lot of them—I would say to the DJ, "Excuse me a second, I have to say something." Then I would say, "Michael go home, son, your mother's crying and she needs you and she misses you." Then I would continue on with the interview like nothing had happened. Michael did hear me and eventually went home to his mother. After I got back home and off tour I wrote this song.

"Why Does Love Got to Be So Sad": Big horn section and a funky track on another one of my favorite songs. I'm playing rhythm guitar and Hammond B3, and Barry Swain is playing lead guitar. With Brady Blade on drums and Darryl Johnson playing bass, this song rocks!

"I Get High on You": CoCo is singing on this one with me. I'm playing acoustic guitar, and Barry is playing the lead guitar.

"It's Only Thunder": This is the only track on this CD that was not recorded at my studio. Jim Keltner is playing drums, Tim Drummond is on bass, Steve Cropper is playing electric guitar, and I'm playing acoustic guitar and Hammond B3.

"Ghost Driver": "Ghost Driver" is about me learning how to drive and wrecking my Daytona Ferrari with the speedometer stuck on 155 mph. This is a driving song just like "Let It Rain." I used to tear down the motorway at night playing that song at full volume and I would wind the engine up to whatever key the song was changing to and then I would shift out into the next gear. Rock and rolling down the road. Awesome! Some things never change. Darryl Johnson plays some very funky bass on this number. Barry Swain plays lead guitar. It was take one on every song he played on. What a fine player.

"There She Goes": This song came to me as I watched my daughter drive away into the night, back to an impossible situation that I could not help her with. I had to let her go.

"I Love You": This song was written by Beau and me. He wrote the chorus while sitting in the swing under an apple tree in our back garden when we lived in Ireland. He had just turned eight. There is a photograph of him at work in the swing. He had my white Strat in his lap and was playing an open E. He finished it and came in and handed me the tape recorder and said, "I hope that you're satisfied." He had been singing under the tree, "I love you, I love the way you always make me feel. I love you, I love you." I finished it and recorded it in Mississippi. I'm playing the acoustic, main electric rhythm and lead guitar and Buddy Miller is doing the fills. I love the ending. The acoustic guitar has a lovely little melody and Ashley is singing at the end, "I love you, I love you." I can't express my feelings with words as to what this means to me. Except that I will always be able to hear her sing and say, "I love you" to me.

"Born to Sing the Blues": My daughter was about four and had just learned to write. One evening I was downstairs sitting on the couch playing my guitar. As usual, I was in the doghouse with her mother again. I was playing a very cool little something when up walks Ashley with pencil in hand and a piece of paper that she had been writing on. She handed it to me and said, "Here, Daddy, this is you." It read, "Born to Sing the Blues." I couldn't believe it! I wrote the song right then and there. I have written two really great songs that were both started by each of my children when they were just that, children. What an inspiration they were.

"Standing in the Rain": This is one of my favorite songs. I really was standing in the rain when the inspiration for this came to me. Buddy Miller plays the tenor guitar and the mandolin. I'm playing the acoustic guitar. The rainstorm was taking place while we were recording. So I had some mikes set up on the porch recording it while it was all happening, thunder, lightning, rain and all.

Vintage

"Who's Been Sleeping in My Bed": Recorded at my studio in Mississippi, Dead Horse Studio, this is the definitive version. I play all of the guitar work and the keyboards as well. Jim Horn is playing the flute. You can hear my voice bleeding through my grandmother's Dobro. That is what I used to record with initially. I added the slide and the other electric guitar.

"Save Your Love for Me": Recorded in 1982 with Chris Thompson at his home in London. I am playing the keyboards. He is playing the guitar and singing background with me.

"Southern Gentleman": Recorded in the early '80s in Nashville with Dee Murray playing bass with Philip Donnelly on guitar. It has the Memphis Horns on it as well. Inadvertently left off of the players list was Tony Newman on drums.

"Streets of L.A.": Recorded at Jack Tempchin's house in Hollywood. I am playing everything on this one.

"Island of Love": Recorded at Roger Greenaway's home just outside of London in 1982. I am playing everything on this as well.

"My Old Pal": This is a song that I wrote after passing Eric Clapton on the Hammersmith Bridge Road in London. We had not seen each other in over ten years. We stopped on the side of the road and did a little catching up. I went back to my home in Wargrave and wrote this song. It was recorded at my studio in Mississippi as well. Barry Swain is playing the lead guitar, Brady Blade is on drums and Darryl Johnson is playing bass. Buddy Miller is playing the tenor guitar on it.

"Perfect Strangers": Recorded at the original Westlake Village Recording Studios when it was first up and running. Steve Cropper is playing electric guitar and I am playing the acoustic. Jim Keltner is on drums and Tim Drummond is playing the bass guitar. Of course I played the keyboards as well. CoCo put her vocal and flute on afterwards.

"Don't Pass Us By": I wrote this in Ireland just after my dad passed. I saw a star in the cold, clear sky that was traveling somewhere far off into the night. I imagined it to be him and was singing to him to "Don't Pass Us By" without telling us what he had found out through his crossing over. It was recorded at Dead Horse as well, at the same time as all of the rest of the songs that were recorded there.

"This Time": Recorded in Nashville. I was walking out the door and my ex-wife said to me in a very loud voice: "You'll be back! You'll come crawling back to me next time!" I told her that "This time there won't be no next time," and drove straight to Roger Greenaway's office in Nashville and got him out of a meeting with this fresh idea. He and I wrote it that afternoon and recorded it the next day. Two weeks later Tom Jones recorded it on *Things That Matter Most to Me*. It has Gene Chrisman playing drums, Mike Leech on bass and Bobby Woods on piano—all of whom were not credited on the record. It was an oversight on my part.

"Your Love": This is the first song that I wrote when I moved to Nashville. I decided to write a song that was nothing but lies about my ex-wife. It turned out to be one of the most beautiful songs that I ever wrote. I finally found my true love and one to whom this song has been dedicated, my CoCo.

"It's About Time": This was written at the beginning of the Gulf War. I did not watch the news for ten years after it started and I have yet to watch it. I figured the best thing that I could do for this world was to write about it.

"Dorothy and John": This is a song that was written about two people that I knew all of my life. He was a farmer and she was the mother of a very large household. They didn't have indoor plumbing and John built their house himself. He plowed with two mules and Dorothy worked at the local doctor's office when I was a little boy. They had a house full of girls and one boy. I used to go over and ride horses with their children when I was young. They didn't have much in the way of material things but they were the richest people that I knew. There was more love between Dorothy and John than I had ever seen in my whole lifetime. They shared a very special love that I would not understand or find until I met CoCo. Theirs was spiritual love. As is ours. I wrote this song and sang it to them when I had finished it. Dorothy asked me, as she lay on her deathbed, to play it at her funeral. I said that I would do that for her. She passed a few moments later. John couldn't live without her and withdrew into a silent shell of the man that he used to be. He passed with Alzheimer's shortly after Dorothy left. I can feel their presence as I write this. I always held those two people in a very special place in my heart. I still do. I recorded this song on a clear summer's night on the porch of my studio that looked out over the valley towards the house where they used to live. You can hear the nightlife as I play my Big Mama's Dobro and sing for Dorothy and John.

Metamorphosis

When CoCo and I left Mississippi in May of 2001 we started writing about our experience. I told her that we should document our life together in song and pictures. And there seems to be a never-ending supply of subject matter because it flows like a river through us. We are in tune with each other and are beholders of our life as it is being played out on the world stage for everyone to see and hear, and now read about. These recordings are a part of that document.

The butterfly on the cover speaks for itself. But if you are aware of it you can plainly see a man on a cross with a crown on his head, Metamorphosis, new life, resurrection. Even though it is a live recording we decided to go ahead and put background vocals and strings and any other thing that we could do to make this a great record. It was produced and engineered by CoCo and the core of it is live and was recorded at our home in New Jersey, on Sirius Radio in New York City, and in Austin, Texas.

"You Don't Know": This song kicks off the record with CoCo playing sax and our band laying it down for her. It's soul music with a positive message of renewal. This was recorded at a very small club in Austin and has the same players who were on our CD *Lovers*. Our band: Brannen Temple, drums; James Fenner, percussion; Andy Salmon, bass; Stephen Bruton, guitar; David Grissom, guitar; CoCo singing and playing sax; me on the Hammond B3.

"Dice of God": The band is kicking it on this song. These guys are the best players in Texas, and CoCo and I fit right in there with them. I told everyone the origin of every song. I guess that's why there is so much emotion in everyone's playing. This song is about that leveling circumstance that takes down the overbearing every time. It's about karmic law that is set in motion. What you do unto another you are doing to yourself. The dice of God are loaded!

"True Love": CoCo never ceases to amaze me. I left home one day in Nashville to go to the store and when I got back she had written and recorded this song while I was buying groceries. I thought that it was about me and I didn't know any different until she told me one evening, crying at the thought of hurting my feelings. It was the same as when Willie asked her what was the origin of the song. She told him that it was about God. How wonderful!

"Best Days of Our Lives": Actually, these are the best days of our lives. But we were going through a valley experience a few years ago, and I turned to CoCo and said, "One day we will look back on this as being the best days of our lives." We sat down and started writing it right then and there.

"My Life": This song is the end result of how I felt upon reading Eric's autobiography. There was very little about Derek and the Dominos and my role in it, and I was crushed. I felt as though I had been left out of the story of my life as a Domino. I was at the dinner table and told CoCo that it was my life, too! That started the song. Then I tried to cover its origin with it being about reincarnation and resurrection. Which it is, but it is really about me and Eric. Just change the word here, to you, and it will be very clear to you the meaning of this song. CoCo did these incredible background vocals and strings.

"He's Gone": This is one funky track. We recorded this with just CoCo and myself playing acoustic guitars and singing live for the planet at 5 in the afternoon high atop Rockefeller Center on Sirius Satellite Radio. CoCo is playing the djembe and bass guitar. I'm playing slide guitar

"One Voice": CoCo's great background vocals really complement this song about the truth.

"Beautiful": This was recorded at our home in Califon, New Jersey, one winter's day. Ahmet Ertegun had called and said that we were soulful and beautiful. We wrote this in our kitchen shortly after his call then recorded it. I played the strings on this one. Then CoCo did her magic with the background vocals. This is probably my favorite song ever.

"Layla": The band just kills this version. This was to be the last live performance with Stephen Bruton and David Grissom together. Stephen told me that he had to get him some of that one. He passed from the visible scene shortly after this show. He was a dear friend and is thought of lovingly by CoCo and me. We miss Stephen Bruton; he left way too soon.

"Thorn Tree in the Garden": This is the first time this song has ever been recorded aside from ending *Layla*. CoCo is playing the harmonics on her acoustic guitar, and Jud Newcomb is playing the acoustic slide. I'm playing the acoustic that Eric gave me, which I played on the original recording.

Index

Abbey Road Studios 75
Abbot, Danny 194
Ables, Joe 220
Albert, Ronnie and Howie 145, 146
All Night Allstars 199, 203, 205
All Things Must Pass (album) 1, 59, 73, 74, 84, 108, 116
Allison, Jerry 59
Allman, Duane 61, 62, 63, 65, 84, 92, 93, 95, 96, 97, 106, 107, 206, 232
Allman, Gregg 106, 162, 199
Allman Brothers 91, 164
Allman Brothers Band 92, 107, 160, 162, 199
Amazing Rhythm Aces 199
Anderle, David 43
Ann-Margret 42
Apple 50, 127
Apple Scruffs 75
Arkansas 31
Arnaz, Desi 152
Arnold, P.P. 73, 82
Ascot
Ashton, Tony 85
Aspinall, Neil 114
Atlanta Rhythm Section 199
Atlantic Records 50, 102, 103
Axton, Estelle 34
Axton, Hoyt 89, 127

Badfinger 76
Baker, Ginger 49, 50, 82
Ballard, Hank 27
The Band 1, 59, 199
Banks, Homer 32
Barberstown Castle 173
Barclay, Eddie 131
Beale Street Riots 28, 32
The Beatles 34, 54, 74, 80, 113
Bee Gees 71, 235
Bell, William 28
Belz, Gary 181
Benno, Marc 39
Benson, Ray 225, 226, 227
Betts, Dickey 92, 162, 163
Big Bopper 16

Black, Mary 189
Blackwell, Chuck 33, 37
Blade, Brady 191
Blaine, Hal 100
Blind Faith 1, 48, 49, 50, 51, 59, 60, 87, 116
Blood, Sweat and Tears 44
Bobby Whitlock (album) 127, 129, 237, 238
Bopper, Big 16
Botnick, Bruce 64
Boxmasters 223, 225
Boyd, Patti 94
Boyd, Paula 74, 112, 113, 116, 117, 118
Bramlett, Bekka 196
Bramlett, Bonnie 44, 45, 48, 52, 55, 56, 118, 196; *see also* Delaney and Bonnie; Delaney & Bonnie & Friends
Bramlett, Delaney 1, 33, 34, 39, 42, 43, 44, 45, 48, 51, 54, 55, 57, 59, 60, 63, 118, 193, 195, 196, 197, 198, 199, 205, 206, 226, 234; *see also* Delaney and Bonnie; Delaney & Bonnie & Friends
Brooker, Gary 75, 80, 81
Brown, James 92
Bruce, Jack 49, 59
Bruton, Stephen 216, 217
Buckingham Palace 98
Byatt, Mick 71
Byrom, Larry 168

Cale, J.J. 37, 40, 41, 59
Canned Heat 44
Capone, Ron 29
Capricorn 161, 164
Carmel, CoCo 29, 51, 116, 120, 193, 194, 195, 196, 197, 198, 199, 201, 202, 203, 204, 205, 206, 207, 209, 210, 211, 212, 213, 214, 217, 219, 220, 223, 224, 225, 226, 227, 228, 229, 231, 232, 235, 236
The Carpenters 43, 44
Carter, President Jimmy 164
Cash, Johnny 26, 97, 104, 105

Cash, June Carter 105
Cecil, Stan 26, 28, 30
Chadie, Steve 221
Charles, Ray 61, 168, 169
Charlier, Olivier 213
Chiffons 56
Clapton, Eric 1, 27, 30, 34, 39, 44, 48, 49, 52, 53, 54, 55, 56, 57, 58, 60, 61, 63, 65, 66, 68, 69, 70, 71, 73, 75, 77, 78, 79, 81, 82, 83, 84, 85, 86, 87, 88, 89, 90, 91, 92, 93, 94, 95, 96, 97, 98, 99, 100, 101, 102, 103, 104, 105, 106, 107, 108, 109, 110, 111, 112, 113, 116, 117, 118, 119, 120, 121, 122, 123, 124, 126, 127, 129, 134, 135, 136, 137, 143, 155, 160, 163, 170, 192, 195, 209, 220, 221, 222, 229, 230, 231, 232, 233, 234, 235, 236
Clapton, Melia 192
Clements, Detective Sergeant John 139, 140, 142, 149, 173
Clifford, Doug Cosmo 164, 165, 166
Cocker, Joe 61, 65
Conaughton, Gary 208
Conaughton, Gig 207, 208
Conaughton, Captain R.G. 208
Conaughton, Sheryl 198, 207, 208
The Contemplative Life (by Joel S. Goldsmith) 231
Cook, Roger 167
Coolidge, Rita 42, 43, 47, 49, 52
Cooper, Joey 33
Cordell, Denny 126
Counts 26, 28
Cream 34, 48, 53, 59, 60, 66, 71, 83, 87, 90, 92
Criteria Studios (Miami) 91, 92, 102, 118, 145
Cropper, Steve 32, 36, 65, 164, 173, 191, 196
Crutcher, Bettye 32

Curtis, King 57, 58
Curtis, Sonny 59

Dalí, Salvador 125
Davis, Jesse (Indian Ed) 39
Davis, Miles 208
Davis, Spencer 27
Dead Horse Studios 190
Dean, James 16
Delaney and Bonnie 1, 33, 34, 35, 36, 37, 38, 39, 40, 41, 42, 43, 45, 49, 52, 53, 58, 61, 62, 62, 64, 65, 73, 84, 92, 115, 117, 128, 160, 233, 234
Delaney & Bonnie & Friends 43, 50, 51, 54, 55, 60, 234; on tour with Eric Clapton 59
Derek & the Dominos 1, 34, 53, 71, 79, 80, 85, 91, 98, 101, 102, 107, 108, 115, 119, 121, 124, 134, 160, 230, 232, 233, 234, 235
Derek & the Dominos In Concert (album) 82, 87, 155
Derek & the Dominos Live at the Fillmore East (album) 60
Diamond, Neil 208
Dick Cavett Show 60
Domingo, Samudio (Sam the Sham) 95, 96
Domino Label 210
Donelly, Philip 175, 187
The Doors 41
Doran, Terry 74, 117
Dougal 130
Dowd, Tom 61, 91, 92, 94, 96, 97, 103, 118
Down the Road (album) 145
Drake, Pete 80, 81
Dude, Aunt 13, 14
Dunn, Donald "Duck" 31, 32, 34, 35, 36, 164, 165, 166
Dunn, June 34, 164
Dylan, Bob 59

Eaton, Michael 230, 231, 235
Edwin Hawkins Singers 127
Eggby, Mr. and Mrs. 67, 109
Elektra 44, 50
Ellis, Keith 128, 131
Ely, Joe 225, 227
Emmons, Don Winker 217, 220
Ertegun, Ahmet 57, 61, 99, 101
Evans, Mal 75, 117
Everly Brothers (Phil and Don) 175
Exile on Main Street (album) 126

Fats Domino 85
Feinstein, Barry 59, 60
Feldman, Marty 66

Feliciano, Jose 125
Fenter, Frank 161
Fillmore East 101
Fitzpatrick, Robert 140
Fleetwood, Mick 119
Fletcher, Freddie 220
Fordham University 207
Forrester, Roger
Franklin, Aretha 34, 91, 140
Friar Park 66, 74, 81, 113
Friedman, Kinky 227
Fumo, John and Kelly 208, 208

Gabor, Zsa Zsa 125
Gallagher, Rory 173
Garris, Sid 127
Good, Jack 33
Gordon, Jim 1, 47, 48, 50, 52, 53, 60, 73, 75, 79, 80, 81, 82, 83, 85, 87, 88, 89, 91, 92, 94, 97, 98, 100, 102, 104, 106, 108, 110, 111, 115, 116, 117, 118, 120, 121, 122, 123, 124
Greif, George 125, 126, 127, 128
Grossman, Albert 59
Guercio, Jim 145
Guermo, Ghia 144, 145
Guy, Buddy 99

Harris, Emmylou 189
Harris, Paul 145
Harrison, Eddie 26, 31, 32
Harrison, George 39, 43, 44, 53, 54, 55, 56, 57, 59, 66, 67, 68, 70, 73, 74, 75, 76, 77, 78, 79, 80, 81, 83, 84, 87, 108, 112, 113, 114, 115, 116, 117, 119, 121, 129, 169, 208, 233
Harrison, Olivia 54
Harrison, Patti Boyd 68, 74, 77, 83, 87, 89, 98, 101, 107, 112, 114, 117, 124
Hasty, Michael 215
Hayes, Isaac 32, 36
Hazel 216
Heffernan, David and Gerald 173
Hell's Angels 44, 45
Helm, Levon 196, 199, 207
Hendrix, Jimi 41, 96, 98, 99, 101
Hillman, Chris 145
The History of Eric Clapton (album) 134
Hoffman, Dustin 152
Holland, Jools 192, 193, 231
Holly, Buddy 16, 68
Holzman, Jac 41, 43, 44, 50
Hopkins, Nicky 83, 125
Horn, Jim 191, 196
Hour Glass 106
Howard, Babe 5
Hughes, Howard 136
Humperdinck, Engelbert 119

Hurtwood Edge 66, 70, 83, 84, 86, 88, 95, 98, 99, 102, 108, 109, 110, 113, 124, 232
Hyde Park 98

Inoue, Takashi 215
It's About Time (album) 191
Iwabe, Yoshiko 215

Jackson, Peter 230, 231
Jagger, Bianca 99, 125, 131
Jagger, Mick 44, 71, 82, 83, 84, 99, 126, 127
James, Catherine 71, 83, 84, 85, 86
James, Etta 199
John, Elton 102
Johnny Cash Show 96, 102, 116
Johns, Andy 115, 116, 117, 118, 119
Johns, Glyn 115
Johns, Will 119
Johnson, Daryll 191
Johnson, Tex 52
Jones, Booker T. 28, 29, 36, 31, 36, 41, 160
Jones, Brian 87
Jones, Tom 114, 119
Joplin, Janis 44
Julianne 138, 140

Kaiser, Bobby 29
Kaiser, Sid 59
Karstein, Jimmy 36, 37, 40, 41
Kay, Carol 100
Keltner, Jim 42, 48, 73, 111, 124
Kennedy, Jackie 207
The Kennedys 208
Keys, Bobby 40, 42, 47, 49, 52, 54, 55, 56, 73, 80, 82, 83, 99, 115, 117, 124, 126, 142, 196; his mother 99
Keys, Judy 117
King, Albert 27, 28, 29, 30, 97
King, "Aunt" Christine 10, 11, 12, 13
King, "Big Mama" 6, 10, 11, 13, 23, 25, 31
King, LaVada Bitsy 5, 8, 9, 11, 12, 13, 14
King, Dr. Martin Luther 30, 32
King, Peapaw 11, 12, 13
King, Troy 11, 12, 1 3
King, Uncle Jimbo 10, 11, 179
Kishida, Kunio 206
Klein, Alan B. 74

Lake, Veronica 221, 222
LaLa, Joe 144
Larkin, Dan 176, 177
Lasker, Jay 127
Later ... with Jools Holland 189, 191

Lawrence, Stewart 169
"Layla" (song) 47, 77, 89, 107, 120, 134, 145, 198, 204, 225, 234
Layla and Other Assorted Love Songs (album) 98, 107, 235
Lazenby, Chrissie 156, 167
Lazenby, George 156, 157, 167
L.C. 20, 21
Leavell, Chuck 84, 163, 196
Led Zeppelin 44
Leitch, Donovan 142, 152, 157, 173
Lennon, John 39, 56, 67, 70, 74, 77, 96, 114, 153; and Yoko 114, 119
Lewis, Jerry Lee 82, 121
Little Richard 61, 62, 82
Long, Dave 130, 134, 135, 138, 153
Lord, Julian 87
Los Angeles Symphony 127, 128
Lovers (album) 120, 238, 239
Luck, Texas 223, 225
Lyceum Ballroom 101
Lynne, Shelby 225, 226, 227
Lynyrd Skynyrd 199

Madison Square Gardens 48, 49
Manassas 144, 145
Maranello's Concessionaires 134, 135
Marquee Club London 90
Mason, Dave 44, 49, 52, 57, 82, 84, 85, 116
Max's Kansas City 128
McCartney, Paul 74
McCaskill, Bruce 60, 63, 88, 89, 101, 102, 105, 106, 110, 119, 123, 127, 128, 129
McGee, Jerry 42
Melton, Steve 203
Memphis 29, 30, 31, 32
Memphis Horns 41
Metamorphosis (album) 207, 242, 243
Miles, Buddy 65
Miller, Bob 140, 147, 148, 149
Miller, Buddy 191
Miller, Jimmy 125, 126, 127, 128
Miller, Tom 165
Millsap, Dave 216
Mississippi 31, 32, 33
Moon, Keith 71, 72, 129, 130, 133, 135, 137, 147, 156
Moon, Kim 129
Moore, Sam 28, 32, 94, 95
Morris 70
Mull, Martin 164
Murray, Dee 102
My Time (album) 175, 192, 239, 240

Nizami 95
Nelson, Paula 226, 227
Nelson, Ricky 41
Nelson, Willie 37, 216, 220, 221, 222, 223, 225, 226, 227, 228
Nevison, Ron 113, 136
Nix, Don 34
Norman Conquest 114
North Mississippi Allstars 191

Oaklands 137, 138, 139, 143, 153, 158, 162
O'Farrell, Bonnie Lynn 33
O'Hara-Smith Singers 75, 80
Olmos, Edward James 59
Olson, Nigel 102
Olympic Studios 117, 120
Onassis, Aristotle 125
One of a Kind (album) 161
O'Neil, Michael 164, 165
Ono, Yoko 56, 77
Oriskany 208
Ormsby-Gore, Alice 86, 113, 124, 136

Pallenberg, Anita 125
Pariser, Alan 41, 43, 48, 50, 51, 60, 64, 233, 234
Parr, John 173
Parsons, Gram 41, 59 , 65, 125
Pedernales Studio 220
Perkins, Carl 23, 105; his parents 24
Phillips, Dewey 31
Phillips, Sam 31
Pickett, Wilson 92
Pink Floyd 88
Plantation 59, 97, 125
Poorboy, Kay 39
Porter, David 32
Prater, Dave 28, 32, 94, 95
Presley, Elvis 10, 24, 31, 62, 167, 169
Preston, Billy 75, 76, 79, 80, 81, 82
Preston, Don 33
Price, Jim 42, 49, 52, 73, 80, 81, 115, 117
Princess Diana 192
Prine, John 167, 175
Priola, David 30
Punter, Sergeant Ken 139, 140

Queen of England 67, 137, 142, 208
Queenie 196, 198, 201, 203, 205

Rabbit 20, 21
Radle, Carl 1, 2, 39, 40, 42, 49, 52, 53, 59, 73, 75, 76, 79, 80, 81, 85, 87, 88, 89, 91, 92, 97, 98, 100, 104, 106, 108, 110, 111, 115, 120, 121, 122, 123, 192

Rainbow Theatre 126
Raw Velvet (album) 129, 238
Rebbenak, Mac 43, 82
Red Headed Stranger (film) 222
Redding, Otis 27, 28, 160
Richards, Keith 71, 83, 84, 125, 126, 127, 143; and Anita 99
Roberty, Marc 234
Rock Your Sox Off (album) 164
Rolling Stones 34, 53, 70, 83, 84, 99, 125, 126
Romeo 218, 219, 235
Rothschild, Baron Philippe de 131
Royal Albert Hall 53, 56, 192
Russell, Leon 33, 34, 38, 39, 40, 42, 43, 49, 59, 61, 113, 115, 126
Ryder, Mitch 32, 34
Ryman Auditorium 104, 196

Sade 208
St. George's Hill 114
Samuels, Fuzzy 145
Schenk, Joe Delaney 23
Schonberg, Emile 88, 89
Schonberg, Frandsen 88
Seger, Bob 199
Shankar, Ravi 94
Shaw, David 71, 134
Sheff, Jerry 62
Simpson, Ritchie 28
Sinatra, Frank 140
Sirius Satellite Radio 207
Slim, Memphis 121
"Slip Away" (song) 169
The Small Faces 34
Smith, Robert 211, 212, 215
Sorenson, Linda 146, 157, 158, 159, 160, 162, 167, 168, 169, 180, 181, 182, 233
Soul Survivors 27
Sowell, Bobby 26
Speakeasy 89, 129
Spector, Phil 74, 76, 77, 134
Spencer Davis Group 53
Spock, Doctor 84, 116
Stainton, Chris 61, 232
The Staple Singers 28, 32
Starr, Maureen 114
Starr, Ringo 40, 76, 79, 80, 81, 114, 119, 233
Stax 27, 28, 29, 30, 32, 35, 36, 37, 44
Steppenwolf 199
Stevens, Chuck 24
Stewart, Ian 83
Stewart, Jim 34, 35, 36
Stewart, Rod 141
Stigwood, Robert 51, 52, 53, 69, 71, 73, 91, 98, 101, 105, 111, 127, 134, 136, 155, 160, 161, 162, 234, 234
Stills, Stephen 144, 146, 157

Index

Sunny Heights 114, 115, 119, 127, 233, 234
Swain, Barry 223
Szabo, Gabor 73

Taj Mahal 33, 39
Taylor, Dallas 145
Taylor, James 104
Taylor, Mick 125
Tempchin, Jack 189, 196
Texas 32
The Band 1, 59, 199
The Carpenters 43, 44
The Doors 41
The Kennedy's 208
The Who 129
Thompson, Wayne 27, 28
Thornton, Billy Bob 223, 224, 225, 226, 227, 228
Todd, Vivian 184, 187, 191, 193, 196, 197, 200, 201, 233
Townshend, Pete 134, 149
Traffic 48, 199
Travis, Randy 182
Trident Studios 82
Trigger 221, 226
Troy, Doris 82
Tuduri, Eddie 128, 131
Tumbleweed Connection (album) 102
Turberville, Ross and Lillian 16, 18
Turner, Ike and Tina 34, 36
Turner, Robin 93, 107
Tutt, Ron 62
Two Virgins (album) 77

Vaughan, Jimmy 225, 226, 227
Vega, David 165
Vietnam War 45
Villa Nellcôte 125
Vintage (album) 232, 241, 242
Visletear, Mike and Sheila 47, 50
Vito, Rick 127, 128, 131
Voorman, Klaus 76, 79, 81, 82, 115, 117, 118

Wages, Dennis 24
Wages, Gertie 24
Wages, Wilson 24, 25
Wages, Woodrow 5, 24, 25, 26
Walden, Alan 163
Walden, Phil 27, 160, 161, 163
Walsh, Joe 145
Ward, Bass 88
Warner/Chappell Publishing 204, 205, 235, 236
Watson, Johnny Guitar 37
Watts, Charlie 71, 125
Wells, Junior 99
Wet Willie 199
Wexler, Jerry 50, 61, 62, 64, 102, 103, 118, 198, 199
White, Alan 81
Whitlock, Alex 6, 7, 8
Whitlock, Ashley 162, 163, 177, 183, 184, 202
Whitlock, Beau Elijah 7, 18, 164, 174, 175, 176, 179, 180, 201, 202, 233
Whitlock, B.J. 7
Whitlock, Debbie Wade 14, 22, 23, 104, 172

Whitlock, Ginger 104
Whitlock, Granny 5, 6, 8, 9, 104, 183
Whitlock, Jimmy 3, 9, 10, 13, 14, 16, 17, 18, 19, 21, 22, 23, 27, 75, 104, 127, 172, 179, 232
Whitlock, LaVada 5, 6, 8, 9, 12, 14, 15, 18, 19, 20, 21, 22, 23, 26, 76, 104, 121, 153, 172, 225, 226
Whitlock, Nathan 22, 153, 172, 201
Whitlock, "Peapaw" 11, 12, 13, 15, 16, 63
Whitlock, Tommy 16, 104
The Who 129
Wilson, Jackie 26
Wilson, Tim 198, 199
Winter, Johnny 44
Winwood, Stevie 27, 53, 59, 230, 231, 232
Wonder, Stevie 71
Wood, Ronnie 71, 117, 142
Wright, Cathy 46, 47, 50, 51, 57, 65, 68
Wright, Gary 75, 80, 81
Wyman, Bill 71, 125

Yeager, Roy 26
Young, Neil 104
Young, Peter 196, 203
Young Rascals 27
Yvelyne 125, 126, 131, 132, 133

Zamek, Paul and Dez 215
Zemaitis, Tony 116

www.ingramcontent.com/pod-product-compliance
Ingram Content Group UK Ltd.
Pitfield, Milton Keynes, MK11 3LW, UK
UKHW050536150426
5217IPUK00026B/1955